An Account of My Life

The Childhood Journals of Helen May Clarke

1915 - 1926

Published by the Mystic River Historical Society
Mystic Connecticut
1997

Acknowledgments

The Mystic River Historical Society would like to thank all of our donors and supporters who helped to make this book, our 25th Anniversary project, a reality.

A special thank you to the "Diary Committee" -- Carol Kimball, Marilyn Comrie, Judy Hicks and Dorrie Hanna -- and to our "Ace Photographer", Jim Burbank.

Finally, our thanks to Dorrance Grimes. Without his generous gift, we would have no story to share with you.

©1997 Mystic River Historical Society, Inc. All rights reserved.

No portion of this book may be reproduced in any form or by any means without prior written permission from the publisher.

ISBN: 0 - 966124 5-0-2

First printed December 1997

10 9 8 7 6 5 4 3 2 1

*Cover design by
Trish Sinsigalli LaPointe, LaPointe Design, Old Mystic CT*

*Manufactured in the United States of America by
Thames Printing, Norwich CT*

Mystic River Historical Society • Box 245 • Mystic CT • 06355

*What is the use of a diary
unless it is passed on?*

*Helen May Clarke
Age 13*

*This book is dedicated to
all those who keep history alive*

Table of Contents

	Page
The Year 1915	15
The Year 1917	20
The Year 1918	69
The Year 1919	74
The Year 1920	120
The Year 1921	170
The Year 1922	203
The Year 1923	256
The Year 1924	311
The Year 1925	313
The Year 1926	332
Index	341

Introduction

One of the missions of the Mystic River Historical Society is to preserve local history. So we were delighted when Dorrance Grimes offered us Helen's diary for our archives. When we read it, we knew almost immediately we wanted to publish it.

The diary is a wonderful slice of Americana, giving a glimpse into life during the early part of this century - a time when society was making the transition from horses to automobiles, from kerosene lamps to electric lights and from dirt roads to paved streets. Moving pictures were the new rage and America was about to plunge into the First World War.

Helen May Clarke was born in Mystic in 1905, a descendant of the Burrows family who helped settle Mystic. She loved to write and kept a diary most of her life. This book includes her writings from 1915 to 1926. The originals were written on various sizes of notebooks, tablets, papers, etc. Later in her life she copied them exactly as written: mis-spellings and all.

In an effort to preserve the character and flavor of the writings, the diary has been published virtually unchanged, except for some minor spelling corrections. The thoughts and opinions expressed are strictly Helen's.

Readers will be struck by Helen's intelligence and her natural gift for writing, even at an early age. She read widely, as is evident from the books she writes about in her journal. She was proud of her ancestry, and stories about the Burrowses and many other people who lived in Mystic figure prominently in the book.

One of Helen's greatest wishes was to see her diary published, and the historical society is please to make that dream come true, albeit posthumously. Although specifically about Mystic, the book transcends time and place and becomes a rich and colorful canvas depicting small-town life in America some 80 years ago.

Readers will become intimately acquainted with Helen's family, her girl friends and boy friends, and some of the unique and delightful characters who populated her world - people like "Umbrella" Bentley, who carried an umbrella rain or shine and walked down the middle of the street keeping the trolleys from running on time, and Rhody Hancock a sweet, pink-cheeked woman who lived in sin with the local Horseradish King.

At the same time, because it is about Mystic, the diary preserves information pertaining to people, places and events that otherwise might have been lost. Everyone associated with this publishing project has delighted in reading Helen's journals and we know that those who purchase this book will have the same enjoyable experience.

The Mystic River Historical Society
December 1997

About Helen...

[From an un-dated letter to Carol W. Kimball from Dorrance H. Grimes]

She was born Helen May Clarke on September 17, 1905 at 12 Noank Road, Mystic, Connecticut, the daughter of Asa Hoxie Clarke and Alice Bowen Hill.

Her line of descent on her father's side was from Joseph Clarke, who was her first English-American ancestor. He emigrated to Rhode Island in 1638 from Boston and resided in Newport and Westerly. (He was the brother of Dr. John Clarke, a founder of Newport). He was a large landholder and the only member of his family who left issue in New England, and from him descended the greater part of the Clarke family living in the Narragansett country.

On her mother's side she was descended from Robert Burrows who after moving about settled on the west bank of the Mystic River. Mr. Burrow's grant was dated April 3, 1651, as "a parcel of land between the west side of the river and a high mountain of rocks." (known as Peace Meeting Grove in Helen's grandmother's day). With his house lot in New London and his estates in Poquonnoc and on the Mystic, he was the third gentleman in the New London settlement in the amount of taxable property.

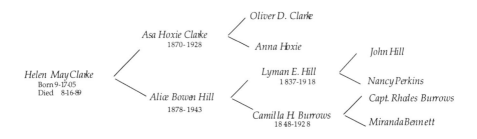

List of Illustrations

Group I - Page 19
    Rudolph Valentino
    Organ Grinder and monkey
    Helen's class at Mystic Academy, 1912

Group II - Page 31
    Lyman Hill [Daddy], Helen's grandfather
    Camilla Burrows Hill, Helen's grandmother
    Helen's grandparents' house, Ashby Street
    Asa Hoxsie Clarke, Helen's father
    Alice Hill Clarke, Helen's mother

Group III - Page 35
    Gilbert Block fire, 1915
    Central Hall, 1865
    Livery Stable

Group IV - Page 47
    Mystic & Noank Library
    Fred Rathburn's car
    Union Baptist Church

Group V - Page 63
    Blacksmith Shop
    Capt. Daniel Packer House, Fort Rachel
    Mrs. Benjamin's Boarding House

Group VI - Page 83
    Mystic River Drawbridge
    Capt. Rhodes Burrows House
    John Green Packer
    The Rev. Byron U. Hatfield

Group VII - Page 119
    Packer's Tar Soap factory
    Helen and Dorrance
    Dan Packer
    Peace Grant House West Main Street

Group VIII - Page 159
    Juliet Haley
    Priscilla "Cill" Lamb
    Dorrance Grimes
    Mary Collins
    Marcus Jones
    Emily Gallup

Group IX - Page 193
    Mystic Island Hotel
    Mystic Island Casino and Beach
    Helen's grandfather fishing at Fort Rachel docks

Group X - Page 213
    Latham Avery's gravestone
    Capt. John Mason statue
    Constance, Helen's sister
    Helen and Constance

Group XI - Page 237
    Dean's Mill
    Community House
    Rossie Velvet Mill

Group XII - Page 266
    Borough School, Stonington
    Trolley car
    Broadway School

Group XIII - Page 300
    Helen's father's fishing boat "Helen"
    Helen's home on Noank Road
    Helen's father's fishing boat "Constance"

Group XIV - Page 319
    Boat Race Day, New London
    Yale crew practices for Yale-Harvard boat race
    Helen at Ocean Beach, New London

All photographs are the property of the Mystic River
Historical Society
and are used with permission

with the exception of that of Juliet Haley
(Loaned by Priscilla Strand and used with permission)

and that of Mary Collins
(Loaned by Barbara Hodgman and used with permission)

Helen's Family and Friends

These individuals are the primary "characters" in Helen's diaries. Their names appear so often in this book that citing them in an index becomes unduly complex.

Allie or Mother	Alice Bowen Clarke	Her mother
Ase or Papa	Asa Hoxie Clarke	Her father
Constance	Constance Clarke	Her sister
Daddy	Lyman Hill	Her grandfather
Grandmother	Camilla Burrows Hill	Her grandmother

Alton	Alton Burrows
Alvin	Alvin Cutler
Anna	Anna Dennison
Cill	Priscilla Lamb
Dorrance	Dorrance Grimes
Elizabeth	Elizabeth Cutler
Emily	Emily Gallup
Howard	Howard Duell
Jerry	
Joe	Joe Walsh
Jr.	Jacob Gallup (known as Junior)
Marcus	Marcus Jones
Mary	Mary Collins
Stanley	Stanley Saunders
Toby	Toby Morgan

Helen as a young woman

1915

12 Noank Road
Fort Rachel Place
Village of Mystic
Town of Groton
State of Connecticut
The year 1915

January 12 My name is Helen May Clarke and I was ten years old in September. Many folks do not think I am so old because I am small for my age. They say I am no bigger than a pint of cidar, which is an old saying. I am a first child, but not an only child. I have a little sister named Constance Anna Clarke. When she was a little baby she called herself Tontann. She is a funny little thing, fat and happy go luckey, but very hard on dolls and play things. She is most four years old. We have yellow hair, dutch cut and brown eyes. A lady said we are Spannish blonds.

I go to Mystic Academy. Grade V. Div. A. Miss Ruby Prentice is my teacher. She is very strik and does not have pretty cloes [clothes]. She puts on flannel shirt waistes every day and silk ones for dress up. I guess she is forty years old. She reads about Greeks out loud for a spell every afternoon. I like that, but lots do not. I do not like long division and she gives hard ones. I can not do them worth a cent. I am not good at number work, I mean I am very bad.

Someday I shall have a moted grange by the sea, with peacockes, a ship in a bottle, swans and two of those big high dogs.

Monday - I broke the old, old cup that never had any handles and that has been in the family for years. It is an airloom. There were 100's and 100's of folks who have had that pretty little cup, then I am born to break it. I shall not blame my children if they hate me. I would give all the money in my Billikin Bank not to have done it.

* * * * * * * * * * * * *

I have seen many nice sceens and the sea is the nicest of all I think. You can see it from under the apple trees and I look every day. Even when in a hurry I look or the Sea would be angery. It is very beautiful to look through the apple blossoms and see the blue sky and the blue sea. Daddy sits on the green bentch and looks far away. He has far away eyes.

There are shells in a case and they are hansome. You can hear the sea in them. Daddy says it is only my ears, but I do not think so. I do not like to have rainbows and fogs egsplained. I feel sorry for shells that are shut up in a case. If I were a shell I should not like it. Daddy and I love the same things. We love boats, trains, woods and plenty of salt water. We walk on the shore and pick up little shells and pretty stones. We let them drop again most always, but it is nice to have felt them we think.

<u>Sunday</u> - When I came home from Sunday School there was Miss Lib Mayo in Grandma's mahogeny chair in the sitting room. She looked at my card and said did I like Sunday School and was I a good little girl. I felt funny because I had been thinking bad things about our Paster, Mr. Welcome Bates. He scares me he asks such fierce questions and he looks cross and suffering even when he smiles. He is a very homely man, but it is ireverend to think such things about a minister of the Gospel specially on Sunday. It is the Devil at my elbow. He is a good God fearing man powerfully concerned with Sin and a hard shelled rock ribed Baptist, but I do not love him. I hope God is not like him.

It is April and Mama has let me take my underdraws off. My! I feel cool and airy. Spring is nice. Pretty soon I will get into sandles and Mary Jane slippers for best. I hate high shoes and socks are much nicer than stockings with ribs. We kids are bouncing balls on elastics. I have had enough of winter. Now I will go out and play. Mama says she is tired of spelling words, she wants to read. Papa says "G-- yes, what in H---(bad word) am I writing. Is it school work? I did not ask many words, only two or three.

<u>July 5</u> - Yesterday was the Fourth. Daddy and I hoisted the flag and set off firecrackers. We went downstreet and bought them a few days ago. I like the Fourth, all but the noise which hurts my ears and stomach. We got a new cap pistol and some caps, also punk, fire crackers and sparkelers. Daddy will not get anything that could hurt our hands or eyes and tells about children who have had things blown clear off. Constance is allowed sparkelers and a horn. The pretty night fire works Daddy set off in the garden. We had rockets and fountans and pin wheels also red fire and green fire. When it got dark Constance and I swung in the swing with sparkelers in our hands. O it was lovely, all the sparks swishing back and forth in the black of night. We swung hard until we touched the leaves and we yelled loud as we could. They said I would be in for a sick spell today being a flightey buntch of nerves, but I feel fine.

The night before the Fourth there was a big comotion. Bells rang and a cannon banged. I did not hear it being asleep. I miss a lot sleeping so hard, but cannot help it. Not much was done by boys. One time they put Aunt Mary Jane's portch chairs up a tree. The real bad boys move privies around. Some times they tip them over and sometimes they move them to some other place like the front yard or in the road. Grandma says she looks first thing Fourth of July morning to see if it is still there. Fences are moved and gates. It is a great nusance but fun.

* * * * * * * * * * *

1915

Capt. Herb Thomas and Capt. Gurd Allen are salts of the earth. Capt. Herb and Gurd and Papa who is Capt. Ace are doing antick [antique] busyness on the side. Capt. Herb says our doors have ships panels. Capt. Gurd went on the menhaden boats before his fall. It was a bad fall alright. The menhaden boats were in and he wanted to earn some money on account of he is thriftey and does not like to be idle when they are tied up, so he helped paint the sie House which is a hotel and quite high. Well, the stagen [staging] broke and let him down three stories to the sidewalk. He says he hit it spang on his butt and like to druv his teeth up through his head. It hurt like Old Harry. It is a good thing he is broad in the beem I guess. He says it was just an averije size before the stern crash, but I think it must have been a little big to start with. He was on the ways for months and Mrs. Gurd has to histe [hoist] him with a takle when she changed his bedden [bedding]. Papa use to shave him and tell him funny stories. Both Capt. Gurd and Mrs. Gurd set a store by Papa on account of all he did. It was certainly a bad fall.

* * * * * * * * * * *

Today Gurden Chapman tried to kiss me and I ran home. I did not think he would do such a thing. I am agast. I shall not tell anyone on account of being mortyfied.

I was a little late for supper tonight though I ran, and was scolded because I smell of the barn. I like to be there when the coal horses come in to supper and to be bedded down for the night. They are noble beasts I think and give me a nice warm feeling in my insides, besides I like the drivers especially Mr. Braxton who being colored does not show the coal dust like the white men. If the coal yard was mine instead of a distant relatives I should hire only colored coal men.

It came on supper time and I had to leave before the big doors slid together. I smelled horsey and knew Mama would snift and know. I hoped she'd think it Caroline's Shetland pony I had been around but I guess I smelt too strong for a little thing like a pony. Mama was specially not pleased with me because that made the second dress I had dirtied that day and look at me now. I was hungry enough to start right in eating but no, I had to take a uer [ewer] of hot water and go upstairs and scrub with Cashmere Bouquet Soap and put on the yellow dress with the blue dots and blue socks. You would think I was a lepper. When I sat down Mama said, "There now, don't you prefer to be a clean, nice little girl? You looked like a stable boy." I certainly do enjoy smelling like a lady when I have not got anything else to do, but when I am having an interesting time I forget how I look and smell.

<u>August 2</u> - I have been thinking up in the apple tree and feel like writing down my thoughts. It is hard some times because some of them do not like to be slapt down on paper and would rather flit off. One thing I was thinking was how awful biggety most grown up people get to be. They think themselves the Head Shinoras of the Universe. They are so puffed

An Account of My Life

up they miss a lot. Some women would rather hear themselves talk than listen to a song sparrow. I think it stupid of them to clack when there is a lovely sound to be listened to. Most kids do not smell either. It has to be a very sweet smell or a bad stink or they do not notice. They do not see either. I mean they look and do not see half. They say how pretty the flowers are but they do not put their faces down and breathe them. They just snift them quick and hard which is no way at all.

Only poets and artists keep on Seeing, Smelling and Hearing after they are grownup.

My other thoughts were about the gippies [Gypsies] that came one day just before dark. They are kind of poor I guess, the poor horses are thin and the vans patchey. I have heard of rich ones with Kings, Queens and gippy Princisses, but have never seen them. Grandma hates and despises the thieving Egyptians, but I do not. I have never had my palm crost with silver, the family will not allow it. Daddy likes them too, but he will not take me to their camp in Haley's Woods. He says because they will steal me, which is a joke because I am not a pretty child.

I feel something the same about them as I do about the organ grinder man and Beppo. I do love that monkey and worry for fear he is not getting enough to eat. I think a big, fat man ought to be ashamed to make a little monkey work for him. Its' little red cap and jacket are faded. I think it earns enough to have a new one. There is no need for fleas either. The man says they always have them and you can not wash a monkey on account of its catching cold and dying. It looks like he feels the same way about water himself. Those sad eyes hurt me. It makes me mad to know the money I put in the cup will mostly go to the man. I do hope he divides fair.

These are all the thoughts I can think of now. A lot got away

1915

Rudolph Valentino
in "The Four
Horsemen of
The Apocalypse"

The Organ Grinder and Monkey

Helen's Class at Mystic Academy, 1912

1917

Helen May Clarke - 11 years old
The Beginning - April 30, 1917

    I am eleven going on twelve and in the 6th grade at Mystic Academy. I have been reading about a girl who kept a Diary and I am going to do so likewise with dates and everything. I use to write things down in a notebook, but it was not like this girl's Diary. I wrote things on pieces of paper and made drawings to give Daddy. I have no real Diary so I made this out of sheets of paper tied together. Daddy likes people to be ingeaneous so I aim to be.
    There are a lot of words I cannot spell although in school I am a good speller being among the last to go down in a Spelling Bee and sometimes the last.
    This pen don't write worth a cent.
    When girls in books start Diarys exciting things start to happen right off the bat. I hope it works for me, oh I certainly do hope so. I shall make this as repleet with description, conversation and antidotes as my life will allow.
    Miss Happy Brown says all children should read the Bible and use the Dictionary dayly. I think some book ought to be written to explain them both. She says she read the Bible all through three times before she was much older than we. I asked if she understood it and she said yes, certainly. Gee, she must of been smart because I do not understand hundreds of words in it at all. As for the Dictionary you have to almost <u>know</u> how spell a word before you can find it.
    Miss Happy read *"The Man Without a Country"* in class and cried bitterly. The kids cried too, even the ones who had not been listening. I did not weep, but felt very sad.
    She says I read more than any child she knows. She cannot understand why I do not like the Uncle Remus stories, she thinks they are fine. Right now I am very fond of Gene Stratton Porter and Joseph Lincoln.
    We have been at war with Germany most a month now. A lady dressed up in bunting sang "The Star Spangled Banner," by the horse troth downtown. She had a very loud voice and bright yellow hair. We must do out bit to lick the Kaiser.
    I hope to be pretty someday, but my nose worries me. Papa has a very dignified one called a Roman nose which would look awful on me. I do not want to be spoiled by a magnificent nose.
    The scab on my arm is very thick and crusty and does not feel sore any although uncomfortable when I write. The Family says maybe I'll stop jumping off things for a spell. I have always enjoyed climbing things in order to jump off which I have done since able to jump, many times a day.

During that time I have had two or three bad falls so the Family thinks whenever I jump I will skin something if not worse, which is not logic. It is a great thrill to be up high and to say, "Ask your mother for fifteen cents, to see the elephant jump the fence. He jumped so high he touched the sky and never came down until Fourth of July" and to land with a pleasant thud on the last word. Grandma says for all my legs look like sticks, my bones must be good else I would have snapped them in two ere this.

Papa approves of me keeping a Diary. He says the school things I write and other such things are tosh and do not sound like me. He says to keep my diaries so that someday I can enjoy a good laugh. I shall not need such things to laugh at then on account of everything nice happening when you are grown up. Besides I do not see anything funny about what I write in here. If I heard more funny stories I could write them in here like a sort of a joke book but I do not hear any very often and they are hard to make funny on paper.

<u>May 5</u> There is not a thing worth writing, so I will just ramble on because I have not got anything to do.

I like Spring because going to and fro to School I see many lovely flowers. Going up to Mary's house to play I pass old man Allen's house. The grass is green and plushey and robins hop all over it. Best of all are clumps of daffydils growing here and there not in beds or borders, but up thru the grass. Many big pines give the big yellow house a stately appearance. Mrs. Allen is nice and Deacon Allen is religious, but purse proud.

I should like a pony. Grandma says we are not John Jacobasters [John Jacob Astor], only comfortable. Caroline has one and a little wicker cart and they are not John Jacobasters either. May Penfield has one, a calico not a Shetland. She is a big girl, but nice and she lets me ride it. It is fun, but like to split my straddle, being a fat horse.

May's Mother is Mrs. Ballentine Penfield who gives dancing lessons. I take dancing lessons and have two lovely dresses just for dancing school, one blue with white embroidery all over it and the other pink with a sash. Mrs. Penfield wears black lace and looks hautey. She use to be rich, but is no more because her father lost his money and died. They live in the gardeners house because there is no gardener or any gardens. They grow plants in the hot house and sell them. One day Daddy let me pick out what plant I wanted. O there were many lovely ones. I took heliotrope because it is so sweet. I love green houses, the earthy smell being one of my favorites. It is lucky they have the gardeners house, because the big mansion never got built before the money was lost. The grounds have grown up all tangled because they cannot keep them tidy. There is mirtle [myrtle] and lily of the valley and all kinds of flowers growing like wild. The ground is made in layers and there is a lovely brook. It is called Aires (Ayres) Woods, but it was not meant to be woods, it has just gone wild. Years ago they took summer people and that is how Mrs. Penfield met her husband. He was just a boy and his folks would not let him stay married to

An Account of My Life

her, so he went back to New York and I have never laid eyes on the man. He is rich they say. Mrs. Penfield is poor as Job's turkey. Papa says she is a gushing fool of a female. She is very strik about manners and thinks deportement is just everything. The girls do not mind, but the boys except Reynolds, hate dancing school and raise Ned all the way home to make up for it.

That awful Harold Chapman scared me today. He chases girls and if he catches them he kisses them. He does not catch them very often he is so fat and he shakes like jelley when he runs, besides he gets tired quick. He is simple minded and Mama says he ought to be shut up before he does someone harm. He is not ugly unless plaged [plagued], but if you say Georgy Porgy Pudden and Pie kissed the girls and made them cry, he gets mad and throws big stones fast and harder. He likes girls but they do not like him he is so gormy. Mama says give him plenty of leeway which I do. Papa says if I plage him he will tan my hide. It makes him swear, he says we are savages. Harold is no relation to Gurdon being another family. Gurdon is plump too, but not pussy.

I think my favorite man is Kent. His name is Mr. Kenneth Payne and he lives on Shelter Island. He is Papa's friend and specially mine. He sends me post cards and brings them to me in his pocket for my album. He says I am an easy one to please because I like pictures of boats, harbors, ocean scenes, ship yards and such and he is handy at picking them out. I like to hear him talk and laugh and watch him eat. We are both hearty eaters. He says we put a fine polish on the plates. He is a great joker and we nearly split each others sides a laughing. I like him better than Hans Shellnick. He gave me a doll because I said I would marry him when I grew up. He is a Swede and very immens. I think I would rather marry Kent even if he is pretty old.

We are at War with Germany to save Democracy. We have Current Events in school so I know all about it.

<u>May 12</u> Mama has given me a little pearle handled pen which she had years ago when she was a girl. I have written in ink without spilling or spotting for most two years now. I like to write, but I hate sewing and am the despair of the women folks.

Daddy says I have pretty hands. Grandma does not like him to say so, because it will make me vain and afraid to soil my hands. He likes fingers to tapper [taper] and he says my nails are very long and narrow for so small a hand. Papa says they are the prettiest damn hands he ever saw on a mortle. More people look at a pretty face than at pretty hands. I wish I had a pretty face and curls.

Grandma says it is a mercy Mama had Constance before I was completely spoiled. She says Daddy and Papa were showing me off just as if I was something out of the ordinary. All but Daddy say I am a spoiled child, but they think the other to blame and not themselves. Grandma has not got over the telegrams Papa sent when I was born and says, "just like a

Clarke." I know what Aunt May's said because I have heard her tell about it. It said, "Helen May born today, your loving brother, Ase."

I do wish I had been born beautiful. Grandma says I will get my come uppance for thinking such vain things. If a Dark Day should come I guess I would be scared. Grandma says her great grandfather lived thru one years and years ago and never forgot it. It must have been fearsome all right.

Teacher brought some pictures of Greek sculpture to school today. One was that one of Hermes with the funny looking baby on his arm. Her picture was cut off at the waist not like the one in the book here which shows much more. She said we could ask questions, but not many did on account of most of the kids were giggling. I said I though Hermes was very beautiful but looked stupid. She got very sarcastic. Well, he does, I think - and sort of silly. I like the Winged Victory. Maybe she had a silly face too, but what is left is grand. It makes me feel like my dream of flying. She does not think the Romans so wonderful as the Greeks, but quite wonderful. I said my father said they were vulgarians and she got red and said I must have mistaken the word. I am sure I did not.

May 26 Teacher said to write a composition about Decoration Day which I did. I quoted "under the sod and dew waiting for Judgement Day, under the one the Blue, under the other the Gray" from Mama's old red reader. It was nice and sad. My thoughts were very plentiful, but if I am not carefull the kids gigle so I keep my real thoughts for myself.

Some of the kids hate compositions and think even 100 words a lot. My trouble is to stop writing once I get started. I have a full feeling so I shall write a sort of composition in here, maybe not all at once, but as the spirit moves.

I love Decoration Day morning and get up early because there is so much to do. After breakfast I hurry up the path to help Daddy get the Flag out of its bag and get it up. It is limp at first until the breeze lifts it and it looks so beautiful on the white pole with the blue sky and the new leaves on the big maples, my eyes smart. I have to be early because if I am not Daddy does it alone on account of Mr. Charles Parks will get his up first and Daddy and he try to be first. It is great fun. Mr. Parks is not as old as Daddy, but he has no little girl to help him which evens things up. Daddy says His flag is the kind you hang from a rope. It too, looks beautiful with the blue sky and the big dark pine trees all around it. Everyone puts out flags or bunting. Old Mrs. Ann Judd Webb and Nell Crary have poles sticking out from the house. When I have a house I shall have the longest Liberty Pole ever seen.

Grandma calls me and hands me the big basket and takes the sheares. She does not let me cut because I am inclined to be wasteful. The grass is wet with dew. I take the branches of lilaks she hands me and smell them with joy. I cannot make up my mind which I like better, the white or the purple. Sometimes it is one, sometimes the other. The white ones are best in the moonlight. There are lillies too, day lillies and flurdelee, also iris.

An Account of My Life

The ends of the stems are slippery wet. There is a pineapple bush with little brown flowers the color of chockalate, not pretty, but oh so spicy smelling. There is also a snow ball bush that never whitens in time, and Grandma's pride and joy, a beautiful samon [salmon] colored azalia [azalea] bush of great loveliness. There are tall lemon yellow tulips, masses of for-get-me-nots and June lillies. When the basket is full and my arms too, she goes in to wash her hands and change her garden hat.

It is only a little walk to the Burrows Burying Ground. We meet lots of folks we know on the way. Elder Miner makes believe he cannot see me behind the flowers in my arms until he parts them. I am too old for that kind of joking, but he has always done it and it is pleasant. He is so old I guess I seem very young to him.

I like to have flowers all around my face and am like to swoon from the sweetness. When we get to the burying ground Grandma casts a critical eye around to see if it is being kept up. Great-Uncle Nelson's line has the care of it. Now it is in Cousin Rollin's hands and after him Kenneth must take care of it. It is a sacred trust. I do not see why the men should have everything. Grandma says Roll never gets all the poison ivy out and he knows she poisons. He says he does. Grandma poisons awful and after every Decoration Day she is a sight being plastered all over with yellow soap, or sody. Mama says it is ridkulous, she is perfectly willing to trim the graves, but Grandma says she guesses she can stand it once a year. Neither Mama or Daddy like to trim graves, but she does and so do I. I get a pail of water and fill the iron flower holders and fix the flowers as pretty as I can. It gives me a good feeling. When it suits her and she has washed off the bird droppings on the stones we take the empty basket and go out latching the gate. We have a few words with the folks at the house, but there is much to be done and we do not tarry long.

Back home we fill the basket again for the Burrowses and Bennetts in Elmgrove. That is too far for her to walk so Mama goes with her on the trolley car. I pick more flowers and hurry to the Grand Army Rooms to help make up the bunches for the Veterans graves and the button hole bouquets with a little silk flag stuck in them. We know the flowers and which gardens they came from. I love to do it and feel put out when the Daughters say they could use a little more flowering almon [almond], don't we want to ask Mrs. Latham if she can spare a little more and while we are about it get some flowering quince from the yard of the old tumble down house next to the stable. They always do it when the talk gets interesting.

Tomorrow or next day I shall write about Decoration Day afternoon, not just this one, but all of them put together.

Mama has my white dress ready because I march with the school kids carrying flags. Daddy is all dressed in his uniform so tall and straight, not like the bent over old men. He makes me feel the way I did when I looked at the flag.

The Parade never starts on time and sometimes we get pretty tired standing around. We stop at the Bridge first for the sailor dead. It is a pretty sight to see the flowers floating down the River. Most rivers are fresh water but ours is as salt as the sea. Next we stop at the Soldiers Monument. It looks very pretty with the green grass inside the iron fense stuck full of little flags. The boys have little flags on their wheels and the rest wound up in bunting and whey they go fast the wheels are a blur of pink. It is very impressive and the marshall [martial] strains are inspiring. It is a hot, dusty march to Elmgrove and lately the Veterans ride in an open trolley car on account of some being so old. They use to march and Daddy says he still can. Elmgrove is a beautiful spot with hundreds and hundreds of old trees. It is the most beautiful in the State. It is very somber marching through the big Mallory gates under the big flag, and the slow, slow steps to the Dead March give me chills.

The Exercises are held near the water between the valt [vault] and the tomb. When the Parade falls out we kids sit on the tomb. It is the kind that goes into the ground except for the front of it. The big mound is grassy and good to sit on. We do not listen much. I like to look down the River. The cool breeze dries up our presperation.

I have been all week writing this. I guess I will finish tomorrow.

After things are over the Veterans are taken back to the Rooms on Pearl Street for coffee and doughnots. The rest of us march back. Before we leave Elmgrove I like to jump down from the tomb and look in at Capt. Williams. The big door is open sometimes and you can see thru the fense thing all the drawers screwed in with names and dates on them. Some have no names yet. Most the old Captains died before my day, but Capt. Williams and I just missed each other by four years. I wish he could of hung on.

I wait for Daddy and we are late getting home. Mama and Grandma are usually cross because we do not know enough to come home until the last gun is fired. By that time all hands are sort of tuckered out and cross.

This is the end of this composition.

June 23 I have had a wonderful time, about the most wonderful time in my life so far I guess and I must write it down before I bust. My Cousin Marion got married and Mama took me to the wedding in New London. It was at night. I do not get out mutch at night not being allowed to stay up late like some girls I know, so it was a very happy time for me. I wore a white dress with a pink satin sash and Mama did my hair up the night before so I would have curls. I prayed it would not rain and take the curls out and it didn't. I wore a big pink satin bow on my head, likewise socks and bran new white slippers. I am homely when my hair is skinned back and braided which is most of the time, but I like looking at myself with curls hanging around my shoulders. If I had real curls and could turn a tune I guess the family would be much prouder of me and who can blame them. I would not like a child like myself. Mama had a new dress of rich blue silk and looked very hansome. Someday I shall have long white gloves. Grandma stayed at home to care for Constance who is too young for night weddings. She looked us over and said I was vain as a peakok and fine feathers do not make fine birds.

When we got to New London we found throngs of people and the house sweet with lovely flowers. They said it was a small wedding, but I did not think so. I was the youngest person there and got a lot of attention. Some of the people who had never seem me looking homely with braids and high shoes thought me a lovely child which was flattering, but made me feel sort of guilty.

The minister was hansome, but quite old. He amused me by saying funny things to me. He said maybe I'd marry his son someday, he would do it and not charge a cent. We liked each other fine.

Cousin Nellie was there and as comical as of yore. She is quite old, but well preserved. She always says as soon as the kissing is over "I am thinner than I was, don't you think so?" but she never is. Then she says, " I hold my age well don't you think?" She is not really old but she is getting on. Marion is not pretty, but she looked nice in her lovely clothes and the veil helped a lot. Walter, the man she married, is very bashful and not hansome, but sort of nice. The day Marion brought him over for Grandma to inspect he sat on the horsehair chair and blushed like fury. It is a very hard chair to sit in unless you know how on account of being slippery.

The bridesmaid was <u>beautiful</u>, simply beautiful with pink cheeks just the color of the pink satin bands on her white tulle dress and <u>pink satin slippers</u>. If I could have pink satin slippers I could die happy.

If I had been Walter I should have married her instead of Marion because he might as well marry a pretty one. But If he had I should not have been there so I am glad he did not. The wedding presents were all put out in one room so everyone could see them. I did not see anything I wanted, but I guess they were pretty fine. Cousin Nellie gave her a great big picture. In it was Moses with a lot of animals, maybe it was David. I do not like Bible pictures. Cousin Nellie was very proud of it and told everyone she had given it.

After the wedding I said to myself, but out loud, "Well, the next thing will be a baby."

Mama said, "Helen!' but Cousin Nell laughed and said, "I'm sorry Allie, but she is funny."

Rev. Lee put his arm around me which showed them I wasn't naughty and he didn't laugh either. I like him. If his son is like him I'd just as soon marry him. Cousin Lena handed me some packedges done up in red tissu and said it was confeti and to throw it when Marion and Walter came down.

I wondered why no one else nearby had any, but I got ready to throw it when Rev. Lee explained the confeti was inside and that you had to open it up first. I was very mortyfied. He said to Mama who came looking me up, "If she had hit poor Walter with one of these, his nerve would have forsaken him completely." Mama said, bitter like, "It would have been safer to have brought the baby." My feelings were hurt because I had been stupid but Rev. Lee undid them and said it was a very natural mistake for me to make. I told him I had never seen any confeti this being my first wedding and he said he hadn't either at my age, but he'd seen a mortle lot of it since.

The supper was awful good. It was a buffay supper and there was chicken salade of which I am very fond. They gave awful little dabs and I was hungry so I told Cousin Lena who was in brown satin and very busy. She did not care if I had more so I looked up the caterers and had several. They are nice men I think. The punch was lovely and I was very thirsty. I wished it was champain, but it was good anyway. There were lots of gentlemen and soldiers around the bowl although it was not intoxicating and when I kept coming back for more a man said I was drinking him under the table which is an interesting expression. I hung around to see if he'd say some more until Mama took me away. Cousin Nell hugged me and said "I wish I had one just like her," and her eyes got wet. Mama smoothed my hair. It was very impressive. Later she said Cousin Nell's little girls died when infants. It is a shame she has no more. I do not care for babies and will most likely have a dozen. It is the way of the world I guess.

I teazed Mama to walk down to the city and not ride because it would take longer and I wanted all of the night I could get. This she did. Being Saturday night the Five and Ten Cent Store was open and we bought a big stand up paper doll for Constance. The stores are exciting when lit up. I do love the night. I have never been on a ferry after dark before and the black waters were thrilling. At last we arrived home. What a time I have had. This Diary has got a fine start.

June 24 Sunny. I did not know Cousin Nellie and Uncle Charlie were going to visit Grandma, but they are and are there now. Uncle Charlie must go back to the city tonight but Cousin Nellie is staying. I love company and she is very jolly. Her feet puff up over her slippers. Grandma says she has the Brayton vanity. Cousin Mildred Carver and her friend Marjory Bradford are coming for a visit this summer. I am glad. Mildred has the prettiest clothes and the other kids envy me. Daddy has fixed me a fine see-saw.

June 25 Sunny. Cousin Nell took me to the picture show and we saw Fatty Arbuckle and he was awful cute. He was dressed like a girl with curls and a sash and socks. She laughed as hard as I did and said that was what made her fat, she guessed. Then she looked at me and said, "<u>Am</u> I fat?" I said, "Oh no, Cousin Nellie, but you know the Braytons are a large people." I did not want to hurt her feelings but she laughed which hurt mine. When I am not takful [tactful] they get mad and when I am I get laughed at.

July 5. There was a big parade in New London yesterday. It was three miles long and cost thousands of dollars.

An Account of My Life

Daddy is deaf and does not know how loud he talks and Mama and Grandma were mortifyed because they said he made himself conspicuous. It provoked them because I shouted things to him and he shouted back. Grandma says I talk with him so much I beller like a bull moose. I cannot tell about the Parade because there was so much I am dayzed. Sometimes I could not breathe. I should like to be on a Float. Oh there were beautiful Floats and so many bands I lost count. I sat on a curb stone and enjoyed an elegant view. It has been a very awspicious ocassion. When we got home Daddy set off fireworks.

Today I have been reading *"The Secret Garden"*. I guess that is about the dozenth time. Sometimes when I finish I turn right back to the front page and start in again. I do love that book.

I wish I had a cousin like Colin and how I should like to live at Misselthwaite Manor and see the moor. Just think of a hundred rooms with closed doors! I can not imagine that many rooms in a house. I do not believe the Hoxsie House has got that many. I always thought Evans Morgans house was big and it has maybe fifteen rooms.

A secret garden must be wonderful. I wish I could know Colin and Mary and Dickon. Before I go to sleep I make believe I am in the garden or looking thru the hundred rooms. My real friends are not as nice as those in books.

I cannot write anymore now because I am going to the spring with the tin peddlar pitcher. We like the water better than fawsut [faucet] water when it is hot. Tin peddlars don't come around any more and Grandma hates drummers.

I am going to have supper with them tomorrow night. I think I am old enough to drink tea that is not half milk. I hate milk. Tea isn't <u>meant</u> to be milky even if Elder Tuttle said, "There is no bad taste to it."

I am tired of having that said to me. Grandma says Old Lady Pyncheon who is no more, was a great believer in cambric tea for the young because tannen [tannin] dries the blood. Still, I don't like it.

An Essay on Cats I Have Had.

As a Familey we are fond of cats. Mama says they are nusances but she likes them and Constance treats them better than most little children. I should like to have a large number of them someday. We have not got one since our last was a viktim of circumstance over which we had no control. I hope to get one soon. I know a lovely cat and when she has her next batch of kittens I shall teaze for one. I just love a blue eyed baby kitten.

My first cat was named Fanny. She was killed by a trolley car and I threw stones at the car every day. I was very young. Then Papa brought home Sailor Cat. He was so named because he came off a boat at Noank and did not like dry land worth a cent. When the telefone was put in he went most crazy and streaked out of the house when it rang. And then Constance was born and her crying was more than he could bear, I guess. Besides he did not like Nurse Reynolds because she thought any old scrap of food was good enough for him and he was use to the best. She fussed when I fed him. She said I was a spoiled child if she ever saw one and it was high time my nose was put out of joint. I did not like her either. It was an unhappy time. Sailor Cat got enough of it and just got up and left. I guess he put out to sea never to return. I do not blame him. Any number of boats would be glad to get him he is such an interesting cat.

After him was a little black and white kitten which got bit to death by Constabul Jim Brown's mean old dog before I had named it. I can not like dogs on account of that mean one. I guess if that dog was a person it would be drummed right out of town. Drunken men and such are afraider of it than of Constabul Jim who is as nice a man as one could meet in a week of Sundays. He has a Livry [livery] Stable which I like, but I am not allowed there. I like all such places that are not lady like. He has buggies, carryalls, surreys, funeral haks [hacks] and a herse. He loves horses. I like them and the hostlers and such. Mr. Duncan drives a beautiful bay horse. He calls his sweet heart, Maud S. after a famous race horse because she is a fast woman. Mr. Jerry Ganu is very funny when he is not sad. He is fat and red and Irish. He gets drunk and very sad, but he is sober quite often and I like him. Grandma and Mama are ashamed of my low tastes. Sometimes funeral processions go by with Jerry sitting up very stiff driving. He does not smile at me, but sometimes he winks. He is a Roman Catholic.

Albertine has got a parrot. I do not think much of it. It is a dingey yellow green with no bright feathers on it and can only say Polly wants a cracker. I thought it would be like the one Capt. Morgan had that Grandma told me about. He brought it from the West Indies or some such place. It was beautiful and could mimik people. They use to put it out on the porch on nice days and it would yell at every one. It did not have a rawcus parrot voice, it was like a persons. People would walk by not seeing anything behind the vines and pretty near jump out of there skins. Then they would see a bit of bright color and say "that dratted bird." It was a profane parrot. They say to go by you would think you were going by a wicked place on the water front in a foreign port. Capt. Morgan said it had lived hard and expressed itself accordenly.

How I wish I had known that bird. What in Time is the good of a parrot that won't really talk? I have been looking at an old Art journal which tells about the ancient stone crosses of England. They don't look like crosses, but that is what they are called. England must be wonderful, we don't have such things around here. It is hard reading because the words are strange to me. I should like to read about them in words I can understand. They give me a funny feeling.

July 6. I had one of my best dreams last night. I dreamed I was skooning over the waves like a ship skoons with its sails full. If I were not human I should like to be a ship or a gull. Grandma says I am an oddity. Daddy says he callates I am one of Mother Carey's chickens.

Mama has a lot of common sense and Grandma's imagination is the kind that sees you getting drown, or lost or come to some harm. Papa says the Burrowses are devoid of imagination and I get mine from the Clarkes. Well anyway the Burrowses are fine people and better ones never stepped on God's green footstool.

Daddy and I took a walk today. Grandma cannot see any sense in tromping all over creation. We like to wander and she wants us to keep to the road. She don't like timid people, but she wishes I had sense enough to know when to be afraid. I said I give bulls plenty of leeway, but that made her mad because a lady does not speak that word. Papa laughs at that. He laughs at lots of things she says. She does not mean to be funny. She says I am getting Daddy's way of looking off as if we saw things not beholden to the human eye. She said the two of us sitting there looked for all the world like an old grizzled Tom and a skinny little kitten. Papa was tikled. I do not think it funny. She says there is no sense in being afraid of the things that scare me, like the stereoptican. The animals are right in my face and I feel as if I were in the Tomb with Napoleon.

July 7. Several women came to call this afternoon. I had to sit still and not talk unless asked a questions. They thought it awful that I do not sew. One woman said her little girl baked a cake, could I cook? When they were looking at fancey work I slid out and hunted up Daddy. He was reading and he looked up with a mad face until he saw it was me. He shut his book and said, "Driven you out too, have they?" And he said he presoomed we had better take a walk or we might get halled in. He takes lovely walks and it is so much fun I did not care if I got scolded for dirtying my dress which is last summer's Sunday go to Meeting dress. Daddy takes the kind of walk that is hard on clothes. They cannot see why we climb over rocks and walls when we can get to Mr. Watson's house by going along the road and turning down Orchard Lane. They do not think much of him anyway.

1917

Lyman Hill [Daddy]
Helen's Grandfather

Camilla Burrows Hill
Helen's Grandmother

Helen's grandparents' house on Ashby Street

Asa Hoxsie Clarke
Helen's Father

Alice Hill Clarke
Helen's Mother

We went to his house today. He putters about and is kind of dirty and speaks bad English. I play with his granddaughter Mildred, but she was not there today. Mr. Watson has spy glasses and he lets me look through them, but they are not fixed right for my eyes and he gets put out if I monkey with them. He says I haven't any meat on my bones which makes me sick. I do not like that expression. One time I had a tooth ake and he said if I put a wad of tobacco all warm and chewed from his mouth on the gum, it would cure it in a shake of a lamb's tail. I said I would rather have the tooth ake. Daddy would not let him. I am sorry for Mildred, it must be awful to have an ignerent old man for a grandfather. Grandma says a body can tell he had no bringing up the way he never scrapes the mud off his shoes and tracks up a clean kitchen floor. Mildred's mother is fat and nice but her father Capt. Rosson is seldom home. Grandma says the Rossons are good stock and why he married old man Watson's daughter she has never fathomed.

When we got home the coast was clear, but I knew I would catch Hale Coulumby on account of my dress and I did. They were not very worried because when they found Daddy had lit out they put one and one together. Grandma started to rake me over the coals because I had slid out without so much as an excuse me, but Daddy said "leave the child alone." Grandma said we were a tryal [trial] and shut her lips tight. She says it is wicked the way we idaleyes [idolize] each other and some day there will come a Day of Rekoning.

July 10. Daddy and I went downstreet this afternoon. We sat on Mr. Ebenezer Morgan's Ice Cream Parlor veranda over the River and ate peatch ice cream which is my favorite. After I ate one saucer full he said, "Want another?" I said yes, but wasn't allowed two on account of spoiling by appetite for my vitels [vittles] come meal time. Daddy said meal times came around regular and I had best eat all the peatch ice cream I could store away while I relished it because some day I might not. I do not believe that day will ever come.

There were row boats on the River that we watched while we ate. Daddy said he had always had one and mist not having one. I said why can't we? I could row.

"I am too old," he said. "Couldn't let those little pipe stems pull around an old hulk like me."

I said I could, and he wasn't, he looked real rugged. He said, "Be as it may, your Grandmother would put her foot down flat and I presoom she is right. She is after me for taking you on long walks. Musn't forget I'm getting long years."

The ice cream stuck in my throat and I almost cried.

He said, "I guess row boats are out, Helen. We'll have to walk along the shore." I said I would rather do that than go to Spain with anyone else. He smiled and the lump in my throat got bigger and bigger. I got the ice cream down and then we walked all around downtown and stopped in lots of stores. On the way back, we stopped at the French people's house which is interesting because there are painted statures of Saints and we ended up at the blacksmith shop. Mr. Chapman gave me some candy. It was nice of him, but the candies were dirty from being lose in his pocket and I had hard work downing them so his feelings would not be hurt.

We were late and they were looking for us. Time goes fast when I am with Daddy. I do not mean to be late. They said I was getting black as a nigger and where was my hat? I went in with Mama and Grandma took Daddy in tow. She scolded him for going out in the heat at his age.

July - The sink dreen [drain] is stopt up and I am glad because it is interesting to have Mr. Hopwood the plumer come to fix it. He is so fat, his boy has to get in the small places, he is a mass of fat. He says he is too fleshy for his calling and this is certainly so. You can hear him before you see him, he puffs and blows so loud, and also wheezes. He says 't'aint the vittles he eats, it's his nature and he bets I put away more than he does. It does not seem possible. He says folks think his big belly is full of food when it is only layers of fat and the inside no bigger than a walnut. I think that is very interesting.

This afternoon we went downtown and into all the stores. We met Mrs. Annie Lathrop and her sister Miss Jennie in Gene's. Miss Jennie is pretty, fat and simply minded. She was not born that way, convulsions did it. They have to watch her all the living time. I do not see why because she is not violent ever.

July 19 I wish something would happen. Daddy and I are pinening for excitement, Grandma says so. We have had many interesting times together. One time an airship came down in a field near Cousin Nelson's house. When Daddy heard he started for it. Grandma says I went up the street after him like the tail to a kite. We had never seen an airship close to. Daddy says they are remarkable contraptions and if he was a young man he would put money in them.

The burning of the Gilbert Block was the most exciting thing that ever happened. I woke up in Mama's room that morning. I could hear talking coming up thru the hot air register. It was hard to open my eyes, then it came to me that I had been sick in the night and that was why I was in Mama's room.

The screen door was shut and Mama came upstairs all excited. She said did I feel like getting up? She supposed I ought to keep quiet, but the Gilbert Block was on fire and there was a lot going on. I jumped out of bed and got my clothes on the fastest ever. She did not make me eat any regular breakfast except an orange, and we were off. Grandma and Constance too.

Downstreet were throngs of people and firemen and fire carts and hoze all over everything. All the windows were out and red with fire, real flames not just a lot of smoke.

The Gilbert Block is our only big building. Mr. Mark Gilbert built it. Calls were sent to all the towns even Westerly and New London, and father off some folks said. People said it was a disgrace that we had only little hand drawn carts with a building that big in town. They said the whole village would go before we got help. I was never so excited. There was broken glass all over everywhere. It was like the burning of Rome.

They finally got it under control but it had burned hours and was a ruin. Being on the River there was considerable breeze.

We met everyone we knew just like a funeral or Kingstown Fair. No one cared how they looked until after and some women even had aprons on.

No one knows how it started to this day. They told about Old Central Halland wondered if there was another fire bug around. Some thought Mr. Rogers who plays the piano in the moving picture theater which is in that block may have dropped one of those cigarettes he is always smoking. Others said maybe the ovens in the bakery got overheated, so Mother and I and other Daughters of Veterans talked with Mrs. Green who is a Daughter too and owns the bake shop, to show we didn't take any stock in it and it was more likely Mr. Roger's cigarette.

Mr. Charles Cameron lost his voice that day and has never found it. He whispers. When they woke him to tell him the place was on fire he rushed downtown to Mr. Noyes Store where he works in the Gilbert Block. He went to the safe and tried to open it. The fire roaring in his ears. He could not think of the numbers thought he knew them as well as his own name and when he did, his fingers were all thumbs and he couldn't do it, he felt as slow as cold mollasses in the winter time. He told Papa that it was a nightmare trying so hard and not being able to. Well, finally he did get it open and he got out without being burned, but when he tried to talk he had no voice. They said it would come back, but it hasn't so far. He says it was scared out of him for all time. Of course he still works there and we are use to him., but when he leans on the counter and whispers to summer people they act sort of taken back at first.

Well, things as exciting as that do not happen every day. I wish something would turn up. Even a ride with Constable Jim or Jerry Ganu would make me happy.

There was the time there was a train wreck in Stonington. Daddy took me over, but when I heard someone say a load of horses were burned in a box car I got sick. I could smell them. Daddy said it was my imagination. I am squeemish. Trolley cars make me sick too and by the time we got home I was all in. Mama and Grandma were provoked by him and he was put out with me. I do not blame him. I felt that way about myself.

Once there was an autymobile accident on the hill. A woman was hurt, but not where it shows.

1917

The Gilbert Block fire, June 25, 1915

Central Hall in 1865 • Burned in 1880 and again in 1910

The Livery Stable at Bank Square

An Account of My Life

<u>July 25</u> Cloudy. There were Naval Reserve men going away today and Daddy took Constance and me to see the Parade downtown. The Home Gards marched and it was very inspiring to see Maj. Williams on his prancing steed and Evan's father Col. Percy prancing behind. Daddy bought us candy. Patricia and Knox came along and sat on the curb with us.

We followed to the station to see them off, the Naval Reservers I mean. This is a terrible war and I do not know what may become of us. It must be very awful to be a Refugee. This country always helps Refugees, but if we were Refugees who would help us? Well, I guess it could not happen we are so big and strong and important.

<u>July 31</u>. This is the hottest day since 1901 which was before I was born so I have never known such a hot day in all my life. The sun is a molting ball of fire. The bedrooms are suffacating and the floors are hot to touch. All the blinds are closed making a dim, green light which is interesting. The veranda is like an oven. Even down on the shore there is no breeze and you are cool only as long as you are in the water. Papa says think of teniment [tenement] children. Constance and I are going to sleep downstairs because it is cooler on the coutch under the window. We will not have to go to bed until late because it is to hot to sleep. I wanted to sleep in the hammock but Grandma thinks night air is bad for one. The moskitoes are awful too. We have had ice cream all day. Vanilla not peatch. Also lemmonade which makes a person ooze worse though cooling going down.

The locuss [locusts] buzzed and it was so hot in my play house back of the purple lilack I could not make believe. Papa has just read what I have written. He says it makes him hot to read it, but when it gets cooler he would like to know why I feel that I must stick t's in everything. He is using the palm leaf fan so hard it is coming undone. There are drops of presperation on his forehead which is high. He is laughing at me. I have spells of putting in t's.

<u>Aug. 2</u> Mama took us down to Maxson's Beach this evening. There is not much sand mostly stones. Mildred Wells and her mother were there.

<u>Aug. 4</u> Mama had to go to Mr. Wheeler's Drug Store this evening and I went with her. I had peach ice cream. We stopped at Mr. Blivens store across the Bridge which smells of pears, chocklates and newspapers, an interesting smell. Mama says I have a nose like a hound dog and I could find my way about by sniffing. I take my sense of smell from Grandma. There is one thing that I do not take from anyone. Constance is the same. We think words are colored. Grandma says foolishness. I do love the night, it is so majical.

<u>Aug. 6</u>. Sunny in the afternoon. Grandma, Mama and I went a calling on Winnie in Noank. Winnie is the woman Cousin Tracy married. Daddy likes her, but Grandma don't. They talked about the man who was blown

up. It was a very trajik thing. His name was Chester and he got dinimite and put it in his orchard and laid down on it and blew himself sky high. My, what a bang that must have made. They found arms and legs in the apple trees and it took a long time to get him together again. When the trolley car past his house I looked to see if I could see something, but I guess they have found everything. Mama was discusted [disgusted] with me. She said I turned myself sick over a dead dog or a birthmark and had a goolish [ghoulish] interest in this.

It was an awful thing to do. Lots of awful things happen. It was awfuller about Mr. Fish. He was a Noank Fish. I mean he was, he is no more.

One day he drove to Town Hall where his wife worked in the office. She was sole alone except for another woman. Mr. Fish pulled out a pistol out of his pocket and shot his wife dead as a doornale. He was gone before the woman who had seen the deed done before her face and eyes, could move. Then she screamed and <u>screamed</u> and screamed until people came a running. It was so quiet and then <u>bang</u> her friend was dead at her feet.

Mr. Fish drove back to Noank where he went to his Mother's house and not saying a word of the thing he had done, said he wanted his little boy who stayed there while his mother was in the office. Mr. Fish said he wanted to take him for a ride. So his Mother and the little boy's grandmother, washed his face and hands and combed his hair, for she could not know the desprate thing her son had done. Well, that man took his own little boy to a barn and killed him and then himself. It was worse than the dinimite man on account of more people got killed. I bet he went to Hell, but maybe not. Grandma says a nicer man never walked the streets. I think a man has got to be real bad to do such a thing. I do not see how he ever could have been good.

There are a lot of interesting stories I may relate someday. I know about Tony Packer's wife who died. They don't know I know about it, but I do. One time Grandma had someone in her sitting room. The window was open and I was on the veranda getting honey out of honeysuckle and they did not know I was there. I did not know I was not meant to hear until it got so exciting I <u>had</u> to listen. It is exciting, sad and true.

One day when Mama and I were down street I saw an interesting happening. There was this little boy, a real child and very homely, no more than four or five, with a hired girl. Mama knew his name but I forget because I do not know him or his family. He had an ice cream cone from Mr. Morgan's Ice Cream Parlor, strawberry, and as we passed he tipped it and the whole scoop fell on the side walk. The hired girl who was also very homely and likewise scrawny, swooped down and picked it up with her bony, red fingers shining from naptha soap and stuck it back in the cone and the little boy started licking again. Mama went tight all over. I said the child must be extremely fond of ice cream because I could never eat any that had been picked up by red skeleton fingers. Later she said to Grandma, "That is what happens when a green girl takes care of your child." Green means ignorant, but I think a better color would be red because she was red up to her elbows and pale the rest of the way.

Well, if the little boy didn't mind I guess no harm was done, because the sidewalk was pretty clean and I did not see any tobacco juice or chewing gum. Just the same with my qualmish stomach I am glad we do not have a hired girl. It is enough of a trial eating fuzzy candy from the pockets of Daddy's friends.

It is not the dirt I would mind so much, but the shiny, skinny red fingers. I am thankful unto God we do not have a hired girl.

Thoughts

When I feel like this I have to write it out of me. Somehow it helps for the time being. I was reading in the leather chair while Grandma and Mother were sewing and talking. I did not pay any attention until I heard Mother say, "It was a mistake to have them so far apart, six years and five months is too much."

"Well that depends on the child," Grandma answered rocking back and forth. "Some children like to mother a little brother or sister but there's nothing motherly about that child as you can see by the way she has always been with her dolls. I've seen a child hug a rag dolly to her and croon over it, and I've known girls who played with dolls secretly after they were in their teens. She's a solitary child if there ever was one."

Mother saw that I was listening and she said gently, "You do love your little Sister don't you, Helen?"

"Yes," I said.

"Then don't you think you could make more of her?"

"I cut out paper dolls for her," I said. "and I read to her and tell her stories."

"Yes," Mother said, and sighed.

She thought I didn't understand, but I did. There is something wrong with me, I guess.

One day a girl who did not know me or anything about me said something about me being an only child.

"I'm not," I told her. "I have a little sister." She said she never would have known it, she was sure I was an only child.

"Why?" I asked her. "Because I am spoiled acting?"

She said no, of course I was bossy but she wouldn't say spoiled, it was just something about me.

Then Grandma said, "She is capable of a blind devotion such as she has for her Grandfather, but she is not a loving child."

All of a sudden I was crying and couldn't stop. They comforted me and Mother said over my head, "We shouldn't discuss the child as if she wasn't there."

I had to get away by myself.

I know it is very hard for me to be affectionate with people. I sometimes think I love <u>things</u> better than people and feel wicked. I like to stroke a tree and sometimes put my cheek against it. I like to kiss flowers and kittens and puppies. I like to snuggle baby animals against me, but I wouldn't give two cents to hold a baby. What makes me so? Why am I so different?

I can imagine but I cannot pretend.

Thoughts

I wonder a lot about Ase, my father. I think I <u>know</u> Grandma and Mother pretty well, but there are so many sides to him I can never be sure. There are flashes of understanding but they don't last long enough to do much good. I guess I don't love him although he is very kind sometimes and it is wicked not to love one's father.

I am proud of him at times and ashamed at others. When he swears such fearful oaths and says vulgar awful things I can't help being ashamed.

The other girls fathers don't care whether they chew gum or not and are not disapproving and sarcastic if they manicure they're nails out of their own room. I don't mind that because he is right, but I do wish he would not call me a son of a b-- when he gets mad. He does not say it because he thinks I am one but because he wants to abuse me. For a long time I did not know what it meant, but I knew it wasn't nice.

Mary's father is not half as smart as Ase, but he does not call her such names. I don't mind plain swearing very much, but when he curses something shakes inside of me. I cannot set down the terrible things he says, they are terrible and show imagination. He makes up all his own curses and they are very awful.

I told him one time that I bet I had heard more oaths than the kids down on the flats, where I am not allowed to go. He swore louder than ever because what I said hurt him.

But I am proud because he carries himself like a king and is hansome when not in his old clothes. He knows all the important men in town, Col. Morgan, Percy Stowe, Charles P. Williams the millionaire, and Kirk, to name a few.

He knows all about politics and history and has opinions on everything which are worth listening to or Kirk would not argue by the hour, because Kirk is rude and eccentric.

Ase is a champion checker player and a perfect shark at mathematics. He is very well read and can write poetry and satyrical essays which he hands around and then throws in the stove. He has a sense of humor and can be very funny. He can make a crowd of men just roar with laughter by telling tall stories which no one can top no matter how much they try.

He is very generous and gives Constance and me lots of presents and always the very best. When I was seven he gave me a little gold watch with blue figures on its face. He just despises anything cheap. Grandma says he thinks he is Lord Mayor of the Universe.

He is good to the poor, but very rash.

Once in a while he will bundle up what he thinks are old clothes and give them away without telling Mother before hand. It makes her extremely angry because there are usually things in the bundle she would not let go. She says if we children have two pair of shoes apiece he is not happy until he has given our second pair away. When Constance was born, Dr. Allyn told of some poor family up back country who were in dire need, so Ase picked up all the clothes and things he could lay hand to and sent it to them. Mother was powerless to prevent it. It was not good sense because most of the things he sent were summer things and not likely to be much use with winter already on. She says if he had only acted sensibly, found out what was needed, Grandma could have made up the bundle. And she asked what good he thought my scalloped dress with elbow sleeves would do the Crouches and why didn't he take the coal from the cellar to give them in the bargain.

He said when Grandma gave the poor anything she made it ugly first, like taking off pretty buttons and putting on plain white ones.

Sometimes I agree with one side, sometimes the other. I don't know. I guess Ase isn't very sensible. I mean, maybe the children like pretty things and maybe they just spoil them. Grandma's good, strong bone buttons are much more practical. If I <u>knew</u> a little girl who wanted a pretty sash or something I'd give it to her, but when I have seen dirty kids wearing my dresses they are always torn and stained till I hardly recognize them. Grandma believes in helping people to help themselves, but when she sees they won't she washes her hands of them. She says water is free and soap is cheap, that she never saw a house so poor and mean it couldn't be kept clean.

Mother makes our clothes by hand, spending hours embroidering them. She feather-stitches at least one row on my everyday petticoats and smocks or cross stitches my school dresses, while my Sunday school dress and Dancing School dress are scalloped or hem stitched or embroidered with French knots and that flat, heavy kind of embroidery. She says if she thought the pains she took would be appreciated she wouldn't say a word and that if he had put the time on them she had, it would be a different story.

He is a very quixartic [quixotic] man. Almost at the same time, before Mother was up and around I made a fuss when Nurse Reynolds tried to make me wear a dress I didn't like. Ase snatched it from her and thrust it into the fire. I was tickled to death to be rid of it, but Mother was not. She was even angrier because he made an exhibition of himself before Nurse Reynolds who would be sure to tell and was still in a shocked state because she had caught him feeding steak to the cat. I don't think that is so terrible, feeding the steak to Sailor Cat, but Nurse Reynolds is frugal.

I think the worse thing about Ase is his changeableness. He hates any sign of snobbishness, but the time he found me talking to the boy from the flats who mows our lawn each week, he sent me into the house and got an old man to come from then on. I did not much like the boy because he smelled, but when he talked to me I felt it my bounden duty to talk to him.

I said if he thought the Bogues kid did it so he could laze on the job he was wrong because I pointed out all the places he missed and saw to it he did them. I use to go down on the docks with Albertine whose father cooked on the *Leander* and eat after the men got thru when the boats were laying up on Saturday. Mr. Rogers is a great cook and quite interesting because he got Albertine's Mother thru a matrimonial agency. It makes me feel sort of responsible for Albertine because it was Ase who put it into Mr. Rogers head. Seems he was looking for a wife, his first being dead, and not finding one to his liking so Ase and some of the others got hold of a matrimonial magazine and gave it to Mr. Rogers. I asked Mother if it were one of Ase's tall stories, or the truth and she said she only knew what Ase said. He has remarkable powers of invention, but Grandma calls it lying.

Well, one day Capt. Rowe saw me eat at there and he chuckled and told Ase and he raged. I couldn't see why. I know from Grandma that a sea cook is very low down the scale, but if he wants me to be democratic why does he care? You simply can't tell from one minute to the next what is going on in his mind. I asked him if he acted so about the docks because he was afraid I'd hear bad language. He swore, then laughed and said I had a sly sense of humor. I have not.

I liked eating there. The beans are no better than Mother's, but the coffee is much stronger and I like the long oil cloth tables with the rim around them and the heavy china even if I do have to use two hands to lift the mugs.

No, Ase is not like anyone else in the world. He says I don't love him. When he feels like it he is very affectionate. He thinks it alright to swear at me one day and kiss me the next, but I don't. I sort of edge away from him in spite of myself which makes him angry. He says, "Why won't you sit on my knee and make friends?" Sometimes I try but I am stiff at first and by the time I have softened up he is tired of holding me. He says, "You know I don't mean a word I say. You know I'm proud as Punch of you."

Maybe, but it doesn't make me like to be sworn at a bit better.

He says "They" meaning the Burrows have set me against him. When he goes out he is always clean and Mother says as a young man he was fastidious to the nth degree, but around the house he is <u>very</u> untidy. I hate whiskers. He says I am a little old woman. Sometimes I have to clean his room which is not pleasant. Grandma says he ought to live in a pig sty.

He drops his clothes on the floor as he takes them off and will not even bother to put his soiled clothes in the hamper. He gets more sarcastic day by day and curses terribly at everything when he rages, his face gets purple.

A True Story

Ella was a lovely girl. She got married and lived down the road apiece. It was long before my day. After awhile she had a baby and almost died. They dispared of her but she got better and left her bed. One day she did her housework and tended the baby and talked with her next door neighbors. They said so afterwards. In the afternoon some one saw her come out of the house with the baby all wrapt up. They wondered where she was going in such a hurry, but she did not look right nor left, just walked till she came to the tracks down the line. She climbed the banking and laid right down on the tracks with her little baby in her arms. Then the train came screetching around the bend where no one can see until right on top of the tracks. The engineer did not see her until he was most on her. He could not stop in time. He said she looked right up at him, not afraid, sort of smiling. And he knew the bundle of clothes must be a baby. No one pulled her out in the nick of time like in the movies. The terrible wheels went right over them. The engineer stopped the train and everyone got out and people popped up from all around. The poor man was not to blame, he could not have forseen in time. He went just about crazy. He said he could never run an engine again. People said he would get over it, but he never did. He kept thinking something was around each bend. I guess he was all right on the straight going. Anyway he was a broken man. I bet he saw her day and night. It was a trajedy of the first water. No one knows why to this day. Her folks said her mind was turned. Some said maybe her husband knew, but Grandma says "Nonsence, Tony Packer wasn't to blame for anything unless it was for being born a man."

In a made story Ella would have lived happily ever after she got married.

<u>Aug. 7</u> This has been a horrible day. First of all Albertine came over this morning. She did not want to play so we sat in the long grass and talked about babies. I did not like it. She said did I know? I said "what," making believe I did not know what she meant. I felt quamish. She said I was a cimp and thought the stork brought them. I said I did not for years and years. She said she bet I thought Dr. Allen brought them in his satchel. I said I didn't, but he certainly had a lot to do with it. Albertine said she sposed he brought cats her kittens and cows there calfs and laughed too silly for words. I said there were animal doctors like Dr. Williams who were called vetenarians. She said, "Oh think you are smart because you know big words and think babies come in satchels. My but you are a cimp."

She is not much older than I am, the mean thing. She asked "what makes babies come?" And I said the woman has to be sick first. She said "what makes them sick?" I replide that I did not know. So she said "they get sick all right, but it aint ordinary sickness. They get it sleeping with a man and its awful."

I said it wasn't so or why weren't married women sick all the time.

Albertine is an only child, but her parents sleep together every night. She said that was what she wanted to know, they did something so wiked they could not talk about it. I know Mama acts funny and shamed when I ask questions, but I do not believe she would do a wiked thing and I told Albertine so. She said they could not help it, everyone did it, and that we would have to someday or be old maids, and that it was as nasty as could be.

Just then Grandma knocked and said, "Come in" and sort of shooed Albertine. She went, looking scared. Grandma did not say a word and she gave me a warm molasses cookie, but I guess she knew what we were talking about because she knows everything. Finally she said why not listen to the Swiss Music Box. "On a week day?" I said very surprized, and she said maybe I had mist a Sunday some where along the line and today will make up for it.

I got Daddy to play it for me. "Nelly Bly" and all of them. When it run down I did not ask him to wind it up because it is bad for the delekit little points and the comb thing. It was a great treat to hear it on a week day and I appreciated it extensively. I felt good again and sat on the wall. Then that horrid Mr. Machet the ice man came by drunk. I do not care if he drinks himself to death and I wish he would, because when he is drunk he lashes his horse. I want to hit him and scream but the time I yelled "Stop it, stop it you pig you!" he hit harder than ever. When he is dead drunk he just hudles up and that poor, dear horse takes him home.

How I hate him. I wish I were a giant and could horse whip him. I'd make him pull the horse and the ice and I'd lash, lash, lash every step of the way. I hate cruel people. I don't care if he is drunk and doesn't know. He ought to be hurt and hurt for every bit of pain he makes.

This has been a horrid, horrid day so far.

<u>Aug.</u> - This morning I found Daddy looking at the orioles in the crabapple tree. They come every year and we love them. We watched them and the humming bird in the trumpet vine until I said, "What shall we do today?" Daddy rubbed his chin and said we might look thru the telescope and site a ship at sea or we might sit still and recite a canto of "The Lady of the [Lake]" or we might walk down to Dell Avery's and see what he thought of the world today. I said lets do them all starting with the last.

He said he sposed we had better tell Them because they got cross if we didn't. Grandma said not to traipse all over creation and Mama said "no trolley cars, remember." That was because one day we took one to Poquonok and got off and walked in some woods where we had never been. Daddy made whistles and a crooked stick into a snake and we picked flowers and ate berries. No one knew where we were and when we got home they said we had been gone for hours and they didn't even know where to hunt.

An Account of My Life

Today we didn't even have to take Constance who is too young to go far because she was playing dolls with those kids.

We went down to old Mrs. Pendleton's. I do not like her, but she has a nice flower garden which runs right down to the waters edge. I like the clam shell lane way too. From there we went to the West Mystic Station and talked to Mr. Bob Bradley. He was cutting the grass around the station. He says West Mystic used to be called Oldfield and way back in those days there was a cradel factory there. We met several people and they said, "You are a very active man for your age, Mr. Hill." And he said, "This young un keeps me on the go so much I don't have time to grow old." Daddy walks fast and climbs over walls and only once in a while needs a hand up steep banking. We worked our way back and cut down to Dell Averys. I played in the water and they sat on the doorstep and talked.

When we got home Grandma said I looked as black as any of Old Sol Sebastiens off spring. He is a colored man. Capt. Ambrose Burrows brought them here years ago and they are Haitians.

I heard an interesting thing. Papa says Mighty Mitchel can't <u>read</u> or hardly <u>write</u>. And Mr. Lamfere who cleans our privys and cess pools can't either except to sign his name and do a little figuring. How can they bear it?

I shall be glad when I can spell everything. The family spells words for me out loud if I ask, unless busy, but they are curious. They will say, "For heavens sake <u>why</u> do you want to use that word?" Or if Papa feels like being amused he will say "do you mine telling me in just what connextion you intend to use that word?"

It is a bother. Well, there is no excuse for me not being a good speller because both Mama and Papa are. I do not think I spelled Mr. Lamferes name right but if I ask Papa will say, "what Lamfere ingages your interest at the moment," and if I say the cess pool one he will laugh and Mama will look amused. If I ask them to spell the same word more than once or twice they get mad and say I am careless and don't try to learn.

<u>Aug. 10</u> - This afternoon Grandma and I went a calling on Mrs. Frank Buckeley. I sort of like to go calling because other peoples houses are interesting even when you are pretty use to them. All houses have their own smell. I wore my pink linnen with black ribbon velvet run thru the beeding and black taffeta hair ribbons. Also white socks with pink borders and black Mary Jane slippers. I carried my pink parasol with an ivry handle and my handkerchief and fancy work in a pretty bag. Grandma wore white with a fine black stripe in it and carried her black parasol and her redicule. She smelled of Floridy water and I of rose water. We were a fine sight and a credit to each other.

Angelina was coming up Meeting House Hill and she thumbed her nose at me, but was to afraid of Grandma to do more. I sailed along magestically. Angelina just hates clean people.

1917

  Mrs. Annie lives in a big square house on High Street with a cupelow and has fine crimson peonies every Spring. She and Grandma have known each other always, but Mrs. Annie is younger though not young and in frale health. It was her sister Liza who was Grandma's school chum. It was like this. Mr. and Mrs. Tift had had a family and put away the cradel once and for all when lo and behold, Annie came. Liza was so mortified at her mother and father she almost died of shame. That is why there are so many years betwix and between. Grandma and Liza were great friends and Grandma felt all cut up about it when Liza went queer in her head and died. So now Grandma and Annie are friends. We had a very nice call. There is a niece named Carolyn Beebe who is a great piano player. Mrs. Annie is fond of talking ancestors. She hasn't got any Robert Burrows or Sir Robert Hempstead in her, but she has got a Tift ancestor she thinks a lot of and one side of her is Brewster and came over in the Mayflower.

  She is also a Methodist. I do not know why. We had lemmonde and cookies and much conversation. Seems we Burrowses and Tifts have always been friends. They came to Mystic a little after us and the very land the house stands on and the older one next to it where Celia Laurence comes summers use to be Burrows land. Robert Burrows who was called Mister which was important in those days had more land than he knew what to do with and in sixteen something he deeded a passel to the Tifts about the same time he gave some to the Fishes. He did this on account of being lonely and wanting near neighbors. Mrs. Annie says she think it is remarkable that we have remained friends to this day. It makes a body feel sort of solem. I mean even if I did not like a Tift I would feel as if I ought to because if Burrowses have liked Tifts all these years the fallt would be in me.

  It is funny about Mrs. Frank's mother. Seems Mrs. Sam went years and years without a sign of a baby to bless theyre home and when she found she was going to have Frank she was just plain <u>mad</u> and would not sew a stitch of baby clothes. Grandma said "Shaw! What good did she think <u>that</u> would do her."

  And Mrs. Annie said solemly, "Frank was born and not a thing to put on him no more than a beggar's child. Some of the family never got over it they felt it so keenly." I said if you won't admit a thing sometimes it seems as if it won't happen, maybe she felt like that. Mrs. Annie said, "Bless the child" and passed the cookies which were good. Her hired girl is first rate.

  On the way home Grandma said I had behaved real well on the whole and had not said anything too startling and she was encouraged to hope I would curb my unruly member more and more. I heard her tell Mama Mrs. Annie said it was a treat to know a well behaved child in this day and age and that Allie <u>did</u> dress me so prettily. It is not often I can half way please Grandma so I feel real set-up. I guess it pays to be good, but somedays I <u>can't</u> be. She says I am not a bad child, but have many fallts and fallts can become vises so I must keep watch. I have got tendercies that bear watching, but she won't tell me what they are.

Well, she is a just woman accorden to her lights. Like the time I tipped the privy. The lege runs along side and I kind of like to sit on a flat part of it and my feet against the side and push. I am not strong enough to push it over which I do not want to do anyway, but sometimes I can rock it back and forth if I shove extry hard. I know it is not ladylike but it is a great temptation.

Well, this day I had it teetering a little when the door opened and Grandma stept out. Her hat was crooked and she was mad. My stars, I liked to of died then and there. I went stiff all over. I said, "oh my, I didn't know you were in there." She said she callated I didn't, how many times had I been told not to do it, if she could not have peace and privicy <u>there</u>, where <u>could</u> she have it short of the burying ground and even then she wouldn't put it past me to push her tombstone over.

I was agast and said "please go back and I will not touch it again."

"I have lost the notion," she said magestically.

She looked sort of skewgee and I asked if it had hurt her any and she said, "Only my dignity, I guess."

Then she said she guessed I had had a scare too by the looks of me and she would not tell Mama this time, but it must never happen again, things like that being upsetting to a woman her age. It was very just of her because when she complains about Constance or me Mama thinks she must get after us and worst of all not let us go up there for a day or so.

I always make sure no one is in it before I do it now.

<u>Aug. 18</u> Spent the afternoon at Maxsons Beach. Constance and I have new bathing suits. All the Bradley tribe was there. We bought candy at the station. Mr. Bob Bradley's flowers look fine.

Mama would not wait for me to pick tiger lilies from Wild Cat Ledge so I am going to tomorrow. She can not see why when we have them on ours and under the wood house window. I think tiger lilies from Wild Cat Ledge are more magnificent. I like to imagine yellow tiger eyes looking out of the caves. It use to scare me because I believed wild cats lived there. I guess they use to long ago. Tigers and wild cats are the same so I think tiger lilies are enchanted tigers. One day I had so many in my arms they came up under my chin and I was afraid they would bite my throat. I threw them down in the road, but could not bear to see them wilting in the white dust so I picked them up again. If they turned to wild cats they would chase me for throwing them away.

1917

Mystic & Noank Library

Fred Rathburn's car that took the family to Point Judith R.I.

Union Baptist Church, Mystic

<u>Aug. 22</u> All hands on deck early this morning because Papa hired Mr. Fred Rathburn to drive us to Point Judith in his big touring car for fifteen dollars. My Aunt Hannah lives on a big farm close to the ocean. Dinner was worthy of a queen and they said they did not see how I could eat so much and stay so thin. Mama was put out because Aunt Hannah compared me with Barbara who is many pounds heavier though I am a couple of months older.

I like farms. Even the hired man is good stock being a Knowles. The ocean is at the foot of the road and in winter there are wrecks.

I like Uncle Charles Tucker. Aunt Hannah calls him Mr. Tucker to his face which is funny because they are man and wife. I cannot imagine Mama calling Papa, Mr. Clarke. He is a nice gentleman and says I have a good vocabulery. Mama looked pleased and Aunt Hannah snift and said my tongue was hung in the middle. Barbara can sew and cook but is kind of dumb. Uncle Charles uses interesting expressions. I would rather listen to him than the women. Papa and he have intelegent discussions about politicks and such.

Barbara has her room done in yellow and white, which is pretty and she has got a glass lighthouse filled with different colored sand from different beaches. We do not like each other a bit which is a pity. I should like to live there but not with her. She is much bigger than I and homely though she has got curly hair. Aunt Hannah is naturally parshall to her own.

I meant to write this down yesterday. We had a bad thunder storm in the night and Mr. Nelson Baker's garage burned down. The flames lit up Papa's room and we all went in and watched. It was exciting, but they put it out awful fast, but not before it was guttered. I guess that will set him back a pretty penny.

It was a miracle the old house did not go. It is very old and dry.

<u>Aug -</u> It is hot and the locuss [locusts] are buzzing. Went to the liberry this morning to get a Little Pepper Book. I do not think much of them, but Mama thinks they are more fitten than the books I pick up. She says they put ideas in my head.

It is cool and shady all the way, but hot just the same even under the big pines. The liberry is cool as a sullar [cellar] being made of marble inside and in no time I was clammy and cool. Miss Bridgeham went to school with Grandma and was a good scholar. Now she is a sweet old lady with a good for nothing brother who is a dead beat. She bears her cross real well. She helps Miss Annie Riker who is liberian. She likes to find books for kids and takes a lot of pains which is why Mama trusts her. If I pick up one that looks good she says it is not suitable, but she is so gentle I give in and do not mind until I get home and start to read. Anyway I go by Elder Miner's, Mrs. Wolf's (our S.S. [Sunday School] Superintendent) and Cousin Mary Fitch's and one or all stop me and ask what I am reading and click their teeth and tut-tut if it is not stupid and goody goody.

1917

Today Nell Crary was working in her garden. The phlox smelled lovely but I do not really like to talk to her because she is deaf and dumb and makes funny sounds. It is because Capt. Jesse Crary married a cousin, which you should not do. Grandma says only two normal children were born out of five. It is sad. Nell use to be a pretty little girl with long curls. I guess curls aren't everything. Daddy says Capt. Crary wasn't much to look at being pigin breasted, but was a very able man. Nell likes to tell about her long curls, and how she and Mama and Mrs. Fanny Fish went bicicling when they were young ladies. Young Jesse, only he isn't really young, lives on Gravel Street summers. Stuart and Dayton are his sons. He is an editor or something on a New York newspaper.

<u>Aug. 25</u>. Angelina has just gone home and I am glad because she is dirt mean and I don't like her. She lives in a little house on Crary Hill and has not been here long. She is a mean, bold girl, but I have to be nice to her just because she is poor and dirty. Papa says he will tan my hide if I am not. I have never had a whipping and know he would not give one to a girl my age, but I do try. I bet he would not be nice to any man he hated like I do Angelina. When she came into the yard I made believe I was glad to see her. She is very hard to amuse and wants to do all the things I am not allowed to do and if I say so she calls me a baby. She is very nosey too and if I do not look out I find I have told things I did not mean to tell, like the price of things or how much coal we burn. I cannot see why she cares, but she is like that. She did not want to do anything, but be mean. She said she didn't like my dress and that she has a swell silk one for best which is no such thing! She says she'd hate to be as skinny as I and that I wasn't pretty and never would be. She said I gave myself airs. So I told her what I thought of her, but there was so much I couldn't say on account of her being poor and no account and not wanting to hurt her feelings that way, she got the best of it until we got to calling names and then I beat her because she has not much imagination or vocabulary. When I called her a white-livered pole cat she could not think of a thing to say and only thumbed her nose at me. She got enough of it and went home and I felt fine until I told Grandma how I had settled <u>her</u> for once. Grandma said, "Do you have to descend to <u>that</u> level." I felt horrid and ashamed.

Today uncle Ase came to see us with Little Ase who is not right in the head though not simple and a good piano player. Uncle Ase is really uncle to Papa who is Ase too. Little Ase is not really little, being older and bigger than I, but called so on account of there being so many Ases in the family. They come from Charlestown in South County in Rhode Island where Papa came from. Uncle Ase is very jolly and nice looking and stoky and I like him an awful lot, but Little Ase is funny looking. He is quite old, I mean he is not younger than twenty something, I guess.

Papa and Uncle Ase got out the black books called Congressional Records going way back to seventeen somethings and talked about things that were not interesting and Little Ase and I got tired of it and went up under the apple trees. He is not very tall and seems sort of like a boy, only he isn't and not like a man either. Sometimes he talks to beat the band, but this was not one of the times. He listened to me and grinned and looked at me until I got tired and said "let's go back to the house. I'll race you to the back door." Well, I started out, but he didn't follow. I kept on going just the same and jumped up the veranda steps landing with a fine thud like I always do and into the house banging the screan door.

Well! I was never so surprized. Uncle Ase dropped the book he had and jumped to his feet and took me by the shoulders and with an awful look in his eyes said, "What did he do to you? Did he frighten you? Did he hurt you? Where is he?" And before I could answer he started all over again, almost crying. Papa said, "Nothing's wrong Uncle Ase. Helen, answer him!" And there I was trying to and getting shook and yelled at. Finally I said no to everything wondering what on earth was the matter.

Uncle Ase said, "You're sure, Helen?" And then, "Why did you leave him? Why were you running as if the devil was after you?" and so on.

Well, Papa and Mama explained I was always running and jumping and making a clatter and they said I just took a notion to come back to the house, they guessed.

Little Ase came in then, and Uncle Ase turned to him and asked him questions and Little Ase grinned and shook his head. I thought Uncle Ase's feelings was hurt so I went over and took Little Ase's hand and he sat down and took me on his knee. And then Mama said, "Helen, get up. You're too big a girl for that." Well, I know I am, but he wanted to and I didn't want to hurt any more feelings.

They went pretty soon and when he left Uncle Ase put his arms around me and kissed me and said "Asy you don't know how lucky you are." and there were tears in his eyes and by that time I was most crying myself everything being so mixed up.

When they drove off, Papa looked at Mama and said "Whew" and wiped his forehead. Then he said to me. "You little idiot why did you scare that fine old man to death." And Mama said, "The child does not know what it is all about, she meant no harm. I am sorry as can be, but he'll find he will not have an easy moment until that-" And Papa said,"He'll break his heart over him first."

"Why did he think Little Ase hurt me?" I asked him. "My goodness why should he, he likes me fine."

But they would not answer anything I believe. And later Mama said to Grandma. "Children can be so seekretive, do you suppose-"

Grandma said, "Nonsense. Nothing bothering her but what killed a cat."

She meant `curiosity' of course. Everyone has been horrid to me to-day except Little Ase and I don't think he is so crazy as lots of people.

<u>Aug -</u> I have not had any fun today. Not having anything more interesting to do I read "Othello the Moor of Venice" by William

Shakespeare. I read quite a ways in it, not liking it much, or getting much sense out of it. Papa is always talking Shakespeare to me because of the beauty of the language, he says. Today he was real put out with me and called me carping purest because I pointed out that the Duke shouldn't have said "more safer." When I asked him to explain certain parts that just did not make sense he told me I did not need to understand them until I was older, and that all I needed to get from it was a baysick something or other.

I was quite shocked about Desmona marrying a colored man. First I thought a Moor was maybe different but Bratiano mentions his sooty bosom, and the Duke gives that idea, and Roderigo speaks of thick lips, so I guess there is no mistaking he was a nigger. I was not as shocked as a Southern girl maybe, but I was shocked considerable.

This evening I sat with Shakespeare in my lap, tired of reading and thinking about Othello, who though noble makes me sort of sick somehow. I do not read Shakespeare for pleasure and I do not think him so all fired wonderful as Papa does, but his people stick in your mind and are real.

I said: "If I married Ralphy Powers I bet you'd act just like Bratiano only more profane."

Mama said what <u>posessed</u> me to even <u>speak</u> of a negro in that way and that I should be ashamed.

I said I only did it to compare Bratiano and Papa.

Well, Papa had come out of his book and so he tried to explain to me.

"That pesky Shakespeare." Mama said, "is imoral. What kind of a father are you."

<u>He</u> said I had better see life thru Shakespeare's eyes than those of immebecilick pap feeders.

<u>I</u> said I read it because it came after Hamlet in the book.

She gathered up her sewing and left the room.

Papa looked at me and said, "Suppose you digest your mentall fodder in silence, hereafter."

Such a fuss about an old play I do not even like!

I learned something interesting the other day. I have just found out the Booshaws are really French and their name is pronounced, I mean <u>spelled</u> B-e-a-u-c-h-a-m-p.

They are poor people and the father is an awful drinking man. They say when he is drunk he tries to make people pronounce his name the French way with tears in his eyes, but it does no good, folks just call him Booshaw. Well, my goodness, most every one calls the Lebaux's Leeboos and they don't care and they are much worthier people than the Booshaws.

Still I guess I wouldn't like it if I were in France and they twisted my name all around. Names are important, some, pretty sounding, some, pretty written, some, both.

Why, Marjorie Beauchamp is a lovely name written out! It sounds like a great lady not like those grimy looking Booshaws. Things like that are sort of interesting, I think.

<u>Aug.28</u>. Today I was sitting on the steps doing nothing. Mrs Spenser was doing nothing on her front veranda and she called me over to talk with her.

Mr. Romey Spenser her husband has a meat market. Some people say Rummey which is not nice because he is not that way all the time. He gives away pretty callendars, the cut out kind with lovely roses and many other flowers and lovely looking people. Mrs. Spenser has them all taked on the walls of her sitting-room. They are very gay. I hung this years over the kitchen table but Papa said it turned his stomach and hung a great big Atlantic Thread callendar with a ship on it over it.

Mrs. Spenser has a player piano. I like to hear the notes go lickety-split. She is not one of my favorite people. She is a pretty woman and sort of silly, also a gad about.

When I came back I sat on the stone wall doing some thinking. There is a flat stone which is not imbellished with ivy where I sit. Maybe I do not give the ivy time to grow. While I was sitting Papa came up the road. He asked did I feel well and it was not natural for a child to sit like a graving image. He said he hoped he had not born a Joan of Arc by mistake. I replide no, I have listened for voices but fear I am too worldly to hear them. He went in laughing. You never can tell with that man. Well, that is the way of the world I guess.

I was thinking what I would be when I grow up. I do not see why anyone has a poky life when there are so many things to do. I was in a store downtown waiting to be waited on one day. The clerck was busy with another man, I mean he was talking to him and not paying any attention to a mere child. He made little drawings on a pile of paper bags and when the man turned them round so he could see them right side up he said. "You mist your calling alright." and the clerck looked sad and said yes, he had mist it. I looked to, but I did not think much of the drawings. If the man wanted to draw things and not work in a store why didn't he? I guess maybe he is shiffless, lots of people are.

After a while, Harry the English boy across the way in Old Ed Burrows house (Old Ed Burrows is no more) came out and said to come over. They have a new hammock with stripes, very pretty. Ours is so old where you sit makes a bag. We sat swinging a while until Harry put his arm around me. I got right up and went home. I guess English boys are just as silly as our kind here.

The other afternoon Mama was showing his Mother my baby pictures. She would look at the pictures and at me and back again. She said I looked so plump in the pictures and look at me now, and she understood I was an ailing baby. Mama laughed and said that it was a family joke how she rushed me to Tingleys in between sick spells whenever I was looking well.

Mrs. Board said that cleared up the mistery. All she could think of was I must of had a twin, or been stuffed for the ocassion. They thought it very funny. I do not.

After that I crawled under the white lilac with the Pansy book Mama had when a child. It has no covers now but she says it had pretty ones with pansies when new. There use to be more but they were lost. Mama also had a big pile of "Chatterboxes" because she got one every Christmas from the time she could read until she was too old for them. My, I should like to have them. Daddy gave the whole pile to a child in Quakertown before I was born. At first it hurt my feelings because he might of known I would be born and want them, but I guess he knew I would have lots of books and the other child wouldn't, so I am glad he did.

Summer People

Summer people are funny people. They think we are funny and we think they are. We do not like to be called natives like Red Indians or Heathens.

This morning there were two in Main's Store saying how quaint everything was. When Charles filled the molasses jug for me he said. "How you folks fixed for sugar? Putting up much stuff this year?"

I said "Yes," only I guess I said `ay'-uh like you do sometimes. One woman said to the other, "That is what I mean! The natives drall it with a dozen inflictions, So tipically Yankee!" Then she said bossy like. "Repeat it little girl."

I looked at her and did not say anything.

"I'll buy you some of this candy if any of it is fit to eat, but I dare say you are innured to it. Pie for breakfast ought to prepare the stomach for anything!" and she laughed.

Charles is real proud of his candy so I said in a dignafied way. "The flyspeks are on the outside of the case. And I am not allowed to take candy from <u>strangers,</u> thank you."

The other woman laughed and said. "You are put in your place again, Mary. Why <u>will</u> you try!"

The woman named Mary looked cross and said she did not espect curtsy from the natives.

Charles looked real cranky by that time and he said. "No call for her to jump through hoops as I can see. Was there anything more you folks wanted?"

They went out of the door, the one not named Mary giggling.

Charles looked after them and said. "Durn fools."

I wonder what makes them so funny? The ones who come every year are friends also the ones who were born here and come back, but there are some very peculiar ones. They act as if we did not know anything and when we do they call it being trickey. Grandma says she guesses they way they made their money wouldn't bear to close inspection sometimes. She has no use for them since the time they tried to buy a ladder back chair out from under her. She just looked at them and said, "I like this chair." He thought she just wanted to put the price up and when he found she meant what she said he told someone down the road a piece she was a crabby old dame.

Why should she sell it just because he wanted it?

Grandma says some folks are strutting full and there's no place a toad feels bigger than in a little puddle. I guess that is so. They do put on airs which is silly and shows they are no bodies. If we went to where they live and asked questions and tried to buy their things - I guess then the shoe would be on the other foot.

I guess they get that way because some people like to sell them things and make money. They are people who would rather have new things from Montgomery and Ward and laugh at summer people for buying junk. Everybody is not like that.

We like old things and so do lots of people we know. If summer people are as smart as they think they are I should think they would know. I do not eat pie for breakfast because I am not hungry in the morning, but I do not see anything wrong with it. Daddy does and so does Grandma. Mama and Papa do not.

Aug. 29 - Today's weather is a mixture. Spent the day at Ocean Beach in New London where we met Cousin Lena, Great Aunt Mary Jane and Marion who looks just the same as ever though married. Walter was not there being busy working. We took snapshots with the Brownie No. 2, and Daddy and I walked the hard sand close to the waves. The sandwiches had sand in them but were good. If I did not know about the Earl of Sandwich I should think they were called sandwiches because of the sand in them.

Sept. 2 - Went downstreet and bought this months St. Nicholas magazine. Mr. Kretzer said, "School starts pretty soon now. I bet you are glad" and laughed in a cruel gloating way.

Sept. 3 - Even though I have been to the moving pictures this afternoon, I feel flat and gloomy. School starts tomorrow. Papa has bought me a hansome pencil box with simply everything in it. Grandma snift. She says in _her_ day she thought she was just _made_ if she had a penny slate pencil. Daddy has got bags of old coins some of which are those big enormous one cent pieces. I can see where a penny would have seemed like a considerable amount even if it was not worth anymore.

Sept. 4 - I hated that school feeling, but it was fun seeing all the kids again. The first day always gives me a funny feeling. I had a new dress and enjoyed seeing what the other girls had new. Two of them wanted to swap pencil boxes but I did not, though I did swap a few pencils. Mary and I got the big rock for our house, because we got there first. It is in the woods where we kids play recesses. I think Jerry was glad to see me. He plaged me but not in a mean way. He says the reason I am so small is because I smoke cigarets. That is an awful thing to say, he says awful things. Mama let me carry my best green pocketbook to carry the tuition in.

<u>Sept. 17</u> - My birthday. I am twelve years old. I had four books, a picture for my room and another pencil box. Daddy made me a little shelf painted white for my new books and hung it in my room. Mama and Grandma made creton [cretonne] curtains with blue birds on them and a bureau scarf cross stitched in blue and white for the new bureau and looking glass Papa just bought for me. Daddy painted the white wooden bed and chair a glossy white to match. Everything is blue and white even the rag rugs on the floor. I am very happy and love my family very much. I shall try to be a good girl and not get mad when Constance rummiges in my things, or jealous when Daddy notices her. I also promise to keep my room ship shape <u>all</u> the time.

<u>Sept. 20</u> Today Daddy gave me his little green and gold Tennyson because I love it so much, particalarly "The Lady of Shalot."
I do not like girls books except some of Miss Meade's. I prefer Daddy's books. Mama says she does not see why I want to read books too old for me. Well, how can I find out things if I don't? I read until the horsehair sofa pricks through my clothes. Grandma says Papa just about wrecked it courting Mama being a nervous man and I am in a fair way to finish it.

<u>Oct. 4</u> - Terrible storm today. Took my lunch and so did most of the kids. We had fun during nooning hour having a mok wedding in the basement.
This evening Daddy got the Majic Lantern out and hung up a sheet on the wall. Constance and I got very excited. It was a great treat.

<u>Oct. 26</u> - No school today on account of Teachers Convention. Nothing happens so how can I make an interesting Diary?
Vivian's Uncle has got the Mr. Horatio Alger books he had when a boy and I have been reading them. They are a lot the same. I have found one of Daddy's that is more interesting partly on account of pictures. It is all about the uncivilized races and their customs. I am now up to the Figians [Fijians]. Daddy says the printed page has a powerful attraction for him and me. That is certainly so. He cannot step out of the house without buying a book, Grandma says and he has put more money in the pockets of book pedalars than she cares to think. She says if she spent one quarter the amount on ornaments he would call her spend thrift. It is the pedalars she minds worse because there is nothing he will not buy being interested in all things.
I know. If I look at the covers of a book I just can't help opening it and reading. They do not let me dust the books anymore. Papa is a well

informed man they say, but he is not the reader Daddy is and does not love to own books the way Daddy does. There is no one like Daddy for understanding, like not stepping on the same part of the steps, or stepping over cracks and things you like to do and people think foolishness. Why we have a lovely time playing a game with candy hearts picking out the mottoes until we have letters to each other.

Lots of kids grandfathers are dead, and the ones who aren't can not hold a candle to Daddy.

<u>Oct. 30</u> - Bad storm. Papa brought lunches to Constance and me and was provoked when it turned out to be one session. It was quite a tempest.

<u>Oct. 31</u> - I have a new pair of bedroom slippers with pom poms, very pretty. I wrote a poem, This is it.

> I like the russets in the grass
> The woodbine on the wall.
> I loved the Spring - then Summer best
> But now I love the Fall.

<u>Thanksgiving Day.</u> I was so full I could not move. I guess my eyes are bigger than my stomach. There was no company, just us. There was turkey and all the fixens, mince pie, punkin pie and two or three kinds of cake. Grandma does not like to have the table cloth show. It is all so good you do not know what to take and they do not like it if you leave food on your plate except a tiny bit to show you are not greedy. They say waste not want not which is an old saying. I took a little of everything so as not to miss anything. Constance certainly ate a lot for one her size. We were so full we had to stand up and shake it down. After we had flaxed around we felt better and sat down to cut out paper dolls. Poor Daddy did not feel hungry, though he says he is not sick. It is terrible not to have an apetite on Thanksgiving Day. Maybe he will be hungry tomorrow. I would rather have caster oil than have him sick. In the afternoon we read "The Washington Tribune" with me sitting in his lap. I am glad I am little because if I was as big as some girls my age he could not hold me. Mama said I was tiring him and to get down, but he would not let me. He said

"Whose girl are you?" like he use to when I was a small child. I said,

"Yours, Daddy" and we hugged each other hard. Then I went out to play.

<u>Dec. 10</u> - It is awful hard to get coal on account of war and strikes and the school is very cold. Today the weather is cold enough to freeze the hair off a dog and the janitor could not get the rooms warm. The teacher kept sending kids down to see why and Jerry said he swore something awful. Finally they let us go out doors to play because running and playing we would be warmer than in our seats. We most froze. After awhile they

let us in, but we had to keep our coats on and do physical exercises every so often to get our blood to circulating. The teacher was blue except her nose which was red. Finally she set us to copying our compositions, but our coat sleeves got in the way and our fingers were sticks. She said paper was to hard to get to waste, so she dismissed us. Then she and the other teachers went into the teachers room and made tea on the sterno, we saw them. We were cold to the marow of our bones. Jerry said we ought to be given rum or who knows how many of us would last the winter.

Dec. 11 - School today. It was warm enough to stay. I am reading a book of Daddy's called *The Vicar of Wakefield* which is very old being printed in 1797. The s's are f's and it is quite a puzzle. I am getting use to it now and get along fine.

The *Art's Treasury* is the same way. On the front piece it says Nancy Wilcox, Her Book, Oct. 25, 1797. and belongs to Papa, Nancy being an ancestor of his. We have a lot of old old books but I have never seen a book worm. They call me one, which is just a joke.

Daddy bought Mama another pretty plate for the plate rail in the diningroom. She has quite a collection, though not so many as Gurdon's mother who is inclined to over do things. She has got one thing I wish we had and that is a portyair [portiere] of tiny, tinkeling shells between the dining room and parlor.

When I got home from school Old Man Clyde was down from the country. The pikle jar was filled with big, worty pickles in brine with prety sprigs of dill. In the big bowl was the huld [hulled] corn Mrs. Clyde makes better than any one in the world I guess. He was emptying russets into the basket when I came in on a run on account of seeing his horse out side. We have russets too, but his are big and smooth, with thin brown skins with a rosy look.

I like Mr. Clyde much better than John Green Packer, who is good and meechy. We get along fine. He likes a young un to have some spise and spunk, he says. He has first rate hard cider, but we buy the sweet kind. He sells it up in the country and there are goings on. I should like to go. I bet they have fun.

He has got two pretty grown up girls. One is Hazel and she substitutes at the Academy sometimes. You would not think any one so pretty could be so mean.

He has a grown up son, a big rawboned man named Frank. He is cheery, but he sort of takes your breath away. I do not really like him, though he would make a fine pirate, I think.

Old Mr. Clyde made Mama cross by talking about my thinness. He says if he had me on the farm, he'd fill me out. She said I couldn't have more milk, eggs and butter if I lived on two farms. He winked at me, and said then it was the village air. It is naughty of him to plage her, but I know how he feels.

The russet I was eating was so cold it cracked where I bit it.

He said how would I like to visit him for a spell. I can be myself with him so I thought it over for a minute. "It sort of depends," I said.

And he chuckled and said. "On Hazel?", knowing we kids are scared of her. "Out of the school house I callate you can give as good as she sends."

When he makes change he pulls up his coat and pulls out a leather poutch with draw strings like a laundry bag and pokes around with his brown stubby fingers. When I was small I use to think the seams in his hands hurt like cuts. He has a little change purse too, with knobs worn brassy.

Mama kept saying for me to take off my coat, but I kept it on so I could go to the wagon with him because I know the horse real well. That is one horse that does not find an apple a treat. He asked me to ride with him, but I said no, I'd like to ride all over town fine, but I would only be allowed to ride over the hill and a teenty ride was worse than no ride. He undertands fine. He said, "You be'ant a nibbler no more than I be."

I went back in and sat in the rocking chair by the stove eating a worty pikle. I imagined it all out. I made believe I had climbed onto the seat with him and he had pulled the robe over me. I could smell the barn smell just as plain! Mama who was skrutizing [scrutinizing] the floor said he had brought something in on his feet, but I imagined it too. I could feel the horse start and the wagon rattle as we went over the hill. I imagined all the houses he'd stop at and how I'd go in to the nice warm kitchens and how people would say "Aren't you Allie's girl?" or the old people would say "Camella's." Old Mr. Clyde would say he'd borrid [borrowed] me and would wink at me.

The most interesting part was when he turned to go home and the lantrun was lit and bobbing against the side and it got black dark and we had all that way to go. It was cold as cold, but we didn't mind and there were lights burning in the windows.

I have never been to his house or seen it, but Grandma says its an ordinary old house like dozens of others. When we got thru Old Mystic the houses would be quite a ways apart and the windows lighted with lamps more often than electric lights. Mr. Clyde and I would joke and laugh and say Mrs. Clyde would be surprized to see me and we'd guess what there'd be for supper. I did not spoil it by thinking of Hazel. Maybe she wouldn't be at home and maybe Frank would go out after a while. He does not like girls younger than fifteen or sixteen.

Oh I had a lovely time rocking and eating and imagining.

I guess the bedrooms would be tarnation cold even with a hot brick and piles of patch work quilts. I am sort of use to the hot air register.

Maybe it is more fun imagining because Hazel might of been there.

But then, something interesting might of happened that I have not thought of and I might have had lots more fun than I imagine.

Well, he was only joking anyway, knowing Mama wouldn't dream of letting me go, on account of the hard cider and things like that.

58

1917

She is cooking sasage for supper. How I love huld corn and sasage. I am glad I did not go except in imagination. It would be terrible to be struck dead right now. I often think that just before something nice is to happen.

Mama says why do I have such unpleasant thoughts? Well, I try to have pretty thoughts, but thoughts are like babies I guess, you have to take what comes.

I am a great meat eater like the Beef Eaters in England except I like any kind of meat as long as it isn't lamb or veal. Lamb tastes wooly. It is horrid to think of eating animals and I don't. When I see a cow or a pig I dont think of them that way, but when Mr. Bert Williams opens the doors of his meat cart I can not help but think. Raw meat makes me sick. Its like eels. Just caught I'd as soon eat snakes, but cut in small pieces and fried crispy brown in batter I can eat my wait [weight] in them.

Grandma says she hopes I'll outgrow my squeamishness, but she is not sure, because Papa is the same. When he lived on the farm he would not stay around for the butchering and would never eat an animal he had known real well.

The queer thing is he loves juicy steaks - they think it's queer. I understand.

I hope he will not have to go to war because he could not stand the killing.

Just reading the newspapers makes him curse terrible. He asks for the "Day" long before it has come and swears at the paperboy for being late even though he isn't.

He send me to the door a dozen times and if I stop to read the head lines he bellers at me.

Wed. Dec. 12 Mabel Collin's brother Sidney has Scarlet Fever so the school is closed until Friday and maybe longer if he really has got it. Elinor has to [?] a new dress. Mama says just the time she has Christmas presents to finish we would be underfoot.

Thurs. Dec. 13 Mama and I did some Christmas shopping.

Friday Dec. 14 School again and they say we must go all day this Saturday and half of next to make up lost time. We are all mad. Seems he didn't have it after all. Well, they were wrong, not us, so why should we have to suffer? Jerry says he won't go to school on Saturday for anybody! Mama says I must. It is mean to make us miss the movies! After school I went up to Mary's and we worked the Ouijie Board. It gives me prickles it is such an awesome thing. After a while we pushed the thing around making it spell words and laughed until we aked [ached].

Dec. 16 Mary had a party and at night too. I wore my rose silk mull with the short waist and looked elegant. There were no boys. We had sandwitches, peanut butter and ham, besides doughnuts, cake, jello, candy

An Account of My Life

and apples, all of which are good but not exartic [exotic]. We sat before the fire and played games. Mary's sister played the piano and we sang. "There's a Long, Long Trail" and others too.

Stella said she would take me home, but Papa came for me. The snow was crunchy the way I like it. A very pleasurable time was had by all.

Did not go to S.S. this morning on account of I have a cold. Had supper with Grandma and Daddy. We had spiced crabapples.

Dec. 17. Constance and I are confined to the house with colds. We have chewed slippery ellum bark until we are slimy. We are rooping quite bad. Grandma says she will stew up a mess of flaxseed. I have been reading aloud from Elmo's *Speaker*. Got blamed because I picked sad ones like "Curfew Shall Not Ring Tonight" and Constance cried. She <u>likes</u> to cry over sad things, but it made her cough worse and I caught old Harry.

Dec. 18. We have salt pork around our necks and are misrable. I do hope we do not have to have antiforgestine on our chests. mustard plasters are bad enough. My voice is an interesting croak.

Dec. 20. We are better and out again. Priscilla says Bill Edwards likes me. She says he says I am pretty. I am dumfoundered. No one ever said so before. I wish it was Jerry.

Tried to make poetry but it would not come right so I sat on the couch with a pile of catalogs. Charles Williams, Montgomery and Wards, Sears Robuck and Bellas Hess. I do love catalogs. We send to Charles Williams most often.

Dec. 25. Christmas Day. There are evergreen wreathes in the front windows and our tree is very hansome. I put Princess Pine around the shandellars, but a piece got loose and tickled Papa's head so he tore it all down. I don't care if he <u>is</u> my father he is a mean thing. We had a fight. That was yesterday.

Today he is cussed and not speaking to Mama and me so all is calm.

I had 34 presents. There were nine books and three of them were the Ruth Fielding series. I had an ink well with a brass cover, a gold pen knife, a cameo ring, a silver mesh bag and half a Liberty Bond.

Constance had the other half. Daddy gave it to us and a whole one to Mama.

Aunt Hannah and Aunt Mary sent money. I have a new sled, a Flexible Flyer, also ice skates. There were handkerchiefs, hair ribbons, and things like that. The afternoon was not pleasant because we are rooping again. More slippery ellum.

Dec. 30 Coldest day in years. 18 (degrees) below some places and 8 (degrees) below here. Daddy says it is tarnation cold and he wishes he was in Floridy. You have to get full rigged to bring the milk pail from the stoop. Constance and I are coughing our heads off.

Mama is most crazy. When one is not barking the other is and some of the time we bark together. Papa is good again. He says we are sorry looking sights and he is going to bring us something nice from the Store. We can not smell or taste.

Dec. 31. No wind, a still cold. Dear me suz this is a long winter.

I don't like *"Little Women"*. They are shocked, but I do not. The Marches are so noble. I think wicked people are more interesting to read about.

I tried doing my hair a new way, but it does not make me pretty. I am skinnier than ever and my hair is straight as an Indian's. This cold has skinned my nose and now it is pealing off and I look awful. If I cannot be pretty when I grow up I would just as soon die. Grandma says it is better to be good than to be beautiful and look at Malviny Dennison. That is what I cannot bear to do on account of her being scarred with small pox. Her father came home not knowing and went to church. The ones in the congregation that didn't catch it thought they would and were scared to death. Some did die but Miss Malviny pulled through. I think it is a pity she did. She seems happy but I don't see how.

They say it is God's will, but why does he want her spoiled?

In my imaginings I have long curls, pink cheeks and am very pretty. Constance is a pretty child and being plump does not look like a picked chicken the way I do.

Old Mr. Geer says I am bound to be pretty with my eyes and such good looking parents, but Grandma says he is an old fool.

I guess I am put together all wrong. I think wicked people are more intresting than good people and I would rather be pretty than noble. I want to be good but I do not care a hoot about being noble. Jo was noble and Amy got the best.

It is no wonder Grandma thinks the devil is in me. Starting the New Year I must try.

There is a story I should like to know. I mean I know it in a way, but the family will not tell me more. It is about Zella Hollaway, old Capt. Hollaway's daughter. He is long dead, and she too for all we know. This Zella was a friend of Mama's, only Mama never really liked her, she says. She had a beautiful skin and was queer acting. Grandma says, small wonder.

The Hollaway house was the old Clift place.

Zella's Mother was Capt. Hollaway's first wife's niece who lived with them. His wife died and he married her and Zella was born and she died (Zella's mother died).

That is sort of mixed up.

Well, when Capt. Hollaway was away Zella stayed with Mrs Chapman who lived where Mr. Welcome Braxton lives now.

Capt. Hollaway had no friends on account of the talk and he didn't want any. He knew he killed his wife, not really, but he broke her heart. She was sickly and the shame killed her. Zella did not grow up happy like other girls and she was very proud.

The Eberhardts are a story too. He is the man who makes the pencils and he married Wainright Bentley's sister. Wainright is Umbrella Bentley's husband.

The Eberhardts came summers to the house on Gravel Street. Mrs. Eberhardt was very pretty with dark eyes and hair and a pink and white skin. For all he was so rich, the folks never thought much of her marrying a foreigner but he turned out to be nice and the money helped.

Imaging stories is fun too. I like to make believe I am a Princess in a midevil [medieval] castle. Another one I like is imagining a courier coming to tell me I am a great heiress which sounds very fairy tale like but can come true because it has. Way, way back there was a man in Groton who was hoeing in a field when a messenger came up on horseback and addressed him as Sir John Davie and told him someone had died in England and he was heir to vast estates and everything. So it can happen. Daddy says it is extremely unlikely as he cannot recollect another such case.

I like it just the same and it helps too. If my hair needs an extry brushing and I do not want to bother I think, suppose the courier came and found me with dull hair and I sail in and brush until my head is sore.

Alice's Aunt Pheobe who lives in Providence, Rhode Island, is very much taken with my party dress which is blue with little pink roses all over and a blue satin sash showing under the bollareo jacket. She has asked Mama for the pattern. I would not care if I liked Alice, but I do not. I do not think it fair. Mama thinks it mean of me. I wish I had a sweet disposition.

1917

The Blacksmith Shop, Mystic

Capt. Daniel Packer House, Fort Rachel

Mrs. Benjamin's Boarding House

An Account of My Life

A Description of the Walk to School

I walk down the road and at Five Corners is Mr. Chapman's Blacksmith Shop. He is no relation to Alton's Mother who was a Chapman. I guess he would like to have a black smith in the family. I would not, because I do not like him or the smell, but the forge and the sparks are fasinating.

I go up the hill, past the big Buckeley house which was a fine place once, and on the corner across from Brown's house is the chestnut tree where I scuff for nuts on frosty mornings. I pass Mr. Ben Davis' house which is old and rambeling. Mrs. Davis never misses the Women's Bible Class and gets a sight of joy out of it. Her skin is very thin and soft looking.

Next comes Capt. Holme's iron fence and his big white house. I like the Chinese jar on the front lawn which he brought back. Besides there are jardineres at the front steps and all along the side walk. There are lots of bushes and flowers which came from foreign parts.

Capt. Holmes had chin whiskers like all of them, and he carried a gold headed walking cane. His first wife had lovely clothes and lots of them. He brought her beautiful shawls and such and she never had so many she didn't want more.

On a Sunday she'd come out the front door between the urns and unfurl her parrasol before stepping into the sun. In Grandma's and Mama's day, ladies did not let themselves get black which is why they give me hail columby.

Mrs. Holmes walked to church because its only two or three houses up the line, and she kept the sun off every step of the way. Sometimes when I am on the way and all the queer, sweet smelling bushes are in bloom, I make believe I see her coming down the walk with her dress trailing unless she held it, her parasol tillted a little, her Bible and sented handkerchief in her hands. Would she wear lace mitts or gloves? Mitts I guess, like great grandmother's black lace one's. And she would have a fan painted all over, or embrodered silk with sticks of ivry or sandelwood. Great Grandmother's had ivry, but it is black and silver and sort of sad. Sometimes I see Mrs. Holmes plain as day, not like a ghost, like a person. I guess you do not die as long as anyone can see you.

Nothing bad should of happened to her, but it did. Grandma says she went queer and had to be shut in one room. There came a Sunday when she no longer russelled to her pew, and there were Sundays when those in church heard her screaming in her room. In those days, crazy people were not sent to Brewster's Neck. One of the Mallory houses on the other side the River, the one with the swan fountain I think, had a room with bars where they kept a Mallory who was violent.

I like that house on account of the fountan and everything, but I am writing about this side of the River.

After Capt. Holmes went on his very last voyage he was very old at the time. Sometime, I don't know just when, he married Mrs. Palmer his housekeeper and died before my day.

1917

Across the street is the Court House with the lock-up in back. And next to Capt. Holmes is Constabul Jim Brown's house right handy to the lock up.

I go past the Baptist Church and then cross over and walk by the Gates house and Frank Buckeley's and then Miss Emily Gates where Juliet Haley comes summers. She is beautiful, Juliet, not Miss Emily who is homly as a mud fence, but a fine woman. Note: Miss Karish, Miss Emily's sister did not live in that house.

On the same side as the Church after passing Evans Morgan's grandfather's house, is Mrs. Benjamin's Boarding House. Mrs. Benjamin does not live with her husband who has a big old house off the lane next to Mr. Heath's on New London Road. It is because he has all kinds of people staying with him and lets tramps sleep in his barn and besides he drinks. No one blames Mrs. Benjamin who is a Daughter of a Veteran and a fine woman too. She runs a first rate Boarding House and the same people come every summer, being mostly artists and such.

I pass great great Aunt Calista Seamon's big square house and old John Green Packer's (I am not bothering to keep to one side of the road). He has yellow roses and many old time flowers. Across from his house next to Aunt Calista's is the house where the Smith boys live. The house use to belong to old Judge Heath before it was made over and Grandma says it was a little one. Grandma use to cross great-great Grandma's yard and climb over Judge Heath's wall short cutting it on the way to the old Academy which stood where our Academy now stands. Great-great Grandmother use to call out to Grandma, "Now Millie get all the education you can, it is the one thing no one can take away from you."

Next to the Smith's is a worn abode where Mr. Mosher lives. When it is hot he wears white suits and shoes and always carries a cane. His clothes are old fashioned, but white as snow and I call him the Immaculate Gentleman. He is tall, wears a considerable mustache and looks like a Southern Colonel. His house needs paint, but the lawn is very neat. It is a treat to look at him.

The house on the corner before turning down to the Academy is a strange place. An old woman and her daughter live there alone. Mr. Cliff is her husband, but there was Trouble and they have not lived together since Miss Ruth was born. I do not understand it, because Mr. Cliff is nice and makes me think of Daddy. The women are queer and scarey, and the big house is painted an ugly brown. They are well fixed, yet they use oil lamps and carry them from room to room. They have a bathroom, but that is because they are too delicate minded to be seen going into a W.C. They do not let anyone in the house, not even a groceryboy. They will not handle money without gloves and they hate children. At least the old woman does, Miss Ruth is sometimes pleasant in a scarey way.

They play the piano at noon every day with the soft pedle on so that the music is soft and blurrey. Miss Ruth studied music when she was young, and went to a conservatory.

Mama says she was full of fun and boy crazy once. She fell in love with Mr. Hollis Price who was Principal of the Academy at that time. He married someone else and now she is growing crazy like her Mother. They have one beautiful thing in their yard, a great wisteria vine all ablow each Spring. I have never been in that house, which shows how queer they are, because I pass by four times a day and always walk slow when the blurry music is coming out, which is always at noon, between twelve and one o'clock.

Across from them on the corner is the big house where Great Aunt Calista Burrows who married Capt. Will Applemen lived once. He wasn't really a captain being lost at sea at the age of 24, but he was bound to be, so we call him so.

Mama says she recalls plain as plain standing on the porch with Henry their child, which makes him Mama's cousin, not long before he died. There was a big red barn across from there where the Clift house is now and Henry pointed at it. Mama says she does not know why she recalls the incidense, such a little thing all these years. When I go by sometimes I look up and say hello to him, but not aloud. I use his silver fork and spoon everyday with his initials on them, so I feel friendly. I guess he is there even if no one can see him. Grandma says I am queer as Dick's hat band, which is an old saying and does not mean anything.

From there it is just a hop, skip and jump to the Academy.

Saloons

Saloons are interesting but bad. Nice people do not go past one unless they have to and then on the opposite side of the street. I think the swinging doors must be fun and always want to slap one open with my hand, but I do not like the sour smell which is very awful. We have got only two or three, but Bank Street in New London has more than a sufficientcy. Grandma and Mama say "disgraceful" and pinch themselves together. It does not matter which side of the street you are on because they are on both sides. I try to peek in as we go by but Grandma and Mama keep their eyes on me. You are not supposed to look right nor left. Well, you miss a lot that way. I am not afraid of drunken men though I make believe I am because the other girls are.

I love New London. The walk up from the station is exciting. There are flower shops and newspaper stores and fruit stores with those big fat red bananas called plantings [plantains] hanging up. There is a little green around the monument.

New London is a big city now but the streets had funny old-time names years ago. Gingerbread Lane is much warmer and spicier than North Bank Street. I do not see any sense in changing names unless they are ugly.

There are not many very old things in New London on account of Benedict Arnold.

A Story about Great Uncle Aborn Burrows

The house where Evans Morgan's grandfather, Mr. Evans lives, use to be a parsonage, and before that a schoolhouse. Grandma's half-brother Aborn went to school there.

She says he never forgot a sleepy warm day when he sat looking out of the open window the way you do, when a neighbor, she can't recollect who, came in the door and spoke a few words to the teacher Mr. Avery. Mr Avery looked at Aborn and said very gently that he was excused from school. Aborn got up feeling scared and important and walked out wondering what was the matter. Then the neighbor told him his baby brother Little Rhodes had had convulsions and died.

Capt. Rhodes was at sea and Aborn must be brave and help his mother because he was the man of the family while his father was away. Aborn was only eight or nine at the time and he did not know how to be brave. Little Rhodes had tried to follow him to school that very morning and he had taken him back, and left him playing in the yard, just a few hours back.

Grandma says he always said he was never as scared and lonely in his life.

When he was ten or twelve there was an exhibition at the school with exercises held upstairs. The school house was pack jam full when the floor began to sag. The platform tipped and Aborn said they were dumped through to the first floor. No one was hurt bad and Aborn thought it a lot of fun.

He was a smart ambitious young man, but he did not like hard work unless there was a good reason for it. During the Civil War when Capt. Rhodes' vessel was captured and he was thrown in Prison, Aborn suported the family. He worked in the old Boiler works for money, and worked the farm for food and studied nights. Great grandmother Miranda said Capt. Rhodes had left money in the bank, but she did not tell Aborn because if he knew he would not do a lick of work until it was gone. She said the way things were, not knowing if Capt. Rhodes would ever come back, she felt she had to keep an anchor to the windward. When Capt. Rhodes came back, Aborn stopt work and went into the Post Office. He was a likable young man and went to Washington and for years had a good position in the Pension place. The only thing he ever did Grandma did not like was marry a woman from Maryland.

She says she remembers when she was small how Aborn would sometimes get breakfast when their Mother was sick. She says she never ate such awful griddle cakes before or since, almost an inch thick and half done. Mary Jane and she would push their plates away but Aborn who had a very bossy way with him, would say sternly, "You eat what's put before you and be thankful its no worse!" And she says they did. Late years she and Aborn laughted over it.

An Account of My Life

I think Great Uncle Aborn was a worthy man. Grandma says he used to say the cleanest smelling things in the world were bayberry, new mown hay, sweet fern and evergreen.

That is so, but how about lavendar? I should ask him if he had not died before my time. I guess he meant wild things. I mean garden lavendar, not sea lavendar from the marshes which has no smell. Some folks say heather, but my folks do not.

I wonder if it is like the heather in Scotland? I should love to go to Scotland.

In order to get the sense of what I have written I have read this over and I guess Papa is right. He says my thoughts hop around like sand fleas. I will try to controll them from now on.

Grandma was proud of Great Uncle Aborn because she says he could have scratched a living from a rock if he'd had to, but that it is a mark of his worth that he never had the need.

1918

January 1918 - 12 yrs. old

New Year's Day. Very cold. Popped corn and made mollasses pop corn balls and candy.

Went up to Grandma's. As a treat she let me go into the parlor and look at the big Civil War books. I hate them, but Grandma thinks I like them. I do not want to be rude when she is being kind so I do not tell her. I had to bundle up warm because the hot air register was closed on account of dirt coming up. The books are most all pictures and are horrible. There is a lovely white horse dying of shot and shell and that makes me want to hurt someone. I try to skip over and generally do, but it is on my eye balls. There are sad pictures of soldiers dead and dying. I do not get in the parlor very often so it is a pleasure in spite of the books.

There is a palm in a tub, very stiff and green and when I can not bear the pictures I look at it and make believe I am in Florida. The carpet is real pretty, sort of a sand color with faded flowers. There are sea shells on the mantle and under it. There is plush and horse hair furniture and a marble topped table. On the mantle is a Japanese cabinet inlaid with mother of pearl and a statue of Carrara marble. The curtains are stiff white lace and touch the floor. The shades are old timey, grey with pictures of castles in gold. The paper is white and gold and the ceiling is papered too, much prettier than the white wash. There is a case of stuffed birds I cannot bear to look at. Most people admire it. I hate it. The pictures are big and in heavy frames. The biggest one over the love seat is a scene of a battlefield. There is a crimson plush album with big clasps and another of black leather. The Bible is very heavy and made of brown leather toold in gold. It is stuck full of clippings.

There is a Japanese box lined with quilted red satin. Its cover is embroidered storks under glass. The lamp on the table has a great big silk shade, a tannish yellow as big as a little parasol. There are no mirrors in the room. Aunt Helen has great grandmother's peer [pier] glass with heavy gold frame and Grandma has never got over being mad, because she is only a married-in. She got the mahogeny gateleg table too, but Grandma has got the chairs.

There is a carved table and on it the carved dogs from Switzerland which Mr. Ben Grovesnor of Pomfret gave Daddy because they were friends when Daddy lived in Putnam.

Pretty soon Grandma looked in and asked hadn't I had enough for a spell? I said yes and Daddy and I looked at "The Saturday Evening Post" until supper time. Daddy does want an automobile so bad, but Grandma says he is too old and he'd have to hire a man to drive it. That makes him mad. He says he will be dummed if he will pay money for one and let some other man have the fun of driving it.

An Account of My Life

<u>Jan. 2</u> We have had a letter from Kent. He is in Norfolk Virginia now. He says he has another batch of neckties saved up for me. I use them for doll's sashes. Kent says he keeps the doll's complections in mind when buying ties.

<u>Jan 5 & 6</u> - I was sick last night. My head and the left side of my face aked and my throat was sore. They were sure I was coming down with something, but today I feel fine. They made me take casteroil. I made a fuss and Papa bought ice cream so I did. Mr. Kretzer gave us a mess of sourcrowt, but I cannot have any until they find out if I am going to be sick or not. It will put my stomach out of kilter. I have been fixing for a sick spell for days, I guess.

After Christmas I do not like winter worth a cent. I feel like going into the woods and eating sassfrass roots, birch bark and such. Grandma is a great believer in roots and herbs but she does not aprove of eating for the taste of them. She says Daddy will poison me to death one of these days. She says he bites into anything that he finds and if it dont kill him he eats it reglarly. He says he knows what he is doing. She says birch bark dries a persons blood. I do like it, but I do not want to dry up.

<u>Jan. 10</u> This arm moving does not improve my writing and I hate it. I cannot write big and sprawly. I write as if I had shaking paulsey.[palsy]

It has rained and got icy and everything is like glass. You cannot walk without spikes fastened around your shoes. They are called creepers. It is hard to walk on them, but fun. You fall down about as much, but they are a help getting up. I am very bad on account of the Clarke weak ankles. So is Papa.

This has been a mean day. Constance has an ear ake and cries pitiously. I have never had one. It sounds very painful, poor child.

<u>Jan. 12</u> - Mama took me to Dr. Congdon for medicine for my cold. He is old and gruf and untidy. He says I am way underweigh[t]. I dont see why, I eat a lot.

<u>Jan. 14</u> - We have a new Principal named Mr. Lowe. He is small and soft and dark complected. He also wears glasses. I am not much taken with him. My cold is still bad. Daddy bought gingerale and choclate candy shaped like little pipes. My nose is all stuffed up and I snort. Mr. Jim Brown had dinner with us. Not Constabul Jim, but Mr. Jim from Noank. He is an afable man and does not mind a few germs, he says.

<u>Jan. 15</u> Rained hard and they kept me home from school on account of my cold. I read *"David Copperfield"* a while this morning. Daddy is pleased because it is about his favorite book, I guess. I hate Mr. Murdstone and could do him a vialent injury with pleasure. Daddy's favorite song is, "Listen to the Mocking Bird," which is very sad.

Jan. 26 - Constance went down to Maine's Store for the first time all alone. She bought a can of evaperated milk, Eagle Brand. Tomorrow she will be six years old. She is getting to be quite a big child. I wish spring would come. One of Daddy's and my favorite occupations is watching the skows dredgen [dredging] the River up above the Draw Bridge. It is done to take the mud out so the big boats can get up and is an interesting sight. The sceen from the south side of the Bridge is fine too. There are fishing boats and yachts and four and five masted schooners at the dock in back of the Gilbert Block. The breeze is cool and salty. Seagulls fly over head and hang around the water back of the Fish Market on account of the scraps dumpt from a barrell. They make strange cries. When the sky is blue and the water too you feel like dancing and singing. On foggy days it is nice to feel the fog in your face. The water comes slapping up around the piles which are green and slimey. Mr. Cort Potter who is the Bridge tender has a little house on the Bridge and can see things all day long. It is a fine job. I wish Daddy was Bridge tender or a light house keeper like Mr. Thaddeus Pecore. He does not need the money, but it would be fun.

Except for snow storms January is not a nice month.

Jan. 27 - Albertine's Mother has a lot of books with paper covers. We read them in the store room. I am reading a good one. This girl is shut up in a dark attic full of rats by her wicked old uncle. It is oh so dark and full of rats. She could hear them russling, then she saw eyes like pinpoints and then they ran all over her and sank their sharp teeth in her fair flesh. She went crazy, but not for long. I should have raved and died.

Feb. 2 I must write this down. Daddy is dead. He died at 4 o'clock this morning. He was 82 years old. Grandma came down to get Papa. I woke up.

I try to get away from people but they will not let me. I cannot stand kind people the way I feel. Mrs. Spencer put her arms around me and wiped my eyes. I did not know I was crying. Things are far off and cloudy.

Never since I was born has there been a day without Daddy. He was not sick, he just played out. Papa says I must remember he is - was an old man and very tired.

Feb. 4 The minister was very sad. I did not listen to the words. There were many flowers. Mama told me not to look at him, but to think of him as he was. Aunt Mary Jane led me up and I looked quick, just once. He was hansome and grey, not Daddy at all. I did not cry. They thought I would take on. Grandma said, "You never can tell with that child." Aunt Mary Jane said I was composed a young one as she ever saw. The things they said came from far off.

I never thought of Daddy dying. I saved a little piece of fern from the flowers on the coffin. I want something not to be taken to the burying ground. I never saw Mama cry before. Aunt Mary Jane is staying awhile. Grandma would rather be alone, but Aunt Mary Jane says she needs her. I wish she would go home. She cried at the funeral. She did not even like Daddy, now she says "poor Lyman." I wish she would go away.

Feb. 6 - The last time I saw Daddy I ran into the buttery for a cookie and spoke to him and ran out again. If I had known I could have got close to him and held tight. If I had known. I wont bear it, I can't. And I have got to. There are years and years I have got to bear it. I will not be preatched at.

I am not myself. Daddy, if I .....

Feb. 9 I am going to stay nights with Grandma. I am to have Daddy's room. It is an honor but it don't seem as if I could bear it. The *Memoirs of Lafayette* are still on the oval table. Nothing seems real.

Grandma put away his things today. She did not cry, so I did not. When his things were around I could pretend he had gone out and would be back. Now I can not pretend. He is in the vault because the ground is too frozen to dig. It makes it worse. I wish Spring would not come now. We planed the things we'd do come Spring and now Daddy is gone.

I cannot think of birds and flowers. O Daddy I cannot pick violets in the spring lot alone. I dreamed he was alive and that he went for a walk and left me behind. I cried and cried and when I woke up it was not just a dream, it was true.

Feb. 11 - No school for a week because there is not feul [fuel] on account of a shortage. Unless enough coal is got into the village the schools will be closed so the feul can be put into homes. We have plenty in our celler.

I love Grandma and am glad to stay with her. I try to be brave. She sits up straight in the ladder back chair and looks out of the window. She does not look out to sea because she is afraid of it. Before she was born Capt. Rhodes ship was overdo so long Great-grandma Mirandy was sick with worryment. She says she guesses she was marked.

When we light the lamp we look at seed catalogs. She does not buy much because she saves her own. She puts them in little packets.

She says she guesses she will have a big bed of Chiny asters. That will be nice.

Feb. 12 Mary came down and we went sliding. We slid on Great Aunt Jane's hill. It was dandy sliding in the morning. After dinner we went back, but the snow had gone pushy and when we spilt we wet our underclothes. I do not feel like doing even the things that are fun.

Feb. 17 - Cousin Howard Wilcox came to see us today. He is in the Coast Guard Service and is an oficer. He is very hansome in his uniform. I like him.

1918

I was never bad to Daddy, but I was careless and I keep thinking how I lost his pearl handled pen knife and how he looked and looked for it, not saying anything, just looking in the tall grass.

<u>Feb. 18</u> - No school. Pipe broke. This is the longest, awfullest, saddest winter I have ever had. Funny things like hearing Justin's sleigh bells make me want to cry and cry I do not know why.

I am not doing well in school. I am glad Daddy saw my last report card because it was good. I got an average of 98 in everything, the highest in the class. He was pleased and proud. I do not know what he would think of me now. I try much harder, but I am hollow inside my body and my head.

Oh I want to be myself and have Daddy again.

<u>March 2</u> - Something has happened to me and I can never be the same again. Mama and Grandma says it happens to all girls else they die They will not tell me why. I would just as soon die, I wish I had when Daddy did. If I can't have Daddy I want to be where he is.

I am not going to keep a Diary anymore. I am too sad and without Daddy nothing nice can ever happen.

Today Gertrude came to school chewing wax so we knew Mrs. Parks had got some in and this noon we kids went down and bought some both bright yellow and bright pink. She lives at the foot of Banks Street which is downstreet and knows when Mrs. Parks gets it in before we kids do.

The Family does not like me to chew this wax because I get a sore feeling throat from it and they say who knows what the dyes and the taste is. I do not care, it is brittle, smooth and flavored good and comes in different pretty shapes. And if dying will take me to Daddy I'd just as lief as not.

Grandma has been telling me about a prodigey. This Margery Fleming was procoious and Grandma thinks she was a wonder. It is in one of the books. I am glad she did not like arithmetic, she said it was more than she could bear.

1919

July 1,1919 I think I will keep a sort of diary again. I am thirteen years old and shall be fourteen in September. It is pleasant to be well embarked upon one's teens.

This Fall I shall start High School having graduated from the Academy this June. I was an Honor Student and might have stood higher on the list if I had not had flu and missed a lot of time. Papa is never satisfied unless a person gets A in everything, something I have never done. Cousin Mary Tucker has always got A's and A+'s in everything. Papa does not expect me to get A in arithmetic, I guess he would faint if I did. He says he never saw anything to equal my sheer incapacity to grasp the elementary principles of arithmetic. That is an exagerration.

Mystic Academy No Kindergarten.
1911 started 1st grade 5 yrs. old. 6 the 17th of September.
Teacher: Miss Jessie Fish.
1912 - 2nd grade 7 yrs. -
Teacher: Miss Annie Rickerman
1913 - 3rd grade - 8 yrs -
Teacher: Miss Clara Chase
1914-1915 - 4th + 5th grades - Grade B (9 yr), Grade A - 10 yrs -
Teacher: Miss Ruby Prentice
1916 - 6th grade - 11 yrs -
Teacher: Miss Happy Brown
1917 - 7th grade - 12 yrs -
Teacher: Miss Connie Williams
1918 - 8th grade - 13 years -
Teacher: Miss Johanna Burnett
Graduated in June

My yearly marks were:
Arithmetic B (Very good for me)
English B+ (Usually get A)
Geography B
History   A
Physiology   B+
Penmanship   A
I never get a good mark in the classes where the teacher believes in arm movement. Miss Burnett does not, only for neatness
Drawing   B+ (Miss Nye was kind I can not draw.)
Civics B
Spelling A

1919

It was Spanish "flu" I had, short for influenza. There was an epidemic of it and many people died. No one else in my Family had it, I am glad to say. Grandma took me in hand and slapped mustard plasters on my chest, salt pork around my throat and a horrible ointment which smelled like skunk oil, though she says "no," all over me. I don't mean all at once, but at one time or another. I was not fit for human eyes to rest upon and smelled simply vile. I was so sick Jerry said he actually worried. Grandma says I have a tough spot somewhere and that must be true else I could not have survived all that was done to me. Even now I have to act lively all the time or she thinks I am fixing for a sick spell and starts in on me.

When I was on my feet again, she started to build me up which was very wearing as I do not like herb teas or sulphur and mollases. Personally I do not believe the dear Lord ever meant sulphur and mollases to go together. I had several bad colds in succession and felt like something dragged thru a knot-hole, so she fed me sirup of onions which is too vile to be put into words without blasphemy. Since then I have been alright, although they say I look like a picked chicken and I certainly hope I stay well. I don't mind the Doctor because he livens things up when he comes, besides generally speaking, his medicine is not a circumstance to Grandma's remedies. She does not think a thing will work unless it smells and tastes like Old Nick. Mother is not old fashioned, but when Constance and I are sick, Grandma sails right in and doses us. She thinks people ought to be on their feet if not laid up and has no patience with shilly-shallying. Great Aunt Mary Jane has a very awful remedy she is forever forcing down our throats. It is castor-oil and rhubarb which has a blasphemous taste. If someone liked it she would have no faith in it, but heavens to Betsey, who could! It is a good thing I like Miles Arabian Balsam because I got plenty of it. Grandma has more rights to me than a visiting Grandmother, because she has been with me since I let out my first squall in her front chamber. Mother was very sick and Grandmother took me in hand and has never let up. I was puny, although I weighed six pounds to start with, because I lost weight long after I should have been gaining. She says they never expected to bring me up. Grandma lost two little girls with disentery and chlorea infantum and she fought hard not to lose me. I had to have a special cow. I am still very spindly as to legs and arms. Grandmother Clarke died when I was six or seven. I remember a little.

My hair is light brown and very long and thick. Aunt Mary Jane says my strength is going into my hair. My eyes are dark brown and too big for my face. Louise Wolfe told Father she thought I was going to make a pretty girl, but he looked me over and said he didn't see where she saw it. Mr. Kretzer says I will never look as well as Mother who was a very pretty girl.

My graduation essay was on Florence Nightingale. I wrote it one evening in Grandma's sitting room on the cherry table with the lamp with little pink roses on it. It was pretty good.

I had my first pair of silk stockings for the exercises. They cost four dollars and I got them at Noyes Store and Mr. Irv. Mercer was very interested and talked about the old days when he went to school with Grandma.

There is a story about him. His heart has been broken for years, although he is very cheerful. Seems he fell in love with a girl who was a Catholic which about broke his Mother's heart. I don't know how it would have turned out if the girl hadn't died. Anyway he <u>turned Catholic.</u> Grandma says the poor soul was out of his head. If you are born Catholic you can't help it, but to <u>turn</u> is terrible. It must have seemed strange to go to church with people who are not your kind. I think it is sad and sort of romantic.

My disposition isn't very good on account of my quick temper and exciteable ways. Grandma says I am <u>clear Clarke</u>. Papa says Capt. Daniel <u>Burrows</u> burst his spleen in a fit of rage. I guess Grandma forgets <u>all</u> Burrowses were not as saintly as Capt. Rhodes is supposed to have been.

Daddy (my Grandfather) is dead. I still miss him terribly. I called him Daddy because Papa was away so much when I was born. Papa was a steamboat captain at that time. He gave it up in 1912 when Constance was born. He owns two fishing boats now. He is not a happy man. Aunt Hannah says he wanted to be a lawyer, but things didn't work out right. Old Leil Bentley says he would make a good minister which is funny because he curses something awful and is an egnostic. Mama says he has had good positions open before him time and again, only his bad temper and unstabel ways have blocked him.

We are by no means rich, but I guess we aren't poor. Not like poor people you read about, anyway. Once I heard a man say Capt. Ase (Papa) avraged $400 a month clear profit if he did a cent. That sounds like a lot of money to me but Papa says "no." He is good at spending money being extravagent and a poor business man, Daddy always said.

I have a good imagination. Priscilla, one of my friends has one to, but Mary is not a kindred spirit. We tried to explain to her how we imagined and she said she bet she could do it if she put her mind to it So the next day when she told us she had imagined we were not surprized. But <u>this</u> is what she said. She said, "We eat lots of coconuts at our house and I imagined I was eating one and a lot of little monkeys jumped right out."

Mary is good at sports which I hate on account of always getting an awful headache. I am not an athletic girl.

I did not like Miss Beaulah Noyes' course in Physical Culture one night a week in Assembly Hall with the chairs pushed back. Miss Noyes is homely as a hedge fence, poor woman. Grandma said it was just another way to spend money.

1919

There was a school party last October, a Halloween Masquerade. I wore a stunning costume which I have carefully preserved. It has a yellow bodice and a white skirt with pumpkins and mice sewn on the skirt.

Not long after school let out in June, Lewis Cromwell had an evening party the first I have ever attended with boys. He lives on Skipper Street, not far from Cutlers. I had no diary then so I will write what I remember of it down now.

It was the first time I ever played Post Office so I remember quite well. I have never let boys kiss me, but a game is different. Jerry has tried to and Gurdon has as well as others but I was never really kissed before. I didn't think much of it. You'd think to hear the girls talk it was simply great, but it is only silly.

I had a new party dress and the girls said it was perfectly sweet. It is pale yellow silk mull with a round neck and bertha collar and trimmed with narrow ribbon of yellow satin.

The Party started early and because it did not get dark for all hours we played outdoors until dark. When we went in we had to play quieter games and everyone acted grown up and much politer - except that Pest who is sort of a cousin of mine - but I am coming to that. He is Lewis' special friend, so I suppose he <u>had</u> to invite him.

Someone said, "Lets play Post Office." Some girls acted mad and some acted silly, and the boys just haw-hawed at the idea. Well, we played games and had refreshments which were very good and then no one could decide what to play next. Somehow the talk of Post Office started again and after much talking it was decided to play it. Most of the girls know all about it, but I being younger than any of my intimate friends had never played it.

Well, numbers were given out - even for girls, uneven for boys, and Bob Mahoney was Post Master. It was sort of exciting at first, but it got poky waiting for our number to be called so we played other games at the same time.

I kind of lost track of who was asking for mail and I hadn't been called, so I was not very interested. Finally some one called "8" which was my number.

"Who is it?" I asked Bob, but he would not tell me. I asked Anna if she had noticed who went in last and she said no. I hung back until the kids laughed at me. They said I was bashful, but I was <u>not</u>; I just didn't want to. Bob grabbed me and shoved me in.

When the door closed I looked around and there was <u>Alton</u> Burrows looking at the ceiling.

"Oh my goodness - <u>you</u>!" I said, glad that I wouldn't have to be kissed and sort of mad too.

"Why didn't you find out my number so this wouldn't happen?" I scolded him. "It would serve you good and right if you had to kiss me. Whats your number?"

"That's for me to know and you to find out," he said and started out.

77

"Say, Alton," I stopt him, "What's Lewis number?"

He looked at me with a devilish look and I knew I had put my self in his clutches.

The excitement must have rendered me insane I guess.

"Eleven," he said, and I asked if he was telling the honest truth.

"Do you suppose I care who your call?" he hollered. "You can kiss the King of England for all I care - or Fatty Arbuckle - or Dink Breed."

He was so rude I thought he must be telling the truth, so I called it. And in the door came Alton! I stared in fury while he yelled with glee.

"You mean thing," I said. "<u>Why</u> I ever believed you! You are the meanest boy in the world."

"You like Lewis - you like Lewis," he yelled until I was so mad I could not see straight.

"You do too. He's your beau. Wait until I tell him."

"You couldn't be <u>that</u> mean," I cried, but knew he was capable of anything awful.

"Yes I can," he grinned starting for the door. I dove after him and grabbed him and he tried to pull away and we hit against the door an awful thud.

"Alton," I begged. "If you've got any natural feeling for your own flesh and blood, I beg, I <u>beseech</u> you please not to be so mean."

You'd think that would have melted a heart of stone, but he has no heart. He broke away from me and I grabbed him again. This time we went down in a heap and I was mad enough to scratch his eyes out.

"You're kind of pretty when you're mad," he said, but I knew he was being sarcastic because my hair was all over my head and I just hated him.

"What the heck is going on in here?" Bob asked sticking his head in and then he began to laugh and the others came to see and the game was spoilt then and there.

Alton <u>didn't</u> tell, not before the others, anyway, but I quaked with a inner turmoil not knowning whether he would or not.

Later, Mary said, "Alton is a funny boy."

"He is a Terror," I said firmly.

"What did he call your number for when you fight all the time?"

"Oh that," I said, "was a mistake to start with. He didn't know it."

"Yes he did," Anna spoke up. "I heard him ask Bob for your number."

"When I asked you who was in there you said you didn't know," I reminded her. "I'm mad at you Anna Dennison. And anyway I don't believe you."

"Honest he did," she said. "If you don't believe me ask Bob."

I believed her. It just goes to show to what awful lengths he will go to torment me. I have not told the worst part because it is unbelievable. Alton kissed me when we were fighting. I blush to think of it and do not want anyone to ever know.

He didn't tell the kids, but it couldn't have been much worse if he had, I suffered so.

To this day I rue my mistake because he has never let up teasing me. I guess when I am old and feeble he will tease me. I do not know a worse boy, although Reginald use to be pretty bad. During the winter I tried to learn to skate, but I have the Clarke weak ankles. Papa had the same trouble as a boy.

However, I went to the Chicken Pond with the others and had lots of fun.

There is nothing as bewitching as moonlight whether it be shining on snow in winter or roses and honeysuckle in the summer.

For three weeks last winter we had an Evangelist at our church. His name was Mr. Evarts and I had never heard one before. He was splendid. Many of the people wept and prayed a loud, which was interesting to watch but not very dignified. Sometimes he would cry and it was quite a spectacle. I never did, but I use to feel like screaming.

One time he had Mr. Jack Reid, a sailor, come and sing for us. He was handsome with dark, curly hair and blue eyes and he was from the South. All the older girls were crazy about him and we younger ones wished we were older. After he went there were a number of baptisms and would have been more if he stayed longer.

During the Spring we had a dialogue in school of the different reasons different nations went into the War. Raymond Edgecomb and I represented France and had dandy costumes. I wore a full red skirt with an apron, a tight black bodice, white muslin blouse, white cap, white stockings and black slippers. I looked very French.

Sarah Ann, our cat, gave birth to four beautiful kittens, her first batch as she is only a year old. They were born while I was at school. One was yellow and we named him Buster because he was the biggest. Our milk-man took him. I did not want to give him up, but I could not keep them all and a milk-man. providing he does not skim all the cream off the milk, ought to be alright I should think.

There was a lovely grey and white I named Fanchon and a Maltese which I named Elaine but Mother called Sukey. The fourth was Maltese and white and very hansome. I named him Michael O'Halloran and he would have made a beautiful cat if the trolley cars had not killed him before he reached his prime.

Grandma is very expert at telling their sex although she does not like to do it and makes me leave the room. I told her I would do it in the future if she would tell me how. She told me not to be indecent. There is <u>nothing</u> indecent about a kitten.

I have two bookcases full of my own books. Daddy made the first one and he and Mama filled the top shelf with new books for Christmas. I am very proud of them, but still like the old bookcase in Grandma's upper hall filled with Daddy's books best.

Recently I re-read *"David Copperfield"* which was Daddy's favorite book and read *"Ivanhoe "* for the first time. I have tried to read Dante, but

An Account of My Life

do not understand it although it is magnificent sounding. One of my favorite books is *"The Mormon Wife "* which is very engrossing.

Life has brought me some trouble, but as a whole I am quite happy except for missing Daddy. Sad to relate, I do not cook very well and am a clumsy sewer, but I am pretty good at housework and like to push furniture around. Mother is not as tidy a housekeeper as Grandma, for when she cooks she gets things around, while Grandma never makes a mess. Daddy use to call Grandma pizen neat. If you track in a grass blade she picks it up with a pained expression.

I aim to keep an account of my Life and I hope it will be interesting. I wish my ancestors had left Diarys, besides Joshua Hempstead, I mean a Burrows or a Clarke. Grandma says they probably kept them but burnt them when they were setting their Earthly Home to rights before passing on. That is silly. What is the use of a diary unless it is passed on? I should love to have read them. They didn't have much faith in their prodgeny, I guess.

We are one of the oldest families, having been in New England for hundreds of years. Before that we were English which is the only thing you can be and not be a foreigner. Grandma boasts there is no foreign blood in our veins. Her people were Burrowses. Robert Burrows was one of the first settlers in Mystic. Alton is named for him - Robert Alton Burrows.

Papa's people are from Rhode Island. The Clarkes just about made Newport in Rhode Island. He and Grandma are always arguing about their families. When I do anything wrong Grandma says I am "clear Clarke" and Papa says "that's the Almighty Burrows in you." Grandma's family ran to sea captains. There was great grandfather Rhodes Burrows, great, great grandfather Capt Daniel, great, great, grandfather Capt. Daniel the first.

Daddy, my grandfather's, father, was a Captain or just about to be one when the ship and all hands were lost. Daddy was only a little boy but he said he could remember his father packing his sea chest for that last voyage. He has no large family connections like the Clarkes, Burrowses, Bennetts, Hempsteads etc, and I am glad.

Great Aunt Calista Burrow's husband, Will Appleman was lost at sea when he was only twenty four years old, which isn't awfully young, but is pretty young to die.

There is a lovely story about Capt. Ambrose Burrows sand his son Brutus which is printed in a history of Mystic.

I won a Four Minute Speaking Contest which was held in Assembly Hall.

Spies ran rampant and there was talk of germs and powdered glass. Of course we did not know much about the war like the ravaged French and still more ravaged Belgiums, for which I am thankful, but we were attacked by those awful Huns in a small way. I mean the time the Kaiser sent a submarine over to fire at the tugs off Orleans on Cape Cod. The Boston papers had big headlines. It all goes to show you can't be too prepared. Why, the Orleans people were in church which although a good place to be is certainly not strategic. The reason the Hunks sunk only barges was because that was all that happened to be in sight. They would have done much worse probably. It was certainly a lesson in Unpreparedness. Grandma said they'd better stay on their own side of the water or they'd get their come uppance.

When I remember the fuss we made over the *Deutschland* and its crew when it was in New London!

Papa was different of course. When he heard someone telephoned the Airport during the sinking and found the aviators had gone to a ball game he thought it funny. It is his sense of humor. He is really very patriotic being the Military Census Agent a couple of years ago. There is a paper with a hansome gold seal signed by Mr. Marcus Holcomb, the Governor.

Of course we use to watch the Home Guards drill which was interesting at first. Some were quite old and others were runty because only the finest and fittest are worthy the slaughter, Papa says. Evans was a mascot. He was in a news picture.

Once a French ship docked at West Mystic and I liked to sit on the porch steps and watch the sailors go by on their way downstreet. It was very good for business and the stores were pleased. Mr. Kretzer said Miss Burnett had got to stop talking French to them because they could not understand it and it scared them away. I guess he thought they would go to Mr. Bliven's store instead of his.

The sailors wore little red pom-poms on their sailor hats and striped V's in the necks of their blouses. They chattered like monkeys. They use to smile and wave to me and sometimes talk a little although we could not understand. Miss Burnett taught us a little French, but not much useful. I guess the Frenchmen were lonesome or they would not have noticed a little girl. I might have picked up a lot of French if the Family hadn't shut down on me. Grandma said in France well brought up little girls didn't sit on walls and talk to strangers and they would think my manners very free. She said a lot of riff-raff got into uniforms, and that when she saw how the girls were acting, she was thankful I was still a child.

There is a Casino at Willow Point where big dances were held and there were goings-on. I had to take my hammock down because soldiers and sailors with their girls were using it nights. They bothered her the noise they made, so she could not sleep a wink and she said she was too old for such catousing.

When I picked up combs and scarves and handkerchiefs she made me throw them away and wash my hands in the soft yellow soap she makes. That was when the hammock came down, but there were bottles and cigarette stubs under the trees in the garden just the same.

When Edith went around with soldiers Grandma was real put out with Cousin Alice for permitting it. Cousin Alice said she (Grandma) did not understand and that Edith was only doing her bit like millions of others and that the poor boys needed cheering up. I thought it a fine,

An Account of My Life

patriotic answer but Grandma sort of snorted and said: "Kahki or navy blue there's male in the uniform. When it comes to dying if needs be, those boys won't die a mite easier for having left a good girl with a bad name. All hands act like something let out of Bedlum. When this is over people will think back and remember the things they gloss over now."

Some of the soldiers at Fort Wright wrote to Papa and Kent sent me a card from France which is about my dearest possession. He took transport boats over, but did not get sunk. Then there was Kirk (Dr. Stillman) who was 1st lieutenant and surgeon in the Medical Corp. Most of my friends had some one in the war. Mary's brother-in-law was in the Merchant Marine and Priscilla's brother Orrin was "somewhere in France."

Of course I am thankful none of my family was in the awful carnege, but I guess it is the first time in the history of our country that it has happened. We have a dearth of young men that is why, all being too old, or like Alton, mere kids. He is a little older than I and he said if it would only last long enough he'd get in see if he didn't.

During the Revolutionary War I had any number of ancestors engaged: Great-great Grandfather Clarke for one and there were Burrowses, Chesebroughs and others from whom I am descended and they were most all officers.

Nathan Burrows carried provisions to Boston troops, a terrible journey in those days because he went by ox-cart and they are hard riding.

During the Civil War, Grandma's father, Great Grandfather Rhodes Burrows had his vessel *Oscilla* captured and burned and he was thrown into Libby Prison where he languished for a long time. He would not have got out when he did if his cell-mate hadn't died. This man had got his release just as he began to die and he told Capt Rhodes to get out on it if he could. So Capt. Rhodes being so desprate he didn't care what happened if he could only get free, changed his indentity and got free under his name. It was certainly a great risk but he had nothing to lose.

He was treated very bad and would have starved if he had not had money with which to buy food. He said he saw men cooking rats.

When he walked in thru the gate on Burrows Street he was a mere shadow of his former self. Great-grandmother Miranda was frying doughnuts and he said he smelled them all the way up the hill.

Grandma says her Mother would give him just so much food and no more and when he asked for more she would refuse with tears in her eyes. They couldn't let him eat much because he was so starved it would have killed him.

She says when she and the other children ate a cookie they'd do it out of his sight because his eyes were so hungry. It was a long time before he could get enough. She says she'll always remember how he spread butter thick on mollases cookies. The first time he did it she looked at her Mother quickly thinking she would be horrified, but Great Grandmother smiled and warned her with her eyes to say nothing.

1919

The Mystic River Drawbridge

The Capt. Rhodes Burrows House

John Green Packer   The Rev. Byron U. Hatfield

Capt. Rhodes was a just and merciful man. Grandma says he was never hard enough to suit old Capt. Daniel his father. He had a lot of his mother's gentleness.

When he found the kids had been taught to hate the Johnny Rebs and specially hated them for putting him in Prison he talked to them and told them things. Grandma says she's never seen any sense to war since.

Capt. Rhodes said while he was in Libby Prison he couldn't think of anything but Mystic and his home and his family. He'd think of what they'd most likely be doing at the moment. He'd smell Mystic smells and hear Mystic sounds. He knew if he ever got out he'd go home and that it was waiting for him just as he left it. And then he got to thinking of the poor Rebel soldiers in Union prisons and how they must be thinking the same things, but there homes weren't waiting for them unharmed like his and their folks might be scattered and dead.

Grandma says she guesses that was the first time she ever thought of the Rebels as people and <u>not just an enemy</u>. I guess Capt. Rhodes was a mighty fine man alright.

Daddy fought with the 25th Massachusetts Vollunteers and caught Swamp Fever and rehumatism from which he never got clear. He had a queer old carved pipe he picked up in a field where a battle had been fought. He was a private because he had no training and at that time was poor and did not know anyone who would help him be an officer. General Burnside gave him a silver medal for being an Armorer which means a custodan of guns and such.

Once I asked him if he ever killed a man. He looked way off and forgot to answer. He is an expert rifle man and has prizes for being a Marksman and a Sharpshooter and a 1st Class Marksman. He does not like to talk about his war days and what he says is not romantic. I loved "Tenting Tonight" because I could see soldiers sitting around a big camp fire looking sad and lonely. I asked him if he looked at the flames and thought sad thoughts and he said when he wasn't marching, fighting, eating, sleeping or laid up in a hospital he had his shirt off hunting for "cooties", although they did not call them that in his day. Of course I know there are many awful things about war besides killing and being killed, but it spoiled the song for me. Now I see a lot of men with their shirts off looking for vermen and scratching like so many monkeys.

Daddy had a very harrowing experience, He nearly got buried alive. He was almost dead of yellow fever, the men were dying like flies, and the burying squad had their hands full. They had a lot of bodies to put under ground, and when they came to Daddy who had been carted out as dead, they made ready to put him under too. Something made him move one hand just a little and one of the men said: "Hell, this one is alive!" So they took him back to the hospital.

I told him he wouldnt be marching in Memorial Day Parades and having bands and speeches and flowers if he hadn't gone to war and he said, "Thats so."

One afternoon in Civics Class whistles blew and as my seat was near a window I looked out and saw flags flying. Jerry saw it too and in a flash we were all out of our seats and hanging out of the windows. The Teacher telephoned someone and she said yes it was the Armistice, that it had been signed. Well from then on everyone went wild. We went to Assembly Hall and sang "Tipperary", "The Long Long Trail", "Keep the Home Fires Burning" and all the war songs and finally "The Star Spangled Banner" and "America". We prayed and then school was let out and we ran down the street yelling with joy and everyone was just crazy. We could do anything we wanted to do and no one cared. Later when we found it was a false alarm we felt flat as a flounder. Jerry cheered up a lot. He said maybe it wasnt going to end and he could get in after all. He is just the kind to get covered with medals if he didn't get killed first. I cannot make up my mind whether he is brave or just plain crazy to do the things he does. The Armistice was signed November 11, 1918.

I wore the flag pin he gave me, but I was very glad when news of the real Armistice came. I began to think if it went on forever I should have to be a nurse or something and with my squeemish stomach I should make a bad one. I even <u>faint</u> at the sight of blood. Of course if it had to be I should have done my duty because there would be nothing else to do. And I hope I never have to roll another bandage. Sometimes I imagined I smelled blood.

Last winter Theodore Roosevelt died. Miss Burnett said it was a sad loss to the nation but Papa didn't seem to think so. Which reminds me of the Spanish War. Daddy and Grandma and Mama had been back in Mystic only a year or so when it broke out. Mama says she remembers Daddy bursting in with a newspaper, puffing with excitement to tell the news. That was before the addition was built and they were using the basement dining-room. It was in the winter because she sat close to the stove - it was before the furnace. Daddy said the *"Maine"* had been sunk and it mixed up with the smell of geraniums and the warm room and the Christmas cactus which was blooming.

I thought that very interesting, so I asked Grandma how <u>she</u> felt and what she was doing when the Civil War broke, but she says she was only a little girl and can't remember.

If some of my Revolutionary ancestors had only written down interesting things! Maybe they did and they were destroyed. Maybe mine will be and all I have set down be lost. I don't like to think of it. Papa asked, didn't I want to know my ancestors reaction to the War of the Roses? I said it would be interesting. So he said, "My God" and left me to my reflections.

Capt. Ambrose and his Son Brutus

Capt. Ambrose had a brig named *"Frederick"* and he carried cargoes costing a great deal of money. One time a ways out from Peru a vessel came up firing guns. The captain, a very rough person, ordered them to send they're boat aboard or be sunk. He was terribly feirce about it and had a

An Account of My Life

evil crew. Capt. Ambrose didn't know what to make of it, but he got in the boat and went aboard. Before he got there a boat full of men armed to the teeth and very evil left this strange vessel and headed straight for the *Frederick*. They drew their cutlasses and made every one of the brig's crew come with them to the pirate ship. There they were locked up. The pirate chief a very-wicked looking man told Capt Ambrose he intended to take the *Frederick* and cargoe to Chilos and as they hadn't anyone to navigate her Capt. Ambrose would have to do it, if he obeyed he would be well treated, if he didn't no knowing. There were maybe a hundred foreigners on that ship so Capt. Ambrose did some tall thinking. The Burrowses are always sensible so he said yes he would if he could take his son Brutus with him. Well, the Pirate Chief didn't care so he did.

There was Capt Ambrose with a pirate crew under him and his own locked up in the pirate ship. The two vessels were soon a part and then Capt. Ambrose plotted action. Somehow he got hold of all the small arms and loaded and hid them in his cabin. One morning when the officer of the pirate crew went to look at the chart (because of course they were not silly enough to trust Capt. Ambrose), he acted. He said to the man, "Here sirs, is where you suppose you are, <u>but</u> sirs, you are deceived: you are not far from land and now stir hand or foot, make but the <u>slightest</u> noise and you are dead men."

They looked up and there was Capt. Ambrose and his son Brutus pointing pistols straight at them. It does not do to trifle with a Burrows and I guess they knew it. They surrendered and were tied up. Next the Captain and his Son went to the man at the wheel and overpowered him. Then they ordered the crew below and made them come up one at a time and be lashed to the gunnls. He said to the pirates, "Take the boat and put to sea, or be carried to Callao and meet your fate." They preferred to take the boat.

Capt. Ambrose was very kind to the two men bound up in the cabin as they had not been unkind to him. He treated them with Christian forbearance and asked them if they would stand by him if he untied them. They said they would and they did. When they parted he gave them a little money and a lot of good advice, of course letting them go scot free. He always believed they reformed, but I don't know. I guess we Clarkes are doubting Thomases. Anyway he was a brave and noble man.

Knowing all about your people is useful in explaining things like Mama's throat. Grandma says it comes from the Chesebro's way back who were a tisichy people. (Great) Aunt Fannie had asthmy till she was black in the face. Second cousins Rhodes and Herbert have hay fever. I hope I do not take after them.

I wish I had kept a good account of the War. My teacher said we lived in stirring times. Father was always arguing about the War and he always thinks differently from anyone else. He was on the German's side until we entered the War ourselves. I was afraid the kids would find out about his views. He got into a lot of arguments.

1919

  I don't remember much before <u>we</u> went to war. I remember reading about some terrible German atrocities in "The Saturday Evening Post" or "The Metropolitan", I forget which, and how angry the Family was with me. Daddy was very interested in the conflict having fought in the War of the Rebellion. I remember talking with Mary about it up under the crab apple tree the day war was declared. I came down to the house and Papa sat by the window reading the paper and cursing. Mother started to heat an iron to curl my hair and I was so excited I kept jumping up and down until Papa told me to pipe down and not be "a damned little fool." Mother spoke crossly to him saying she hoped there would be an end to his everlasting arguments before he disgraced us all. He said he intended to say what he thought so long as he had breath to say it. Mother scolded bitterly and curled my hair and that is all I remember until the heatless, meatless, wheatless days struck on. I had to learn to knit because everyone was doing it. Everyone had big cretonne knitting bags over their arms. Mary is good at knitting but I am not. I joined the Junior Red Cross and made bandages. We made trench candles in school of tightly rolled newspapers, thousands of them. There were Red Cross plays and pageants. There were many parades. Seems so nearly every day someone in some kind of a uniform spoke in Assembly Hall. We bought Thrift Stamps equal to twenty five cents and War Savings Stamps equal to four dollars. I own two. There were Liberty Bond Campaigns and Daddy bought us fifty dollar ones and a five thousand dollar one for Grandma. We saved peach stones for gas masks although I cannot understand how they were used.

  We made posters in drawing class, but mine did not come out very well. Miss Nye says I have more imagination than ability and I guess that is so.

  Sugar was very scarce, no more than two pounds to a family at a time. I was going to the store for Grandma or Mother most of the time it seemed. Grandma said it was the first time in her life she couldn't buy all the sugar she wanted providing she had the money to buy it. She didn't see any sense to it, but made the best of it despising hoarders and such.

  One day I dressed Constance up like a Red Cross nurse and she looked so cute Mother got out the Brownie No. 2 and took her picture which came out good and is much admired. It was most real because I dug out a legless doll and tied a bandage around its head for her to hold.

  I am very thankful the carnege is over before any more terrible things happened. Parades and soldiers and big, black headlines are exciting, but I am sort of tired of it all. Sometimes it seems as if there had always been a war and I'd just as soon try peace for awhile. It is a great comfort to know there will be no more wars, although Papa says not to count on it. I cannot believe anyone can ever want to fight again now they know what modern warfare is like.

  I shall never forget a moving picture Grandma and I saw. It was about Preparedness and what would happen to us if we were not. I am generally a good one to take to the movies because I do not laugh loud, ask questions

An Account of My Life

or cry very often, but I disgraced myself that time, for I was horrified out of my wits. Grandma never moved a muscle and was very provoked with me, saying, "Its only a picture!" I knew it just as well as she did, but I cried and hid my eyes just the same. She said I was nothing but a bunch of nerves and imagination and she hoped and prayed I'd never be called upon to look at anything worse than make believe. I hope so too. Grandma is as calm as a wooden Indian.

When Mary's brother-in law came back he brought loads of souvenirs and I wished I had a brother-in-law in the Merchant Marine. I think that is better than a real brother because you would worry about a real brother. Mary had a real trench hat.

Of course everything is topsy-turvy and the high cost of living is simply awful. Cars and railroads are striking and in cities there is a dreadful congestion of traffic. Of course we have no traffic to speak of here in Mystic.

We are all hoping that the unsettled conditions will not prevail for long and that eventually we will rid our country completely of these terrible Reds.

<u>Aug. 1</u> - Elizabeth came down early this morning. I was just getting on deck and hadn't had my breakfast. Grandma likes Elizabeth. She had breakfasted but she had some more with me.

She is expecting her father soon. Mr. Cutler is quite hansome specially in evening clothes, while her Mother though nice, is homely. How do homely women get good looking husbands? He is romantic too. being some kind of an engineer. They have lived all around, in South America, Panama and other places. I first knew Elizabeth in the sixth grade when she and her Mother and Alvin were living in Mystic while her father went off somewhere. Now they live in New York winters. She says Mystic is the best place in the world, but I guess she would get tired of living here the year round forever and ever. She dances with joy when she comes and cries when she leaves. but I bet she would get sick of it if she could never get away from it.

I am reading "*The Mill On The Floss*." Elizabeth says "*Adam Bede*" is very good.

<u>Aug. 3</u> - Alvin, Elizabeth, Alton, Stanley, Anna, Mary, Pat and I walked up to the old burying ground and sat on the wall talking. Stanley makes me mad! Just because he summers here and is maybe a year or two older, he puts on airs. He thinks any girl under sixteen is a baby. He does put on the most sickening airs!

One day Elizabeth asked me why I didn't like him because she thinks he is quite wonderful and I told her I didn't like the cut of his jib and hadn't liked him since I saw him kill a cat. She told him today and he laughed, the heartless brute, and said, "Don't hold the sins of my childhood agaist me, Little One."

A little later he sort of whispered, "Still mad at me?" just as if he were a Lord, and when I walked off with my head in the air he followed me.

"Kindly leave me alone," I said haughtily, but he made a grab for me which I ducked away from behind a gravestone. The others laughed except Alvin who said, "Whats the big idea, you bum." Then Elizabeth said, "I believe you have charmed the Charmer, Helen."

Alvin looked at her crossly and said, "Shut up."

Stanley just smiled and said, "Don't get jealous Alvin, I knew her first."

"Yes," I told him with great pleasure, "You did. You use to come down all decked out in a little white suit and beg Mother to let you wheel me in my baby carriage. I've heard say we looked just too sweet for words."

Well, if the kids laughed before, they shrieked at that, especially Alvin. Stanley turned red for a minute, but he is stubborn or he wanted to make Alvin mad because he acted silly about me and the more offish I acted the sillier he acted. It was as if he couldn't believe I didn't like him and I don't, the old Smarty! I was nicer than usual to Alvin just to show him. Anyway I like Alvin pretty well, because he isn't silly and I don't think he is cruel. I can't see where Stanley is so wonderful looking either. I told Elizabeth so and she exclaimed, "And you can stand Alvin's face! It could stop a clock."

"Not this Clarke," I said, and she said I was about the wittiest girl she ever knew. Of course I am not, but any praise from her is double praise.

Alton tried to interfere, darn him. He said if I didn't stop flirting with every boy in sight he'd tell my folks on me. That's a nice thing to say to a relative, especially after the way I snubbed Stan!

Aug. 4 - Expressions are certainly something to wonder about!

For instance "son of a b---" is one of the worst in the world I guess, yet people say quite affectionately and not meaning anything shameful, "you little jack ass" or "don't be a jackass."

Now it seems to me just as bad to be an offspring of a "male ass and a mare" as to be the offspring of a female dog. And where did such expressions start in the first place? They are pretty silly and meaningless if one stops to think of it. These are what Grandmother calls unlady-like thoughts, I suppose, but seeing Mr. Neff's big mules go by started me off.

Those mules are the only ones in town and the only ones beside the Borax Twenty Mule Team I have ever seen.

A donkey is often cute, but a mule is just a horse whose looks are spoiled by jack ass ears of which they always seem sort of ashamed.

Aug. 7 Grandma has been giving me a calling down. Cousin Mattie, Alton's Mother, has told her the girls and boys call Alton, "Boob Mc Nutt", and she thinks I thought it up, or at least tacked it on him. Well, I didn't and I don't know who started it. He looks like Boob Mc Nutt in the funny papers, red hair, freckles and all, although perhaps not so simple, and everyone calls him that. Grandma was cross with me, but not so much as sometimes. She told Mother that it was the first time Cousin Mattie had forgotten her <u>Grief</u> long enough to feel anything for Alton beyond duty and if she could feel indignant it was a healthy sign.

When Cousin Nelson died a few years ago, her heart broke and she has worn black and wept ever since. It was before Daddy died I remember, maybe the year before. Cousin Nelson had a cold, then pneumonia, then died. We were eating dinner when Daddy broke the news to us. I stopped eating before he spoke a word because his face let me know he was sad.

"Nelson is dead, Allie," he said to Mama.

She grew up with him more or less and I must say she seems to have liked him a lot better than I like Alton. Maybe I should feel a little sad if Alton was suddenly deceased, but not very much, I verily believe. Daddy was no blood relation of Cousin Nelson's, but they were very good companions on account of both loved hunting, fishing and other things.

Grandma says she was never so sorry for anyone as for Alton the day of the funeral because he was orphaned to all intents and purposes, Mattie being so mad with grief. She led him to the coffin again and again crying

"Look Alton look! You'll never again see him on earth."

And Alton tried to pull away, crying himself and saying,"I see Mama, I <u>see</u>."

Cousin Mattie just worshiped the ground Nelson walked upon. Getting married and having a baby didnt change it a bit, it was always as it was in the beginning when she loved him at first sight. Of course she cared for her baby, but I guess Alton was just something extra thrown in for good measure. Grandma says any woman who worships a man like that is sinning against God.

If ordinary people are wicked to be jealous I don't think the Lord should be guilty of it himself. Poor Cousin Mattie cried for days and nights, in fact she has never let up entirely which is sad for Alton. Grandma says that is why the boy has such wild spirits away from home. Mattie wears layers of black and they look as if they were wet to the skin with tears. It would be romantic, but she is dumpy and not a bit beautiful. It seems queer such a plain woman could have loved so <u>hard</u>.

Grandma loved Nelson but she is Spartan and does not believe in showing all of her feelings. Mattie wanted to die and instead has many long years to live, most likely and when her time comes she may not want to at all. I have had sorrow to, so I know.

When I remember all this I try to be kind to Alton, but he is such a pesky tease I forget. He went to the West Mystic School until he was ready for the 7th grade and then he came to the Academy. The West Mystic School is a funny little place with two teachers who teach them to read with funny expressions, counting three at every period and one at every comma. That is what he says, and he certainly reads something awful. The class was in histerics when he read aloud. He sat beside me and made my life a torment all that year long.

One time I flipped my skirt too much when I sat down and showed a ways above my knees. As if I wasn't mortified enough he called me a ballet dancer, though I am sure he knows nothing about such people. I never saw one he has never been anywhere I haven't. He shouldn't say a thing like that to his own flesh and blood. Night after night he snatched my hat and just laughed when I stamped my foot. Oh he is a pest of the first water and I cannot begin to name all the mean things he has done to me.

Grandma says we were both naughty babies and that he'd plunk down on a sidewalk or in the middle of the road and scream with rage, and that I use to kick trolley car conductors in the shins without fail. I cannot remember why I didn't like them, but I must have had some reason.

Although Alton is smart in Arithmetic he never would do my examples for me which shows his meanness. He did once, but just because I showed Jerry the answers he never would again. Jerry is always generous with his when he has them so I don't see why Alton should be so onery. Jerry is smart, though lazy. He is much quicker than Alton but he has so much fun he does not get much work done. It shows how smart he is that he passes at all. When Jerry teazes the girls they like it, although we pretend to be mad, but Alton just torments past human endurance.

Aug. 8. I took "The Wind In The Rose Bush and Other Stories" by Mary E. Wilkins from the library last afternoon and Priscilla and I sat on Old Man Allyn's wall and read it. It was very scary even in the day light. What we should have done in the dark I shudder to comptemplate. There were illustrations in the book and one was of a lost dead child with straight wet hair, a bulgy forehead and big staring eyes. Priscilla and I stuck together in fear and trembling and parted the same way. Even after I was safe home and had supper I was scared. Ghost stories about haunted castles in foreign places never seem really real, but these stories were everydayish and you might see things like that in your own yard. I was scared to go to bed and scared to look in the mirror for fear of seeing an old woman's face in place of mine. I did not dare to hang my clothes in the clothes press for fear of seeing other clothes not mine hanging there, but was also afraid of what Grandma would say if I didn't, so I did. The lamp made awful shadows and I was afraid to get in bed and afraid to stay out and paralized when I thought of what might be looking over my shoulder. I did not dare let my hand dangle out of bed for fear of bony fingers clutching it. The maple bough whished against the window screen and I wondered what was trying to find its way in. I did not dare tell Grandmother so I suffered in silence. I hugged myself tight and hid under the pillow, but kept imagining a spectral figure bending over me. I should have died of fright or gone crazy if I had not fallen asleep.

Today I met Jerry downtown going in Kretzers store. I like him pretty well even if he does say terrible things. Today he told me I was growing up to be a vamp like Theda Bara and that my eyes were like hers. I am too modest to be a vamp and dress half naked, besides the family would never allow it.

Ase told me once that nothing is ever completely forgotten, it is just folded away in the creases of your brain to be brought forth when the majic associations unlock the memories. It is certainly true!

Mother and Grandmother who are rocking and talking as they do of an afternoon, have made me remember something so vividly I wonder I ever forgot it.

I was about eight years old and Constance was a baby in a carriage. It was a sunny, summer afternoon and we were walking downtown, Mother pushing the carriage and I walking along side. We were going along Water Street and were at the foot of Crary Hill when we heard a run away horse and saw it coming straight toward us, the driver hanging on for dear life and the carryall swaying like mad.

Mother snatched Constance from her baby cart, grabbed my hand and ran for a doorway. The horse missed the carriage and kept on into town before some one caught it. That was all. I hadn't had time to be frightened, Constance certainly wasn't and I don't remember Mother being all of a tremble as she says she was.

But I am surprized at what I do remember. The door way was one in the wooden building of stores and flats next to the Car Barn where trashy people live, and a funny, dark sort of a smell came from the hall. The paint inside was the color of liver, what there was of it, and there was tobacco juice on the stairs.

An old woman with snaggle teeth came down the stairs and she and Mother talked together although Mother had never spoken to her before, and I guess, never did again.

It doesn't seen to me I took my eyes away from the horse, yet I can smell the odors and feel the scaly paint as if it were now.

And I remember something else, probably because I saw it at exactly the same place on Water Street at the foot of the hill.

At least five span of oxen and one horse in the lead were drawing a great long flat carrier loaded with - and this I don't clearly recall, not being able to look at anything but the oxen and horse, the like of which I had never seen before - but I think, great long granite columns.

Aug.10 Not much has happened today. Priscilla is visiting. I got tired of reading and walked around looking for something interesting. It was one of those times when I missed Daddy. I walked to Five Corners thinking maybe I'd get some gum from Maine's Store, but Mrs Gardiner called me in. They do not like to have me go there because she has got consumption, the lingering kind. There is another kind not so common as

1919

when Grandma was a girl, which was called galoping consumption because it took you off as quick.

I did not want to say no to Mrs. Gardiner so I went in. She coughs awful and spits in clean rags. She knows I like her garden so we talked about it. Her seringa bush is the biggest one anywhere around and heavenly sweet specially on hot nights. The big violets were there when she bought the house. Mr Moon owned it first - maybe he built it, I don't know. I think he was a summer person. He owned the land across the street where Mr. Chapman's Blacksmith Shop now stands, but it was a garden then. Mother can remember it. There were walks, garden seats and lovely flowers.

I didn't stay very long and I went up the road instead of down to the store and I hadn't got past the Buckely House which is next, when Mrs. Buckely leaned over the fence. Grandma says somedays she can go downtown and back in fair time, but once in so often she meets everyone she knows and spends the whole afternoon stopping to chat. It was sort of like that with me, I stopped all along the pike.

Mrs. Buckeley is a nice little old woman and Mr. Buckely is practically blind and seems to be always pushing a wheel barrow. They are Cockney English and cannot say h's when they should and put them on where they shouldn't. Mrs. Buckely always says "'Ello 'Ellen." They are the <u>G</u>ene <u>B</u>uckeley's and no relation to the Frank Buckeleys.

Grandma says it was an ill avised venture buying that great house. One of my people built it, one of the Packers. It is across from the little old Packer house where the Mulaney brothers live now. I think it was George Packer. Anyway he was rich and he built this great house. It was a mansion in its day. There are three Packer houses in a row besides the old one. Grandma says it is wonderfully built. It is high with terraces and when he didn't like the shabby houses on the street below he bought then and tore them down. The summer house is still there. All that was before my time of course. I can't remember when the Buckeley's didnt own it.

They are poor hard working people and cannot afford such a place so they have chopped it up inside and rented different parts of it. Mr. Rogers who plays the piano at the theater lives there in one part. Albertine use to live there too. And one time I think the Duhaimes who own the theater.

Mrs. Buckely thinks it a most elegant house though it isn't anymore.

I guess George Packer would turn in his grave if he could see how ragged his terraces have got to be. She is a funny woman. She acts as if it were my house when I never even saw it when it was a Packer house I have explained again and again that they are only connections, the Packers not really relatives.

It is ages since a Burrows married a Packer and when Mama and Grandma say Uncle Dan Packer he is not really an uncle at all, but it makes no diffrenece. No matter how clean a chair is she gives it a swipe with her apron before she lets me sit down. It is queer. She and Mr. Buckeley live way up top in the servants quarters and rent all the rest. Once when there was an empty place I said "Why don't you move down?"

An Account of My Life

and she looked shocked. It use to make Albertine mad the way she made of me because she didn't of her and there they were paying rent every month. One time when I was telling Papa about how Mrs. Buckely acted he said she was class conscius. It does not make much sense to me.

I guess old people like me pretty well because I am quiet and I like to hear them talk.

Mrs. Ben Davis was outside her house and she stopped me too. I did not stay long because she is very religious. I went up the hill past Nell Crary's and then down Latham Street and back to the house.

Mama said, "Where on earth have you been?"

And when I told her she said it couldn't <u>possibly</u> have taken all that time, I could have walked around the head of the River. So I told them I had stopped in here and there. Grandma said, "Just like her grandfather! Stop at every house along the pike! You know better than hang around old Mrs. Gardiner."

Mama said, "<u>Why</u> she hasn't died long ago!" meaning Mrs. G and they began to talk among themselves.

Lots of girls my age have exciting times. Why, if I didn't write about just <u>everything</u> I'd never write in here at all! I can count the good times I've had this summer on my fingers.

When I first came in they were talking about someone, but I didn't catch the name and they shut up when they saw me. I heard Grandmother says "it use to be town talk." When they say that it is usually something pretty interesting.

I took *Barnabas* by Marie Corelli out of the bookcase but I cannot get interested in it. Albertine has some books of Laura Jean Libby. I am not allowed to read dime novels at home They let me read Miss Mary Jane Holmes and Miss Myrtle M. Reed, but not Laura Jean Libby.

Mama thinks Miss Mead's are more suitable for one my age.

I am very fond of the *World of Girls* and *Bad Little Hannah* and I have read most everything she ever wrote, but a person likes a <u>change</u>, mercy me. I also love *The Little Princess of Tower Hill*. I thought it would be about the little Princes shut in the Tower of London when I heard the name, but it is about a beautiful little girl as rich and lovely as a princess who lived in this place called Tower Hill.

<u>Aug. 15</u> Old John Green Packer does not approve of Shakespeare. He says "The Youth's Companion" is the only paper young people should read because there are no impure thoughts in it ever; and he has met Mr. Butterworth, the editor and regards him as a god-fearing man. He (John Green) is a goody-goody little man and as crooked as a crooked stick, Grandma says. He thinks he has some say so about me because he married Grandma's Cousin Tany and this Tany is not only a cousin on the Burrows side, but some kind of a relative on the Parks side and all that with my Packer blood makes some kind of a relationship.

He does not like me because I answer back.

Some ancestors are sort of interesting, the long dead ones, I mean. There was a Babcock who kissed the Queen and there was Desire and the Chopping Bowl. Sometimes Papa tells me about South County in Rhode Island. He says all I know is Connecticut and the eternal Burrowses but someday I must know Providence Plantations. There used to be real plantations like down South, not just farms and we actually had negro slaves. I was shocked at that.

We had Indians too and they married the niggers which made half breeds. He says most of the colored people down that way are descended from slaves. He remembers a girl Grandmother Clarke had for years. She was part Indian.

There was a special kind of horse called Narragansett pacers. It could carry a pail of water on its back with out spilling, its gate [gait] was so even and could go hundreds of miles without getting tired. I think that is very interesting. They are no more. He says I am descended from Governors and better, and not to forget I am well born just because the line is petered out and that it takes years to make wrists and ankles like mine.

I do not like all my relatives by a long shot, so I suppose I should not like all my ancestors, but I like to pick out this one and that one and imagine them out.

Aug. 17 - Went to church this morning, then S.S. Wore my white dotted swiss muslin. Walked with Anna, Mary and Elizabeth this afternoon. B.Y.P.U. in the evening and evening service following.

Aug. 18 Nothing interesting. Did my customary duties.

My stomach does not feel very good. Daddy use to say I got out of kilter as reglarly as the French clock in the parlor.

I am reading a <u>very</u> good S.S. book called *Pearl of Orrs Island*. I just love it.

Aug. 20 - What a time I have had! Elizabeth gave a party. I wore the new rose viole and my new black slippers.

Alvin says <u>Alton</u> likes me and says I am his girl. I laughed merrily it was so funny a notion. And then what did Alvin do but say to Alton right before me, "Didn't you say Helen was your girl?"

Well, Alton's face got red as fire and he yelled. "I did not. Just wait till I get you outside Alvin Cutler!"

I was mortified. "You needn't feel so bad about it," I said. "I feel just as insulted as you do." and I tossed my head and was miffed with them both. I let Red and Harold come home with me.

Aug. 21 Went to the library this morning and spent the afternoon reading on the veranda. Also made a cake which was eatable. Made a new handkerchief bag out of sateen. Grandma calls sateen "farmer's satin." They had funny names in her day, like "dead silk" for taffeta.

Aug. 22 Went to the moving pictures this afternoon. It was "Old Wives for New" and was very interesting. Old John Green Packer says the moving pictures will prove the ruination of us young people. I must tell him about this movie. It is fun to pester him he is such an old tattle tale.

Jerry is back in the hospital with something to do with the appendix he had out last winter.

Aug. 24 - Church and S.S. this morning. Preacher was Albany Smith who is son of "Gypsy" Smith, the great evangelist. They live in Noank and Jack, who is Albany's son, has a pony. However, he is very homely. Walked in the afternoon. Attended B.Y.P.U. and evening service which was more interesting than usual on account of a thunderstorm which put the lights out and caused old Mr. Wilson the colored janitor to light lamps and lanterns.

Aug. 25 - A horrid rainy day and no fun whatsoever. Grandma says all I think of is fun and someday I will realize that life is a vale of tears more or less.

It is still thundering and I am reading *The Fall of the House of Usher*, by Edgar Allen Poe. I like dank, romantic stories, but I do not want to suffer as much as he did in order to write them. I also like to hear the rain on the tin roof of the ell while I am reading them.

Aug. 26 Mrs. Morgan hasn't come to give me my piano lesson, but I don't care. Something has detained her no doubt. Mother bought some cloth to make me two smocks. She is smocking the pumpkin yellow one in brown and the blue one in lemon yellow.

I guess this Diary isn't going to be worth keeping, because nothing exciting every happens to me.

Aug. 27 S.S. Picnic. Used large trucks instead of trolley cars. It was held at Atlantic Beach. Went on the merry-go-round and other things with Alvin until our money gave out. A very entertaining day.

Thursday. Aug. 28 I have been sitting under the purple lilacks thinking of things I like. Someday I shall think of the things I do not like, like this boney-fish smell from the fish works when the wind is that way.

One of the things I like besides fog horns and boats blowing for the draw to open, is the salt that hardens on the black dirt sidewalks down on Rotten Row. When the tide is high it brings it in and the sidewalks get like iron and make lovely plunky sounds when ladies walk over it in high heeled shoes. It has fascinated me since early childhood and the first pair of high heels I have, I shall walk up and down and listen to my heels plunk and click. Flat heels won't do it worth a cent.

Rotten Row is not a nice place on account of the dirty houses along it. They have a very bad smell on hot summer nights. It is a sort of interesting stink. I am not supposed to use that word but I think a stink and a smell are different. Smells can be sweet, stinks can not. Odor is both, but not so expressive. Like "horses sweat, gentlemen perspire, ladies glow." I have seen ladies that did more than glow.

The real name of Rotten Row is Water Street. There is a grand place in England by that name although it is of French origin. Well, anyway, our Rotten Row is so called because it is rotten. It is on the water front and I kind of like it. The boat yard is across from the row of houses and the docks are within stones throw and then comes Bogue Town. The Bogueses live way down on the water edge, some are built out over. The houses they have built are shacks, but some live in the nice residents in Grandma's day. Deacon Allyn and lots of old people lived there and the Bogueses were unheard of. No one seems to know where they came from or ever heard them before the rail road was built. First a few came and lo there was a hundred. Grandma says she guesses the tide washed them in. Well, it is the only washing they ever had, thats sure. They propangate freely and are tow-headed and dirty as pigs. The small children are pretty although usually gormy and some of the big girls are kind of pretty too, but in no time they are horrid looking with dirty fat.

Mary Hannah Packer Keeler still lives in her old house which has been there since Revolutionary days. It takes more than Boguses or the coal yard to get her out. I think it was her husband's mother who was cut open on an old kitchen table which is now in the attic. There was no ether in those days so they just cut into her and took out a growth. It took several to hold her down and you could hear her screaming a mile away. When I have played with Caroline, Mary Hannah's grandchild who is round my age, I have felt shuddery as if that pain and dreadful agony lingered behind.

Lots of things have happened in that house and of course Mary Hannah can not leave. There are three generations of them there now and there use to be four when her mother was alive.

I like Mr. Welcome Braxton's little house. White people always lived there before and there was talk when a colored man got it. He is very nice, with a church in Noank where he preaches of a Sunday. Week days he drives a coal wagon. He uses very stiff English and never says don't or isn't, but always do not, is not, and for shan't and can't the same etc. It makes everything he says sound very important. I guess likely because he reads the Bible so much. He sits on the wagon seat as if it were a golden throne and he certainly looks fine of a Sunday, all dressed up in black with a long tailed coat. He does not pretend he has Indian blood in him.

Mrs. Braxton does our washing. In the summer she brings the tub out under the big elm trees and wears a bandanna tied over her head like Uncle Tom's cabin. She is not one of our colored people captains brought home, but from the South. She will not truck with trash and calls the Boguses poor whites. They are nice people. I like to hear her say "honey" because she makes it sound the way it looks and tastes. Mr. Braxton is nice too, but very stern.

Summer people think BogueTown and the docks very quaint and of course they do have local color as the artists say. Bogue Town is dirty but I like it. It smells of tar and rope and paint and drying nets, besides the salt from the river and a good big whiff of fish thrown in. It is one of my favorite smells. There are others underneath, more like stinks, because the Boguseses are not very sanitary.

There are other people living there besides them. One is Emma Gurnsey who has only one tooth and smokes a pipe. Grandma says she came of good family and her father was an editor. I like Emma she is so good natured. She likes chewing gum and manages with her tooth real well. It looks like fun.

Nice people don't walk along Rotten Row very much. When they go downtown they go past Miss Lurindy Dudleys house, but the other way is more interesting I think. They are awful mean about letting me go down on the docks. Daddy use to take me, but those dear days are gone. I like the little pebbly beach and Dell Avery's tar paper shack. He is a hermit fisherman and gets along somehow. He chews tobacco and calls engine, "ingine" with a long "i".

Fred Whipple is queer too. He comes from the Island and is a hermit too.

Even as a small child I was allowed to go to the Store which backs on the Dock and is between Rotten Row and Bogue Town. It is very old, so old Grandma says it was old when she was young. I guess it use to be a house, it sort of looks that way. How I should like a house on a dock! Sometimes I think the Boguses have more sense than we have.

The store has a very wobbly floor with high, wide boards that have hollows and bumps. The door sill is a shadow of its former self. It is dark and cool no matter how hot the day and it smells more of salt water than groceries. As you come in on the right is a case of tobacco, corn cob pipes and clay pipes, and next to it a big, long case of penny candy. Charles, the old man who runs the store, has a lot because the Bogues kids are always buying it. Mother says their shiftless parents let them have candy when they are too lazy to cook a meal.

Well, on the left there is a little room used by the Burrows Coal Company for an office. It is small and crowded. Mr. Ben Burrows sits there at a big desk and yells hello to me when I come in. He is a family connection, but not close. Elizabeth and Alice Colby are his granddaughters. Elizabeth is nice, but Alice is a mean one.

In the store there is a long counter of cereals and such. It is so dark you can hardly see what is on it, which is just as well as quite often rats run along it simply terrifying me. There is a fat round stove up farther and in the winter time the fishermen who come in in their rubber boots and yellow oilskins for supplies and canvas gloves, spit on it until all you hear is it hissing. Sometimes they get their feet too close and presently you smell burnt rubber which is an awful smell.

Sometimes Charles will come around sniffing to find out which one has got too close. They cut great slices of smarty, yellow cheese and eat it though we think it very constipating. The store cats, and Charles usually has half a dozen [of] all sizes, on account of rats and mice, circle around and miow until Charles cuts slices for them too.

Charles is quite a nice old man though he is subject to cranky spells. He has lots of fingers missing and the shiny nobs use to make me sick but not anymore. He does up packeges like lightning twisting the string around the nobs some way. Ase has a loft over the store but I have been there only once or twice. I am not allowed there. Ase is very kind to the Bogueses and all they have to do is to look sad and he gives them money. They call him Mayor of Bogue Town.

Aug. 29 - Went to New London and down to Ocean Beach. It is not as nice as it use to be on account of Jews. We like our Jews in Mystic and there are four or five familys, but these are not like them. Some of them make me sick to my stomach. Called on the New London relatives and saw Vivian Martin in "Louisiana" at the Crown Theatre. I am crazy over the South and wish I were a Southerner.

Great Uncle Aborn's wife came from the South and the family does not like Southerners on account of her. Besides Grandma hasn't forgotten the Civil War though it was so long ago.

Sept. 2 - Started in High School. Expected to like it and am surprized to find I don't. Lesson haven't commenced yet. We are all split up, those of us from the Academy.

Cill has started at Williams Memorial in New London.

I am taking English, Latin, French, Algebra and General Science.

Sept. 3 Elizabeth and Alvin left for New York and I am bereft. Still don't like school.

Sept. 6 Wrote a long letter to Elizabeth. Mary and Anna came home with me after school. Anna says Alvin told Alton I was pretty and he told Lewis and he told her. When Anna had to go home Mary and I walked home with her. On the way back Mrs. Kate Perkins came out on her porch and asked us in. We didn't mind because we saw Leander's aviator coat airing and knew she would be full of stories about him. Leander was in the War and Mrs. Kate loves to talk about him. She airs his coat very often and calls in people to talk to. She says Leander never talks about the war. Well, where does she get all these accounts of his experiences? Mary says Billy says he couldn't have packed all that in one war.

It would have been very sad if Leander had been killed, but he wasn't.

An Account of My Life

> "Latham Avery died 17th day, 9th month in his 13th year, the only son of Jerusha and Latham Avery"

I want to write in here something that is Very Private. One Sunday last Spring when the swamp apple blossoms were in bloom - no it was the Spring before because I was thirteen then, Mary, Priscilla and I walked to the Old Burying Ground on top of Fort Hill. In it are Averys and others, most of them connections of mine. It is a haunting spot. First, it is walled in by a high faced wall with steps leading up to the very top of it and going down the other side. The top is very wide and they say they use to rest the coffin there.

It is a very tiny Burying Ground with some table stones and although automobiles pass along the road, it is still and hushed inside the walls.

There is one little stone marking the grave of Latham Avery who died nearly one hundred and fifty years ago at the age of thirteen just my age when I found him. I dropped some azealia on his grave and sat down to imagine him out. Since then I have dropped in to visit him quite often.

The other day Mary and I went for a walk and ended up there. It was a little coffin for Latham I guess. Grandma has told me about old time funerals where men carried the coffin thru the fields on their shoulders and lowered it into the grave they had dug. I could see them walking up the steps and down the other side. It was three years before the Revolution. The men wore knee breeches and long coats and cocked hats which they held against their chests at the grave side. The women wore long volumnious skirts and bonnets. The ninth month would be September. He died on September 17th, my birthday! I never thought of that!

The day Mary and I were there the breeze blew the grass on his grave and I felt Latham there and loved him. Mary makes jokes about him, so I do not say anymore. It is a very private feeling. I should never have said he was my dearest friend, because she said I couldn't be friends with a dead person. I said Latham wasn't dead and she said, "You are loony. He is as dead as a door nail. He's been dead so long he is deader than dead."

I do not feel that way. I think he is part of the breeze ruffling the grass and part of the grass too. If he were a ghost it would be spooky. I am afraid of ghosts. I think he is alive only no one can see him. He is frightened and a littly shy, but he likes me. I can feel him.

I wish the Burying Ground was nearer. I like it better than the Packer Burying Ground where a British soldier is buried.

Poor Latham did not live to grow up, a sad pity, because all the nicest things happen then.

Sept. 5 - There is one little Blue Book I read over and over, called *The Olympian Gods* by H. M. Tichenor. I knew a lot about the gods before I read it, but he has opened my mind to many things. I know Grandma would call them evil things, but they don't seem so to me.

"The ancient Pagans possessed gloomy and vindictive dieties; they also possessed beautiful and kind ones. The beautiful and kind gods and goddesses of mythology were discarded by the priests of Christianity; only the gloomy and vindictive ones were preserved. Jehova, with horns on his hands and a sword in his mouth was saved, while Apollo, ancient god of the Sun, charming and graceful, with a crown of laurels above his brow, guardian deity of the nine Muses that filled the world with music and song, with the drama and dance, with the liberal arts and sciences, was repudiated by the priests of sack cloth and ashes, of damnation and hell. Venus, goddess of love and passion, born of the froth of surging sea and cradled in a shell of pearl, was dethroned, and a holy virgin, to whom love was a vice and sex a sin, was made queen of heaven. The woodland Pan of milk and honey who played such sweet strains on his pipe of reeds that nature paused to listen, was forgotten, and a tortured diety, sacrificed to appease the wrath of the God that begat him was offered in his stead. The jovial Bacchus, god of wine and mirth, adorned with leaves of grape and ivy, was cast aside, and a melancholy holy ghost, created in the image of a pigeon, made men most over the everlasting judgement. Charon, boatman of departed souls, ever wailing on the shore of the sea of Avernus, into whose waters flowed the river Lethe, of which unhappy souls might drink and rest in dreamless sleep was turned away for Satan, demon of a brimstone pit, where Jehovah plunges unbelieving souls. The graceful fairies of the fountains and the streams, the green hills and groves, pased away, and the widows of a dead deity in funeral garb, walk the earth. It were better had we kept some of the fairer gods, than the gods we have. Better to adore Apollo, with his harp strung with golden chords, than Jehovah, with nostrils filled with fumes of burning blood; better the silence of the dark waters of the Lethe, than the shrieks of the eternally lost from the red flames of hell; better the voluptuous Venus with form divine, than a sexless virgin with passionless face. Better to worship Ceres. Better to be with the jolly rustics at the ancient feast of Ambarvalia, where the golden corn is ripe, and sing songs to Ceres, than to kneel in confession to an immaculate priest, or weep at a mourner's bench. Better to join with the Pagan poet, than with the saints in dismal doxologies. Terpsikkore, Muse of dance and song, of gayety and grace, that distinguishes healthy minds from puritans.

* * * * * * * * * * * * *

The fair gods fled when Hypotia, last of the Pagan philosophers, was flayed alive by Christian priests, and the sacred tripods, torn from the demolished temple of Apollo at Delphi, were placed in the hippodrome of the bloody Constantine, arbiter of the Christian creed."

And in *"Sun Worship and Later Beliefs"* by the same Mr. H.M. Tichenor there is this beautiful hymn from the Rig-veda a part of the Sanscrit of India a thousand years before our Hebrew Scriptures were known. It is so beautiful and comforting I wish I had heard it said over Daddy's grave.

"To Yama, mighty king, be gifts and homage paid.
He was the first of men that died, the first to brave
Death's rapid rushing stream, the first to point the road
To heaven and welcome others to that bright abode.
No power can rob us of the home thus won by thee.
Oh king, we come; the born must die, must tread the path
That thou hast trod - the path by which each race of men
In long succession, and our fathers, too, have passed.
Soul of the dead! depart; fear not to take the road -
The ancient road - by which thy ancestors have gone.
Ascend to meet thy God - to meet thy happy fathers,
Who dwell in bliss with him. Fear not to pass the guards -
The four-eyed brindle dogs - that watch for the departed.
Return unto thy home, soul! Thy sin and shame
Leave thou behind on earth; assume a shining form.
Thy ancient shape - refined and from all taint set free."

How beautiful that is! "The ancient road - by which thy ancestors have gone." I can understand that.

I think the story of Marie the Persian is interesting. He belonged to a sect called <u>Babtists</u> in Babylonia. He believed man was begotten of Satan and I'll swear Grandmother unconsciously follows that belief, or how can one account for her low opinion of all men save Capt. Rhodes?

I think the wisest words I have ever read are these of Buddha:

"Believe not because some old manuscripts are produced, believe not because it is your national belief, believe not because you have been made to believe from your childhood, but reason truth out, and after you have analyzed it, then, if you find it will do good to one and all, believe it, live up to it, and help others to live up to it."

I hate to think of the expression on Miss Hattie's face if I brought that out in S.S.! She gets put out with me for asking questions about the scripture. She simply accepts unquestioningly. I suppose I am without faith. Grandmother is the same. I mean like Miss Hattie. Well, I suppose its right for them - somehow they manage to evolve a quiet philosophy, a hidden strength, a serenity of mind.

<u>Sept. 7</u> - Sunday - Church: morning service, Sunday School, in the evening Christian Endeavor and vespers. Band concert this afternoon. Mary and I went. Am reading *"The Deerslayer"* with manifest pleasure.

<u>Sept. 11</u> - Nothing interesting. I am getting use to High School, but I do not like it. Mary told me she thought I was very dignified. When she is not good natured she says I am stuck-up. I am not.

1919

Sept. 14 Church. Band concert. Cousin Herbert May, Great Aunt Mary Jane and John Eldredge and wife who are family connections spent the afternoon with us. Christian Endeavor, vespers and bed.

Sept. 15 - Warm days, but the nights are chilly. Do not like school any better. I do not seem to fit in.

Sept. 17 - Today is my fourteenth birthday and I have such a cold I cannot let go of my nose long enough to write. Nice presents, but too miserable to enjoy anything.

Sept. 19 - Day sunny. Cold Better. Letter from Elizabeth. She wants me to spend Christmas with her in New York. How wonderful if I could! The Family will not give an answer because it is a long way off, but I know from their faces. Grandma says I am not old enough to go to New York alone. I am not a child.

Sept. 20 Anna, Mary and I decorated the church with cosmos, dahlias and all the late flowers we could get hold of. The old church people find fault if it is not attended to, but they are awful tight with their flowers. Not all, but some.

Sept. 22 I am not sick, but I do not feel well. It is very strange, this all gone feeling.

Sept. 23 - Dr. Allyn says my nerves are bad. He said he said last spring after flu I was in no shape to make up work and cram for the finals, and that apparently the summer has strung me up tighter than ever. I would not admit it. I would not tell him I can't remember the things I learned last and that I can't memorize now the way I use to. I could read a poem over a few times and get it. Now I learn almost word by word. Last spring, I got sort of panicky before exams but they came out pretty good and I felt fine. All summer I have not had to remember or learn or concentrate and I had no idea it would be like this. I am miserable. No one understands why least of all myself.

Oct. 1 - We are having "*Treasure Island*" in English. I was surprized that few of the kids had read it. We have a very stupid teacher. She isn't a lady either and we do not like each other.

Oct. 3 The Family got worried because I am losing weight and have decided to let me take lessons from Miss Greene and not go to High for a little while until I feel like going back to school. Well, anyway, Miss Greene and Miss Nye, the Academy drawing teacher live together. Miss Greene is very intellectual having taken several degrees. She speaks

An Account of My Life

several languages and has books in foreign languages. She is old, but she is still studying because she likes to.

They live in a darling little house on a ledge with a rustic gate and a winding path leading to the door. It is very interesting.

Oct. 6 Miss Greene is a kindred spirit. I wish I liked her more, I admire her, but I cannot seem to get fond of her. There are books everywhere and portfolios and curios on tables and shelves. There is a piano in one corner and on it battered tankards. I did not know what they were until I asked. I said I thought it would be fun to drink nut brown ale from them and she agreed, but said she never had. Sometimes when I come in she tells me to amuse myself until she does a few more pages. Even since she has found that I know how to handle books she has let me take them from the shelves. Today I got interested and kept so still she forgot about me and I about her. It is such a quiet place nothing distracts. After a while she looked at me and said, "Bless my soul, you're a quiet child. We must get to work."

She is not like a teacher at all. She explains the Algebra assignment to me and goes back to her reading while I work. The queer part of it is I am almost smart in it. She says I wouldn't be bad at mathmatics if I had been taught properly. She is contemptuous of public schools. I don't know whether they are good or bad, but I know I have never had a teacher who approached knowing as much as Miss Greene.

We had a very little French at the Academy, not as a subject, but because Miss Burnett use to be good in it, and of course I have had a little more at High. Miss Greene speaks it fluently, but I cannot understand it and she says what I have learned is atrocious.

I was surprized when she said my hands were beautiful. People have thought so, but she does not look like the kind who would take notice.

She said gruffly: "I suppose you would rather have a doll baby-pretty face?"

I have thought if I could be really pretty, I'd gladly take a different pair of hands and I turned rather red. She said "Bah!" in a disgusted way. She is a very noticing person. She asked me if I wrote a lot. "I never saw anyone write legible long hand at such a rate of speed; it takes practice."
If I like her really, I should tell her about my diary and note books, but I do not feel close enough to her, so I just said, "I like to write."

Oct. 8 In one of the old "Art Journals" there is a set of articles about the stately homes of England with engravings. I mean there is a set, but this number I read is about Burleigh House where the Lord of Burleigh, Tennyson tells about use to live. It gave me a queer, pleasant feeling, but sad.

Then I got out Tennyson and read the poem. All the times I have read it I never knew there was an honest to goodness Lord Burleigh! That is the wonderful part of finding out things, one thing leads to another. I studied the engravings all over again imagining Lord Burleigh leading his lady from hall to hall. Tennyson said it so true: "Parks with oak and chestnut shady, Ancient homes of lord and lady, Built for pleasure and for state"...."Till a gateway she discerns, with aurorial bearings stately."

I don't see why she died. It says, "But a trouble weighed upon her and perplexed her night and morn, with the burden of an honor, unto which she was not born," but that is nothing to die of. She was quite young, twenty four or so. And then poor Lord Burleigh went "weeping, weeping late and early, walking up and pacing down. It is so sad. It has become very real because there actually is a Lord Burleigh now, or was when this was written in 1875. I guess he'd be pretty old now because his youngest daughter Lady Louisa Alexandrina Cecil was eleven years old then and so must be along in her forties now.

I told the Family all about it, but they didn't see anything to get excited about. Well, I do. Someday I shall see Burleigh House and just about die of joy I guess.

Grandma says if I don't stop hunching over dusty magazines in the store room when I should be out doors, she'll call a junk man in. She knows that scares me. Anyway I was out doors in my imagination, walking in the Park at Burleigh.

<u>Oct. 9</u> This has been a pleasant day although nothing spectacular has happened. When I got back from Miss Greene's I went up to Grandmas. She had been putting up picallili and chili sauce and the kitchen smelled warm and spicy. A little sauce pan of chili-sauce was still simmering on the stove and she said it was from the last batch and she was saving it for me, because I never wait until it has seasoned properly before wanting to eat it. She poured it in a bowl and set it in a cool place in the buttery where I could find it. I said I was already for it so she gave me a little sauce dish of it and cut fresh home made bread to eat with it. She makes the most wonderful bread! Mother does not make bread or riz biscuits very often because she is modern.

Grandma said on the strength of that I could help her take in the rest of the geraniums in the big urn. The choicest ones were taken in weeks ago and the ones left go downstairs in the basement until spring.

It was chilly out and Grandma tied the cape under her chin and handed me the heavy red sweater. I was warm enough but there was no use saying so. The geraniums we potted smelled spicy and the Inch plant was so thick it was hard to untangle the vines.

I like the urn in the front yard and consider it elegant. It is shaped like a great lily with leaves and buds at its base. The girls admire it too, and it certainly looks lovely when the geraniums are a riot of color: coral, and magenta, scarlet and apple blossom pink, deep, dark red and white; plain geraniums, ivy geraniums and Martha Washingtons.

I paused in my labours once in awhile to eat a ripe tomato from the row on the south fence corner. Grandma told me not to spoil my appetite I

An Account of My Life

don't think she quite trusts tomatoes although she eats them, because years ago people called them Love Apples and believed they were poison and certain death. What quaint beliefs they had! Imagine being afraid of a luscious red tomato! I am sorry for all the children who longed to bite into one and never dared. I guess it proves that it doesn't pay to be too cautious.

We did not talk and all was quiet except for the shrieks from the ledge where Constance and a bunch of kids were playing.

Well, when I had helped tote the pots to the basement, Grandma went to put the kettle on for tea. I hoped she would ask me to stay for supper, but she said she was having nothing but a little picked out codfish, being all out of everything and that I needed something more sustaining than that. She has given up cooking hearty meals since Daddy died. I said I would fill out with fresh bread and chili-sauce but she said I needed real vittles, so I gave in.

On the way down the path I paused to look off to sea and found myself sitting on the bench under the Baldwin tree eating apples. It was so very quiet but for the fall sounds, the whisper of leaves and the dull thud of a falling apple.

I heard Grandma step on the squeaky board in the buttery as she went about preparing her tea. Presently she noticed me from the little window and rapped for me to go home before Mother had to call me. Her rap said, "stop mooning and go home," so I mogged along.

Mother poured my tea while we talked about the plants. There was sasage and newly baked potato, tomatoes, apple sauce and hot gingerbread of which I am very fond.

After supper I reached for my sweater and tam and went out on the ledge and ate grapes. It was very pleasant out there, with the sound of people passing on the road below.

The hop vines have tangled with the grape vine so it is like picking grapes from the hop vines themselves. Grandma makes little pillows of dried hops to hold between your cheek and the real pillow when you want to sleep sweetly.

The dark came on and the lighthouse brightened. It is fascinating to watch a light house blink. You wait for the next wink of light and the next until it is later than you think.

The grapes are beautiful big ones - the Family says too big to swallow, but I do not have any trouble after the first two or three. They don't know how to stretch their gullets.

I suck the silvery blue skin until it pops and the frosty, slippery insides slide into my mouth and down my throat. If you suck the empty skin just a little you get a lovely sweetness, but if you keep on it gets sour and winey tasting. I guess it proves you can't get too much out of anything. Grandma makes grape juice and wine every fall, but we don't get any wine unless we are sick.

1919

I didn't do any serious thinking, but let little thoughts come and go. I sat there until Grandma who could see me from her kitchen, hailed me in. I was not cold, but as I said, it does no good to say so. No, I was not cold, but the stove felt good and the yellow lamp light made the outdoors so black it did not seem as if I had just left it.

This time of the year makes me think of Daddy, but I guess most any time of the year does that - growthy April days, May days when the violets are out, hot days when the locusts buzz and leave their shells sticking to trees, and snowy days when I bring a bowl of russets from the apple barrel. Daddy could pare them without breaking the ring and we loved the scent that comes with throwing the parings in the fire.

Mr. Brenton Copp misses Daddy too. He says he was a fine old gentleman and Mr. Ed George said just the other day that there are not many left of the old school.

I guess seeing me on the ledge reminded Grandma of something because she began to talk of the old days when Ashby Street was no more than a lane. Summer people think that now! When she was a girl she use to come down to Old Margaret Burrows house on the corner, but of course she was not <u>old</u> Margaret then. At that time this house hadn't been built, nor Great Aunt Mary Jane's. I guess the Hazard and Ashby houses and Capt. Lamb's were the only ones at this end of the street except the Burrows house at this end. The lane came to a dead end with a wall running across the end over which she had to climb to get to Noank Road.

<u>Oct. 10</u> A rainy day but a lovely one for me. I had lunch with Miss Greene. I helped her get it ready in the tiny kitchen and all the while we talked books. She said thank God I had evidently read something besides girls series. She made a Spanish omelet with all sorts of things in it and we talked about Spain. I am going to read "*The Alhambra*" by Washington Irving.

The table cloth was Japanese and we talked about Japan. She has been Abroad and knows everything. She explained about Darwin when I told her I was reading *"The Origin of the Species."* There is a big picture of him hanging over one of the many bookcases and when I recognized him she acted surprised. She said she'd had had several ask if it was a picture of a relative.

<u>Oct. 11</u> - World Wide Guild Meeting at Miss Coat's house this afternoon. I like that house a lot and besides she gives us a wonderful tea. The walls of the living room are lined with books, many of them belonging to the old Doctor who is dead and gone. We have an old dictionary of his. He made medicine which can still be bought. They are small black pills called Dr. Coat's Pills, but I call them Black Majic and the family calls them that too.

Oct. 12 - Usual church attendance. Rained all afternoon, but I did not mind it because I read *Dorothy Vernon of Haddon Hall* which I took from the S.S. library

Oct. 18 - Downtown with Mary on an errand. Studied two hours, practiced my piano lesson, read more of "*The Last Days of Pompeii*" which is very thrilling and cross stitched another rose on the sofa pillow top I am supposed to be making. Later, Mary and I went for a walk in the woods which are very lovely now. Ended up in old Mr. Heath's orchard. He lets us have all we can eat, but we musn't pick any or shake any down which we never do anyway, because the piles stacked under the trees are more than sufficient.

I love to sit in the grass with my lap full of winesaps which are my favorite at present. It is pleasant when the dusk begins to creep in under the trees and you know the dark is soon to come. I love apples almost as much as Mother. Daddy use to say she should have been named Pomona. I am glad she was not. It is a good name for a goddess but not for a Mother.

Sometimes Mr. Heath comes stumping over to say a few words, mostly grunts before turning away. I am probably one of the few young people on this side of the River who is not afraid of him. He is on the School Board and when he came to inspect us at the Academy, the school room became as still as a grave and some of the girls and boys got goose flesh. He is a strick disciplinarian for one thing and for another he doesn't hold with new-fangled ways. He won't let the teacher show us off and examines us his own way. I mean he did when we were at the Academy. He use to make every pupil do a sum in his or her head. He says that is "practical learning." The smartest use to freeze in their tracks, but I think he put me on my metal because I could do even the mental arithmetic correctly which is quite a feat for me. And besides, you can't spend hours in a man's orchard, walk off fairly bursting with apples inside and out, and still be afraid.

His wife is little and like a rosy apple, Grandmother knew her as a girl when she was a Fish. Mr. Heath has apple cheeks too, and all his grown up children likewise.

I like their kitchen which is very large, very clean and bare, with geraniums on the window sill and a faint whiff of the barn in the corners. Mr. Heath looks like a gentle person being pink cheeked, with a little grey beard and blue eyes, but he can speak sharply when he so minds.

Oct. 19 - Sunday - Florence lead the B.Y.P.U. meeting tonight.

Anna is going to have a party Friday, she says. I have a new dress, blue poplin with embroidered butterflies on the cape.

She likes Marcus Jones who comes to our church and plays the piano very well and so she has invited him to her party. I like him too.

Oct. 21 - Miss Greene had callers and let me go early. I think Marcus looks a little like that picture of Sir Galahad with his white charger. Marcus is a Latin name.

Oct. 24 - The Party. Had a good time. I think Marcus likes me. I wanted him to, but did not see why he ever would when Anna is so much prettier. I always thought a boy liked you or he didn't and I did not know until Sunday night that I could make a boy like me so easily. It was after B.Y.P.U. when a number of us were in the church kitchen, getting a drink of water. Marcus was there and he did not look at me until I smiled and said "hello Marcus." He looked at me as if he had never seen me and said "Oh, hello!'

A little later he talked to me, but he went home with Anna so I wasn't sure.

Harold and he came home with me from the Party. That does not prove a thing, because he could not very well take Anna home when she was already there.

Oct. 25 - Went up to Mary's house this afternoon. We went for a walk in the woods and ended up at the Stanton farm. Dink Breed the boy who is not right in the head was skinning a rabbit. It made me sick.

Oct. 26 - A lovely letter from Elizabeth.

Oct. 27 - Piano lesson today.

Althea wrote a note to me in Study Hall. She says Marcus likes me and not Anna. Yes, I am back in school and I still hate it. Ase could not afford Miss Greene who is expensive. She offered to teach me for less too. I think really Grandma and Mother want me to go back to school. They are afraid she will make me peculiar.

Oct. 28 - Paul Massey, a Senior noticed me today. I don't like him very well because he is showy and impudent, but the girls were quite impressed that a Senior boy noticed me.

Oct. 31 - Halloween - Mary, Constance and I dressed up in sheets and went around ringing door bells. We did not make mischief and most people were glad to see us. Constance looked so comical, a funny little roly-poly because of a heavy coat under the sheet.

My mask was very fiendish. All our masks got soggy about our noses and mouths as usual, but I like the funny smell of them and of candle drippings in the pumpkin moon shine lanterns.

I love Halloween; it is just about my favorite day. I got Daddy's big leather bound Burns and read "Tam O. Shanter" which I dearly love and then I read "Halloween," too.

Nov. 1 - We had our Halloween Social in the church basement tonight. Red apples and cider and dougnuts and pumpkins and rustly corn shocks give me a strange, exciting feeling. I wonder why?

Marcus does like me. Everyone has noticed it and Anna is mad at me. I am surprised, for I cannot see why he should prefer me to such a pretty girl as Anna. He walked home with me.

The funny part of it is that now I know he likes me I don't care whether he does or not and would just as soon have him like Anna again.

Nov. 2 - Church, Sunday School, Christian Endeavour, Church. Marcus walked with me. Anna really mad at me. I did not think a little smile could do all this. All the girls smile at him, because he is good looking and popular, so why am I so bad?

Nov. 3 - Mary likes a French boy at school. She says I'd better not try my tricks on him or she will never speak to me again. I do not like the boy anyway. My goodness!

Nov. 6 - Got 90 percent in French today.

Nov. 8 - Walked up to the old Peace Meeting Grove this afternoon. We hadn't been there since we picked Indian moccasins and found a few yellow violets.

Priscilla said it must have been a pretty exciting place when people came from all over for the meetings, because her mother said famous people came there. It is hard to imagine it now. There can't have been any meetings for many years now, although Grandma says they have had a few since I was born. The land once belonged to us and I guess if she had it now it would never have been sold for the meetings. It started out well enough, but there was soon drinking and it became like a circus or fair.

I once heard her speaking of someone as a "Peace Meeting baby," so I guess there must have been plenty of excitement. It would be pretty embarassing and inconvenient to have a baby at a meeting, but I can't see why it is so shameful one uses a certain tone of voice.

Nov. 9 - This afternoon Mary and I walked to the Fort Hill Burying Ground. We talked of many things and Mary did not guess that I was seeing and talking to Latham all the time.

In the evening we went to the Congregational Church on the other side of the River to hear a man give a lecture on Africa which was interesting. I am to have a new dress I did not expect. Grandmother bought the cloth. She says I don't need it anymore than a dog needs two tails, but it was a bargain and will work in handy.

I am reading Jane Austin's short stories of olden days with great interest. It is strange, yet familiar to see the name of Sam Chesebro on a page when I know a Sam Chesbrough. Then there is Althea and Nelson and their Cousin Paul who is clever as well as handsome. I am descended from the Chesebrough's myself Mother says. And the Carver name in print looks <u>so</u> familiar because of Cousin Mildred Carver. And Pitcher. Mr. Pitcher was once Principal of the Academy and I knew Molly Pitcher when they lived in the big yellow house next to Elder Miner's before they moved away. Mr. Pitcher was Editor as well as principal and very cross and irritable. It does not surprize me to see familiar names in town histories and records and such, but it gives me an odd feeling to find them in stories. I wonder why?

I never liked Saturdays and Sundays quite so much before and I never dreaded Mondays so much. I don't like high-school - and I don't know why. Maybe I shall get over it, I hope so. Its odd because I never gave a thought to whether I should like it or not, never felt any doubts at all, but from the first day I have been lost in a thick, dark mist. Of <u>course</u> it sounds crazy, but its the only way I can express it. None of the others feel that way so the queerness is within me.

Stonington itself is interesting, but somehow I can't love it even though I love so many things about it. The Main Street; and only business street, is tinsty and narrow. There arent any stores as good as those in Mystic, but I do like the way it meets the ocean. In Mystic you see the ocean, but you can't hear it. And I love the Breakwater and the narrow road and the sagging old houses, and the old light house. Parts of the town are plain shabby, but the residential section with its shady streets and fine old house, is lovely.

There is a little common too, something Mystic hasn't got, and on it little piles of cannon balls because the British shelled Stonington. One of my ancestors was the first settler, so I ought to feel a part of it, but I don't.

One noon I found the house where Capt. Nate Palmer use to live. He discovered the Antartic or something, and was a <u>very</u> domineering person. All the interesting people seem to have died before I was born.

Sometimes I tease some of the girls into walking down to the Breakwater with me, but they talk boys, boys boys! I would rather go alone, but no one can do <u>anything</u> in Stonington without <u>everyone</u> knowing it - its worse than Mystic - and it would look strange and cause talk.

When I'm out there I think so many things! I'd like to have lived in the days of clipper- ships. Maybe I did, and died before I got half enough of it. When I stop to think that I have never been to sea, have never felt a deck beneath me, I - well I just can't believe it. I seems I <u>must</u> have, I know the feel and the sounds so well.

Those were brutal hard days, the captains were often mean devils, but though it meant yellow fever, scurvy, being buried at sea or knifed in a foreign port I should go to sea if I were a boy and now were then.

Someday I am going abroad and while I shall love being out of sight of land it will not be the same. I cannot get any feeling for steamships at all.

An Account of My Life

<u>Nov. 10</u> Nothing interesting to write. Old Leil Bentley was on the school car tonight with her umbrella up, paying no attention to anyone. The kids laugh at her, and so do I sometimes, but I feel ashamed. Everyone calls her Umbrella Bentley because she keeps it up in doors and out, and even in the moving picture house. She says its drafts. Grandmother and she have been friends since their girlhood. Her name is Lelia and she was as pretty as her name they say, but now she is white and swollen like the crawly things you find under rocks. Her clothes are fastened any old how with safety pins and she carries her money in a paper bag. Although she is rather dirty most ways, she is afraid of germs and washes her hands a hundred times a day. Another odd trick is the way she walks spang in the middle of the trolley tracks with the car crawling along behind. She will not get out no matter how much the motor man clangs the bell. Talking does not do any good either, and when the car is late everyone says Leil must be on the tracks.

Gurd Allyn says she would try the patience of a saint which he don't pretend to be. One of her aggravating tricks is to go to his W.C., bolt the door, and stay for hours. She will not come out until she feels like it no matter how much you need to come in.

She cannot bear her husband and keeps saying she will kill him one of these days, but no one really believes it, although she throws skillets at him, and they say, has chased him with a bread knife. When she gets one of her spells she is a terror. Several years ago when Grandma and I were in the garden she came by and stopped. Wainwright, she said, was a viper. He had everyone fooled with his looks and taking ways, but he was a viper.

Then she hollered that the happiest day of her life would be when she stood beside his open grave throwing rocks down on him. Grandmother looked at me and said "Go away." So I did and heard no more. But I have heard Grandma tell about her to Mama over their sewing, afternoons. If I keep quiet I hear a lot, but if I forget and ask questions they say "it doesn't concern you. Be quiet, or leave the room."

Grandma says she minds as if it were yesterday the day Leila stopped her (they were young women at the time) and said, "Camelia, Wainright has asked me to marry him."

"You don't seem much taken with the idea," Grandma said, and Leil said, no she wasn't.

"Well," Grandma said. "Theres a number would like to be in your shoes. He's got a way with him."

Leil admitted it, but wasn't sure she wanted to get married.

Grandmother told her there was no law compelling her to if she didn't want to.

All at once Leil clutched her hard and said, "Well, I'm scared of it!"

"I guess you'll live thru it," Grandma told her, and then seeing she was really up-set spoke more kindly.

1919

"I told her," Grandma says, "that Wainright Bentley was a good man and if she felt like that she'd better wait. And then she switched right around and said she always intended to get married and she liked Wainright.

Well, he was possessed to marry her and he did, and he hasn't drawn an easy breath since. There's a queer strain in her family, but none were like Leil. Maybe she'd have been different with another man, I don't know. In a way she sets quite a store by him and she is jealous if a woman so much as looks at him. There never was a man with nicer ways."

I can imagine the pretty Lelia Bailey Grandmother knew, but I <u>cannot</u> see how she became queer old Leil Bentley.

<u>Nov. 11</u> - I have been in the upper hall sitting on the horsehair sofa reading an old book of Daddy's called "*A Memoir of Capt. W.T. Bate R.N. (Royal Navy)*" by the Rev. John Baillie.

Capt. Bate was a very noble seafaring man and the Rev. Baillie is very pious and much given to poetry and prose quotations. Some of the poetry is nice. I like this - "His eye is quick to observe, his memory storeth in secret: His ear is greedy of knowledge, and his mind is plastic as soft wax." I am not so sure about the being "plastic as soft wax" because that means any old thing would make an impression which would make a messy sort of mind, I should think, but the sentiment is noble. I hate another line he quotes - that one about "not lost, but gone before." I think it is stuff and nonsense.

Grandma and Mother are downstairs in the sitting room talking what Ase calls mid-wife talk. A midwife is the nurse who takes care of a baby. The door is open so I guess they do not care if I hear. Anyway they are talking so low I was not interested until I heard my name. I don't think it is evesdropping when you listen to something as far back as me being born. Of course I know that Mother almost died at the time. It took hours from midnight until six the next night and was very hard on the both of us and also on poor old Doctor Barber. When he was having coffee his hands shook so the cup rattled. He did not practice much after that and soon died. He was very old, but the experience didn't help him any I guess. He had to use instruments, I don't know what kind, but he did and he pulled my head all out of shape and I had scars for months and months.

Grandma said, "What a mercy she is alright! Mrs. Buffum's little boy was crippled. The instrument slipped pressing his spine at the nape of his neck, I've heard say."

Suppose I had been crippled! Indeed I have a great deal to be thankful for. I wonder what kind of a cripple I would have been? Sweet and patient like the ones you read about or mean and onery like the ones in real life? I don't blame cripples for being onery, but it is hard to get along with them. Take Lee. <u>He</u> is crippled and goes on crutches, infantile paralisis did it. He can do anything the other boys do. He can swim, ride a bicycle and he can even run on his crutches getting over the ground slick as a whistle. I admire his pluckiness, but he is not fair. He makes the boys fighting mad and then says, "You can't hit a cripple," and of course they can't. Sometimes a boy will get so mad he will take a step towards Lee with his fists doubled up, but that is all, because Lee says, "Go on, hit a cripple, will you! I <u>dare</u> you hit me."

It is not fair to the other boys when he <u>tries</u> to get them mad. And if they <u>don't</u> get mad, but act good natured <u>he</u> gets mad. He bothers <u>girls</u> too. His arms and hands are awful strong and when he twists your arm the hurt most kills you. One time when he hurt me I said, "Stop Lee or I will slap you."

And he said grinning, "Hit a cripple, would you?"

"Yes," I said, and slapped him hard. He was very surprized. I stood there so he could hit back if he wanted to so it was not cowardly like running away, although he can travel fast.

"You can't strike a girl," I said. He looked queer for a minute.

I should not have done it because he is afflicted and I am not. When I told Jerry I felt bad about it, he said, "Cut it out booby. He asked for it, now don't spoil it all. Remember in the 7th grade the time you cracked Warren?"

I sound very brutal, but I am not. This Warren is a colored boy who use to make sounds with his lips like kissing sounds, when he passed me. I told him to stop but he kept right on day in, day out. One day he did it right close to my face and I hauled off and slapped his face with all my might and main. It made a loud sound like a pistol going of and most broke my hand. He looked very surprized and his head bobbed back. The teacher saw it all. "Helen!" she said, then went off biting her lips and never mentioned it again. I told Jerry I should not have done it with my bare hand, but he said what else could I use there not being any ten foot poles or gauntelets handy? He said I did a good job and that you could hear that smack the length of the hall.

I guess it was wrong, but I could not help it.

<u>Nov. 13</u> Anna had another party . When she gave Marcus his invitation he asked her if I was coming. She didn't like it very well. It was fun walking to the party breathing in the crisp air. Marcus hung around me all evening. I wanted him to like me some but not too much. He walked home with me and so did Harold Maine.

<u>Nov. 20</u> Today we held a Mass Meeting in Study Hall. Game with Westerly tomorrow. Very important.

<u>Nov. 22</u> Saw William Hart in "Wagon Tracks." Extremely good.

<u>Nov. 23</u> Usual thing. Marcus leads B.Y.P.U. next Sunday.

1919

Nov. 27 Today is Thanksgiving. Had turkey and a pleasant time. No school until Monday.

Nov. 28 Long walk to Noank with Mary. This afternoon we walked in the woods and picked Princess Pine. I am always light and happy in the woods.

Nov. 29 Marcus walked by the house a few minutes ago. Constance was playing in the yard and he gave her a note to give me. I am getting sick of it!
The Family won't let me spend Christmas in New York and are hurt that I want to. Oh why can't they understand! Darn everything!

Nov. 30 Marcus acting downright silly. Anna still mad. Didn't know she could stay mad so long. If he acted so silly with her I should think she'd be glad to be rid of him

Dec. 4 Anna asked me to write in her Birthday Book so I guess she is alright again. I am glad; no boy is worth it.

Dec. 6 Held World Wide Guild Sale. Mary and I got the alderberries for the decorations. Sale well attended. I bought a string of rose pink beads Miss Coats had donated. Guild took in $15.85.

Dec. 7 Usual Sunday. They handed out Christmas recitations today and I got one of course.

Dec. 9 Rehearsed Christmas program at Church and had an awfully good time.

Dec. 13 Mary and I went to the movies. Serial very exciting. I feel that I cannot wait for the next episode.

Dec. 17 I wish you weren't supposed to like boys. They are not necessary. If other girls would stop talking about them I would be glad, but unless you want to be left out of things and pitied, you just have to be popular. I like it alright when a boy is just beginning to get interested in me, but just as soon as he gets silly I am nauseated.
Have nearly finished my Christmas shopping.

Dec. 18 Rehearsed at Church. Marcus came home with me.

Dec. 25 A wonderful white Christmas. Had everything I wanted within reason. Mary came down in the afternoon. Stanley is in Mystic. His Grandmother is dead. Grandma and Mother have been in , but I haven't yet. I am sorry for Stanley and don't know what to say.

An Account of My Life

Dec. 28 - Went to Elm Grove with Mary while she placed an evergreen wreath on her brother's grave. Awful cold in my head.

Dec. 29 Sliding fine. Spent afternoon on Stanton's Hill. Mary asked me to-day if Marcus kissed me. I was shocked. She laughed at me. She says all the others do. Well I won't. Why can't I be like the others?

As a general thing I like old people better than do most girls my age. I like to hear them talk and they like me except the very prissy ones. Once in awhile however, there is one who tries ones soul. Today I met one of the old Mr Whipples from Quakertown, which one I don't know because they all seem alike to me and seldom come to town. He spoke to me as if he knew me, so I stopped.

"Whose girl are you?" he wheezed. "You look familiar."

I said I was Helen May Clarke and he said: "Only Clark I can call to mind is Dummy Clark You don't look like any kin of his. New family?"

"I'm not!" I exclaimed, too indignant to be polite. "and my father has been here fifteen-sixteen years and I was born here."

"T'ain't no time at all," he said and spit tobacco juice." Durned if you don't look familiar just the same."

Seeing he meant to keep me there while he scratched his head I thought I might as well help him out.

"It's probably the Burrows look," I told him with dignity." My Grandmother is a Burrows."

"Well now," he pricked up his hairy old ears. "Now we're getting somewhere. Which ones your granny? I've known more Burrowes n' you can shake a stick at. Fine people, best there is. One of the first families, some say the first barring the Injuns, I dunno. Fishes, Parkes, Packers, Dennison, Hempstead. Folks think highly of 'em, most of 'em least wise.

"Guess my old eyes aint gone back on me yet. I saw the look, Girl, now didn't I see the look?"

And so it went on and on wheezing and talking.

After I got away I forgot the every day ordinary things by imagining I lived in a castle. I swept gracefully thru my marble halls in a robe of velvet. There were butlers and footmen in scarlet livery, tall and motionless as statures. Rare paintings and tapestries decked the walls. Tall candles gleamed in great golden candlelabra. I descended the great staircase, my hands white on a carved railing.

I wonder what a princess in a castle dreams about?

An Essay on The Smell of Tar

One of the nicest, cleanest smells in the world is the smell of tar. We get it in three forms. First, from the ropes and nets on the docks and from the boatyard. Second, from the tar wagon when it spreads it on the roads in Spring. And third from Packers Tar Soap Manufacturing Company.

In the spring after the March winds have dried the mud and the roads are white and dusty, the tar cart comes out. It never goes on Ashbey

Street because it is sort of a side street, but Noank Road leads to New London and sees a lot of travel. The tar flows out in a lazy way, all thick and black and shining and men follow along throwing sand and gravel over it. My, how it does shine in the sun! Mother thinks it nasty looking stuff, but I think it is beautiful. Of course it makes a mess until it is worked down hard. You naturally track it on the veranda if not in the house and we kids sometimes get it on our clothes. Some of the boys manage to get simply <u>covered</u>, and it is terrible for long skirts too. Everyone says, "that devilish stuff, " but later they are glad of it. When it is hard is when I <u>don't</u> like it. I like roads to be white and soft with dust. Our road never used to be tarred. It is on account of there being more automobiles every year. The sprinkling cart came by during dry spells and we'd wait for it to wet down the dust before we went for a stroll - Mother, I mean, Daddy never let dust bother him.

It is not enough now. When the road has just been done, the smell of tar is very strong and punget.

Packer's Tar Soap is a more refined scent. We use it and the shampoo on account of Uncle Dan Packer who started it being a family connection. He began to make this tar soap in the high basement of the Packer house on the corner of High Street and Dudley Hill just up the hill from here. He got to be a rich man. At first he wrapped the soap himself and Aunt P. helped. Later, he built a place to make it in and he needed more help. Aunt P. said she would not have foreigners brought in, it was a nice lady-like work and she only wanted girls she knew root and branch. So one day, Mother says, Uncle Dan came up the path just as they were going to have dinner. He couldn't stop for a bite he said, though that pie did look powerful good, he was out getting girls to help him wrap. There was Prue Waterman, Laura Packer, Emily Weeks and he wanted Allie. Aunt P. told him to be sure to get Allie. He'd pay $5.00 a week. Grandma said, "Dan Packer, the women in our family don't work - the men are perfectly able to support them. You ought to know that."

Uncle Dan tried to talk her around, but it was Daddy who did the deciding. Mother says he took a drink from his mustache cup and said, "T'won't hurt the girl, Teach her the value of money."

Mother says she was just <u>wild</u> to, because it sounded like fun and it was so dull at home embroidering and reading, with Grandma being so strick about going out nights and all that.

It caused bad feeling in one of her friends, though. Uncle Dan didn't want Lucy and Aunt P. said 'no.' she would not have any but the best girls in the best families and relatives or family connections when ever possible. She said she would have to associate with them and she guessed she'd have her own kind or know the reason why. Well, it got so it was sort of a social honor. Uncle Dan didn't hire - I mean if anyone went to him asking for work he wouldn't like as not. He just picked out the ones they wanted and called on the parents.

Mother says she never had so much fun in her life. In the afternnoon they stopped for afternoon tea and they vied in seeing who could bring the nicest things to eat. At the end of the week they had five dollars and later seven. It was only so many months in the year so they had plenty of vacation too. Some of the girls spent their money as they got it, but Mother saved hers until vacation and then she spent it all on clothes and good times.

It is not like that now, now that it has grown so big.

I have told the three forms of tar common to Mystic, all of which I enjoy smelling and I have thought of one other, the tar on the trolley tracks. A little man with a bucket of tar and a long handled thing swabs it in certain places on the tracks. It does not smell so strong because there is not so much of it. We like to walk the trolley tracks, but where they have been tarred we get it on our heels when we slip off of them. That makes our parents the maddest because there is no need of walking there. When it is on the road they are resigned to a mess, but when we deliberately seek it out they are scolding full. After all, I am going on fifteen and pretty old for such tricks, I guess.

Grandma does not like the idea of me writing poetry. She says she hopes I wont turn out to be another Ida Whipple Bennum [Benham]. This Ida Whipple use to live in the house I have always known as Elder Miner's house, and she wrote poetry and had it printed. Grandma says she never could make out if she was an extra smart woman, or a plain fool until that business about a baby, and then she knew. Seems Ida Whipple decided she was going to have a baby. She told every one so and got the clothes ready for it and then it turned out she only thought she was going to have one. Every one said with disgust," If that isn't just like Ida Whipple [Benham]!"

People are so queer. There was Mr. Buckeley's mother who would not make a stitch of clothes for the baby when she knew she was expecting and let it lie bare naked for want of them, and here was Ida Whipple [Benham] making clothes for a baby that never was outside her own mind. It is very interesting.

1919

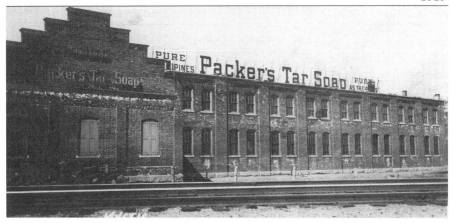

Packer's Tar Soap building, Mystic

Helen and Dorrance

Dan Packer

The Peace Grant House, West Main Street, Mystic

1920

<u>Wed. Jan. 21</u> - Mary and I went sliding on the Three Hills after school. They are supposed to be dangerous, but we had a good time and nothing befell us until the last slide which came near to being our last slide more ways than one.

It had grown dark, the road was icy, the sled simply flew and somehow we went into a gutter hitting a drain-pipe with terrible force. Mary was steering and I was on her back. I simply flopped over her head, turned a somersault and lay in the snow laughing. Then I looked for Mary. She was lying in such a queer heap I stopped laughing and touched her. When she held her head up I saw that blood was pouring from a deep gash over one eye. I tried to stop the blood but couldn't. A man who came from somewhere wanted us to go into the neighboring house, but she wouldn't. My house was nearer than hers so I helped her there and Mother patched her up temporarily and when she felt better I took her home. On the way back the street lights went out. As a rule I am not afraid of the dark, but I was just nervous enough to imagine things. I kept thinking suppose when I touched Mary she had been dead. Thank you God that awful thing didn't happen.

<u>Jan. 24</u> - Queer weather, but interesting, it has been raining, hailing and snow by turns and all together. The sliding is ruined of course. We had been planning to go somewhere seeing it is Saturday and Priscilla, Mary, Anna and I have been at the telephone all morning. The family got tired of hearing the it ring and of what Father calls "giggling jibber-jabbering," but my goodness, with the weather too bad to do anything, we had to do something. By afternoon the weather had calmed down and I went up to Mary's house. Her mother is English with a funny accent. The best room is clean, but the kitchen is not. I am not being critical, just interested, because I have never seen a kitchen like it. There are no curtains at the windows, everything is on top of something else, and nothing shines.

<u>Jan. 25</u> - The minister had a bad cold, poor man.

<u>Jan. 29</u> - Althea gave a small birthday party this afternoon,. She is sixteen. Priscilla and I are now the youngest girls in our crowd and Priscilla never lets me forget than I am two months younger than she.

Althea's mother has some fine geraniums in bloom which made the whole room look bright, and warm especially with the sun on them. I like a farm.

1920

Jan. 31 - Marcus has been asking me to have supper at his house and today his mother asked me special. His parents are estmable people I am sure, but I do not find them interesting. They haven't a book in the house. I do not mind poor English if the person is interesting, but they are so dull, And I think Mr. Jones is the silliest man I have ever met.

Sun. Feb 1 - The usual church going. Priscilla and I had tea alone. Mother let me use one of the best tea clothes and the solid silver spoons and embroidered napkins.

Feb. 4 - Mary and I have small parts in the School Minstrel Show.

Feb. 5 - This is an extra fine winter with a lot of snow. We are having a blizzard now and the trolley cars are not running. Have been popping corn and reading "Evangeline." Sarah, our cat likes pop corn first rate.

Feb. 6 - Labourers are trying to shovel the car tracks out, but as it is still snowing they are not making much head way. They say all the snow plows are busy. There are cars stalled here and there and it is called the worst blizzard since 1888.

We don't have any such storms as they had in 1740 or there abouts, when Desire Packer Burrows who I think was my great, great, great, great grandmother, slid from her bedroom window in a big chopping bowl over the frozen River to the Dennison house on the opposite side. What fun that must have been.

Feb. 7 - The snow plow has dug us out. There are great drifts in our back yard.

This afternoon the World Wide Guild met at Mrs Osborne's, the minister's wife. I like the parsonage because it is homey. They have a great many books, although no exciting ones, and marble statues and groups stuck all around. The tea was good with a great sufficiency of odd little sandwiches. Mrs. Osborne had mixed bayberries and bittersweet in a squatty brown bowl and it pleased me so I could not keep my eyes away from it.

When the sun set it touched the brick library to rose gold and bathed the white church spire in a lovely light. Our Society is prosperous with $14 in the treasury. When the meeting came to an end we walked across the street to the library and I took out *The Chronicles of Avonlea*, by Miss Montgomery. We had a snow fight on the way home during which Alice Colby broke her pocket mirror. She says she is not superstitious, but I think she looked pale. Seven years bad luck would be very hard on her as she is a great one to complain anyway.

Feb. 9 - Mon. No school because the trolley cars are not running yet and won't be before Wednesday. It is like having a new lease on life.

Music lesson today after which Mary and I went sliding in the side hill lot. The sunset was glorious, the whole sky bursting into flame.

Feb. 10 - Snowing again. Have been feeding the birds and reading Whittier.

Feb. 11- Same as yesterday. Fed birds again and read more of Whittier. I love "Magg Megone" and "The Bridal of Pennacook" and all those about Maine. I don't know why but the names, both Indian and white thrill me. Castine, for instance, sings in my mind. I think Maine must be very different from the New England I know - grand and frightening and wild. Someday I shall go there and if the majic is Maine majic, not just Whittier majic, I shall stay a long, long time. Casco, Dark Isles, Katahdin are such fairy tale names I cannot explain how they make me feel.

Feb. 12 - We girls have been buying valentines to send to each other. We think it is very bold to send valentines to boys, although it is alright for them to send to us.

Feb. 14 - Several unsigned valentines among the rest, I could guess pretty well. Marcus sent me a handsome one, but the verse was too sticky sweet for my stomach.

Feb. 17 - Minstrel practice at Boro Hall in Stonington. It would have been fun but for Marion Rose a big clumsy Portygee from the Flats who hates me for no reason at all. She was horrid to day and I ignored her. She would like me to quarrel with her, when she could yell me down, but I won't and that makes her furious as she would rather be insulted than ignored any day in the week. I heard her telling a girl that I was "a little stuck up snipe." probably because I don't say "aint got none" and keep my finger nails clean. I just look thru her, not at her. I might not mind what she says, but it burns inside of me. She reminds me of Angeline, that awful little brat I knew as a child. I am willing to leave her entirely alone, but she won't be let. It's not that I have ever done anything to her; it's simply that she can't abide me. Well, I can't abide her either. She is as mean as a halfbreed Indian.

Most of the Portuguese from the Flats are pleasant people. Some of them have been here for several generations and most of them bear Yankee names because they took the name the Captain bore who brought them over.

Mary isn't like Priscilla or Elizabeth for instance. We are friends because we have been to school together rather than for any other reason. In Stonington we go different ways and never like the same girls. The ones I like she thinks are "snooty." I should have gone to New London with Cill I suppose, but Stonington High is directly on the sea - and oh I don't really know why I decided the way I did.

1920

<u>Wed. Feb. 18</u> Bought a "Vogue" magazine at Kretzers. I love nice paper. Just touching the glossy, smooth pages eases the ache in me, which is the sort of remark I can not make without Mary saying, "You <u>do</u> say the funniest things!"

<u>Thur. Feb. 19</u> Mr. Jones sat in back of us on the car tonight. When he saw me he acted very silly and even told the man with him that I was "one cute kid!" He didn't care who heard and Mary thought I was crazy not to feel pleased. Instead, I felt sick.

Just a little while ago Mother asked me about him. She said she didn't believe in putting ideas into my head, but Ase had heard men talking about him and he insisted that she ask me. I said he was a regular Baron Whats-His-Name - I mean Mr. Jones, of course, except that his lies were never interesting. She said `yes,' everyone laughed at him. When I didn't say anymore, she asked if he acted `silly.' I said "over me?" and she said "Well, yes," looking very embarassed. She explained that he had a bad name with women and girls and even if one discounted a good half of what was said, one could never be sure how much truth there was in his talk. I laughed. Imagine that little runt! Marcus takes his height from his Mother who is a massive woman. No, he doesn't act silly the way she means, but he makes silly remarks and looks sly.

<u>Sun. Feb. 22</u> We are all curling our hair, but it is not very successful in this damp air. Anyone as fond of salt water as I am should have been born with curly hair.

We are going to have some of Mr. Edgecomb's sausage for supper. He is a cranky, taciturn person, but his sausage is wonderful. It is the best anyone has ever eaten. Just to smell it cooking is enough to make one's mouth water. It is a Secret which Mr. Edgecomb got from John Green Packer and <u>he</u> got it from Sam Buckley.

People taste it knowning what goes into sausage, naming the different spices with knowing nods, but when they go to put it together it is just plain sausage such as anyone would make. The worst torture I can think of beyond being gnawed by rats is to be bound starving in a chair with Mr. Edgecombs sausage cooking under my nose. I think Tantallus would have suffered worse if he had smelled it.

Mr. Edgecomb ought to advertize it as the sausage that tantalized Tantallus, but of course he does not advertize. He has an immaculate meat market and wears clean straw cuffs. He also wears an orange colored wig and most of his teeth are solid gold.

I <u>do</u> wish we had Camp Fire Girls here, I should so like to belong. They use to have them, but it has been given up, I don't know why. Reading the series about Camp Fire Girls has got me just crazy to belong.

<u>Feb.</u> - Although I had fun this afternoon I feel let down and out of sorts. Cill, Mary, Marion, Marcus, Pat and I met the rest of the crowd down

at Anna's and went sliding across the lots. Someone laid boards over the little brook at the foot of the slope, packing them with snow so that our sleds could cross over and keep on going. All went well until Marcus with a too heavy load on the big sled, lost control and tipped us into the icy water. We scrambled out of the shallow water, some of us wet to the knees, some of us wet underneath. We laughed until we were limp and aching. Anna said we must hurry to her house as fast as possible before we caught cold.

Well, we did head in that direction, but we were so warm from the exertion of snow balling and climbing the slope we didn't feel cold.

Cill who had wet underneath was uncomfortable and we girls almost burst trying not to laugh at her funny gait.

My gloves were wringing wet because I had thrown my hands out as we tipped, and Marcus pulled them off and slipped his big mittens on my cold hands. They looked so funny we almost died of laughing.

I told him his hands would be cold, but he said `no' he'd stick them in his reefer pockets.

"I told him, "Have one mitten, I can get both hands in one. See?"

Well, he just rolled in the snow laughing at me, but he wouldn't hear of it.

When the others had got a little ahead of us he said, "Gosh Helen, you look pretty with that red cap on. Your eyes are awfully pretty."

I couldn't help looking at him sideways once in awhile as we climbed the hill. He is the tallest and broadest of the boys and not a bit gawky. I guessed how my eyes looked because his are dark too and the snow and bright blue sky made them very clear and liquid. Cill's eyes look that way out in the snow I've noticed. Marcus has an olive skin and today it was flushed and warm looking. A lock of hair black as a crow's wing hung down on his forehead from under his red and blue knitted cap. I had a funny feeling that he was important - I mean against the sky he seemed very large and splendid.

Thinking of hair made me think of my own which felt rather loose and strange. I knew what had happened. "Darn it," I said, pulling my braid over my shoulder where I could look at it. "That's the second hair ribbon I've lost in a week. I guess I shall be reduced to shoe-strings before long."

"Want to go back and look for it?" he asked, stopping short.

"What's a hair ribbon!" I said. "Come on lets run after the others." He caught my hair where it was fast unbraiding and shook it loose until it spread all over my back. I wasn't really angry though I pretended. I had just washed it (which brought out the golden lights) and it crinkled and waved from its tight braiding. Usually it is merely light brown and straight as an Indians.

"I wish you'd leave it that way," he said, running his hand through it. I said I guessed I'd have to until I got a comb and something to tie it with.

1920

When we were drying out around the sitting-room stove and the wettest had changed to dry things, Mrs. Dennison brought in hot chocolate and cake. I think she is a fine step-mother, but Anna, who remembers her own Mother, does not pretend to like her.

Then Justin came in (no one calls him Mr. Dennison) red as an apple, breezy as a March day and full of fun. He has a voice like a bull and can't say "good-day" without bellowing it. Mother tells about the time the little boy who would be older than Anna if he had lived, died unexpectedly. She was in the front chamber late at night when she heard a horse and buggy coming up over the hill. Next she recognized the bellowing voice and wondered what brought Justin out so late at night - late for a farmer anyway. He was roaring about his little boy's death, the first anyone had heard about it - at the top of his lungs. Before morning everyone on the road knew all about it and how he felt. When he whispers in church it is like a gust of wind.

Well, he joked with the boys and teased the girls saying comical things until we were in an uproar. He is such a tease, sometimes he makes us mad, but not for long.

Mrs. Dennison who likes to paint in her spare time, of which she has very little, and is interested in child education and geneaology, thinks him sort of coarse, I guess. I think he acts all the rougher just to bother her. She was Linda Richmond before she married him, and an old maid schoolteacher, they say. She says we are related thru the Bennetts she believes. Of course I have a Dennison line too, so that makes us all connected.

Well, she wanted to calm things down a little I guess, so she asked Marcus to play for us. When he walked over to the piano Justin shouted, "My God, boy, you must be nigh on to six feet and no where near got your growth. How old are you? Fourteen? Jesus Christ, but you're a buster!"

Justin can't stand much classical music and in no time he was calling for something lively. Marcus then played old songs and new in a sort of slap dash way which pleased Justin mightily. He said he could tickle the ivories for fair, but with a build like that he ought to be on a farm. Then he looked at me and then at Marcus and said, "Never knew it to fail. Why don't you pick some one your size?"

Mrs. Dennison said "Justin" in a terrible voice and Marcus and I felt like fools. When he went out to do the chores with the hired man we began to get ready to go. He told us to stay for supper, but I didn't want to see any more of him, besides we had sense enough to see Mrs. Dennison looked tired and twelve extras are a lot even if we girls helped. Justin only lets her have a hired girl in the summer. Besides it meant calling up our parents and some of the kids didn't think they could stay. We paired off as soon as we were out of doors, a couple to a sled and Marcus and I were the last to send our sled skimming down Justin's hill. As I got on with him he said,

"You tied your hair back."

"You wouldn't want it in your face," I told him practically. "Look, if we get a good start it would be a shame to stop at the foot. It ought to carry us down the corner hill, across the road and down to the Railroad Station."

"Suppose an automobile comes up Noank Road," he argued, "we couldn't stop. And crossing the trolley tracks is risky the way they tear thru this stretch."

"And maybe a train will come along just as we hit the railroad tracks," I mocked. "We can't die but once. Are you afraid?"

"I feel responsible for you," he said, weakening a little.

"Come on!" I cried.

He gave in. So down the long hill we sailed with the wind sweeping us, and at the bottom he swerved without tipping and while we slowed a little, our speed carried us down the hill which in turn gave us force enough to carry us whizzing across the trolley tracks and down almost to the railroad tracks. It was grand!

I said so when he pulled me from the sled and that it was too bad we couldn't go on and on.

"You'd have to stop somewhere!" he laughed. "Unless you want to go into the River and I should think you'd had enough of a wetting for one day."

"Its the best slide I ever had," I said. "Thank you Marcus."

Well, the only sensible thing to have done was to have walked along Noank Road until we came to my house seeing we were so near, but he said: "Helen, lets walk back up and along Skipper Street and around. I'll take you down Three Hills." I gave a little hop of joy and he laughed.

"Marcus," I said. "You're swell."

Well, we hadn't gone but a little way before he began to tell silly jokes explaining each one although a child could have got whatever point there was.

I knew for a few hours I had again fooled myself into thinking him a Prince Charming when he is only plain Marcus and nothing more.

I tried to think of him with the blue sky behind him and his eyes full of laughter, but it was as if I had read about it long ago.

I sat on the couch with Constance cutting out paperdolls from the old Charles Williams catalogue. Of course I dont play with them, but I sort of like to cut them out.

Why can't people enjoy things when they have them? On sweltering hot days I often think of crunchy snow and snow flakes hissing against the window panes, and now that it is winter I long for summer and the scent of sweet fern.

It all started when Mother said she guessed we'd have a huckleberry slump tomorrow. In a flash I was thinking of huckleberries warm from the sun and all the summer smells around me. Why can't I think of the steaming hot slump with the berry juices running into the plate and the butter melting down the sides?

And why must I always like Marcus best when I am not with him?

1920

Of course I liked him for quite a spell today, but I wasn't really with him. I guess I fooled myself into thinking he was something he never was or will be.

From now on I vow I shall see him as he is: and I vow I shall enjoy all good things as they are when they are.

I have been thinking. If a woman lives with a man who is not her husband, she is a bad woman and her family is disgraced. But if she became a King's mistress her decendants are proud for ever more. If it is wrong for one why not the other? Of course it is much more elegant than the ordinary kind, but if one is bad the other is too. I know the King can't marry an ordinary woman which is some excuse, but wrong is wrong. The trouble is I'm not sure either are - always.

In the old days people were ashamed of any suspicion of Indian blood: now people boast of it. Mother says generally speaking only the worst men married Indian women. And Father says its been many moons since the Indian was noble if he ever was. He says for years they were pitiful objects having been debassed by us whites. Well then, why be proud?

Its the same with Pirates. If you have any folks in jail you are disgraced, but if you had a Pirate Ancestor who was hung, you are proud. I feel that way myself. I feel that a Kings Mistress or a Pirate are treasured ancestors to have, but my common sense wonders why?

Grandma always says, "Wrong is wrong," but she explains ancestor's misbehavior by saying times were different then and we can't understand. I said times are different now from what they were when _you_ were young, so maybe what was wrong then is right now and vice versa.

She blames Father for encouraging my unlady like thoughts. She cannot see why I must tear everything apart. Well, I know it doesn't get you anywhere, but I can't help thinking about things.

I do not think I shall ever become religious, but lately the spiritual side of me has been giving me a little trouble. Things I can't understand or thrash out. I have read enough old books and heard enough old people talk to know that in those days everyone thought of hell constantly. They were scared to death of it: they ate it, drank it and brooded over it. It must have been gloomy business. You had to be so very good in order to be thought good at all and so very little bad to be called a wicked sinner it must have been discouraging.

Grandmother is good, she never turns from the path, but for years she has never gone to church. Neither has Mother except when we speak pieces. Grandmother is a member of the Congregational Church in Putnam, though brought up a Baptist. Mother belongs to no church. Ase is an agnostic and swears like an atheist. We never say grace, and outside of requiring me to know my S.S. lesson no one rams the Bible down my throat. It would seem the Family has rid itself of the fear of hell. I don't believe in hell, though I feel uneasy when I say so.

There are so many puzzling angles. If I hear for instance that Mr. So and So is a "bad man" I know he may be a thief, he may be cruel, he may be bad on any one of a dozen counts, but if I hear Miss So and So or Mrs. So and So is a "bad" woman I know it means just one thing: adultery.

Why? Adultery isn't the only sin a woman can commit, or even the most frequent one. There are women who never have a kind thought in their lives, who are selfish, cruel and malicious, who spread gossip, whip up scandal and drive people to desperation, yet are "good women" because they "never look at another man."

Lately I have been looking the congregation over and wondering. A few are good, most are not. They may be trying but only on Sunday and only in church. Miss Hattie my S.S. teacher is good. I dont believe she ever did a wrong thing in her life, she's good to the marrow of her bones and happy in her goodness. I can never be like her. There is just one man in her life next to God and that is the minister. She is so rich in spiritual grace she looks like a nun though she would be horrified at the comparison, and practically is one. I respect her kind of goodness so much that I try not to ask upsetting questions (she is not an intelligent woman) and she looks so hurt and lost thinking she has failed as a teacher. If she prays over me it is in private. She is so <u>darn</u> good it is exasperating. She baked and sold a quantity of pies and cakes in order to give everyone of us a little testament which none of us wanted in the least. She'll go without a new dress in order to give to the missions. And she is happy doing so.

I like fun and good stories and even profanity if its sort of picturesque. I like lesser sinners. When Bill - or maybe it was Mike Mullaney (brothers, Roman Catholics, who drive for Jim Brown's Livery Stable) said. "Timperince be damned! I've rid many a hearse full of heathen Protestants to the cimitery that never warmed their guts with divil a thing but mullein tea." I thought it funny, but Miss Hattie thought it vulgar and shocking. Is it? Why?

<u>Feb. 29</u> - Church with Priscilla. I thought Walter was away at the Boys Convention, but he was there. He and Marcus do not get along.

<u>Mar. 3</u> - Public speaking in English class. I enjoy it, but most of the kids do not, so I pretend I hate it too so that they will not think I am putting it on.

<u>Mar. 4</u> - We have finished "*Treasure Island*." I do hope the next book won't be one I know by heart. Elizabeth Austin is a very sweet girl. It is odd, but every Elizabeth I have ever been friends with has been nice: Elizabeth Cutler, Elizabeth Colby and now Elizabeth Austin.

Elizabeth was one of the Clarke family names, but it was spelled <u>Elisabeth</u> which I think is prettier to look at and softer sounding. And then too, it does away with Lizzie which is the ugliest nickname in the world.

1920

Mar. 6th - A blizzard! Father read, "As You Like It" aloud, and then we talked about it.

Mother made fudge. When Father was tired of me I sat in the big leather chair with my legs over the arm and read Miss Meade's *"A World of Girls"* for about the fortieth time. Mother sat at the piano and played soft, sad things. It was very comfortable.

Mar. 7 - Communion Sunday. Walter came home with me from S.S. and Marcus is mad. In the afternoon I went up to Mary's. The snow was so crunchy and the sky so blue I tingled all over with happiness. Mary felt that way too, or she caught it from me, and I guess we were just too silly for words. We walked as far as old Danny Brown's.

Mar. 9 - Assembly Hall today. Book report for English. I do not like our book list and said so when the teacher asked which one I had chosen.

"I suppose you prefer the Senior list," she said with a sarcastic laugh.

"Yes," I answered flatly.

"I am afraid you are not quite up to that," she said, and the class knowing she wouldn't mind and half expected it of them, laughed.

I said nothing more. I know I could report on any book on the Senior list, for I have already read many on it. On our list there are only books I have read and re-read, and perhaps a few by Joseph Lincoln, or Gene Stratton Porter or even Harold Bell Wright.

Mar. 10 - Minstrel practice. I like Tommy O'Conner who is chief of police and belongs to the Stonington Fire Department. He is very popular with all the high school crowd because he is a good sport. Mouse in French class. As a rule I hate them, but this one is tame and friendly.

Mar. 11 Stereoptican lecture at church. Japan. I enjoyed it very much although the man slid in every other plate upside down.

Mar. 13 - All week I have longed for Saturday and now it is pouring!

Mar. 14 - Usual thing except that both Marcus and Walter walked home with me when I would not choose between them.

Mar. 15 - This morning I noticed the sunshine was more golden and the air actually spring like. I have been longing for Spring and yet it has taken me by surprize.

Mar. 16 - Today is cloudy, but I can still smell Spring. Bought a moving picture magazine today. Maybe I shall be an actress.

Mar. 17 - Saint Patrick's Day. Mary wore a green ribbon which I think is rather silly as she is a Protestant.

It is more fun practicing now because we have a new piano. Grandma bought it for Mother and it is a very hansome one. When Grandma spends she does it nobly.

<u>Mar. 19</u> - Fri.- Stereoptican lecture at the Community House. China. Walter sat with me. One of the slides showed a beautiful Chinese garden.

<u>Mar. 21</u> - Sunday. Church was wonderful this morning because the air was so warm and sweet with Spring everything seemed to have a special meaning.

A new girl is visiting here. Her name is Martha Dickey and she is pretty in a large way. The boys are acting interested in her, especially Lewis Cromwell. I <u>think</u> it is Marcus she likes best. I don't care much about him but I can't let a strange girl do this to me can I?

<u>Mar. 25</u> - Shed our winter coats today. What a glorious feeling!

<u>Mar. 26</u> - Fri. - Last night I dreamed I met the Queen of England and the Prince of WalesThe Prince kissed me and his lips were salty. A queer dream, but enjoyable.

<u>Mar. 29</u> - I suppose all compliments are pleasant, but the ones one most wants to hear are never forth coming.

Tonight, there was a woman on the school car. Perhaps she didn't know the regular car followed, but she didn't seem to mind the noise. Of course there is no law against taking the school car, but most people would rather not. We had to stand up, Mary and I, and she was nearer this stranger, while I was a little way down the aisle. We were joking and laughing as we generally do and having a pretty good time. I saw her watching me and when she smiled I smiled back for fear she was someone I ought to know or one of those distant relatives one only sees once a year and forgets all about.

I have overlooked relations, or rather, connections, quite unintentionally and received merry hell for so doing.

When we had left the car and were walking up the hill I noticed Mary was acting sour and catty. I tried to find out why, whereupon she told me I was stuck on myself.

"I'm not!" I said indignantly. "What's eating you, anyway?"

She wouldn't tell me at first, but finally said the strange woman on the car asked her who I was and then said, "What an amusing child! And her eyes are magnificent!"

"There!" Mary said. "I suppose you'll be more stuck on yourself than ever. I don't know why I told you."

I could feel my face fall at the "child" part. Why did she have to say that!

Just because I am small must I be called a child all my life?

And as for my eyes, that didn't mean anything to me, because I am use to people speaking about them and anyway nothing but violet eyes would satisfy me.

"<u>Well</u>!" Mary said sarcastically. "You are hard to please."

"<u>If she had only said</u> I was beautiful and had a pretty nose," I mourned.

"You're not and it ain't," she returned flatly, and, I suspect, with keen enjoyment.

And I know it. Common sense tells me that one can't praise what isn't worth praise, but somehow I never enjoy compliments the way I should.

I wish I were pretty like Anna, who stays pretty. I am almost pretty sometimes, really pretty very rarely and quite plain oftener than I like.

Still, I looked like Old Mike Raferty when I was first born, Father says. so I have improved quite a lot.

Mary is wrong: I am not vain, but oh! how I should enjoy being vain if I had anything to be vain about.

<u>Mar. 31</u> I've been trying on school dresses. They are almost done and are very pretty. Mother hates to try things on me because I can't keep still for long.

Grandma is making us some underclothes because they are better than any one can buy, and Mother has her hands full making spring dresses for Constance and me. I am very grateful, but I can't help being more interested in the dresses. Grandma says I am like the man with several ruffled stocks, but nary a shirt on his back. When she was my age she was making her own under wear and sewing for the younger children as well. I can never hope to be the woman she is, I'm afraid.

<u>Thur. Apr. 1</u>- The grass is getting very green. Have an awful cold. We were excused at 10 o'clock for minstrel practice. Steroptican on the Phillipines this evening. Marcus came home with me. Oh! I nearly forgot - and how could I! Sarah, our cat, has just given birth to three superb kittens. Constance and I are in estacies.

<u>Sat. Apr. 3</u> -It is one of those days when the sky and the sunshine all melt into one. Can't explain what I mean. You feel it, rather than see it. Have been cleaning the flower beds out. Tomorrow is Easter. We trimmed the church this afternoon. There are to be several baptisms tomorrow night, Marcus among them. Mr. Evarts converted him and Marcus has been trying to convert me ever since. He simply <u>entreated</u> me to get baptised with him, but I refused. If I ever get converted it will be by a regular converter, <u>not</u> by Marcus.

<u>Easter Sunday, Apr. 4</u> The church was beautiful with its lillies, jonquils and tulips. I felt very holy. Of course I have new clothes, but it isn't fitting to describe them now. The Baptisms were very thrilling.

An Account of My Life

Marcus loomed up over Rev. Osborne and I wondered how he was going to manage, but he did. There must be something wrong with my soul because I kept thinking how long and ugly Marcus' neck was without a collar.

<u>Apr. 5th</u> I have a new school hat, very becoming. The kittens are too sweet for words.

Of all the awful books I think *"The Wandering Jew"* by Eugene Sue is the meanest! I get so upset and angry and baffled I could cry. Nothing comes out right. I feel tired out and weighed down. I hate Jesuits.

<u>Apr. 9</u> The Minstrels were very exhilerating. My part was a mere nothing but the costumes were cute, although babyish.

<u>Sat. Apr. 10</u> Anna has been hurt in an accident. She was coming home from the church. Lebeau's auto hit her, but did not kill her.

Her head and ears are cut, she is badly bruised and shaken up and they fear internal injuries. Mary says the cuts on her face will probably leave scars, but I will not believe it. She is so pretty, the only really pretty one among us. Mary always believes the worst. As soon as she is well enough, I must see her. We have always been friends except for the time she liked Marcus. I never got over being surprised because she is so pretty. Anyway the joke is on me.

<u>Apr. 11</u> Anna isn't badly hurt and we can see her in a few days. Priscilla, Marcus, Marvin, and I went for a walk this afternoon. At times I like Marcus, but at others not at all, but no matter how I feel he likes me too much to be any fun. I have a cold, darn it.

<u>Apr. 12</u> Couldn't go with the Minstrels to Westerly because my cold is so bad I can barely speak. Wept and pled to no avail. Grandma did not want me to go anyway. She says no good comes of traipsing around from here to yonder mark her words! She is <u>so</u> old fashioned.

<u>Apr. 15</u> - The sky is a mass of white clouds to-day. We were allowed to see Anna this afternoon. She looked flushed and pretty and was pleased with the flowers we brought her.

<u>Apr. 16</u> April showers. April is a lovely word, but I like Aprilly better. It is a nosegay with a lacy frill around it. I could not bear it if such a lovely month had an ugly name. Crocuses are in bloom and the grass is bestrewn with them.

<u>Apr. 17</u> Foggy day. I think it a shame that school days should be so golden and full of Spring while Saturdays when we <u>can</u> get into the woods, it turns foggy. All week I have longed for the woods, and now look at it! I'd get soaked and most likely lose my bearings. I suppose I can go to the

storeroom for old Atlantics, Murrays and Harpers as I often do on rainy days. The very old ones are funny and it is interesting to read stories by Charles Dickens and people like that.

<u>Sun. Apr. 18</u> Church. We all went to see Anna in the afternoon. The kittens are walking now, their hind legs wobbling adorably.

<u>Wed. Apr. 21</u> Miss Collins was simply awful today, so sarcastic. She doesn't like anyone much, but I guess she hates me. I hate her too!

<u>Sat. Apr. 24</u> - Gave my room its usual Saturday cleaning and ran out of doors. Grandma would call it a lick and a promise. Today is all the little notes of April put together in a song.
Father is not well, but they say it is not serious. Kirk and Dr. Lew are tending him. He cusses so much he does not sound sick.

<u>Sun. Apr 25</u> - Several men spoke on the Inter-Church Movement: Mr. Gray and Deacon Elias Wilcox spoke. It was very dull. I used up the time trying to imagine what Capt Elias was like as a boy. He was one of the boys who spent Sunday afternoons with Grandma and Aunt Mary Jane and Calista. They were musical and spent the afternoon playing and singing mostly hymns, at the old grand piano. Why Capt. Elias must have sat on the little mahogany chair. How funny! And he looks like a Bible character now. I think they had very dull times, but Grandma says 'no.'
This Day Light Saving Time is a bother. Grandma says it is going against nature and ignores it which mixes me up. It confuses Mother too, and Father has to straighten us out. He says we are feather brained, dithering fools.
Priscilla, Marcus, Marion and I walked to Elm Grove this afternoon. Priscilla put flowers on her father's grave. I am thankful that my Father is so much better.

<u>Mon. Apr. 26</u> - Awoke early this morning and jumped out of bed with joy the day was so wonderful. The sky had the palest blush of pink dawn left and a thousand birds were singing in the garden. The grass was dewy and little white puff clouds floated in the fresh blue sky. Daffodils nodded primly, while the crocuses held all the gold of the sun and white of the little lazy clouds.
Robins dug in the newly spaded earth and overall something I can not write down. No one was around so I hummed and talked and made poetry. This is the best.

     Peach tree in bloom
     Breeze from the sea
      Silky petals
      Covering me

All the enchanted feeling ended when the time came to catch the school car.

<u>Thur. Apr 29</u> The yellow maples are in bloom outside my window and it is like living in a golden bower. Grandma keeps saying they must be trimmed before they rub the paint off the house, but I love them as they are. They tap against the window or rustle against the screen in such a friendly way. I am sort of thin this spring so Grandma is brewing some stuff on the stove. There is no romance <u>in</u> her! She says I look like a Shanghai rooster.

I love April showers, especially when they pitter-patter on the tin roof.

<u>Sat. May 1</u> Anna and I went to a movie and she cried steadily. She says I am hard hearted, but I am not; I do not enjoy crying.

On the way home we met Miss Liny who stopped to talk with us. Anna was bored and when we finally got away said: "How <u>can</u> you stand old people! They smell musty." Well, so do old books and papers, and they are interesting too.

Miss Liny and Miss Hattie are always spoken of as "the Burrows girls" though they are old.

This morning I cleaned the upstairs rooms. Mother's asthmy is bad again and the dust has collected. Rolls of soft grey lint in a dust pan give me a horrid feeling and I dump it as quick as I can. Grandma said: "If you don't like it, don't let it collect." She is the most <u>sensible</u> woman!

I am reading *Eben Holden*; it is very good. Father gave it to Mother before they were married so it is quite an old book. The paper is heavy with gilt edges. Daddy never cared if a book cost ten cents or ten dollars, but Father likes things to be handsome. Grandma says he will drive to the Poor House in his own carriage.

Earl Batty who is a rich banker wanted to marry Mother years ago. I guess he never said so to her but he approached Daddy who was agreeable. Mother would not so much as look at him because he was lean, dark and homely, likewise tight as the bark on a tree. Grandma said she'd live to rue the choice she made but I don't think she does because otherwise, she would not have Constance or me, though she might have had very much nicer children. The first time I remember seeing Mr. Batty - his brother Frank is Cousin Addie's husband - he looked at me and said,"So you're Alice's girl." He is very stiff and stern. I should have thought he'd feel sad, but I guess he is not romantic. And he has got a girl older than I.

<u>Sun. May 2</u> - Took Constance to church this morning. Here after Sunday School will be her limit until she learns not to wriggle all over the place. I knew I'd get blamed if I didn't make her behave, and tried my best, though she almost wore me out.

1920

Stayed home this afternoon. I could have gone for a walk with Cill and Gladys and Marcus and Marvin but I did not feel in the mood. Mother was sure I was sick or had had a misunderstanding with one of them, but it was neither of those things. I just <u>didn't want</u> to.

<u>May 5</u> - Wed. Some people think it very cold for May, but I don't think so.

Went down to Vivian's house this afternoon after school. I love that place because it is old, rambling and interesting.

Her Grandfather hanged himself in one of the door ways. I do not know which one. He was coal black when they cut him down.

There are tall trees on the front lawn from which the place takes it name of "Buttonwoods," and there is a little brook cutting across the foot of the lawn. I <u>do</u> envy the brook.

There is a hill behind the house where tall cedars grow and violets and myrtle cover its slopes having spread from the garden planted at the bottom years ago.

Vivian says she hates the place which is something I <u>cannot</u> understand. I love the brook and the trees and all the glassy leaves of the myrtle and the shut up rooms and the dusty old book case in the hall spilling over with old books. And then there is the privy.

Years ago, Vivian's Grandmother having spent all her money on her husband, opened a select school for females in that very house. The privy was built to accomodate the school and so is unlike any of the common garden variety. From the outside it looks like a closed in summer house. Stone steps lead to the roomy interior which has seats on three sides of it of all sizes. I guess Mrs. Avery must have had some quite small pupils judging by the size of the smallest holes. There is nothing common about that privy, it is a most comfortable, commodious affair. It is interesting to have such a variety of seats, I think.

<u>May 7th</u> - Had supper at Priscilla's. Her mother went to a Rebecca Meeting, but Norman was there and she said we could ask a few friends in for the evening which we did by telephone. We didn't do much but talk and laugh, but it was fun. The evening being chilly we lighted the fireplace and sat crossed legged on the wide hearthstone until our faces were flushed red. This has been one of the times when I like Marcus.

<u>May 8th</u> - Elizabeth paid a flying visit to Mystic today! Her uncle left her at her Grandmother's while he went to Boston on business. When I heard her voice on the telephone I could not <u>believe</u> she was in town. She asked me to get the other girls together and come up as quickly as we could. In no time at all we were there. We had <u>so</u> much to tell each other, because you can't remember to put everything in a letter no matter how much or how often you write. Elizabeth says Alvin says he guesses summer will never come. She says I'll spoil everything if I don't pair off with him

and forget Marcus of whom she has heard, but never met. She says she thinks it positively romantic that of all the hundreds of girls and thousands of beautiful women he sees in New York, he still remembers me.

<u>May 10</u> We are reading "The Ancient Mariner" in English. It isn't that I don't <u>like</u> to re-read books because I do; however we have it in the big bookcase where I can get it any time.

<u>May 11</u> - After school Elizabeth Colby and I walked up to Priscilla's. We went into the little burying ground in the cedars where we sat in the grass talking about this and that. After awhile we went into the woods and picked violets and stuck shad bloom in our hair. Shad bloom has a queer smell, not unpleasant, not really sweet, but like nothing else. We can't make up our minds whether we like it or not.

<u>May 13</u> - Letter from Elizabeth. It is raining and I am reading *Guy Mannering*, of Daddy's books. Meg Merrill is fascinating.

<u>May 15</u> - Mary and I gathered pale swamp violets this morning. We walked deep in the woods and of course got our feet wet which was natural seeing it is a swamp, but impossible to explain to Mother. The trees are tall and there is a strange, heavy stilllness which gives one a queer <u>alone</u> feeling.

We sat on a fallen tree and talked - at least Mary talked and I listened for the most part. I am just as anxious to get this baby business straightened out as anyone, but I <u>hate</u> these talks. Neither Mother nor Grandmother will tell me a thing and I don't know anything, really. Mary hears all kind of things, but she contradicts herself and I don't believe she knows what she is talking about. I make believe I know far more than I do, because I should be deeply mortified if the girls found out how little I do know. Some of the things Mary says can't be true, they are too awful and make me sick to my stomach. Grandma says she didn't know <u>all</u> until she was married. She must have been brave. Catch <u>me</u> marrying until I know everything!

<u>May 17</u> - We are having a contest in Christian Endeavour. We are divided into two classes, the Reds and the Blues. Rev. Osborne thinks it will stimulate us which it probably will as long as it lasts.

<u>May 20</u> - The sky is still faintly pink, but fading fast and twilight is descending so rapidly I cannot see to write for any length of time. A soft breeze stirs my hair as it ruffles the edges of this notebook. The cherry tree is a drift of bloom and its fragrance comes in waves.

Priscilla and I talked for hours on the doorstep. Mary came down the road and joined us. We all agreed and felt in tune which is pretty rare.

1920

May 21 - Having trouble with that darn contest! There are continual squabbles about points.

I do wish Grandmother would stop giving me hot chocolate to drink every day. I have just about reached the saturation point! She thinks I need extra nourishment even though I eat like a stevedore. Just because I don't get fat and maybe am a little thinner than usual. Left alone, I have a good, clear skin though coloress, but <u>now</u> I am breaking out into pimples. She says the impurities are better out than in. I prefer them where they don't show. I've drunk it all winter and now I've had enough. She isn't so insistent and maybe she thinks so too, though she hints at yeast cakes which will be even worse. You wouldn't think she'd want her own grandchild to look like a freak, but she gazes upon the biggest pimple with the utmost calm. And I saw her shake the box of Pink Pills to see how many were in it.

May 22 - Mary's Mother sent us down to the Stanton Farm for cabbage plants this afternoon. It was so showery she made us carry an umbrella.

First we stopped across the road to call on Old Giles Stanton, uncle to Jimmie and Billy Stanton. Billy married Mary's sister Jennie. Old Giles is a magnificent old man. It is too bad that all old people cannot look like him. I don't believe he was a bit better looking or half as imposing when a young man. I should like to have my husband and look like that when he is old.

His daughter Lucy was busy in the kitchen so we did not stay long before going across to Frank Stanton's. Jimmie put the cabbage plants in our basket and we started back up the hill. We carried it between us and took turns holding the umbrella which was a big old thing belonging to Mary's father. We began to laugh and couldn't stop. We staggered all over the road laughing until we cried and our sides ached. Then I saw some white violets near the wall so I went after them while Mary stood there holding the umbrella and basket, scolding like a blue jay while I got them.

Sun. May 23 - This Contest may make us learn bible verses, but it is causing more fights than anything else on account of the rivalry. Someone is nearly always mad. Marcus and I are not speaking. Anyway, I am not speaking to him.

To-night Anna told Rev. Osborne that I was flirting with the boys and getting them to join the Reds. He just laughed, he likes me anyway, and said he thought she was mistaken, but she said she wasn't. So he said he was glad we were so in earnest, but not to get carried away by it. I never thought it of Anna! How can you make them learn verses to raise the score and how can you get candidates if you are not especially nice to them? Boys don't like to do such things and you just have to make them want to. Its no fun being nice to boys you don't care a cent about, and I felt noble and proud of the good I was doing, until Anna said that, and now I feel terrible. Oh my soul and body, maybe I've been too forward!

Mon. May 24th - Priscilla says I am mean to Marcus. If I want to stop liking a boy why can't I? You'd think he'd have too much <u>pride</u> to tell her such things. Wait till I get a hold of him!

Tues. May 25th - I had a ticket to the "Cantata of Flowers" in which Marcus sang, so I went with the others. He looked very hansome in the distance and I heard several girls rave about him. Well, I can't rave about him, but I do feel a littler more kindly toward him.

Wed. May 26 - Marcus and I have made up, but I feel it in my bones it won't last. I like him best when we are mad. Everyone is spring cleaning. We are going to have new curtains in the dining room.

Thur. May 27 - I am sitting under the Baldwin tree. The wistaria is hanging in heavy clumps of fragrance and the sea is deep, deep blue. I guess I'll just dream.

Sat. May 29 - What a day! Mother received a letter from Aunt Hannah saying that she and Mr. Tucker and Barbara and Aunt May were driving up Monday. We have been cleaning house and everything is upset. Mother gave a wild glance and say, "Get busy! We've got to get this straightened out. Tomorrow's Sunday."
We worked like mad until we were so tired everything went wrong. I tripped over a rolled up rug with a bowl of water and went sprawling, had a squabble with Constance who is plenty old enough to do <u>some</u> things, and hit against some freshly painted woodwork that was dry but not hard, leaving a long mark. Just when I was in the middle of the third book case, with my hair down, my face dirty and my temper simply <u>vile</u>, in walked Walter. You'd think he'd have <u>known</u> we were in no state to see callers, but no! He sat in the middle of everything, got in everyone's way and talked and talked and talked. Mother was so provoked she showed it. He was willing to help but he didn't know where anything went and only made it worse. I am tired and mad at everything.

Sun. May 30 - I don't seem to grow up fast as I should and at times find myself doing childish things. Today in Sunday School, Marvin who sits near by, threw a flower at me which went down my neck causing me to say "Oh" out loud while the Superintendent was talking. When Marvin turned his back I stuck the flower which I had fished out, in the belt at the back of his coat. How was I to know that the minister was going to call him up front to give him his nine months pin? Still, that does not excuse me.

Tues. June 1st - Today Mary, Anna and I discussed our ambitions. Mary said she used to want to be a teacher like her sisters,, but now she felt that by the time she got thru with school herself, she would never want to darken the door. Anna wants to be a nurse. I said I didn't want to do anything but have exciting times and travel and read and write about it all. They think it a queer idea and no ambition at all. Oh my stars of Bethlehem, am I put together all wrong?

Wed. June 2 - Reviewing for finals.

Mon June 7 - Exams in French and Algebra today. Latin tomorrow.

Thur. June 10 - English to-day. If all were as easy as that! Mary says I'm crazy, it's the hardest yet. We both had the afternoon free so we went for a walk over Fishtown way. Mary told some more stories about Capt. Fish who is a really wicked man. We stopped in the school which has one room and eleven scholars, practically all back wood Moshers. How they stared at us! Mabel is substituting there. She went to Grammar school with us, but not to High. She was always very stupid, but I guess you don't have to know much to teach at the Fishtown school.

In the evening Mary and I walked down to the Ice Cream Parlor for college ices.

Fri. June 11 - Broadway School graduation. Marcus graduated. His essay was on "Nathan Hale." and wasn't bad. The teacher must have fixed it up a lot. Terribly hot and everyone stuck to their seats. He is having a party tomorrow night.

Sat. June 12 - Busy all morning getting flowers, busy all afternoon trimming the church. This morning Mary and I who are on the Flower Committee, decided to go in the woods for flowers. We were glad of the chance for it was a golden day. A red-winged blackbird flashed over the swamp lighting on a branch of a tilted tree. There was the sound of growing things everywhere: I could almost feel <u>myself</u> grow. Mary said for heavens sakes, don't - she was fat as she wanted to be. We waded out in the marshy land for blue iris and picked gigantic ferns by the armload. We found a cute little turtle and wasted time playing with it, and we picked cardinal flowers and swamp apple blossom forgetting all about the time. We had the church a bower of beauty though perhaps that is not a good orthodox description. Anyway, we worked so late we had to rush home to dress for the evening party. We had been gone since early morning and were practically starved to death. Also our Mothers had been telephoning all around and were just three jumps from being cross. I never knew a day to go so fast.

Mother had my white ruffled dotted-swiss laid out on the bed and plenty of hot water which I sadly needed. I looked quite pretty, although brown as a nut. Mother says <u>why</u> will I go without a hat, do I <u>like</u> to look like a Portygee?

It was quite a good party and we had fun. I don't see why Marcus likes me so well, it makes me feel embarassed and guilty. When he kissed me he took hold of me as if I'd break any moment. He has never kissed me before - not even at Anna's party and he acted - well, I was sorry I couldn't feel the way he did. He just looked down at me for a minute and when I lifted my face because I knew what was coming and wanted to get it over with, he looked almost <u>reverent</u>. It made me feel awfully queer.

I like the way he kisses pretty well - sort of soft and gentle, but firm. It is alright once in a while at parties.

Afterwards he told Priscilla that it was much more wonderful than he ever thought, and said. "Gee, she is so little and sweet I was almost afraid to touch her."

I am sorry she told me.

There was a boy there who seemed to like me pretty well, but I didn't really like him, although he was good-looking.

Marcus took me home. He said it was the happiest night of his life and asked if he could kiss me goodnight. I said 'no' I couldn't permit it outside of parties and he said "Well, I hope there will be lots of parties. I smiled at him and said goodnight. I was half asleep on my feet.

<u>Sun. June 13</u> - In the afternoon Priscilla, Marvin, Marcus and I walked up to Bindloss Brook and sat down by the old mill. I don't like Marcus as well as I did last night. He carved our initials on a tree and I felt provoked and ashamed. I was cross and he was hurt. Darn boys anyway.

<u>Fri. June 18</u> - Well, I'm thru this year after a fashion. A year ago I was graduating with honorable mention. I shall have to crowd on more canvas.

<u>Sat. June 19</u> - I am going to enjoy this summer if I never do another thing! Mary brought little Billy down with her and we spent the morning on the beach. Stella, Mary's sister, came flying down and said the baby hadn't had anything to eat since 9:30 and that Mary had simply walked off with it without saying a word to any of them. Mary said she thought they'd be glad to have it off their hands for awhile. The baby <u>had</u> cried a lot, but when we found there were no pins sticking in it we decided it was merely developing its lungs in the manner of all small children. Mary had remembered to bring diapers and had changed it. Stella said neither of us had sense enough to go in when it rained!

When I got home I found the grey kitten, Paderewski, had had a fit and had run up the broom handle spitting. Nice day, I must say. I love "Dardenela." It is queer neither Constance nor I can turn a tune.

<u>Mon. June 21</u>   Priscilla's sister Marion is home for the summer.

There had been an artist painting next door, I don't know this one, but Father does. He will not let me look over his shoulder or talk to him. Ase won't, I mean.

1920

Tues. June 22 A horrid, horrid day. Saw a dog run over by an automobile. I held my breath and said "please don't let it get hit, God, please don't let it!" The car passed on and there it lay - not dead, but with its paws and one side crushed. Its owner came and got it and I sat on the wall and cried and cried. I shall never <u>never</u> get its pitiful howls out of my ears. One minute it was trotting along with its ears up and its tail wagging and the next it was dying of its hurt.

Not to be able to help it - that was the worst.

Fri. June 25 Today has been a full of fun day! Priscilla's school closed today and I went over with her. It is Boat Race Day too and although the race doesn't come off until late afternoon, the city was alive with hawkers and peddlars: and the harbor was jammed with yachts. We bought balloons, Priscilla broke hers almost at once, but Elizabeth and I carried ours home safely - and then within a stones throw of my house I let mine slip between my fingers and before I could catch it, it was high above my head, where it floated serenely upward, a bright blue bubble against a pale blue sky, until it was out of sight. I was going to give it to Constance, but maybe it was a better fate than hitting against earthly things and breaking: it has it's way.

In the afternoon, Mary and I went down street. We happened to meet Ase so I asked him for money, although I had some, and he gave me a dollar. Mary thinks he is wonderful because he is so generous. We bought college ices and candy and went to the movies. The picture was Mildred Harris Chaplin in "The Inferior Sex" which showed plainly that women get blamed for everything. After the movie it was time to dress for the Church Social.

It was a basket picnic and began at 6:30. Mother had my basket packed and my new dress spread out on the bed. It is pale green trimmed with white ruffled organdy. She does make me the sweetest dresses. Mary stopped for me and as we had plenty of time we walked up to meet Priscilla. They have a lovely, old fashioned garden, which Norman tends devotedly. He gave me two pale pink rosebuds.

At the church we sat at long tables and ate from the baskets. Cocoa was served and Priscilla spilled some on my dress. We went to the dressing room to sponge it off with cold water. "There is one thing about you Helen," she said. "You never fuss when anything happens to your clothes, though I suppose that is because you have so many." I never thought of that before. I have always hated fussy people and have taken accidents matter of factedly, but I guess it's no credit to me. I must think it out.

Raymond Hatfield was there - he is the son of Rev. Byron Ulrich, and he payed a lot of attention to me so of course Marcus began to droop. Mrs. Wheeler, who was a sort of chaperone, sent us home at 9:30. We pretended to go with the rest, but Mary, Pat, Cill, Harold, Lewis, Marcus and I came back. We gathered in the grove of trees between the church and the library. The moonlight shone thru the trees silvering everything. We told ghost stories and had a mock wedding. Pat knows the most gruesome ghost stories - I guess gruesome isnt the word.

With Ray out of the way, Marcus felt better. Ever since the Party he has been perfectly sickening. The only way to manage him is to be cruel.

<u>Sun. July 4th</u> - Elizabeth (Cutler) met Marcus this morning. She says he is good looking, but uses the worst English she ever heard. He does.

<u>Mon. July 5</u> - The legal date to celebrate the Fourth. Nothing much doing. Sat on Mary's verandah and watched the fireworks some of which were beautiful. I like displays, but noises tie me up in knots.

<u>Tues. July 6</u> - Spent afternoon with Elizabeth. Alton was around of course. He lives nearby.

<u>Fri. July 9</u> - Elizabeth came down before I was out of bed. Spent the day together. I admire her more than anyone I know.

<u>Sat. July 10th</u> - Spent the afternoon in New London. Mother took us, Constance and me, to a restaurant and a matinee at the Crown. Enjoyed ourselves thoroughly.

Thoughts.

When Mary came into the garden this morning I was picking forget-me-nots from the bed beside the stone steps. It was a perfect June day, the sky as blue as the forget-me-nots and the grass still wet with dew.

"I've got to go to Noyeses on an errand," Mary said. "Come on with me."

I went with her carrying the bunch of flowers in my hand because they pleased me so much I could not bear to put them down.

Mary had to go to the grocery store too and in there was Miss Annie Fiedler who spoke to us. She is a Jew though blond. Her eyes are blue and she does something to her hair to make it golden. She wears blue a lot and unless you look at her nose she is as pretty as a calendar picture. When she saw the for-get-met-nots she said "how lovely, are they from your garden? I never saw such lovely ones." She wasn't pretending, she really loves flowers.

I'd been thinking how well they matched the blue of her dress, so I held them out and said, "Would you like them?"

"Oh, <u>yes</u>," she exclaimed, holding out her hands gladly.

Then she looked at me with such a glad, greatful look I felt queer.

"My dear, it's sweet of you," she said.

After we had left, Mary said, "Well, you've got yourself in solid with her alright. But why?"

"I was tired of holding them and they looked pretty with her dress," I told her and changed the subject.

But I've been thinking of it ever since - that look in her eyes sticks. She thought I was so nice and I wasn't at all. I did not tell the truth when I said I was tired of holding the flowers, I never get tired of holding flowers, but I did give them to her because they belonged with her dress and for no other reason. It wasn't kindness, it wasn't neighborliness, it wasn't because I thought it would please her. Sometimes I think I haven't a soul. I do not think I am old enough or wicked enough to have lost my soul, so perhaps I was born without any. In church they talk all about saving souls, but it doesn't mean anything to me.

Never have I felt as full of God as I do in the woods or by the sea. I never felt as much reverence for our minister as I do for a sprig of arbutus. In church God is a mystery to me, but lying in the sun with violets touching my face, I feel him, not the God of Mr. Osborne or of the Sunday School teachers but a Presence. Isn't it enough to be glad of the sun and the moon, of shadows and sparkling sea, of bumble bees powdered with pollen? If you are glad and happy and pleased you <u>want</u> to be good, That's it! The lovely morning and the for-get-me-nots and the blue of Miss Fiedler's dress made me happy and being happy I was good without thinking or trying, just automatically. That makes me feel a lot better even if it isn't a bit orthodox. I still think there is something wrong with my soul, but maybe it will develop as time goes on.

<u>Sun. July 11th</u> - Alvin came today. He is awfully fresh and slangy. Elizabeth says he gets that way every winter and it takes the family all summer to get him toned down and by September when he is at his best, he goes back to school and the whole thing starts again.

He asked me if Marcus was my "fellow." It makes me sore to have anyone use that word in that way. He said he wouldn't <u>dream</u> of cutting him out, but he thought he had a heck of nerve crowding in on him. I told him maybe Marcus felt the same way which made him mad and we started to squabble. Elizabeth made us stop because she wants Alvin to go around with me because it makes it easier for her when she has dates, for while Alvin is younger than she their Grandmother thinks it quite proper for her to be out at night as long as Alvin is in the vicinity. Elizabeth says its enough to make a horse laugh because <u>she</u> looks out for Alvin and Alvin's protection isn't worth a cent. She says he isn't naturally obliging and unless it interests him to side with her, he won't.

The poor girl is upset on account of her Grandmother not wanting her to have anything to do with Harold M. It's like this. Old Mrs. Cutler is very religious and belongs to all sorts of societies for doing good. She thinks drink the devil and all young people bear careful watching. Elizabeth has lived such a roving life from Panama to New York she feels that she must counteract the influence.

Daddy knew Old Mr. Cutler and Old Mrs. Cutler and Grandma share the same views on Drink and all like evils, although Grandma is not so active about it. Anyway they think Prohibition is wonderful and are very W.C.T U.

Well, Mrs. Cutler made Elizabeth stop asking Pat to her house because his father drinks and his Mother is a doubtful sort of person. Elizabeth didn't mind that because she thinks Pat common, but <u>now</u> her Grandmother says Harold's Uncle is a Bootlegger. I'll bet that will be news to a lot of people. She may be wrong, but she is on so many purity leagues and things it isn't likely. Harold's father is dead and he lives with his Uncle. I have to admit she is true to her views because he is one of our leading citizens and owns more land and houses than you can shake a stick at, even if he is a skinflint and sort of crude.

Elizabeth and Harold like each other pretty well and it is hard on them.

<u>Mon, July 12</u> - Bought some black patent leather pumps which I didn't need but couldn't bear to get along without. Mrs. Morgan came and left me a stack of Etudes.

I wonder what the story is about Oscar Wilde? Ase won't tell me. I think he is wonderful. I love "Panthea" and there are such luscious words in it: gorgeous-mailed snakes," "diapered frittillaries" and purple lidded sleep." I get a thrill from "grand white feet flecked with saffron dust." wind-stirred lillies, "hot and amber foaming mist, the blue Ionian air." And this beautiful, <u>beautiful</u> bit, "We who are god like now were once a mass of quivering purple flecked with bars of gold." Oh it is all lovely, rich and lovely, like putting your hands into a jewel casket and letting the jewels caskade thru your fingers. There is another poem called "The New Helen," which is dripping with color: "sullen blooming poppies, purple galley and crimson waves of war.

Mr. Wilde knows the right color for the words too! So many people don't and just laugh. Of <u>course</u> a galley is purple. He didn't use it because the galley was purple or had purple sails, but because the <u>word</u> is purple

If the words were written down in colums with no connection to one another it would still be poetry.

<u>Thur. July 22</u> Marcus' Mother asked me to supper, darn it. Mother says I must have him here next. I cannot bear it. Father always makes a fool of him, not that Marcus knows it, but I do and Father knows I do.

Stanley is here again for the summer, a little bit more of everything than he was a year ago. He calls me Little One and says <u>when</u> I am sixteen and if I turn out to be as cute as he thinks I'm going to be, <u>maybe</u> he'll take me to dances.

"When I'm sixteen and cute maybe you won't get a chance," I told him.

By and By Elizabeth stopped on the way home from downtown. She says Stan and I adore fighting. We don't; we just can't help it.

He told her I was still a baby. "Every summer she's just as darn young as ever," he said.

1920

"You grow so fast you'll be like a gone to seed dandelion blowing all over the place before long," I said, which struck Elizabeth and me funny, so we laughed even when Stan got indignant. He said we made him sick.

Of course Elizabeth is older than I and he had to treat her with some respect, but he told me I had a nerve being ironical when I was just a kid and couldn't dance anything but dancing school stuff and he said I put on airs which is a joke coming from him. Why he is so stuck-up he calls his grandmother's hired girl a maid, but not when she can hear him!

I guess we'll never get along and I don't care. Grandma says as a child I'd play with Gurdon and Royce contentedly enough, but the moment Stan hove into sight there'd be trouble. I use to hit Gurdon over the head with his little red chair when I wanted my way, but I never hit Stan. He'd probably have hit back. Finally Elizabeth started home and he walked up the street with her.

Sun. July 25 This afternoon a crowd of us walked to the Haunted House under Lovers Leap. Tramps use to hang around before it got so tumbled down. We did find a man in the barn, but he got out when he saw us. If the folks knew they'd have a fit, being funny that way. "Fools walk where angels fear to tread" or something like that.

I don't believe the place is haunted, but I should not care to be there alone at midnight. If any thing is haunted it is Porter's Rock which rises in back of the house.

Tues. July 27 I have been reading the Little Colonel books again. I wonder what Lloyd would have made of my life?

Sun. Aug. 8 I am so tired of Mystic, I have never been any where. We started out to walk to Noank but only got as far as Devil Foot Hill.

Mon. Aug. 9 A very hot day. Priscilla asked me to go on an errand with her to Stonington. Marion has been having some clothes hemstitched and as they were done she offered to pay our fairs [fares] if we'd go after them.

We stopped at a little house and were met at the door by a woman wearing a soiled dress and who was perspiring freely. I was so sorry for her, though I must say she seemed happy enough. I wonder if she is brave or just isn't over particular?

Priscilla and I discussed it on the way home and agreed we would rather die than live such a life. The Chataqua has been and gone. I love Hawaian music.

Tues. Aug. 10 B.Y.P.U. Picnic. Rowland Colman was there. He is spoiled and arrogant, but he is interesting. He has dark, curly hair cut close and a dark skin, but his eyes are grey.

An Account of My Life

He is Capt. Rowland Wilcox's grandson and is named for him. He lives in North Carolina winters where his father is a Professor. Rowland speaks French and has a nice voice, but he is rather sentimental. I'd like him if he weren't so selfish. I don't give in to him, so we argue a great deal.

<u>Fri. Aug. 13</u> Rowland, Cill and I went rowing this afternoon. He says I am petite, piquante and have eclat.

<u>Mon. Aug. 16</u> Last evening when Young People's was over we stood around wondering what to do because none of us felt like going to church. Stan, Elizabeth, Harold, Alvin and I stood talking and Elizabeth said, "Let's go to my house. We'll have to be quiet, but we can sit on the veranda and there is lemonade in the ice box. Anyway, its better than sitting thru another sermon."

So we walked up the hill and down Skipper Street and sat on the veranda. There were plenty of chairs, but we prefer steps and railings. I was almost overcome when Stanley got cushions for E. and me!

We spoke of croquet, but Elizabeth's Grandmother makes them put away the set Saturday nights and it seemed like too much trouble to get it out when it would be too dark to see soon.

If some of the crowd had been there would have been a lot of shrieking and fooling, which is why E. didn't ask them. All the neighbors weren't in church by a long sight and her Grandmother would be bound to get reports of how we behaved ourselves.

Only Alvin acted crazy. He got on one of his fresh, show-off moods, but with no one to aid and abet him it did not amount to much. We talked about any number of things and Stanley told about Stuart his brother who was an aviator and got killed. I had forgotten he had so many grown up brothers, for he is the last one and like an only child.

There were Walter, Alden, Stuart, and Ashbey who died when a baby, and another whose name I cannot recall. We talked about movies and actors and this and that, anyway it was very pleasant. Even Stan didn't tease or act as if he owned the earth. The peep-frogs began and the scent of roses and honeysuckle and sweet peas came from here and there, warm and dizzy sweet. The light house blinked, the elm trees made a soft shushing sound and then were still. And the mosquitoes came out. Alvin told that joke about the fireflies being mosquitoes with lanterns, which is really very funny. A moth fluttered against my hair and Stan caught it.

I said, "Let it go, don't kill it please."

And he did, not saying a word which is very unlike him.

Instead of a stab of anger I felt a warm flash of liking for him which was very unusual too. Elizabeth acted puzzled too, because he gets bored if he is not entertained, and she asked him if he felt alright.

"Sure," he said. "Where's that lemonade, Queen Elizabeth?"

Which is one of the reasons why girls like him.

I keep saying this and that isn't <u>like</u> him. How do I know what he is really like? I've known him ever since I can remember - he's about three years older, but he doesn't know the me I am writing down anymore than the Man in the Moon.

I went into the kitchen with F. and put the glasses on a tray while she was getting the pitcher and the sponge cake. She said she thought Stan the best looking thing!

Well, I suppose he is good looking - his is a good-looking family, but somehow he never strikes me that way.

We left the hall light on so it shone out on the veranda and we all gathered in its glow. Stan took the tray and the cookies from us in a very courtly way. He <u>has</u> nice manners. I found myself forgetting about the cat he killed, and how mean he was to the hired girl and how overbearing he can be to people he considers beneath him. I sort of looked at him over the rim of my glass and he caught me at it.

"What is it, Little One?" he asked, knowing full well that name makes me mad!

So I said, "I'm trying to see why people think you are so all-fired good looking."

Elizabeth said, "Helen, you are the limit!" and giggled. Harold asked if he wasn't hansome too and Alvin yelled with laughter, then stopped off short as if he didn't know why.

Stan tipped his glass for the last drop and said "Do they?"

Finally I realized it was past time for church to be out and I'd better get home.

Harold stayed a little longer, but Stan came with me. I expected Alvin, but he was sulky by that time. It was the first time Stan and I had ever been really alone since we were children and it seemed strange, somehow not to be fighting.

When we crossed the street he put his hand under my elbow and he bent his head and said, "I won't call you `Little One' if you don't like it, but why don't you? I like it. Everyone calls you Helen, but you are `Little One' to me."

"It depends on how you say it," I told him. "I don't like to be mocked."

He laughed and said, "What an idea! Don't you see its because you are so sweet? And you mock me and always have. You always preferred Gurdon and that was why I was mean."

"No," I said flatly. "I preferred Gurdon because you <u>were</u> mean."

"Forget about it," he laughed, just as if <u>he</u> hadn't brought up the subject. "How'd I know you'd turn out to be so pretty?"

"Am I?" I asked, so eagerly he laughed and my cheeks burned though he couldn't see them. We were passing a fence covered with honeysuckle and he pulled off a spray and made me stand still while he put it in my hair.

"Pretty and sweet and I'm going to kiss you."

I said, "No you're not Stanley Saunders, don't you dare!"

"I'll wait until you want me to, if it don't take too long," he whispered.

When he didn't I sort of wished he would, but I knew if he did I'd want to slap him. I felt as if I were dreaming it all. He didn't even try to put his arm around me, just held my hand in his as we walked along, and it seemed wonderful that the boy I'd detested for <u>so</u> many years and squabbled with should be this person. There was still something deep in me way down that didn't <u>quite</u> like him, but I guess I am stubborn.

We walked by his house and stopped under the maples for a minute before I went into Grandmother's. I thought this time he would surely kiss me and was wondering if I should let him or not when he laughed and said,

"Let's sit on the front steps awhile and talk about you."

I knew I shouldn't, but I didn't feel like myself anymore, so I let him lead me over to the front steps and we sat down. Stan put his arm around me and bent his head. And <u>then</u>, at that <u>very</u> minute, Grandma came to the door on the war path!

Naturally, we pulled apart and hoped she hadn't seen.

She said, "Helen, do you know what time it is? You march in this house! Who is that with you?"

I told her, hoping it would calm her down, but she peered harder and said to Stan, "You're folks will wonder where you are. Time you were both in bed."

And then Stan did something I admire. Most boys would have run into the middle of next week because they think she is a terrible old woman, but he stood his ground and asked, "Can't we sit on the steps for a few minutes, Mrs. Hill? I'm practically home and so long as you know where Helen is, you won't worry."

Grandma spoke back sharply, "Nonesense, boy! What would your Grandma say if I let you roost on my steps at this hour of a Sunday night? Now you mag along home. If you two've got any talking to do, do it by daylight. There's another day a coming."

I almost <u>died</u>. "Roost"! <u>Why</u> does she use such inelegant expressions?

"I'll be right in," I told her, mortified nearly to <u>death</u>, hoping she'd at least go away from the door, but she wouldn't budge. So we said goodnight, and I could tell by the way he said it, politely, but <u>coldly</u>, that he was mad.

Well, she gave me Hail Columby for being so late. She said it never took any such time to walk home from church and where had I been. And she said she'd like to know how long since we two could be together without fighting like cats and dogs.

"We are children no longer," I said haughtily. But she flattened me right out.

"That's so," she said and looked at me hard. "I won't have any lally-gagging, Young Lady."

I was almost crying with rage by then and I yelled, "You don't act like this about any of the others and I've been this late lots of times."

1920

"When any of those boys," she answered, "Keep you out until going on twelve of a Sunday night and then have the gall to ask you to sit out with them, I'll send them humping and you can count on it."

All the niceness was gone and it was all her fault. How <u>can</u> she be so terrible!

<u>Aug. 18</u> <u>I want to have my hair bobbed!</u> All the girls are teasing very hard. It makes me tired the way they act! After all the years of having Aunt Mary Jane shake her head and say all my strength is going into my hair, they act like this! I am so mad I can't write straight. She use to almost convince them my hair should be cropped, not <u>caring</u> how ugly it made me, but the thoughts were too terrible for the Family to contemplate I guess, because even Grandma said I'd look like a picked chicken and Ase said people would think I was something the cat brought in.

I told Aunt Mary Jane she knew what happened to Samson and she was practically a Philistine because if my strength did prove to be in my hair, I'd be ruined.

She said she'd always heard the Devil could quote the Scriptures to suit his ends. She'll remember it. The only reason they can have for not letting me bob my hair is that its a new style and that is no reason at all. I don't see why they act so mean. Mother says for heavens sake do I have to keep things in a turmoil <u>all</u> the time. That is not fair! Just because Grandma says I need a firm hand she is trying to be stern.

And yesterday, Rowland who is leaving sooner than he expected, came down, and Ase got into a state because he stayed so long Capt. Rowl called up trying to locate him. Ase said he'd like to know what we found to chin-wag about by the hour and Capt. Rowl said to send the dod-dratted boy home even if it took a stick of dynamite to do it.

We had spent an interesting afternoon discussing the colored race about which Rowland thinks he knows a lot because he lives South winters. He has read more than most boys and is quite a conversationlist.

I haven't done a <u>thing</u>! <u>They</u> make all the fuss and then blame me.

<u>Aug. 19</u> Walter brought me a great bunch of pond lilies, so sweet, with long wet, rubbery stems. I was so pleased Walter thought it was with <u>him</u>. Mother said practically, "They are lovely, but what are you going to do with them? Pond lilies should never be gathered. I suppose we must have that boy to supper some night."

Most people put them in tall jars and I did the same, but the heads just hung over in a folorn and droopy way reproaching me. After awhile I could stand it no longer so I got a big shallow bowl and started to cut the stems. Two or three of the big flat leaves were in the bunch and I cut them too. Then I floated the flowers and the leaves in the water just as they look in a pond. It was beautiful! Mother was pleased and Grandma was surprized. She is a great hand at <u>growing</u> flowers, but she can not fix them worth a cent. She picks hard, tight little bouquets and stuffs them in things. I <u>think</u> she looked at me with respect. She said she'd never seen them fixed that way, but it was really pretty. It is so simple and easy I can't think why I never thought of it before. Other people must have, but not around here, that I ever saw. I think unless you can make flowers look as pretty picked as they did growing it is a shame to pick them. Sometimes you can make them even prettier by combining colors and species that grow miles apart and would never get together but for you. They laugh at me for picking "weeds" and grasses, but you can <u>do</u> things with them. So far, I have not been able to make them see the loveliness of Queen Anne's Lace. I didn't myself until I saw a summer person picking it. We kids laughed, but after I had really <u>looked</u> at its laciness, white and faintest pink, I stopped laughing because it is beautiful. Grandma was almost proud of me, but she would be prouder if I had embroidered pond lillies on a table scarf because it would be useful as well as pretty.

<u>Sat. 21</u> - Last evening Elizabeth invited so many of us to her Grandmother's house it turned into a party though it did not start out to be one. That house is another one of my favorite places, for it is big and also old except for the long veranda running around it; there is a large lawn, fine trees and a beautiful view of the River and the Sound.

Elizabeth complains because it is so old fashioned and tries to get her Grandmother to make more improvements. Even the big grand piano is so old it just tinkles and is more suited to candlelight, curls and "Loves Old Sweet Song" than to popular songs like "Smiles."

The name of the street has been changed from Skipper Street to West Mystic Avenue. However, to all the older people including Mrs. Cutler and Grandmother it is still Skipper Street, regardless, though all the skippers are dead and gone. Grandma still calls Baptist Hill, "Meeting House Hill" and Mistuxet Ave., "Slaughterhouse Hill". She still measures distances by the Halfway House though it hasn't been standing since I can remember, and when summer people ask directions from her, I have to translate.

Stanley wasn't at the party because he had gone to a club dance in white flannels. Alvin who is still in knickers, said he bet he looked a perfect sap. Stan, I mean, but that is too much to hope as he always looks like a fashion plate, drat him. I have decided I do not like him any better than I ever did - at least by daylight.

Alvin embarassed Elizabeth considerably by showing snapshots and baby pictures of her. In revenge she showed his too, but he thought it funny while she quite naturally didn't.

I <u>do</u> love Elizabeth! She isn't pretty, but she knows all about clothes and when she says she likes yours you know they are just <u>right</u>.

Alton was there, the pest, and he came up to me and said: "You stop telling people we are only 5th cousins, because its no such thing! We've got the same great grandfather and you know it. Capt Rhodes Burrows was a great old boy and I look like him."

1920

"I bet you don't," I said. "Just because your father did is no sign you do."

Alton was very indignant. "You never saw a tin type of him without whiskers I bet! If I had whiskers I'd be the spitting image of him. And if we had the same identicle great grandfather and I'm the son of his son's son and you're the daughter of his daughter's daughter we're a long sight nearer than 5th cousins. My father and your mother were own first cousins."

"Such a tempest in a teapot!" I said very coldly.

This morning Grandma went to see Judge Hinckley at his house and she let me go with her. I like to go there because it is shady and pleasant and Judge and Mrs. Hinckley are very nice. The Judge's Mother who is still alive is very aged. She was married just a little while when her husband died and she never married again, but this is the interesting part, the Judge was not born until after his death and is therefor posthumus.

Grandmother gave me advise against the day I may need it. "Judge Hinckley is our Family Lawyer. He had charge of your Grandfather's affairs, he looks after my interests and he will look after your Mother's when I am dead and gone. Most lawyers are kittle-kattle. Frank read law with Abel Tanner who is just my age and a fine man."

I said I thought him a very estimable man, at which she nodded and warned me never to forget how Caro Partridge got <u>her</u> comeuppance.

This Caro is way before my day: She is older than Mother I guess if she is still alive. I have not related her story before because it is not romantic and has a Moral. Still, I guess I had better. Well, to begin with Caro lived in the big, white house that stood where the Library is now on land Capt. Rhodes sold to them. At first they were summer people, Mr. and Mrs. Partridge, Caro and her sister Robbie. It was a very pleasant house they built, and even their privy was so roomy and elegant people said it was an ornament to the grounds. When the house was torn down in later years to make room for Capt. Spicer's Public Library, Great Uncle Nelson Burrows bought the Privy and set it up on his own land. Grandma says he could never bear to have anyone have anything better than he had.

After a time Mr. Patridge died leaving his wife and daughters not nearly as well off as they had expected, and when Capt. Spicer wanted the land they were only to glad to sell. I feel sorry. I never saw the house of course, but it would hurt to sell the pines and to this day white violets push up thru the cracks in the slate walk because the slabs were laid over Caro's white violet bed. The Spicer gardener sprinkles salt between the cracks and I hate him for it, but every year the white violets spring up again. Any man who can sprinkle <u>salt</u> on <u>white violets</u> hasn't any soul.

There was very little money beside the house and the land which was a great shock. Mrs. Patridge had always been looked after, so she turned to the girls who knew no more about money than she did. When Capt Spicer paid the money to them, they decided to put the money in the bank for the time being until they could have devised some plan. If they had gone to Judge Hinckley or taken it to Mr. Evans, president of the Mystic Bank, what follows could not have happened. But no, Caro took the train to New London with the money safely in her keeping intending to bank it there when whom should she meet upon the train but Mr. Tinker, who was uncle by marriage to Constance and Virginia who were at the Academy with me. Mr. Tinker told Caro she was extremely foolish to put her money in the bank when it just so happened he knew of a good thing which would bring in a fine income.

Caro had always had plenty and she began to see that just a enough to live on wouldn't be nearly enough. They were not Mystic people and living here the year around seemed awful to her, and it looked as if they would never have money enough to live anywhere but in a little village. Well, Mr. Tinker got the money and that was the last the Partridges ever saw of it. Mr. Tinker was not a scamp or a thief or anything like that, he was just a gentleman who was mistaken in his hopes.

I do not know what happened to the rest of their money - maybe there wasn't so much left as people said. The house was gone, the land was gone, the money was gone and soon Caro and Robbie were obliged to earn money. Caro taught school and Robbie opened a kindagarten, the first ever known to Mystic. Neither married because they could not marry just _anybody_, and all her life Caro knew she brought poverty to their lives.

The Moral is, never give your money to anyone to invest even if you know him without seeing a _trustworthy_ lawyer.

Oh yes, Grandma talked about the Bank too. She says ever since there has been a Mystic Bank our Family has banked a part of its money there. Mr. Evans, Evans Morgan's grandfather, who is president is tighter than the bark on a tree. He _couldn't_ be rash with money, even someone else's money just because it _is_ money. At one time, Grandma says, he owned a dry goods store where Wheeler's use to be. When his wife wanted anything above her very small allowance she sewed for people, and when she bought her thread and material at his store he charged her just the same as any customer. Grandma says he is a just man, but a little penurious. _I_ call him a skin-flint.

<u>Sun. Aug. 22</u> - This afternoon Ernest Post took me out in his motor boat as far as Fishers Island. We had a wonderful time - gulls, salt air and fun, but on the way home the engine stopped dead. Ernest said it did that once in awhile but after a short rest usually started up all right. I didn't mind because the sun was setting over the water leaving a golden path and an aeroplane flew against the sun. However, we were so long getting started we put Warren ashore at Groton to call up our families and tell them we were all right.

Well, it was dark before we got home and I caught the very devil. It seems Ase knows the boat and says it was such hopeless junk he (Mr. Post) gave it to Ernest to monkey around with, never dreaming he'd take it out on the Sound. There wasn't a life preserver on it and a storm was brewing.

He called me a witless, heedless, no-nothing and Ernest even worse. I was sorry on Mother's account and on Grandmother's, but he made me so mad I was glad he had been worried. I tried to explain to both of them, but was not successful because they had arrived at the angry stage. Mother says Grandma walked the floor. Oh I am sorry.

Aug. 23 - Mr. Jim Brown, the Constable, not the Noank one, took Constance and me on a picnic supper at Deans Mills this evening. He has a Ford automobile. Deans Mills is a lovely place and it was a treat to be taken there because you cannot get there except by automobile or by horse and buggy which happens very seldom. The road is a narrow white ribbon with a twist in it here and there closely wooded on both sides. There are very few houses and those are old and gray and after awhile there are none at all. One little weather beaten house was smothered in the orange red flowers and rank green of a trumpet vine. The flaming red against the gray shingles gave me a warm glow inside of me.

A little shower came up lasting just long enough to leave a glittering drop on every leaf. We toasted marshmallows over a fireplace made of stone. There was an orange colored sunset and just before dark came down, the sky became a wonderful pale apple green. It was so breathtaking I let my marshmallow burn to a crisp which amused Mr. Jim considerably.

I had a feeling that a sunset like that couldn't just happen, that it must be a special manifestation of Something.

Aug. 27 - Today has been a lovely blue and gold day. Early this morning I went up to Cill's carrying the letter I had written to Miss . Both of us love the Anne books and decided several days ago to write to Miss Montgomery who must be a wonderful person.

As I walked into the yard I was engulfed in the fragrance of phlox which grows in a deep border along the garden wall. The hot sun was simply pouring down on it.

Priscilla had her letter ready so we mailed them, feeling stirred to our depths. Then we went back to the house and sat on the sunny doorstep reading a whole stack of her grandfather's diaries which she had run across. We were very disappointed by those diaries. There were thirty two and not an interesting entry among them. Sometimes the only entry for a whole day would be "Cow calved," or something similar. A good man no doubt, but sadly lacking in imagination.

Aug. 29 - Spent the afternoon at the Fish Farm. They are an old family too and we have known them at least a couple of hundred years, I guess. Robert Burrows gave land to the Fishes because he wanted them for neighbours. We certainly owned a lot of land in those days, for our farm stretched from the Bridge to the Peace Meeting Grove and west to the top of Pequot Hill. Seems queer to think that Robert Burrows and John Fish were friends just as Warren and Sands and Robert Alton and I are now. I like to hear about old times.

For a long time I have been tortured underneath with thoughts of this school term which is approaching. I hate to lose all this - and oh how I <u>hate</u> to go back!

Had a letter from Rowland. He writes a good letter, but it shows up all the things I don't like about him, but which I excuse when I am with him.

<u>Mon. Aug. 30</u> - I am in my room at Grandmothers with my notebook spread upon on the oval shaped walnut table and nothing special to write about, although I feel like writing. I love this room. Grandma does something to a room, I don't know what. Her rooms even have a certain smell no other rooms ever have. Everything is old fashioned and awfully prim and <u>terribly</u> clean, but instead of being un-homelike it is the homiest room I know. She won't let me bring flowers into it and allows only a few books on the table, and <u>they</u> have to be placed just so! If I don't fold my clothes neatly before I get into bed she does it for me without a word, but looking so grim I don't forget again for awhile.

She blows out the lamp and takes the matches so I can't read in bed. She scolds if there is the least bit of mud on my shoes. She won't let me push the curtains aside and has a fit if I spill talcum powder on the bureau scarf. And yet I like staying here.

The paper is faded, there are rag rugs on the floor, which is painted; the white woodwork is ivory colored it hasn't been painted in so long. Her sheets and pillow cases are always smoother and sweeter smelling than any others and the muslin curtains a little whiter and stiffer. The window shade must always be <u>exactly</u> even. It is a good thing I am not a boy!

The old fashioned wash stand has a quaint toilet set covered with wild roses and the splasher behind the stand is a crane and water lilies embroidered in red by Mother when a young girl. All Grandmother's towels are of glossy linen, not so good as turkish towels to dry yourself, but lovely to look at and to feel.

The room is so much mine in feeling that the little naggings don't count. It has but one window, however the square upper hall opens off it and as she does not allow me to close my door at night, I can look out of the hall window at the sea. On moonlight nights I tiptoe out and kneel by that window. The scent from the lilacs and the wisteria, the apple blossoms or the roses floats all around me and everything is still except for the night sounds. Grandma does not approve of it: sensible people go to bed to sleep. I suppose it is the Clarke in me.

<u>Aug. 31</u> - I have done things that went against my grain many times, but never anything as <u>mysteriously</u> hard to do as to go back to school. I who use to rather like school. I am <u>forcing</u> myself to write about it when

1920

everything in me shrinks and ties up into knots. Why? I do not know. I have only to apply myself to get good marks, yet I deliberately shirk studying and have often gone to class unprepared. When I am out of school I cannot bear anything that reminds me of it. The worst of all is this sick, scared, helpless feeling that something is wrong with me - something that makes me unlike the others. I don't want to be queer - oh I don't.

I am going to try this year as hard as possible, but oh! how sick it makes me feel!

Sept. 1 - Big Warren took Cill, Leona and me out in his canoe today and we spent hours lazily paddling along the river bank.

Warren goes to Kingstown College very shortly. He asked me to write to him, I promised. If I didn't write amusing letters they wouldn't want me to. I suppose I could stop, but I guess I'd rather be bothered answering letters than lose my reputation for good letter writing.

Sept. 3 - The wild grapes are ripe on our Ledge, and Mary and I sat there until it was too dark to see and we had to feel under the big, rough leaves for the smooth, cool grapes. The air was frosty and tangy and a fringe of golden rod peered over the edge at the tangle of hop vines below.

We talked of many things - of "sailing ships and sealing wax and cabbages and Kings." The first star offered us a wish and we said "Starlight, star bright, first star I've seen tonight, I wish I may, I wish I might" and wished in silence.

The night sounds began while Ayres Woods became a place of shadows. It was so very, very beautiful even Mary remained quiet. Straight ahead Fort Rachel loomed up like a dark mountain.

There was a Burrows and several Packers defending that fort once, for it was an honest to goodness fort. Mary did not know how Fort Rachel got its name and wanted to know how I knew or if I were making it up. I know because I was curious about a Fort having a woman's name and asked. Mary admitted that she had never stopped to think that it was a feminine name, being so used to it. I verily believe she is curious about little besides what boy walked home with what girl.

Well, she likes stories providing they are told to her, so she asked about Fort Rachel. An old woman named Rachel lived at the foot of the hill years and years ago. She was very good natured and witty although poor, and she like Grandmother knew herbs and how to cure people's ailments although she did not keep her knowledge private as does Grandmother. She sold herbs and told fortunes, too.

There was an ice cold spring bubbling up in her green door yard where the soldiers came to drink and sometimes she would carry pails of water to them while they worked. They grew so fond of her they called the new fort Fort Rachel for in a way she had helped them build it.

An Account of My Life

I suppose Burrows men joked with her daily, and here I am over a hundred years later looking at Fort Rachel every day. I gives me a comfortable feeling.

I told Mary about Capt. Ambrose Burrows and his son Brutus in the year 1812 when as captain of the sloop *"Hero,"* Capt. Ambrose did battle with a British sloop a little off Block Island which we can see from the ledge on clear days.

It was an April day I think, when they did battle, and the British sloop turned out to be none other than the *"Fox"* which the British had captured from Capt. Jesse Crary not long before! Well, the *"Hero"* and the *"Fox"* had a hand to hand fight and Capt. Ambrose won.

When Mother came to Mystic from Putnam in the late 18's, a family by the name of Worden lived there, a widow with two pretty daughters. Mrs. Worden was burned to death when she struck a glass container filled with kerosene against the stove. So far haven't been able to find out who built the house - for some reason Mother doesn't remember. Although she thinks that the Heydeckers (four brothers from Germany) lived there before they built the house to the left of it. Old Hat Gabriel lived in the house to the left of it and it is from that well that she carried her water.

Sun. Sept. 12 Wonderful thunderstorm while we were in church. It grew so dark the lights had to be burning to see around at all. Rev Osborne's sermon fitted in splendid for just as he said "Give us Light Oh God!" - I mean prayer, meaning it in a religious way of course, every blame light went out! We kids giggled, but it thundered so hard no one heard us. We wouldn't have been surprized if a bolt struck us dead, but none did.

Went up to Cill's in the afternoon. Miriam and Mary came up as did Harold and Marcus. Emily and her brother Junior were visiting their Grandmother Slack next door and they came over. Junior is either shy or offish, but I think he likes me. Anyway Marcus thinks so and is jealous. Had a very good time.

Fri. Sept. 17 - My birthday. I am fifteen years old to-day. Had many presents, but it is too childish to enumerate them, so I won't. Christian Endeavour Business Meeting this evening. Marcus tried to find out how much I like Junior, but I was very mysterious Anyway, I don't know.

Sat. Sept. 18 World Wide Guild met at Miss Hattie Fish's, our Sunday School teacher's house. Today she told me the sampler in the parlor was made by a Burrows. She played on the spinet for us. I like to go to that house because it is the one Capt. Rhodes built for his growing family. It isn't the first one of course as that was built by Robert Burrows. That burned but in seventeen something another Burrows built the one now standing on the same site around the same chimney. This is sort of mixed up I guess. Aunt Jane owns it now although she does not live in it, but in a newer house next to Miss Hattie's. She is very wealthy, because Uncle Tom

1920

her husband was a rich man, although a scamp, Grandma says. I don't know what he did exactly, but he made a lot of money when a lot of people in Mystic lost theirs.

I stopped at Mr. Evans' on the way home and got some hyderangeas from him for the church. He is awful tight and very rich.

<u>Sun. Sept. 19</u> - Marcus played a piano selection at Christian Endeavour. He plays awfully well and is quite musical. I mean he really likes classical music, although he never reads and doesn't know who Rembrandt was. I felt quite pleased with him until I found he had swiped some snapshots of me from one of the girls. <u>Why</u> does he have to act so silly!

<u>Wed. Sept. 22</u> I should like to shut Marcus up in a dark, dank dungeon for at least a week, so I could have a little peace. He gets sillier and sillier. I never realized a boy could be such an infernal nuisance. He sits with me on the car, he has managed to get both study periods with me and he waits for me here, there and everywhere. It was bad enough to have him Sundays but every day is more than I can bear. I <u>won't</u> be made ridiculous and I <u>won't</u> be teased about him. He is nothing to me. I asked him to please leave me alone for a spell: I tried to avoid him and finally I told him I was sick of the sight of him. It hurt his feelings and I had to say I was sorry. Yesterday I hadn't got to the corner before I met him! I've been mean, I've been sarcastic and I have been icily cold, but <u>nothing</u> does any good. I am in the last throes of desperation. If he wasn't stupid as an ox he'd realize how he annoys me. If he wasn't so silly he would be very likable. What has gotten into him I don't know. He can't like me any better than he did because he already liked me as much as possible.

<u>Thur. Sept. 23</u> Marcus says he has put my snapshots in his family album! I cannot bear it. If it were romantic, but this is just plain sickening. The girls know I am raw with mortification. Ase says he has never seen a worse case of puppy-love. How I hate that expression! It makes it even sillier than it is.

Well, I have a new scarlet sweater which is very becoming, but I am too <u>bothered</u> to enjoy it. How I rue the day I ever imagined I liked that pest!

<u>Sat Sept. 25</u> - A sleepy, Indian Summer day with the hills veiled in the smoke from the ghostly peace-pipes of long dead chieftans. Our S.S. class held its picnic today in Mr. Horace Cliff's woods. Priscilla, Mary, Adelaide, Alice, Elizabeth and I met at the foot of Pequot Hill and joined the others at John Mason's monument where Miss Fish and Miss Coats got us in order for our walk to the Jonathan Jesse place - what was his place, for now there is nothing left but the cellar and the doorstep.

Jonathan Jesse built or bought this house way off in the woods years and years ago. Grandma says it was because he wanted no mortal witnesses to his deviltry. She can remember hearing him drive his team home at night, ripraring drunk and singing wildly as he lashed his horses on to a faster pace. She use to snuggle down under the quilts and lie there wondering if his smashed and frozen body would be found in the days to come. And in the morning her mother would say, "Old Jonathan Jesse rode by last night. I hope he made port safe and sound." It seemed that the wilder the wind or the rain, the deeper the snow, the better he liked it and the louder he sang.

But the devil was good to his own and for all I know to the contrary, he died peacefully in bed when his time came. The house burned one night and time has tangled his doorstep with vines. There is quite a stretch of woodland to pass thru before you come anywhere near the place. We walked Indian file down the narrow, twisty path fringed with late golden rod and wild rose bushes bearing the scarlet hips as farewell gift of summer. In some places the trees arched completely making a long green tunnel, in another purple asters grew among a stretch of birches. When I see a white birch I believe hamadryads and many things. The maple trees were a flame here and there.

After we climbed the little stone steps leading over the wall to the stretch of overgrown pasture land, we came to more woodland, and here we crossed the bridge made from a single log that spans a gurgling brown brook. Here the path became so overgrown we only felt it with our feet as we pushed thru the undergrowth until we came to clearer slopes of Jonathan Jesse's door yard. A big fir tree guards the cellar hole and the apple trees and lilac bushes have long since gone wild. I expect on wild and stormy nights Old Jonathan still laughs madly as he clatters up the stony cart path.

1920

Juliet Haley

Priscilla "Cill" Lamb

Dorrance Grimes

Mary Collins

Marcus Jones

Emily Gallup

An Account of My Life

Miss Hattie brought forth a book on home missions and began to read aloud. It does seem that home missions belong in church not in the midst of autumn woods, but she is a good woman and perhaps knows best. I was glad when our picnic lunch was spread under the biggest apple tree, for food as Miss Fish and Miss Coats prepare it, is sheer poetry and enough to bring Old Jonathan sniffing around. I said so, without thinking, and they were both pleased and shocked their usual reaction to most of my remarks.

We were herded together and started home long before dusk fell. Miss Fish and Miss Coats act rather frightened of the woods. Old people are like that. Grandma won't admit it, but she never sets foot in them and she says in her grandmother's and great grandmother's day they rejoiced to see a tree cut. How could they? It goes thru me like a knife.

<u>Sun. Sept. 26</u> Marcus and I have had a fight, although I did it all, practically. It is like pounding a stone wall.

I am sad tonight. I have lost Latham. I sat by his grave this afternoon and it was so quiet, so beautiful, with the ocean blue and serene and a little chipmunk running along the wall, and the smell of autumn in the air. I looked at his gravestone, not thinking - and one thing stood out and hit me. Thirteen years old ! A little boy! How can a little boy be my secret friend when he was never fifteen! Next year I shall be sixteen and the next seventeen, and Latham Avery can never grow older. I tried to feel him there, to bring him out of the breeze and the grass and the haze, but I couldn't no matter how I tried. I know now that I never can and I am sad because he is dead to me. I wonder if he misses me! I wonder if there will ever be another of his age and kin who will be a friend to him? Or will he be lonely for a hundred years? I know he is dead to me because I felt as if he'd gone and a little ghost stood at a distance and watched me, but when I put my hands out, he shrank back, because <u>he</u> knows too. He was never a ghost before - he was real and my dearly beloved friend. I suppose this is silly, but I've simply got to cry. He was so different from other boys - not rough or silly, for Latham was a gentle man.

<u>Sept. 27</u> Cill has had her hair bobbed and I want mine done too. Marcus said he would never speak to me again if I cut my "pretty hair." I guess I looked as if I didn't care if he did or not because he said quickly that he didn't mean it, he'd like me <u>any-way</u>, but he <u>preferred</u> my hair long! This hair is coming off just as soon as I win the Family over.

<u>Sept. 28</u> Anna, Mary and I stuffed on apples until we could hardly see! There we lay in the thick grass looking up through the leaves at the sky, talking of this and that, stray leaves dropping on our faces, feeling full and contented. As soon as we felt a little better we reached for another apple! If one's taste stopped automatically as soon as the contents of one's stomach reached a certain level - but such is not the case. Anna said she was breaking off by reducing the size of the apples until she got down to

crab apples. It seemed a good idea. She bit a piece from a Dennison Redding and being almost too full to chew, studied the white flesh streaked with red. "You know," she said slowly, "I think these are the best of all. Lady Anne certainly knew her apples!"

I laughed, while Mary asked with quick curiosity, "Lady Anne who?"

"Our ancestress," Anna said with an elegant simper. "Lady Anne Dennison. She's buried somewhere around here."

Now this is the funny thing, Anna and I think of her as a nice romantic sort of an ancestor and that's all, but Mary who is half English - the English are so queer that way - was mad!

She said, "Anna Dennison you are making every bit of it up on account of your name being the same!" And she said Anna and I were <u>no</u> relation to each other and we were just plain ordinary girls and not titled even if we <u>thought</u> we were better than anyone else. Anna and I said indignantly we didn't make up such stories, that we weren't related, but we were connected, and that we both <u>were</u> descended from Lady Anne Dennison and could prove it!

Mary likes stories sometimes, so I told her how years and years ago Lady Anne brought apple cuttings from England and our Dennison Reddings grew from them. Mary sniffed and said she didn't think it much of a story.

I said, "Well, it explains what Anna meant! And it could be made into a story easily enough. Now stop being so mean!"

It must have been the way I said it or something because she actually swallowed hard and stopped. After we had left her on the way home Anna said with awe, "Golly, if I'd known Lady Anne would make her behave I'd have trotted her out long before this."

<u>Oct. 9</u> Last night Mary and I went to the Evangelist Meeting at our church. Instead of <u>one</u> evangelist there were five called the Glory Band. They come from over Westerly way - Potters Hill, I think, and are workmen by day and evangelists by night. Mr. Hart is the leader, although they all speak at one time or another. Mr. Bailey the youngest and best looking plays the piano - the organ only being used for regular services. Mr. Hart is an old man and the others youngish- oldish and not very interesting, although they sing duets and trios with great fervor. They all get together when begging for converts and if one evangelist is nerve racking, five are devastating. After a fiery sermon, Mr. Hart exhorted while the other four went around from pew to pew pleading personally. Almost every one was deeply moved including Cill and I tried to feel exhalted, not wanting to be a lone, sad sinner. Mr. Bailey seemed to know that Cill was softer than I for he pled with her long and earnestly. I listened with considerable interest until he suddenly switched to me. I was embarassed. He held my hand and would not let go asking me questions which I answered by "yes" or "no" hardly listening until I found he was trying to lead me forward. I balked, whereupon he acted hurt, speaking of

sinful pride etc. Then he asked, "Why won't you give yourself to Jesus?" I couldn't do anything but shake my head. After awhile I couldn't make sense to what he was saying. I looked down because I couldn't bear to have him look in my eyes so compelling and I tried to get my hand free. Cill was crying, the old negro janitor moaned out loud; men and women were holding handerchiefs to their eyes and Capt. Elias' beard waggled as his lips moved in prayer. I felt frightened. There were all those good, kind people being deeply moved, while I felt mad, cross and embarassed. I felt like a monster or something and that I'd better get my soul saved while there was any left to save. Every time someone went forward to be greeted by open arms I felt more alone in my wickedness. I just plain didn't want to go forward, because I hate to make a holy show of myself and because I don't believe God puts too much stock in public confessions. And then Cill started on me. She said she was going. I must go with her. We must go together into our Saviours arms. I said "No! and meant it, so I can't explain how it happened. "I'm going," Cill said, her face wet with tears, while I hadn't shed one. She got up and to my amazement I got up too. I thought the Spirit must be prevailing over the Devil. Next thing I knew everyone was crying and praying over me and I was feeling glad, mad and sad. Am I different from everyone else? Am I bad? Oh I am all mixed up!

Oct. 11 Went to the movies; John Barrymore in "Dr. Jekyl & Mr. Hyde." I have read it several times but Mr. Barrymore made it so real I was terrified of my evil nature.

Oct. 13 Another meeting at the church. It was a wonderful evening with a crescent moon in a clear, high sky. At the church I found the kids waiting on the steps because it was early. Nellie Brooks who sings, though not very well, and is both religious and fond of men, asked Cill, Glad, Elizabeth and I if we would like to drive out to meet the Glory Band. We are all sort of stuck on Mr. Bailey so we went with her. It created quite a stir when we walked down the aisle with them. The sermon was very exciting and a large number came forward. I think Mr. Bailey is wonderful and so do the others.

Oct. 15 The last night of The Glory Band. All the girls asked Mr. Bailey to write in their birthday books and so did I, but I was afraid the other members of the Band would feel slighted so I asked them too, though I didn't really want them. After the service I sat on the platform and talked with Mr. Bailey. He makes it seem right and natural that I should have doubts and fears and he says I am a good Christian girl. Sometimes I don't feel like one. Mr. Bailey is married, but it is alright to love him religiously.

Oct. 18 Letter from Warren who is at Kingston College. One of the things I like about Alvin is his flat refusal to write to me. Not that I asked

1920

him to, but Elizabeth tried to and he said if he had to write to a girl every week he'd hate her and she'd hate him. He has sense. If he weren't so Smark Alicky I'd like him better than any of the others.

Today Ase and I had one of our arguments. I mean we were just disagreeing about a book. Of course when he couldn't convince me he lost his temper and said mean things and I lost mine and said mean things too. When I try to think back now, it doesn't make <u>sense</u>. Well, anyway, Ase got madder and redder and more ornery - we'd got miles away from the subject by that time - and all of a sudden he struck me in the face.

I just stood there too surprized to do anything but look at him. He is often abusive with his tongue, but he never touched me. The color went out of his face and he looked sick and shamed enough to die. One part of me, the good part, I guess, felt sick with pity for him, and then like a prairie fire, shame and humiliation burned over me. Something ticked in my head like a clock, "he struck you, he dared to strike you, he struck you, Helen Clarke."

I'd like not to write down how awful I was, but it's not fair to tell on him and not myself and I've to get this awfulness out of me or die.

I knew he was sorry, that he'd give anything to have it undone. I knew if I'd shown fear or shed a tear he would have gone on his knees before me as he does before Mother. And I felt that I could stand anything but that. Hate is strong and fierce - oh I can't explain it. I didn't seem to be myself at all. I swore at him using words I never <u>dreamed</u> I'd ever use. Swore at him and defied him and dared him to touch me again. He looked so surprized, as surprized as I had when he struck me, I guess. After awhile he turned and walked away. I stood there stiff and hard and furious until I began to shake. I shook and shook till I thought I'd fall apart. I was so sick with shame for myself I almost forgot what he had done and said. It was like waking up in the morning to find oneself turned to a scaly monster.

There's no one to tell - to talk to. Mother, Grandmother they'd be horror struck and there'd be an awful battle. Besides its between Ase and me. So I mixed some aromatic spirits of ammonia and after the awful shaking stopped I went to sleep. And when I work up I reached for this. Now, I guess I will have a bath.

<u>Oct. 22</u> Business meeting at church. Wore my new scarlet sweater. Mr. Bailey was there on business. He shook hands with me and didn't let go until I almost melted with joy.

<u>Nov. 4</u> Harding has been elected President. Very exciting time - big parade, speeches, streets crowded, colored flares, whistles and horns this evening. Mary and I went with Althea and her father in their car. Marcus appeared and hung around until I wanted to <u>scream</u>. Seems as though all Life's most glorious moments are marred by him, if not completely ruined. I couldn't refrain from asking him why he wasn't with the boys and he said,

An Account of My Life

"You know why." I felt like slapping him, honestly. Thea whispered, "he's crazy about you, Helen." Just as if I didn't know it!

Still, everything considered I had an interesting evening. The Parade was splendid. Three bands and some bag pipes, not to mention the fire engines. The dark makes everything more wonderful. I mean things you know to be ordinary by light of day, take on a note of mystery. Having been kept in all my life and being put to bed so early all my younger years, I am unjaded.

Althea's kid sister was with us and I verily believe she will make a good rag man or woman for all it is a low walk of life, because she picked up bits of colored buthing [bunting] and paper and even found a good leather belt someone had lost. Thea tried to make her throw the stuff away, but she insisted upon taking it to Nelson.

Senator Brandygee was supposed to speak, but didnt. I have never seen a Senator to know it.

Nov. 20 - Larry Thompson is going to have a party Tuesday, but I am not sure they will let me go.

Nov. 28 Marcus and I have had our final blow out. He has been simply persecuting me with his unwelcome attentions. If I treat him kindly, he acts silly, if I don't he tells everyone expecting them to comfort him. Until recently the boys have liked him well enough, but he has become so darn mawkish, they can't stand it. Ase says he is a blubbering mooncalf and it serves me right.

I am haunted by him, literally haunted. Seems if I can't go anywhere but what he will pop up from somewhere. I have stamped and raged to no avail. Nothing did any good and whatever I did or said he persisted in liking me

Well, Sunday night he slipped a note to Pat to give to me, and Pat the idiot, slipped it to me so that Mr. Osborne saw the transaction and was very cross. Later I scribbled an answer to Marcus and told Pat to give it to him.

I know it was blistering, but I cannot remember what I wrote. I know that sounds odd, but I was so distraught I was literally beside myself.

When I was at the piano the other night, Mother came into the room.

"Helen," she said sternly. "Explain this if you can. What have you been up to now?

I swung around on the stool in astonishment. I couldn't think of a thing she'd be likely to hear about.

And then she held a letter under my nose. It was from Marcus to her saying how cruel I had been and how I had hurt him and how much he thought of me and how he had tried to please me and oh - everything!

I was shocked speechless. To think he'd do such a thing! Write to Mother!

Its the most absurd thing I ever heard of. If <u>that</u> doesn't prove that he is next to being half witted!

Mother said I must write an apology for anything I said - and that's when I began to come to life. I refused flatly and nothing she said moved me. I would not apologize because he had driven me to desperation and it served him right. If I felt like that, she said, I must tell him gently but firmly that we were much too young for a sentimental attachment, but that we could always be friends. She was brought up on "Hill's Manual", so I did not tell her how useless and ridiculous such a reply would be. Tell him "gently and firmly'"! Tell him gently but firmly when I've done everything! I told her anything I wrote in my present mood would be twice as bad as anything I had said or written - and that unless she wanted him sobbing on her shoulder she'd better not make me do it. I guess she thought he'd be capable of it because she looked bothered and uncertain.

"You'll write what I tell you to write!" she said firmly.

"No," I said. "I'm sorry, but I can't do that."

At this point Ase came in, which was like dynamite dropping into a bonfire. When he got the gist of it all, he simply raised the roof. He called Marcus a string of names without end and never once repeated himself. He was profane but magnificent. He threw the letter into the fire and forbade me to write or even speak to that "lummox" again. Mother told him not to be ridiculous and said <u>she'd</u> answer the poor boy's letter, and then the trouble really started.

The storm had been hitting on all sides of me and suddenly he realized it and landed on me. He said I was always keeping things stirred up, but this was the limit and only fifteen, a mere child. He said he'd send me away to a school if he had to borrow money to do it and that he'd be damned if he'd be worried to death by all this adolescent fol-de-rol.

Well, two more letters came to Mother and after the third, I broke. I wrote to him and told him I was sorry I hurt him, but it was his own fault.

I wrote it on some ugly, lavendar paper some one gave me and I can never bear to use. I did it for Mother's sake, because she was beginning to look harried. Ase has now arrived at the stage where he thinks it funny and the remarks he makes are hard to bear. If he tells it around among the men - to Kirk and Dr. Lew and Perce Morgan I shall leave home.

I told Ase that I had supplied them with enough laughs first and last and I considered myself too old to be made the butt of ribald laughter. He only laughed at me. A parent with a sense of humor is hard to bear. He doesn't seem to realize that I am ashamed and mortified and sick about it all. When he isn't blasting me sky high he is laughing at me. If I ever have children I shall try to understand them and to treat them like human beings.

Guess I'll go out and hunt for russet nubbins in the dead grass. When they get frosty they taste far better than the picked apples in the barrels.

An Account of My Life

This November landscape suits my mood. The branches are practically bare and the grass is sere and twisted. The melancholy days are here again and I am melancholy too.

I've just thought of a couple of things I have not written down.

Nellie took us to Potter's Hill to hear the Glory Band, but we all knew she wanted to see Mr. Bailey. They have a little chapel there and were quite surprized to see us. Mr. Bailey's wife was there too which sort of put a reef in Nellie's sails. The ride over was fun.

One day Priscilla and I went into Cliff's Woods for alderberries.

It was a grey, sharp day, cold enough to make our blood tingle pleasantly. We found plenty of berries near the tumbled down wall and filled our arms with them.

Last evening I went to the Library. It was pleasant being soul alone in the quiet dark. I made believe as I always do when alone. The Library is a castle and I walk slowly up the great staircase, my train a rich crimson velvet whispering on each step. It was a <u>blow</u> to have her ask me if I didn't want to read "*Little Women*" again. I was very firm and took out a biography of Robert Louis Stevenson because I love the story of The Road of the Loving Heart. Trisitala is a lovely name.

There is not much satisfaction in being fifteen when one looks not more than thirteen. The old people will not believe I am actually growing up. It is inconvenient too, for if I say something perfectly suitable to one of fifteen they are shocked and think I am precocious. I heard Grandma tell Mother that Miss Livy actually told her I was just a little girl and too young to have "beaus." <u>How</u> I hate that word! Grandma said she told her "the girl is fifteen" and Miss Livy said she just couldn't believe it, it made her feel old. Heavenly days, she <u>is</u> old!

<u>Dec. 6</u> - Dr. Mac Gown has run away with Cousin Tracy's first wife's sister. Mrs. Mac Gown is one of the Daughters of Veterans and if Dr. Mac Gown ever returns everyone who counts is going to ostracise him.

Dr. Mac Gown is middle aged and more, while Winnie's sister is not at all pretty. There isn't a vestage of Romance to it: it is just plain ugly.

<u>Why</u> do people that age do such silly things! There was the case of Cousin Gene and Dr. Smith's wife, Jack and Orville's Mother. It was embarassing for we were at the Academy together, but we ignored the subject, even when their father sued Gene for $25,000.

Grandma said Mrs. Smith chased Gene and that she and Aunt Calisty had marked it time and again. She doesn't hold with sinners. let them reap what they sow, only in this case Mrs. Smith did the sowing and poor Gene all the reaping.

She has never approved of Gene, not liking that red and black full blooded type, but she says any man would have behaved the same.

I do not like Dr. Mac Gown or Winnie's sister. I hope they come to some bad end, but they probably won't. Poor Mrs. Mac Gown. I always suspicioned he was pretty small potatoes.

1920

<u>Wed. Dec. 20</u> I saw murder committed today. A movie has been made of Anne of Green Gables which I have been simply <u>dying</u> to see Well, today I did and it was awful beyond belief. <u>Their</u> Anne was a pretty blond, while Gilbert was fat and stupid. Even worse than Marcus who isn't fat. Mrs. Lynd was left out, Matthew was ruined and Marilla wasn't right. There wasn't any point to it all, but was wishy-washy and sickening If Miss Montgomery ever sees it I bet she'll want to <u>die</u>. Why, on why did they do it ! I'm mad clear thru. The minute I go home I started reading Anne, but that actress's face kept coming between me and Anne. I hoped the movie would make it more real, but all it did was mess up the mental pictures I already had. I have often been provoked by illustrations in books which did the same thing. but I have never minded as much as this. I am very bitter.

Clam chowder for supper. I like it, but not enthusiastically, preferring meat to fish any day, except lobsters and crabs of which I can never get enough. Of course, I am very fond of cunners, but scallops and oysters I do <u>not</u> like.

Mary says Jimmie Chesebro had the worst fit of his life yesterday falling into the wood pile and frothing at the mouth,

Poor Jimmie is alright except when these fits come upon him. It if weren't for them he would be sort of a romantic character, being good looking like most of the Chesebroughs, even though he is not young. He is usually very melancholy on the full of the moon at which times he plays queer wavery airs on his violin. He plays by ear and the fiddle isn't much good, but there is something lovely and strange in the music he makes. Mary says it is "spooky." I think eerie is a better word. I like to hear him play. Spooky has a humorous sound and there is nothing funny about Jimmie's music.

<u>Thur. Dec. 23rd</u> - Christmas Tree Night at the Church. Marcus acted like a sick cat, but I ignored him until what transpired later, but I am coming to that. Anna said he told her he'd give anything to have me like him and that he must have been crazy to write to my Mother. Anna felt sorry for him. So should I, maybe, if I weren't the victim. I told her to tell him to leave me alone and not even speak to me.

That was before the presents were taken from the tree. Among mine, was a long, narrow box. I opened it and it contained a gold pencil from <u>Marcus</u>.

I felt like shedding tears of rage, I was <u>unnerved</u>.

Althea said, "He says he's going to marry you someday."

"I shouldn't wonder," I replied, weary to my heart's core.

"Do you <u>want</u> to?" Althea asked in surprize knowing my feelings for him.

"No," I said. "I'd rather die, but if this goes on for years and years and <u>years</u> I shall be in a weakened condition."

Well, I hunted him up and thanked him bitterly. I couldn't throw it at him, although I longed to.

"Can we be friends?" he asked.

"I suppose so," I said with resignation.

When I got home with the presents the Family saw the pencil of course and Ase exploded again. I just sat down and cried. He stopped roaring long enough to ask me what was the matter. I replied that I could not bear any more and he let up a little. He says he would know how to deal with the affair if I were older, but that it is so damned ridiculous -

Mother said the "poor boy must have been saving his spending money for weeks, Helen."

So what with Mother's reproach and Ase's condemnation I am about ready to die. If Life is like this, I don't care much about living.

<u>Dec. 25</u> A lovely day in spite of everything.

Before that terrible time Christmas Tree Night, I noticed an awful nice looking boy who played a violin solo. He was in the Cantata too. I <u>think</u> he goes to the Congregational Church and his name is Dorence. He is friends with Marcus so I suppose he is a darn fool too.

<u>Wed. Dec. 29</u>   I am glad this is the last entry. Oh I suppose I shall keep another Diary. Ase says I am a true Clarke with "the itch if not the gift." This, I think has been the worse year I have known since Daddy died.

Ase still raving about Marcus. "And to think," he said with sarcasm, "To <u>think</u> I smiled when the nurse said, `you have a little daughter, Captain'!" I laughed and he said he was glad I was developing a sense of humor, because I was as a child so serious and humorless he was afraid I was a Burrows.

I have been reading Grandma's *Historic Groton* again. The story of Groton Heights and the brave men who fell there make me feel all choked up. The wounded were piled into a cart and jolted down the hill to the Avery house where the women of Groton cared for them as best they could.

These words give me a strange thrill everytime I read them.

"There were more than forty women of the Congregational Church in Groton who that day were made widows, and no man was left at the next communion to pass the bread and wine."

To think of the awful suffering necessary to make those thrilling lines!

I don't suppose those poor women taking the wine and bread felt at all heroic.

I am glad I have Avery blood in my veins.

Thoughts

We had a cherry tree in the garden and when Spring came, it petalled the ground and filled the air with white flakes more fragile than old china. I like to watch them float down upon the grass and cling there, pretending to be grass flowers.

Grandma said, "It must be cut down, because the fruit is sour."

"But the flowers are sweet," I reminded her. She said I was not practical and much too notional.

The man forget to come and when he brought the ax it had burst into bloom.

A few sharp chops and it was down. It was a rather little tree, slender and young. I watched it wither in the sun. It looked like a giant boquet. It died slowly, although the little breezes tried to cool it.

Sometimes on moonlight nights I think I see it. Perhaps after all ghosts are memories that will not die.

1921

January 1921 - 15 years old

<u>Saturday, 15th</u> - Once upon a time I was childish enough to believe every new year <u>must</u> be happier than the old; now I know better. Still, this year has started wonderfully with a long, long letter from Miss Montgomery. Her husband it seems, is a minister the name of Mac Donald, but I cannot think of her except as Miss Montgomery. She says she has two children, both boys. I telephoned Cill immediately and she said hers had come too, so we met and read each others. Mine was longer and Cill said it was because I wrote such a long letter myself. I wonder if I bored her? I hurt all over when I think of her skipping. Ase says I mustn't make a practice of writing because she is a busy woman and I must not make an infernal nuisance of myself. I shall treasure this letter all my life.

<u>Jan. 27</u> I am staying at Grandmother's all the time because Constance has scarlet fever and I am quarantined out. It is her birthday, too, poor child, a very tragic way to spend a birthday. In the olden days scarlet fever was very dangerous, but they say modern doctors keep it pretty well under control. They use to not get well quite often, but it is better not to think of that I guess. Doctors have learned such an enormous lot since then.

When evening comes Grandma puts off lighting the lamp as long as possible, because she likes the dusk. So do I, specially when she sings old songs and tells of clipper ship days. She was born the year of the Gold Rush and one of the first songs she can remember is "Oh Susannah."

Those were exciting days in Mystic when the shipyards were so busy you could hear the pounding of hammers and the clinking of metal on both sides of the river all the day long. Then the launchings. I reminded her I had seen a three master launched from the Pendleton Yards, but she says I have no idea of the launchings in the old days when there was music, speeches and everyone dressed up for the occasion. Great-Grandmother knew when all the Mystic ships were launched, but Grandma says she can only recall the tail end of them. I guess I am getting the <u>tale</u> end of that! There was plenty of building during the World War, but <u>not</u> clippers. There was a Burrows yard at the Head of the River around a hundred years ago. And where Bindloss is now use to be D.O. Richmond's boat yard and before him way back in the beginning a Packer had a yard. I guess that strip of land has seen as many ships built as any in the world.

Great Uncle Phillip Iron's grandfather was named Resolved Irons, a very firm sounding name I think, and he was the Irons of Irons and Grinnell who had a big yard on Pistol Point. Next to him was the Greenman yard. And the Grinnell part is us too, because great great Aunt Jane Packer's daughter Tret married a Grinnell About the only ship yard we don't seem to be connected with was the Mallory yard and Grandma knows Miss Lizzie and the hunchback Julius.

I think Irons and Grinnell built the *Andrew Jackson*. Capt. Williams sailed her to the Golden Gate in one hundred days beating Capt. Gurdon Gates on the *Twilight* by just a few hours. Capt. Williams was an awful driver. Grandma thinks the Andrew Jackson was superior to the *Flying Cloud*. The latter has the lovelier name by far, but naturally I want our ship to be the faster. I think Capt. Williams sailed the *Liza Mallory* too. I am quite fond of him because I only missed him by a few years. I mean he died just a few years before I was born. They still call the square house on Gravel Street the Capt. Jack Williams' place.

Capt. Holmes sailed around the Horn 84 times before he left the sea and he was just about that old before he really retired. Grandma says his retiring was a standing joke. He was always saying each voyage was his last and every time he'd sail again. One time he really did retire and went into the fish business in New York, but within a year he was sailing again. Maybe he is still sailing.

As I said, Grandma knows the Mallorys. There are a lot of Mallory houses about town on the other side of the river but most of them are lived in by strangers and are not kept up as they use to be. Miss Lizzie is an old maid like the rest of old maids, but Julius makes me sad to look at him You know he was meant to be tall and straight and handsome, fit to build or sail the finest ship in the world. The sight of his face and the fountain that doesn't play makes me ache with sadness. Grandma says tosh, he is doing real well in New York.

She can remember when Capt. Spicer took the *Mary E. Sutton* around in 110 days trying to break his own record of 108 days. His portrait hangs in the Library over the fireplace so I know his face almost as well as my own.

The *Charles Mallory* was a noble vessel. Capt. Hull's heart broke when she piled up off the Brazil coast, and he never sailed again. There is nothing so bad as losing one's ship even if it is not one's fault. It is best to go down with it.

I wish I could remember all she tells me - I forget some of it before I have chance to write it down. She knew the old captains and grew up with their stories. She was a grown woman when they made a coal barge of the *David Crockett*. She says its a pity, but I could cry with rage. And while it is a lovely name I would never name a ship *Twilight*, because it makes me think of the twilight of the gods. They thought those days would go on forever, Grandma said, or rather they didn't think, simply took it for granted. It was the most thrilling way to make a fortune in the world. If I could have chosen when to live I should have chosen that era. Then almost every house held a captain - not all clippers or whalers, but some kind. There was Capt. Cunningham of the China trade and Capt. Pray, Capt. Holwell, Capt. Wilbur - oh I could go on forever.

An Account of My Life

Well anyway, I saw the *Kingsway* launched at Pistol Point and during the war launchings at Noank were common place.

Jan. 29 - This is terrible! Constance is worse. Dr. Allyn doesn't think she will get any worse, but doctors often say that. It seems as if nothing could happen like that to us, but there was Daddy.

I got out the old music box, but its tinkly tunes brought it all back until I stopped it. Grandmother looks stiff and rocky. She lost two little girls and while I have never seen her cry, her eyes grow misty when she speaks of them even unto this day. I do not dare to give away to my feelings before her.

When we sat looking out of the window before the lamp was lit, I put my head down in her lap and she patted my head. Her fingers are not gentle, but I love the feeling of them and the smell of her starched white apron - such a comforting smell. She says in time I will learn to accept God's will.

I may learn to accept, but I shall not call it God's will.

Feb. 12 - Constance is so much better they let me talk thru the window to her. There is no further cause for worry as she shows no signs of complications. There hasn't been a snow really fit for sliding this year; however we have had some of the most beautiful snow falls imaginable. Yesterday was damp and all the snow that fell thru the night clung to the branches and twigs so that the world was a crystal palace this morning.

A valentine from Rowland. When I am not with him I like him a lot.

Feb. 20 A splendid blizzard. Am simply enthralled by *The Count of Monte Crisco* and am experiencing a wide variety of emotions.

Grandmother is rather put out with me. It is my own fault because I know she does not like my light moods and I should save them for Ase who does. She has been treating me like a child while insisting I am a young lady and must not do this and that, among other things, sit with my feet over the arm of the easy chair while I read.

"If I'm really grown up," I said. "Where are the eight large oysters for my tail and the lilies for my hair?"

"Have you taken leave of your senses?" she snapped.

So I asked her if she didn't remember the Anderson Fairy tales she use to read to me and how I asked for "The Little Mermaid" again and again. She remembered reading fairy nonsense but she didn't remember a thing about it!

"Don't you remember the old grandmother who always wore twelve oysters on her tail because she was so proud of her birth?" I cried. "And how when her grandaughters came up to see the world when they were fifteen?"

It was no use. She was angry and thought me impertinent. As if I'd dare to be!

1921

Feb. 21 Wind blew the snow into great drifts and the street cars are not running. Read "Snowbound" again. Mother says she always read it on snowy days when she was a girl.

Had supper early and went up to Grandma's. She was just having hers: tea and bread and butter and preserved pears, so I sat down with her and ate again. She says it is beyond her where I stow it away.

Later we talked and she sang, but mostly hymns. I cannot like hymns except a few like "The Little Brown Church in the Vale," and "I walked in the Garden Alone." I detest "Rescue the Perishing, Care for the Dying" and "When the Roll Is Called Up Yonder." Moody and Sankey are so grim.

I shall never cease to regret I cannot carry a tune, for Grandmother's sake. She looks at me and says sadly. "We were all such sweet singers, it must be the Clarke and the Hill in you. Your mother never could turn a tune either."

She likes to hear me play the piano, but to <u>her</u> way of thinking, a piano was made to accompany a voice and for no other reason.

She had hopes that Constance would have a voice, but no, she cannot turn tune any better than I. However, knowing I can't, I will not try, but Constance likes to sing.

She will sit in the rocking chair opposite Grandmother and sing happily for an hour. Sometimes she almost turns a tune. She really does "John Brown's Body" quite well with Grandmother to carry her along.

Grandma would like a grand daughter with blue eyes and gentle ways. One with a pink and white complexion who <u>never</u> let herself get brown. One who would sit with her afternoons, who could sew and embroider beautifully. She would like to speak with pride of my fine stitches and beautiful singing voice. If I sang in the choir she'd burst with pride I think.

She'd like a grandaughter who was modest and shy, one who would never look at a man until the time came for her to marry a much respected man of old family, with a bank account and splendid prospects.

I know what <u>she</u> wants, but it isn't in me to be it.

<u>Mar. 4-5-6</u> - Friday, Saturday, Sunday

I was never before so <u>furious</u> my internal organs actually quaked, but I have just recently undergone such an experience. And after having so <u>much</u> fun and I could have had infinitely <u>more</u> fun if he had let me alone! I am referring to Marcus of course. Oh it is useless to repine, but I can't help it!

In the first place, the Boy's Conference was held in Mystic this year, the boys coming from all over the Country. The girls looked forward to a wonderful good time, because the Social and some of the services were to be held at our Church.

Anna, Mary and I happened to be in Kretzers store when quite a crowd of boys stepped off the trolley car. Naturally, after seeing the same boys year in year out with monotonous regularity, it was interesting to have scores of new ones literally swarming about. We kept picking out the ones we liked the looks of and changing our minds as soon as we saw a better looking one, like the soldier in the Anderson fairy tale who threw away the coppers in the chest in one room for the silver in the next, then the silver for the gold. Or to be more apt, like the dream I sometimes have when I find pennies all over the ground, then nickles and throw away the pennies to pick up the nickles, find dimes and throw away the nickles and so on, waking up with nothing at all. After all, the soldier had the gold and the tinder-box.

Well, eventually I saw the one I liked the looks of best and made up my mind then and there, because I knew there couldn't be anyone hansomer than Clarence (I didn't know his name then), and there wasn't. Trouble was, Anna and Mary decided on him too. He was tall and hansome and well dressed, so it wasn't strange.

The Social was the next night and I had a new dress, green with gold embroidery, made sort of Russian tunic effect, so I felt sure of looking well.

I hadn't been there long before I heard Mrs. Gremley telling another woman I was the prettiest girl there which made me happy until I reminded myself Anna hadn't arrived. I have quite a clear, smooth skin, but Anna has a Complexion and naturally curly hair. However, she wasn't any prettier than usual and I was, which sort of evened up things.

The regular boys just didn't exist for us! Even unpopular girls had several conference boys in their train. It's a marvellous feeling to be able to be so pick and choosey. I don't suppose one can expect that much popularity many times in ones life. At first it seemed as though all the boys I had passed over with a glance, took a <u>preverse</u> delight in falling for me, while Clarence who was very much in demand in spite of the supply, seemed to think no more of me than of half a dozen others until we were playing "Wink". It was his turn and all the girls were looking at him expectantly. So I didn't, I looked away. Well, if I wouldn't look it didn't do any good to wink at me so he winked at Anna, but he continued to look at me in a puzzled sort of way, and when someone winked at Anna he was too inattentive to catch her in time.

With his chair vacant he looked at me and winked. Marcus dug his fingers into my shoulders and held me in my chair. Clarence scowled.

Knowing that if I showed any eagerness to go, Marcus would be on guard and hold me there all night, I acted indifferent, and sure enough he became less watchful. Clarence who wasn't exactly dumb! seized the opportunity - and that time I slid from under Marcus' hands neatly and whirled into Clarence's chair.

"Got you!" he said triumphantly, dropping his hands on my shoulders. Which was swell. I knew however, that if I didn't make it exciting he'd think I wasn't so wonderful, after all, so at the first opportunity I slipped out of his hands and into Pat's chair. Well, from there on it was a battle, and by the time we were ready to leave I had him interested. He was waiting for me, but when I came from the dressing room whom should I crash into but Marcus.

"Ready?" he asked.

"Go away," I said impatiently. "You can go home with me some other time."

And as I tried to pass he stepped in front of me. "I'm taking you home tonight." he said firmly. "I've told that fellow you are my girl and not to wait. He's gone with Anna."

You!" I exploded, furious that my evenings work should go up in smoke. And I jerked away from him and ran out of the door. Several boys came up and asked if they could take me home, but that big <u>Mutt</u> caught up with me and said, "<u>I'm</u> taking her home."

"You're not! He is not!" I snapped.

Well, the boys laughed and one of them said: "You're not married to her, you Big Stiff."

Then Rev. Osborne came along. He <u>would</u>.

"What's this, what's this? No loitering boys." he said severely, and then, seeing me, began to chuckle.

"Well boys. I guess this lad has prior claim. Come along. Time you were in bed." And they all walked off, leaving me fairly dithering with rage.

"Come on," Marcus said smugly. I said to myself, "maybe I won't give <u>you</u> a time of it!" And I thought of how every girl would have interesting things to tell - even the prunes, and the awful joking I'd get and felt utterly without mercy. Of course after a time I felt tired and the fight went out of me.

"How <u>could</u> you," I said sadly. "How <u>could</u> you do this to me! A special occasion like this and <u>you</u> butting in. If you were the least bit noble you'd <u>want</u> me to enjoy myself."

He grunted.

"You don't really like me or you wouldn't be so selfish!" I cried.

He acted so mulish I gave up to despair again. I told him I hoped he was satisfied, he'd ruined the best time I had ever had.

"Best hunting," he muttered.

"Go ahead insult me!" I said coldly. "It's what I expect from you!"

He said he wasn't and we argued that for a while.

Finally he said, and I noted with satisfaction that he sounded just about exhausted.

"You can raise more hell than ten girls."

"Marcus," I said wistfully. "Will you keep out of my way tomorrow?"

"No!" he yelled in my ear.

"I shall hate you if you don't."

"Alright," he gave in suddenly. "I'll tell those fellows I was only kidding and that I don't care anything about you."

"I don't expect you to lie!" I said, very shocked.

He said he wasn't so darn dumb as I thought and I said quickly, "Of course not, Marcus. It's nice of you to give in to me."

Sunday the boys were supposed to go to the Methodist Church, but they could go to another if they chose and a goodly number chose the Baptist.

Well, we all sat together and had an amusing time reading hymn titles. It is funny how many have sentimental meanings if you take them that way. When Clarence came to "Side By Side," he added in a whisper, "under the sheets!"

I gave him the Burrows look which withered him

It is always that way, <u>always</u>. Am I forever doomed to find interesting boys fresh and nice boys <u>unbearably</u> stupid?

Mar. 13 - Albro is dead. He is - <u>was</u> a little older than I. I don't - didn't know him well enough to feel really sad, but I feel shocked.

Forgot to record that I have had a letter form my Cousin Oliver whom I have never seen. When Mother sent my photograph to Aunt Catherine I wrote to him. He says judging from my photograph New England girls are better looking than those out there. Ase chuckled and said it was just the sort of thing Oliver (his father) would have said at that age.

Young Oliver is studying to be a violinist and is very talented. They use to live in Tacoma but have moved to Berkeley California. Seems odd for a Clarke to live out of New England and the last male of the line too.

I <u>would</u> have an interesting cousin way out there and one like Alton <u>here</u>.

I can not <u>imagine</u> Alton with a violin.

<u>Mar. 15</u> - This morning Grandma called me at the usual time and when I came down into the kitchen I smelled bacon cooking and saw her break an egg into the pan.

I thought she gave me an odd look so I went into the buttery but I didn't think much about it being still very sleepy. Then she said calmly in an everyday manner, "Is my face much twisted? Last night I had a shock, I think."

I leaned against the door jam and looked at her. "Your mouth is - just a little," I said.

"I thought likely you'd notice it first off," she went on. "But seeing you didn't it can't be too noticeable. Well, sit down and eat your breakfast."

I was beginning to get my senses back and to feel an awful sense of guilt.

"Why are you up? Why didn't you call me? And getting breakfast! I'm going to get a doctor. I thought I was here in case you needed me," I fired out, almost crying.

"My legs are alright and so are my hands," she said shortly. "What's done is done, it came to me and now its gone. Eat before everything turns stone cold."

1921

It was a terrible meal. I didn't want to eat, but she made me: I didn't want her to see me looking at her mouth, but I didn't want her to think I was avoiding it.

I caught one of her hands and rubbed my cheek against it, not saying anything.

"Go along, Soft Soap," she said quite affectionately for her. I could barely force the food down.

She is Spartan. Why I have seen her scald her arm, pull the sleeve down and keep on working! She never complains and calls those who do, spleeny.

If I had only known! As far as I could see she was fit as a fiddle at bedtime. And of course I slept like a log.

"When you tell your Mother, don't frighten her to death," she said as I left for school - I always stop in before taking the trolley. So I managed to say quite calmly, "Grandma says not to get excited. She has had a slight shock. She is up and around and her mouth is only a little twisted." Mother stared at me for a moment and flew up the path.

The kettle was spouting steam and I pushed it back. I wondered if I ought to get Constance ready for school. Then I decided to let her sleep. If Mother got back in time to get her off alright and if she didn't it wouldn't matter. I went out to the car stop. Later. The Doctor says it is only slight facial paralysis and that it will pass off.

I shall try to sleep lightly now. She is so <u>splendid</u> in the way she faces things. Pain, sickness and death frighten me dreadfully. I have always thought an imagination a wonderful thing to have. But now I am not so sure.

Maybe the reason she faces things so bravely is because she never confuses Right and Wrong as I do. Sometimes I feel frightened because she says if one sins one can never alter the fact. One can repent and be forgiven, but if ones sinned, ones sinned and the burden of your conscience is the load you bear for wrong doing You can never be as good as you were before, you are a mended vessel.

<u>Mar. 21</u> - The lamp is lighted and Grandma is reading. The door is open and the frogs are croaking in the swamp. I hate nights now for I wake up cold with fear thinking she may have called and I not heard. One night I heard a dog baying and my heart stopped. I get up and tiptoe to her door and listen.

She seems well and her mouth has straightened somewhat.

Priscilla and I are going to be baptized Easter Sunday.

<u>Apr. 22</u> - I am sitting in a chair on the back porch and glad to be out again, for I have been sick with scarlet fever. This morning I helped Grandma dig leaves from the flower beds and tie up the pink rambler blown loose in the last wind.

An Account of My Life

There are several daffodils blooming in the south corner which seemed so wonderful I had to recite, "I wandered lonely as a cloud."

Grandma said I had the lightest case of fever she ever say. Well, it was light but any sort of sickness leaves me weak on my pins and I nearly keeled over when I first tried to walk.

It is really Spring now and the crimson maples are showing a haze of red against the bright blue sky, and the sea is glittering in the sunlight and there are robins everywhere.

Grandma has just remarked that it wont be long before the summer people and painters are all over everywhere. That's what I like, but Grandma doesn't care for out siders.

Apr. 28 For years and years Grandma has subscribed to a funny little paper called the "Comfort." It has a list of shut-ins and needy people among other things. Well, I wrote a letter to an invalid boy of fifteen and sent a dime to an old woman who asked for a dime shower. The Family does not approve.

May 9th Leona and I were baptized last night; a very holy experience. The church was sweet with apple blossoms and I felt very spiritual.

Miss Coats remembered when two hundred were baptized at one time. It must have taken a wonderful evangelist to prevail on so many.

Priscilla was baptized while I had scarlet fever. She said she didn't want to be without me, but she was on the list for that date and couldn't change.

May. 28 - Yesterday was a most interesting day. The Sophomore class of W.M.I. gave a Cabaret and Cill, having the interests of her class at heart, sold tickets to Anna and to me. We took the 4 o'clock trolley to Groton.

The ferry boat, *Governor Winthrop,* has been sold and they run the *Nelseco* built during the war and used by the Groton Iron Works workers. Cill, Leona and another girl were waiting at the Ferry House on the New London side and because we were early we spent part of the spare time in the Public Library. I enjoyed it, but Anna who is smart in school but never reads outside if she can help it, figetted all over the place.

When the time came we walked to the school where we were introduced to many girls, among them Frederica Hunt who seemed very popular, but a trifle loud. Her father is dead and her Mother is now married to a Congressman. The dance floor was made to resemble a cabaret. I have never seen a cabaret of course, but I have read. Small tables were placed along the sides leaving the center free for the entertainers and the dancing. It was very pretty, but a cabaret without any boys or men seemed rather unreal to me.

1921

    When we were seated at our table I noticed the loveliest girl! She was about my age, had bobbed hair (light brown), blue eyes and a fair skin. I have seen prettier girls, but none so interesting. Her dress was dark blue voile with a thin white collar and she wore high heels. I noticed that she walked with a slight limp and some one said she was thrown from a horse as a child. Her name is Harriet, - Harriet Chappell.

    Cill is forever having crushes herself, but she gets jealous when I have one. I <u>did</u> have such a wonderful time.

    <u>June 13</u> I have had my hair bobbed at last after months of teasing. I admit I felt sort of sick when I heard my braids thud on the floor, but was enchanted with the result. Mother would have let me had it done months ago.

    Have a new dress and a floppy hat of pinky orchid organdy. This is a nice summer, so far.

    <u>June 17</u> - Last night Cill, Gladys and I went to the Broadway School graduation. We were late and had to stand at the back of the hall as every seat was taken. We were next to Jerry and Everett and as we had an open window at our backs and a fairly good view of the stage, we endured our aching feet. It was very tiresome, the graduation, I mean, and I looked the graduates over again and again for an interesting face. There was only one really pretty girl and upon looking the boys over I decided that the one who plays the violin at our church sometimes, was the best looking. I never can remember his name, because it is an odd one, so I asked Everett and he said Dorence Grimes and I needn't flirt with him because he had no use for girls. I withered Everett with a glance.

    Nine girls gave a scarf dance dressed in white with little tinkling bells sewn to their scarfs. It was very pretty and the best thing on the program, until Dorence Grimes played a violin solo. I don't know what he played, but it was refreshing and the entire audience including Jerry, stopped rustling and squeaking their chairs to listen. When Jerry quiets down, <u>that</u> is a tribute of great magnitude. He looks as if he ought to play a violin - and I like his name. He gave an encore and that was so heartily applauded he gave another. He sounds and looks too perfect - there must be something wrong with him as there is with Rowland. Everett walked home with me. I bet if I had the chance I could make him like me.

    <u>June 23</u> - School is out, praise be! Boat Race Day tomorrow. I want <u>to go</u>!

    I'm to sleep at home now. The family has decided. Grandma says I gad about too much and probably will do more so the older I get and she is too old to keep an eye on me. The two houses have been wired and she has only to press a button in her bedroom to have it ring in Mother's. Secretly I am hurt; I know I sleep like a log but I have honestly tried to look out for her. I feel that I have failed in my duty.

June 24 - Boat Race Day. It was sublime! Although Cill and I wanted to go terribly it looked for a time as if we wouldn't get there, simply because our Mothers said we could not go unchaperoned on such a day in such a crowd! and neither one would go themselves. We were nearly desperate until Cill found out that Doris Peckham, who is in her twenties, was going and we arranged to go with her.

The car was very crowded and hot, but we did not mind, being too intent upon the thrills to come. The harbour was a glorious sight with destroyers, Coast Guard cutters, yachts, launches, sailboats, row boats, even canoes all bright with flags and happy people.

The ferry passed close enough to one of the millionaire yachts to give us a glimpse of wicker chairs and tables. I felt envious, but it didn't last, although it is unpleasant being poor. There is such a vast, vast difference between a dirty ferry boat and a beautiful yacht. I intend to be rich myself, someday.

I love New London on Race Day, when the streets are jammed and the peddlars with their great bunches of crimson and blue balloons, and the whole pushing crowd of people. It seemed to get hotter every minute and we perspired freely. As we passed the Mohican Hotel I *think* I saw Charles Dana Gibson coming out. There were any number of nice looking boys, brown and careless. I thought of Marcus and shuddered. I noticed a little girl looking from the hotel and I simply choked with envy. I don't think generally speaking I am given to envy. I find it a very unpleasant sensation.

I imagined myself stepping from the Mohican into a roadster drawn up to the curb, wearing white except for blue (red?) flowers at my waist, with one of those brown boys, at my side, the admiration of all eyes, but completely unconscious of it. It was grand imagining but did not relieve my discomfort. I thought of myself aboard a yacht, seated in a wicker chair sipping a frosty drink with ice clinking in it while the Captain bent forward attentively. It was very real, so real I had to quit it because I was about to choke to death from thirst. We went to the Candy Kitchen and had a soda. It was still early and our feet were tired so we went to the Station and sat down. It is the best place to study human nature I know.

Someday I shall eat at that lunch counter! I know it is far from elegant, but it is interesting. I like the pyramids of oranges and polished apples. The waitresses in neat black and white, the thick white china and the whole tinkling, clinking, banging business.

I like the steaming coffee urn (but *not* on a hot day) and the smell of hearty food. It is best on a snowy evening when the Train Announcer is powdered white and the Thames is lost in a blur of snow.

The people who eat there are interesting: sailors, drummers, jitney drivers and you never know who. I have wanted to eat at that counter ever since I can remember and someday I shall. Also go to the magazine counter and buy all the magazines with gaudy covers.

1921

We cast longing eyes at the Observation Cars, but found them beyond our means, being five dollars a seat. Except for Doris Peckham we didn't have that much money all put together. After a time we decided that it was time to find ourselves a vantage point on the shore, so we walked along dirty streets, slid down a banking and found ourselves along the waters edge with a lot of people most of whom were foreigners - the smelly kind. I knew if one ate garlic one could smell it a mile away, but I did not know that if eaten in large enough quantities over a long enough period one <u>perspired</u> it. Those people did. The man next to me reeked of garlic and <u>sweat</u> - perspiration is not the word for it. I felt hot and sick, but when the Race started we forgot everything with thrills racing up and down us. Of course we didn't see the start as they were rowing down stream, but we saw the finish. I was so excited I could not stand still. Yale won and I was thrilled to my innermost depths. The noise was tremendous, shouts, whistles, bells and horns. I shall finish this account tomorrow.

<u>June 25</u> - Continued - Well, here I am on the front veranda with a slice of warm gingerbread in my left hand and my pencil in my right. If no one stops by I shall finish my thrilling adventures of yesterday.

After the Race was over we returned to the Station and a scene of indescribable confusion. There were officers from the Fort, Coast Guardsmen and gentlemen in flannels everywhere. A tall man with a boy about 12 or 13 years of age came into the station A red cap carried bags and golf sticks, but the boy held a violin case firmly. The man disappeared in the crowd before I could more than note that he was dark and hansome. The boy placed the violin case beside him on the bench and waited, meanwhile opening a copy of "Life" which he had bought at the newsstand. He must have been very traveled, because he paid no attention to the multitudes and kept on reading. I should never be able to do that. Cill and I decided the man was the boy's father and that his Mother was dead hence their devotion to one another. Cill said, how did we know they were devoted, being together didn't prove anything. I said we must assume they were for the sake of the plot and she agreed. Two girls about my age came by and I abandoned the boy to study them.

One wore a dream of a peach organdy dress which caused me to feel bitter because I had wanted to wear my pale pink and Mother put out a middy blouse and pleated skirt. As if I didn't look young enough as it is! I said I felt like an Inmate of an Institution, but she said if I went to a place like New London on Race Day, the least I could do was not to call attention to myself. She and Grandmother think it is a sin. I like to have people notice me. Mother says I ought to be ashamed. It doesn't embarrass me to be gazed upon, I feel all lit up inside. They think it would be better if I had less self possession and more sense.

Doris had to get a bag which she had checked upon our arrival as she wasn't coming back to Mystic but was going on a visit. We had to wait in the baggage room. I mean we went in, and I had a wonderful time reading

An Account of My Life

labels. I was sorry when she got it being loath to leave such interesting luggage. Doris told us to go straight home which we did eventually.

We found a very interesting looking man, very tall, brown and strong with sinicle expression. His lips were locked tightly and a pipe dangled from the corner of his mouth. He stood right beside me and looked over my head. I guess I looked longer than I should because I was deciding whether to have his heart broken or have him happily in love, anyway he looked down at me once and away again. If I were only startlingly beautiful he would have looked again.

Cill found a tall, stately elderly gentleman who looked like a Kentucky Colonel although I don't think they get this far north even on Boat Race Day. He was a good find, but I preferred the tall man as having a wider scope.

We wanted to stay after dark but did not on account of the Families and besides Doris trusted us to go home. It was a wonderful day and has given me a glimpse of life. Here I am part of Mystic. It gives me an excited, impatient feeling filled with longing to think of all the world I don't know of which I am not a part. Cill and I can hardly wait for next year.

<u>June 29</u> - First Chatauqua Day - Went with Grandma, who buys a season ticket because she approves of it. Went with Mother in the evening. The lectures are educational and sometimes interesting. I prefer the other things. The Columbia Artists are swell and it is interesting to see in the flesh people important enough to make victrola records.

I had a party about a week ago. Mother and the kids thought it was a surprise, but it wasn't. We had a lot of fun and I was too tired to write it down that night and later I put off doing so because the excitement was over, in which case I am likely to feel flat.

Roland Coleman came. I think he likes me, but of course he is really little more than a kid. He paid me compliments in French, which is more than some of the older boys would think of doing! Marcus would <u>never</u> think of calling me "chic" for instance. He doesn't like Rowland and Rowland is <u>contemptuous</u> of Marcus.

I say I had fun because I cannot imagine a party without fun, but really I enjoyed it far less than many others. Being hostess so to speak, I wasn't free to do as I pleased. I knew it would be bad manners to monopolize Rowland, and didn't. I really tried to make Marcus notice someone besides me, but gave it up. Both helped me serve the refreshments, which isn't the custom at all - -

This is the first mixed party I have ever had, because Ase will not have noise and racket and does not like to have boys around. He says he is jealous of them, which is silly, of course. However I am so afraid he will have an ugly mood I never enjoy having a large crowd around. When he is good natured he monopolizes the conversation, and when he isn't, he mutters and growls.

The boys as a general thing, are sort of afraid of him, but most of the girls like him because he flatters them.

Mother sympathizes with me because she cannot entertain without feeling uneasy since the time he sat in the next room and grumbled and swore because a group of the Daughters of the Veterans stayed too long.

I asked her if it was safe to have them the minute the party started and she said yes, he was in a good mood.

June 30 - Second Day - Rained cats and dogs - I should say it rained torrents. Went with Gladys in the afternoon. It was a long walk but we had a good time sloshing thru puddles. The tent was dry inside of course but the rain made such a dreadful roar upon it it was hard to hear anything. The lecture was interesting (Ase says I use that word too much). It is not paucity of words but because so many things are interesting. There was a concert by the Shirley-Leadbetter Co. The women wore lovely evening gowns. The dampness kept the harpist busy replacing strings which broke as fast as she put them up. Did not go in the evening as the downpour continued and the Family said `no.'

July 1st - Still pouring. Anna, Gladys and I sloshed over, dripping wet inspite of our umbrellas. Today we heard the Ladies Pittsburgh Orchestra. There were two beautiful blondes in it. The best part was the ten year old Wonder Boy who played on several instruments. Anna who is very tender hearted said he didn't look as if he'd live very long and she bet his father was cruel to him, because think of the practicing the poor child must have undergone. Maybe the man wasn't his real father. I saw that boy, Dorence Grimes. It's got to be accidental or appear to be.

Saturday - Fourth Day - Went both afternoon and evening. The lecture was quite inspirational and the Pilgrim Entertainers were good, but the big thrill was the evening and the play "Nothing But The Truth." It was wonderful. The program says it was a Broadway and London success. It is thrilling to think of people in New York and especially London having seen it.

Sunday - The Sunday program was so suitable it was not much better than church. Mother saw Marcus across the aisle and said, "Heavens does that boy always have so many pimples?" He never does, it was something he ate.

Monday - Paul Fleming the Majician is simply marvellous!

He is quite good looking - in the distance, anyway. I have been dissapointed so many times. Anyway, evening clothes help: I think a man must be pretty terrible to look at not to look well in evening clothes.

An Account of My Life

<u>July 10</u> I wish I knew more. I read, read, <u>read</u>, but I want to live things. What's the good of reading art reviews when you've never seen more than the Summer Show by Mystic artists? Whats the use reading music reviews when you've never heard a really great artist in person? I am not good at learning by myself because I don't know exactly what I want, but I learn quickly from people. I want to get <u>out</u> of Mystic!

Grandma and Mother are different. Grandma in particular, fits in here. Mystic was made by the Burrowses <u>for</u> the Burrowses. I don't say she has always been contented, but she knows what she wants. She said once that she had wanted to go places but in her young days there were babies, or there was sickness etc. and now she just doesn't care, which is pathetic I think, like never looking on Carcasonne.

Besides, she is uncrushable. She isn't just a person, she is a personage. Practically every one knows her. She always wears black for best, plain and unadorned except for a lace collar or a small jet or gold pin, or perhaps her fat gold beads. Sometimes she wears a narrow band of black velvet around her throat. If she wore a white cap and a ruff she would bear a striking resemblance to that portrait of an Old Lady by Rembrandt.

I like to have the older ones call me "Camelia Burrows' granddaughter." I guess she is the kind of woman who could be married a dozen times and still be called by her maiden name, not that Daddy was by any manner of means a meachy or hen-pecked husband, but because her personality is such that it cannot blend into anothers, or take on any of its color.

Mother has dreams I suppose, but she doesn't understand plain restlessness, and asks, "If <u>you</u> don't know what you want, how do you expect me to?"

Ase might help me if he would, but he doesn't want to be bothered and never notices me in a kindly way except when the mood strikes him.

<u>July 19th</u> - Nothing of interest to record, nor any prospects of anything. I guess it is only in books that nice things happen and that Shakespeare is right when he says "how weary, stale, flat and unprofitable, seems to me all the uses of the world:" but I don't really believe it.

Last night Marion, Cill, Di, Glad and I went over to the Community House dock. We rowed over and the water was rose and opal from the glowing west. As soon as we were around the bend we heard laughter from the club dock where there was a number of boys and girls in the water.

Teddy Mosher, his sister Caroline who is pretty but has no palate, and their Mother were there. Teddy was spic and span as usual. He attended the Academy at one time, we were in the 5th grade together, but since he moved away he considers himself a summer person and regards his Grandmother Pomeroy's house across from Miss Emily Gates' on High Street, as his summer residence.

Marcus came over later. However, I felt cross with him albeit for no good reason, and acted so. Someday he will be fat.

We stayed until the moon came up, then rowed slowy to shore, the river banks sending back our voices, the oars dripping phosporous.

Mrs. Benjamin's Boarding House veranda was lighted brightly, and the sound of music and dancing met our ears as Cill and Glad walked part way home with me.

That man, Eddie LaChapelle, who is an actor, was dancing alone while the others applauded. Some people have such good times!

Leona's brother Lowell knows him, but when she asked him to introduce him to us, he said Eddie wasn't interested in children. Naturally, Leona was outraged as she is older than I, and I am within two months of being sixteen. A great many girls have really lived by the time they are as old as I. Sometimes it makes me wild to think of all I am missing!

July 20 - Club dock again. Foggy and very sultry. Mary says if you cut your eyelashes they grow out curly. Mine are thick and long and straight. I haven't any curl in my system. I wonder if I dare?

July 23 - This afternoon Mary had the World Wide Guild meet at her house. We sat on the veranda and when the chairs and couch hammock were filled, sat on the railing and steps. We talked and sewed all afternoon for the Red Cross babies, making blankets and booties of pale blue flannel; no pink ones. I remarked that they must be expecting a crop of boy babies, which shocked Miss Harriet, though I can't see why.

We may give a play in September called "Patty Makes Things Hum."

July 25 - Went up to Cill's this afternoon. Met Miss Bertha Foote coming up Meeting House Hill and walked with her as far as the foot of Burrows Street. She lives in the old Burrows homestead now owned by Great, great Aunt Jane.

I like Miss Foote, although she is prim and makes one mind ones P's and Q's. Years ago I renamed her Matilda and though the Family scolded it has got the habit of referring to her in like manner privately. She has had a Romance in her life for years. Mr. George Greenman started his attentions years and years ago - oh, as many as twenty five or thirty I guess, and he still calls on her once or twice a week. He has pressed her to marry him many times, but she will not do so until he earns a living, which he is unable to do although an architect. It does not matter so much because he has the Greenman Family in back of him and will not starve, but Matilda having taken a stand, is not to be budged.

I have thought of something that will amuse Ase: George Greenman is not yet tired of pressing his wedding suit!

July 30 - We spent the day at Ocean Beach. Mother, Grandmother, Constance and I. It was cloudy in the early morning and Grandma who is weatherwise, said it would not clear and would surely rain before night. However, we had made all preparations and decided to risk it.

The Harbor was filled with yachts from the New York Yacht Club, and at noon they set sail for Long Island, like white birds on the wing.

There was sadness at the Beach to-day: the New York Tribune sent twelve or more little cripples to the Beach for a two week vacation. The children were in bathing suits which of course exposed their deformities pitifully.

Someday, when I make money, or earn money, or both, I shall help poor little cripples and hurt and helpless animals. There are so many big things in the world waiting to be done!

It started to rain just before we left, and while Grandma did not <u>say</u> "I-told-you-so," she looked it. Well, we had a lot more than as if we had stayed at home. None of us was surprized. She is really a wonderful weather prophet. Ase even asks her opinion when the barometer's acting cussed. Grandma respects the barometer, but says it can't be expected to see as far as she can. She claims generations of sea captains have made her "weather wise."

She's wise lots of ways, although she is not clever. I guess good people never are.

She knows all about the moon without an almanach and can tell what quarter it is and when it will be full, without looking it up. Then too, she pays attention to the Line Storms and Sun Dogs and St. Swithins day and the last Friday in a month because it sets the weather for the next month. When water boils away fast its going to rain and she calls the nicest days weather breeders which I think is very pessimistic of her. Then there is: Mackerel sky, rain is nigh. Red in the morning, sailors take warning, red at night sailor's delight." When the sun goes down orange so many nights we are in for a drought and when locusts shrill its going to be hot. "Rain before seven it will clear before eleven and when its foggy in the morning its likely to burn off by noon. If the wind is in the east its good for neither man nor beast and when there are cobwebs on the grass its going to be a fair day. When it snows she marks the day and the moon and knows about how many storms there will be that winter.

Then theres that about March coming in like a lamb and going out like a lion - and of course the Hedge Hogs. When there are lots of leaves and the animals thicker fur than usual its going to be a long cold winter. When I point out that she is sometimes wrong she looks majestic and says, "I am only human," which leaves me without anything to say. Well - to return to my knitting, in other words, to go on with my account.

On the car I discovered interesting material. A man, I think he was in his forties, very hansome with grey eyes and a firm chin with a cleft in it. I like clefts in chins although Alva Chapman, Gurdon's father who has one, says it is a damn nuisance because he always cuts his chin when

1921

shaving. I named this man Hamilton Grant. His lips were set in a straight line and he looked as though he could say scathing things. His nose was perfect and his ears nice. I stared at him so hard he looked at me. Mother was horrified at my lack of manners and because I attracted the attention of a strange man, which is a thing a lady never does. I was foolish enough to say I always looked at interesting men. I saw her exchange looks with Grandma, so I said quickly, "You needn't worry. They never pay any attention to me. I look younger than my years." Grandma gave me the Burrows look and I said no more. I hope they forget about it before another Boat Race Day.

Aug. 3 Life is very dull. We are brown as berries, although I never saw any brown berries, but there is nothing in our lives but the Church, the Community House, the Library and the movies. All the girls are simply pining for excitement, but there is none forth coming. I wish I were seventeen or eighteen, or even sixteen! Fifteen is a horrid age. Treated like a child when I'm not. I want to grow up. I want to leave Mystic. I want to be the admiration of all eyes.

I am reading "*Jane Eyre*" and think it wonderful. Ase laughed at me because I pronounced it Jane Ear. How should I know?

Aug. 7 - Cill, Glad, Elizabeth Colby, Alice, Leona, Florence, and I went on a hike to Deans Mills - at least such were our intentions. but as it happened, we did very little walking. We made the arrangements Friday, and at nine Saturday I met the others at our regular meeting place, the church. We wore middies, bloomers, socks and sneakers.

Leona's Mother made her take Lorna on a leash. She said it made her feel safer which Leona says is a joke if she only knew it, because the only time she was ever frightened and ran, [Lorna] thought it was a game and ran too. I was the last to appear, so according to a previous arrangement, I had to carry the watermellon first. Fortunately, Mr. Spencer from whom we bought it, took pity on me and let me take a basket. There was a gleam of disappointment in Florence's eyes for she hoped to see me bearing it in my arms, but all she said was, "Trust Helen to find a way out."

I did not like her tone and told her so. Outside of that there was no unpleasantness. She is several years older and doesn't like me although she pretends to most of the time.

Her father is usually three sheets to the wind and I am sorry for her, when I am not provoked at her. She is nasty mean and there is nearly always one of us not speaking to her. We were so heavily loaded we were tired by the time we labored up Slaughter House Hill, though none of us would admit it. And then Luck befell us in the guise of a pleasant faced man in an empty delivery auto who told us to hop in, which we did, putting Lorna in the front seat with him. He drove along the dusty road with golden rifts of sunlight making yellow openings on the dark leaf designs patterned on the road. Cill started to sing "Heaven Seems

Nearer." In church it doesn't mean much to me, but heard as jogged along the bumpy road, it seemed <u>fraught</u> with meaning.

In a short time we were there and we simply spilled out of the delivery wagon. We thanked the man profusely and he smiled and said he'd enjoyed it too, which was very wise of him. Lorna got quite attached to him and was loath to move. She is a very affectionate dog and is forever becoming friendly with strangers.

We started on a voyage of discovery and first of all we found a shining pond and on its banks grew cardinal flowers, nearly as high as our heads and of a perfectly regal color. We hunted out our own little camp, where the stone seats and table and fireplace were to our liking and as there were no other people around we had everything to ourselves. The land belongs to the Mystic Valley Water Co. from which source our drinking water eminates, and when Lorna, free from her leash ran for the water and waded in, we all squealed with horror and waded in after her because she would not come at our calls. We got her tied to a tree and nicely settled in some bushes when the Keeper came by. He said dogs werent allowed but if we kept her leashed he guessed it would be alright. Lorna had only wet her legs and the long hair on her stomach all of which was concealed by the bushes, but being a friendly dog, we were afraid she would bound up to the man, thereby disclosing everything. We got as close to her as possible and determined to fall on her if she moved. The man seemed to like us pretty well and hung around so long we were on tenterhooks. We cut the mellon and gave him an enormous wedge. He simply fell on it and after that we were firm friends, besides he said he had to go and after thanking us, went off happily, dripping mellon at every step. We watched him out of sight, before making preperations for dinner. Leona, Alice and I gathered dry wood and got very scratched and dirty. We toasted frankfurters and marshmallows of which we thought we had an enormous quantity, but all disappeared like snow beneath the mid-day sun. We had the watermellon for dessert and it was simply wonderful, being the juciest and pinkest I have ever seen. After we ate our fill we stretched out and went to sleep. but not for long. We explored, took snap shots, played games, and ate blue berries and green apples.

In no time at all it was sunset and we sat in stone seat on the Big Rock and watched the sky. We hoped Lowell, Leona's brother would come for us in his touring car. Leona asked him to, but he wouldn't promise for sure. Still, as she said, left to himself he probably would being a good sport, but if Molly Palmer or some other one of his girl friends phoned him, we'd probably be sacrificed to them. The very prospects fatigued us and was with bated breath that we awaited his coming. Presently we saw Lowell in a cloud of dust and were much relieved. He is very hansome in a blue sweater with the crimson letter on the front. He laughed when he saw us and said it was about time civilization claimed us once more. We <u>were</u> pretty dirty, but he said without a looking-glass we couldn't appreciate <u>how</u> dirty. He drives quite fast and our hair blew all over our heads. We had to stop at the market to leave Mr. Spencer's basket and before we could get under way, Molly Palmer hove into sight. She stopped short and surveyed us. Needless to say <u>she</u> was spotless. Well, we surveyed <u>her</u> coldly.

"Well, Lowell! Robbing the cradle? Was this the pressing engagement?"

Lowell laughed, but he was embarased. <u>We</u> were furious. Gladys and Alice are the youngest and they are fourteen. Leona was practically speechless for she adores Lowell and it simply infuriates her to have Molly Palmer butting in all the time. She says she supposes she could bear it if Lowell was deeply in love with her, but he isnt. According to her she simply pursues Lowell. Well, I <u>don't</u> see what he can see in her. I think she is homely. Of course she isnt bad in a riding habit but she can't go to the altar on horse back very well.

When we passed Mrs. Benjamin's Boarding House, Eddie La Chapell said, "My God, Lowell! Playing nurse maid or do you like them that young?"

I don't think I like him even if he is in vaudeville.

First we stopped at Leona's and played leap frog in the back yard as we do not enjoy the freedom of bloomers every day. We decided to go to choir practice as we were - at least Florence decided to and set about convincing the others. I didn't want to, really, because when I am not in the woods I like to be clean and properly dressed. Florence called me a poor sport, a kill-joy and a Miss Nancy until I said sweetly, "Alright I'll do it. If being a sport means going dirty and trying to attract attention as you seem bent on doing!"

We had a little money left and being hungry again we stopped at Mr. Iver's Store for candy and ice cream.

When we passed Mrs. Benjamin's Boarding House and I saw all the cool, clean girls on the veranda I felt awful inside of me - like a dream when you find yourself walking down a street in a night gown. Florence watched me and guessing my feelings said, "Having a good time, Miss Nancy?"

"No," I replied. "I'm not. <u>I</u> don't feel natural this way." and I sort of inflected the "I".

I think Josie Ennaking, the artist is a very nice man. Of course his name is Joseph, but we call him Josie.

Well, we went to choir practice, but the conglomeration in our stomachs began to kick up and we felt none too good. It was a perfect day.

<u>Aug. 8</u> - I've found some interesting material here in Mystic. <u>She</u> is lovely and <u>he</u> is interesting. I don't know their names, but it doesn't matter. They are married and really in love with one another. He has a crippled foot and walks with a cane. They say he is an illustrator and designed posters during the war. She is lovely and she dresses <u>beautifully</u>.

When she smiles at me I want to do something great for her. I am glad I have seen a case of real love.

<u>Aug. 10</u> - I have been reading Materlenck's "Bluebird". Oh I'd give anything to see it on the stage. I have never seen <u>anything</u> on the stage except "Uncle Tom's Cabin" years and years ago.

"The Land of Memory," "The Palace of the Night". I can not endow them with a millioneth part of their rightful beauty. There are so <u>many</u> things I have never seen - lovely things! I should think anyone who has money might be happy, yet you read of people who have all the lovely things money can buy and are tired of the world. I cannot grasp such an impossible thing!

<u>Aug. 14</u> - Yesterday the Mystic Theatre re-opened having been closed since June for a complete rennovation. Our crowd went last night. The movie was Jackie Coogan in "Peck's Bad Boy" and was very amusing. Mr. Duhaime the manager was there and he asked us how we liked it. Ernest and Marguerite were there too. They went to the Academy before they went away to school - Marguerite to a convent and Ernest to a boy's school.

Mr. Duhaime is French, Mrs. Duhaime is Irish and Marguerite is lovely. I love misty dark hair and grey eyes. She wore a pale blue dress and a wide brimmed hat of yellow straw. I enjoyed looking at her.

<u>Aug. 15</u> - I have just finished *"La Bodega"* by Blasco Ibanez. Parts of it sort of shocked me. There is a whole shelf of Ibanez at the library.

<u>Aug. 21</u> - Rev. Osborne is away and the Rev. Jones preached in his stead. He looks exactly like the White King. Kent came up from Shelter Island today and had supper with us. We don't see much of him now that he is married.

<u>Aug. 24th</u> - Cill phoned that they were going to the Camp Mystic raft and did I want to come? I said yes and started out, meeting Elizabeth, Alice and Eleanor on the way. We went down Starr Lane where an artist was painting. He looked very cross when he saw us, but we did not bother him. The boat was at Bert William's and as we went thru his orchard we stuffed our pockets with his big, juicy, red-striped summer apples. The river was ruffled making rowing rather hard. The Camp Mystic girls were on the raft and of course we have no real right there, but Mr. De Groat the swimming instructor who is very pleasant, told us to stay. He isn't tall and he is very homely, but his muscles are like ropes and he is a beautiful bronze color. The Camp closes this week and some of the girls have gone. The station wagon was plying back [and] forth from the station all day. One girl whose home is in Ohio said she was leaving tomorrow because she had to buy a wardrobe before going back to school.

The Chaperone sat under a purple silk parosol and dozed. On the way home we stopped at Roland Perry's and swapped some of Bert's apples for his yellow ones. It is unbelievable how such a pretty woman as Mrs. Perry can have as homely a son as Roland.

<u>Aug. 28</u> - Today Ase took Mother, Constance and me to Mystic Island. On it is an abandoned hotel with tumbled down cottages, bath houses and what is left of a once fine bathing beach. When Mother was a girl the Island was at the height of its popularity. Now, the great pier stretching far out that steamers might dock is gone, and we tied up at a small rotting landing on the other side of the Island. The place is a tangle of under brush and the hotel nothing but a ruin. There it stands with its eyes picked out and the great verandahs sagging, yet bearing itself with folorn dignity. Men have built cottages, father says, from the lumber torn from it, carrying it away in row boats. Even up until five years ago or thereabouts it was well furnished and in a fair state, but no account people have cleaned it out.

We went up the steps and across the wide veranda into the lobby. I stopped at the desk imagining it was the way it use to be and I was about to sign my name in the register. Mother said she was glad it wasn't within walking distance because I'd spend hours mooning around. There were tatters of carpet hanging to the stairs which creaked under our tread. We explored the ball room, the dining hall, the kitchens and pantries, then the bedrooms, corridor after corridor, room after room. There are bits of broken furniture in nearly all the rooms and the kitchen is a clutter of rusty ovens, shattered china and battered pans. People have written their names on walls and woodwork, many Mystic names.

"They leave prints don't they, like animal tracks around a carcass," I said. Mighty looked at me as if he thought me touched in the head.

Some of the bedrooms were wonderful - or must have been. I imagined being there with the moon lighting the sea and wondered how anyone could have slept a wink.

Mighty said he guessed a moon couldn't keep awake what liquor had put to sleep. I knew from the way he rolled his tobacco quid to the other cheek and spat that he was going to tell stories about the place, but Mother looked at him and he shut up like a clam. I hope of all the people who gazed from those windows, at least one felt as I do about the sea.

We even looked in the servants quarters - little rooms just big enough for a bed, a chair and a wash stand. Ase was oppressed by them and when I lingered, Mother said impatiently that she couldn't see what there was to hold anyone's interest.

Ase says a moving picture company tried to buy the place in order to burn it for a scene in some picture they were making, but the owner wouldn't sell. I think Mr. Osgood was the last owner, and that it was he who gave the place a bad name. Ase use to know him and he says he was slippery as an eel.

Mother can remember when it was a nice place long before gambling, drinking and bad women from New York spoiled it for decent people. Seems to me they might have picked a less lovely place for their sinning.

After it had been closed a few years, the care taker was withdrawn. At the time the place was completely furnished.

Before we left we went down on the beach where to my utter surprize I found Alice, Betty, Jack, and Roland Perry in swimming. I felt as if I had been <u>miles</u> away! Seems the boys were headed for the Island in Roland's motor boat when they saw Alice and Betty out rowing and brought them along.

I wanted to go to Fishers Island - Alma Gluck summers there, but Ase wouldn't. He never lets me stay out as long as I like.

The sun was sinking when we turned homeward, and a fleet of little sailboats bobbed like egg shells on the tinted waves.

This has been a very interesting day.

1921

Mystic Island Hotel from an 1895 photo

Mystic Island Casino and Beach

Daddy,
Helen's grandfather,
at the Fort Rachel
docks

An Account of My Life

Aug. 31 - At last I can sit back and take account of stock. A lot has happened since Monday. To begin with Junior and Bob have been visiting Junior's Grandmother who lives next door to Cill. Junior is Emily's brother and while he isn't as homely as she, he is not handsome. Emily is the homeliest girl I have ever seen - in fact she is so homely she makes fun of her face. Junior is very tall, very lanky, with enormous bones. His Grandmother says it is going to take time to fill out that frame, but she guesses he will if he ever stops growing in one direction. He is a couple of years older than I, but up till now has never shown any interest in girls.

Early Monday morning we rowed to the raft. It was a splendid day with the water as calm as a mill pond. We laughed and talked and joked about little things I can't even remember now. When we got to the raft we found Johnnie, Phip and Pewee already there and not a bit glad to see us because they had planned to swim naked. I guess they figured if they teased us enough we'd be glad to leave, with that horrid Pewee muttering about "darn girls." They wanted Junior and Bob to stay and when they wouldn't were rude and fresh.

When we were hungry we landed at Mrs. Rogers, filled the boat with apples and rowed out again spending the whole day on the water.

In the evening the boys took us to the movies; it was Marguerite Clarke in "Scrambled Wives." Jr. said I looked like her which is a compliment, although she is not the type I admire.

On the way home we stopped at Mr. Ivers store for ice cream and then Junior walked home with me.

We spent the next day on the river, too, but this time we caught crabs.

At noon we went ashore - the boys to Jr's Grandmother's, while I stayed at Cill's. Everyone else had eaten, but we managed to make out and by the time the dishes were done, the boys were over again. We had a water fight at the well, and as usual, I was the one to get soaked to the skin. While I was drying out in the hot sun, Jr's Grandmother called us in and gave us home made ice cream, all we could eat.

She reminds me of Grandmother. I made her laugh by saying if we hung our family pictures in her sitting room and hers in ours, they'd feel right at home. The boys were supposed to go home that night, but she said they could stay another day if they telephoned Norwich for permission, which they did.

Junior is double jointed and can twist himself into all manner of awful, yet funny shapes. There is nothing romantic about double joints, but they are comical.

At 5:30 we rowed over to the raft where we stayed until dark. After supper we played Authors until we were tired of it, and then we made peanut butter fudge which turned out very good considering the way the boys bothered.

Junior walked home with me and was very quiet most of the way. He said he hated to leave in the morning, but he knew better than to ask his father to let him stay longer. The cost of the toll call would give him fits.

1921

I guess he must be tight fisted - Junior's father I mean. I said I couldn't recall ever having had more fun than I had had the past two days, and he said the same went for him too. I don't know whether I imagined it or not, but there seemed to be a <u>significant</u> tone in his voice. Then he went on to say Bob was a prince and Cill a lot of fun. I wanted for him to say something about <u>me</u>, but he only looked down and opened the gate. I had the queerest feeling that maybe he didn't like me after all. Of course being some older and taller he might think me just a kid. I felt put out with him.

"Bob is <u>awfully</u> nice, isn't he?" I said.

"Sure, he's alright." he answered sort of short like.

But he isn't my type," I added. "Besides he likes Cill."

"What type do you like?" he asked point-blank. "That Marcus guy?"

I said I liked several types and Marcus wasn't all of them.

He didn't seem to know what to say. I guess he didn't have nerve enough to ask if I liked him, and maybe he knew I wouldn't tell him. He said goodnight, but he didn't move; he said it again and didn't; finally he said "goodnight" and did.

Ase was up when I went in, and pretty good natured for a wonder. He said I looked like a cat that had eaten a canary.

They left at eight the next morning and Cill and I are at loose ends. She says Junior has a crush on me and that if I'd ever seen how he use to act with girls, I'd know it. She says he would never be alone with a girl if he could help it, and when he not only took me home, but made it plain he didn't want them tailing along too, she thought she'd <u>die</u> and Emily would never believe it. She said he acted sore when she mentioned Marcus, too. Then she tried to find out what I thought of him, but I was very cautious, because I don't know, exactly. I knew she wanted me to say Bob was crazy over her, so I did which pleased her very much. She also said something that sort of pricked me. "I <u>know</u> Jr's got a crush on you," she laughed. "Because he thinks you are pretty."

"What do you mean?" I asked.

"Well," she said. "Boys think you are pretty <u>after</u> they fall for you, but they never think so before."

"I know I'm not, really," I tossed my head. "But if they don't think I'm pretty <u>before</u>, why do they fall for me?"

"I don't know," Cill said. "I've often wondered."

Maybe she was only being frank, but if I said it she'd call it being catty! We rubbed each other the wrong way all morning. Mother will say we've been seeing too much of one another and that an overdose will bring on a quarrel any time. If Anna had made such a remark it would have been one thing, but for Cill who is <u>never</u> pretty - well, I think she had a nerve!

<u>Sept. 4</u> Ella has left for the Seminary and Elizabeth goes to Boston on the 12th. Wednesday Elizabeth Cutler left for New York. Every autumn we have to stay behind while the summer crowd goes back, but this year many of our year round crowd are leaving for school.

An Account of My Life

Sept. 17 - At last I am sixteen!

It is the dream of my life to go abroad. Imagine having something interesting to write about! The sea voyage would be <u>marvellous</u>, but when I think of Paris in the spring with the horse chestnut trees in bloom and wine at the cafes I almost <u>burst</u>. I want to see the Louvre and the Bastille and all the wicked interesting places, and the home of Jeanne D'Arc and Carcasonne and the Bridge at Avignon. I want to see the linden trees in Germany and drink beer and go thru the Black Forest. I want to see the Tower of London and the changing of the guards, and stop at the Cheshire Cheese and go to Suffolk because some of my people came from there, and see Stonehenge in the moonlight. Then I want to feed the pigeons at St. Marks and ride in a gondola past the Palaces of the Doges. When I think there are literally thousands of girls my age and <u>less</u> who have seen these things and more, I could die of envy. I should return an entirely different person.

The Old Randall Place

I think old houses like to be remembered. It is easy to forget them when they burn or are torn down. I think their stories or obituaries should appear in the newspapers without fail. A house does not have to have been slept in by Washington to make it interesting. There are a number around Mystic. Some have lost their families and are sad and lone, while others have dirty and careless people under their rooftrees. Perhaps it is better to burn than to have a scarred and dirty door.

Why! I never knew there was an old house torn down so that the Car Barn could be put up about the time I was born! I might never have known if Grandmother didn't speak of the old Randall place now and then. Today, from idle curiosity I asked, "Where is this old Randall houses anyway?" She told me. The car barn is so ugly. There was a ferry there too. Everything was ferried until the Bridge was built about a hundred years ago, and even later.

Old Jedediah Randall died before her day, Grandmother says. He wasn't a Mystic man, came from up Norwich Town way, she'd heard say, but he married Mary Burrows, old Elder Silas Burrow's daughter from out Fort Hill way, a Burrows connection. He kept a ship's store and ship yard on the land between the house and Main's Store, which was Batty's store in Grandmother's day and Jim Fish's before that, and he made money hand over fist.

In the War of 1812, wounded British soldiers were taken to the Randall house. That was when the British soldier was buried in the Packer Burying Ground. I always thought he went back to the Revolution, but she says no, she remembers her Grandmother Hempstead - that's my great, great, grandmother telling about it. Mary Hempstead was a young girl during the War of 1812. I said I didn't see why they didn't put him in the Burrows Burying Ground; it would be interesting to have a British soldier in ones graveyard. She said lands sake, how should she know! But she thought a while and said, "Unless because Capt. Packer's wife was related to Jedediah." I couldn't see what that had to do with it, so she said it was a Packer house before it was called the Randall place. I asked "why?" again and she said she presumed because it was Capt. Packer's, who built it so far as she knew. And then she told me to see what Horace Clift had to say in her *Historic Groton*. I did.

"Jedediah Randall was born in Norwich, April 1773 and moved to Mystic in 1807."

Young man in his thirties," Grandmother nodded. "I've heard that he was."

I skipped a line. "He located at the ferry landing with Capt. Edward Packer whose wife was Prudence Crary, a connection of Mr. Randall's."

"Both the Crary's and the Randalls were newcomers," she commented.

I skipped a few more lines because she told me practically everything. "Mr. Randall purchased from Capt. Packer, besides the buildings, a number of acres. -"

"He had a lot of git up and git," Grandma said approvingly. "Grandmother Hempstead knew him. She was a little girl when he came to Mystic. When does it say he died, or did Horace forget to put it in?"

"Eighteen fifty one," I read.

"I was a baby," she said. "I told you 'twas before my time. There was a son, I believe. My how that line has petered out."

It will be interesting imagining it out someday. I wonder if Mary Burrows and Prudence Crary laid out the dead British soldier because they were sorry for him and he was so far from home? I should think likely, because they needn't have given him a spot in their Burying Ground, carrying him up all those hills. They could have dug a hole anywhere or thrown him in the river - if they had been the kind of people to do such a thing.

Mother says she always loved that house. "I hated to see it torn down," she said, "but of course it was badly run down and rented out to just anyone. It was a big house with an ell and in the ell one of those divided doors - Dutch doors I guess they call them. No, not inside, it was an outside door. The top part was always open in warm weather. When we came back from Putnam an old man lived there. Seems to me his name was Richmond, though I can't say. After that, I remember when he died, someone lived there with a raft of children. It use to have a lovely garden running right down to the river's edge. Mary Hannah Packer's house must have been the nearest to the south."

To think of all that living - and now a car barn!

Sept. 20 Received a letter from Ella. She says she likes Northfield. Doesn't sound very exciting, but it must be better than Stonington High except in its distance from the sea. <u>That</u> I would find hard to bear. In Stonington, the rocks come almost under the windows and in high tide the waves break over them. We eat our lunches on the rocks with waves

An Account of My Life

slapping against them. There are water rats, great loathsome things, but I shut my eyes and wait for them to slither away.

The school is ugly as a jail inside, and to me, as oppressive. Sometimes I feel the noon hour will never come. When it comes at last I feel that nothing can be more heavenly than the breeze in my hair, the salt in my nostrils, the cleanness of it all after hours of dust, chalk and smelly school books. And when the bell rings it is like being hit in the stomach with a stone. In English class I sit near a window, a window purposely placed high, but affording me the sky a patch of sea and a wheeling gull. If I stretch or stand I can look upon the waves glittering in the sun and upon the boats like specks on the horizon. I love it stormy days when the fishing-boats are in and the grey waves wear white caps and the gulls are chalk white against the leaden sky. But fair days are the best. When I look back into the school room I am blind for a minute - and then faces emerge, and sounds, and scratched desks and the long expanse of greyish black board.

<u>Sept. 24</u> - A surprize party on Warren Fish last night. Juliet Haley and Byron Hatfield were there. Byron is Raymond's elder brother, but you'd never guess it as he is dark, hansome and romantic looking. Beside that, he has a wonderful voice.

Juliet is in her late twenties and very exotic looking. They make a perfectly stunning pair. She wore a scarlet skirt with a black sweater; her hair and eyes are black as night and her lips and cheeks are scarlet. How two women as plain as her mother and her sister, Juliet's Aunt Emily, can be any relation is beyond me. She lives in New York winters and the first day she comes back to Mystic is always special just because she is back. I adore her.

Most of the girls she grew up with are married and seem practically middle aged with babies and all that, but Juliet doesn't change exept to grow a little richer and a little lovelier.

Byron is simply mad about her. Some of the catty older people who don't know Romance when they meet it face to face, say he is after her money, because he is too good looking and artistic to care for work. I might believe it if Juliet weren't so lovely. One <u>couldn't</u> marry her for her money. Her clothes are exquisite and she uses divine perfume - the kind you can't smell all the time, but which comes out in exciting little puffs. I don't suppose I shall ever be like her.

<u>Oct. 8</u> Sometimes Grandma sings a song about "jolly good ale." To-day I found it in a book of English verse. It was written by John Still who was the Bishop of Bath back in the sixteenth century. She sings only a few of the verses, so I showed her the whole poem at which she sniffed saying she didn't think the lines she didn't know were any great loss. I asked her where she first came by it and she replied that she had never read it; in fact, never knew it was in print or who wrote it. She'd always known it

and thought her Mother had learned it from <u>her</u> mother. It would be interesting to trace it back thru the Burrowses to the first one who heard or read it.

The Glory Band conducted our B.Y.P.U. Meeting to-night. I shall never feel the same toward them though it isn't their fault. Of course, I have previously written, all of us were rather gone on Mr. Bailey, but only because it was exciting and rather fun, but Nellie, Miss Brooks, who is at <u>least</u> twenty seven went <u>really</u> crazy over him. That is why she took us to Potters Hill. The first time she needed us to take the cuss off it so to speak, but after that she went several times <u>alone</u>. Of course she is very religious and sings in the choir which I suppose she considers a bond between them. Well, they say Mr. Bailey said he would not be made a conquest of "that woman." Seems his wife didn't like it. They say Nellie even wrote letters to him. The darn fool! I have all the sympathy in the world for Romance, but when I think of how strick she has been with us, and of the times she has tattled on us for whispering and talking to boys! I do despise a hypocrite! Grandma says she is carrying too much sail now a days.

<u>Oct. 14</u> - The living-room floor is being painted and I am sitting on a sofa surrounded by furniture shoved out of place.

Junior and Emily are down for the week-end. Cill has always wanted Emily and Jr. to like me and now that they do she acts sort of jealous.

<u>Oct. 17</u> - We have had a glorious time. Last evening we went for a walk - Emily, Jr., Cill and I. I don't believe I ever laughed so much in my life! Such fun!

They went back to Norwich late Sunday afternoon. Emily says Junior talks about me all the time and doesn't care now much they tease him though hithertofor very touchy on the subject of girls. He even wanted to spend the summer in Mystic with his Grandmother, the coming summer, I mean, but he is not going to be allowed to do it.

After they left, Cill, Glad and I sat lonesomely on the garden wall and talked.

<u>Nov. 1</u> Cill and I are going to Norwich on a visit, I don't know just when.

>   Alone, on the rim of a curving beach
> 'Twixt the rippling waves and the sand
>   My face full turned to the open sea
>   And my back to the dull, dry land

<u>Nov. 3</u> I have just found a picture of Miss Montgomery in a book catalogue and have cut it out for my scrap book. I'd love to write to her again, but Ase says "don't be a damn nuisance," I wish I <u>knew</u>.

Sat with Grandma this evening until the lamp was lit. She sang her special songs which is a treat. Her voice is sweet although cracked. I wish I could sing because it would please her to have me join in, but I have no voice at all and cannot even carry a tune.

She sang "Scotlands Burning", "Tenting Tonight", "Lorena," "The Daring Young Man on The Flying Trapeze," "Little Nell of Narragansett Bay" "Three Black Crows", We'll Hang Jeff Davis To a Sour Apple Tree" and "Polly-waddle-doodle all the Day." She knows lots more, but she gets tired. "Poor Old Ned" makes me sad to the bone.

When she's like this - quiet, with her hands in her lap, I forget all about her strictures and her scolding. She isn't a pretty woman - not even a good looking one now, but she use to be pale and interesting looking when she was young.

Once, someone told her she was as white as the flower for which she was named. She was named for a New York girl who summered in Mystic: Camelia McManus was her name.

<u>Nov. 6</u> Harold Smith is one of the nicest boys I have ever known. When he and Billy Maxson were at Camp last summer, Billy says he was just swell. Poor Billy was dropped by his nurse when a baby and doesn't grow anymore. When the boys went on long hikes and Billy got tired, Harold stayed behind and even carried him. He read to him nights too. It wouldn't mean much for some boys to drop behind but Harold is just about Billy's age and like his father Dr. Smith, tall and strong and broad shouldered.

<u>Nov. 11</u> It is Armistice Day and at two minutes past twelve all traffic and commerce came to a stand still and every head was supposed to be bowed in honor of the Unknown Soldier who was buried at that time. And I forgot! I thought of it a few minutes before - and then forgot, thereby cheating myself of a solemn moment. It is far more thrilling than when the great Caruso Memorial Candle was lighted.

<u>Nov. 12</u> Today while Glad and I were at the C.H., Mr. Wright phoned in for the Yale-Princeton football score. It was 13-7 in favor of Yale. Marshall Foche was a spectator. I should like to have been there wearing a crysanthemum.

<u>Nov. 13</u> Father pulled a nice trick on me! He said, "Have you seen the picture of the Unknown Soldier in the paper? A fine looking chap." I started to say "no" when the little warning bell tingled inside of me.

"No, and I'm not likely to," I snapped, feeling cross at my narrow escape. For if I had fallen for it, he would have twitted me mercilessly. As it was, he was quite pleased that I was mentally alert even when entirely off my guard. He said he had tried it on several people and every one of

1921

them said, "No, let me see it." He told them he bet I wouldn't be caught and they bet I would.

It sounds terribly dumb - but he says these impossible things in such a casual, disarming way! If you are thinking of other things and attending with only half a mind, it is <u>fatally</u> easy to make a stupid answer.

<u>Nov. 18</u> - Nearly a week has passed. My life is so monotonous. After piano practice, I do my homework and go to bed. Up at 6:30, eat breakfast and start out again. Last quarter I was third on the Honor Roll. If I hadn't made such heavy sailing of the first year! However, it is useless to repine.

<u>Nov. 21</u> Dick Wheeler came for me this morning in his flivver. He lives in North Stonington. I didn't know he was coming, but Florence will never believe it.

<u>The Day After Thanksgiving</u> - Wednesday night a Thanksgiving service was held in place of Prayer Meeting. Anna and Elizabeth Cutler are here for the holidays, but Ella remains at Northfield. It was snowing when the meeting came to an end and we walked home with soft, feathery flakes melting against our warm faces. Anna made us promise to come down to her house Thanksgiving afternoon. She told some of her experiences in the hospital, some of which were funny, but many were disgusting although necessary. Ugh! none of that for me!

<u>Christmas Eve</u> - There are <u>weeks</u> when I don't write a word in this Diary, but sooner or later the craving comes and I itch for pen and ink and fair white paper.

Junior has sent a big box of candy and Emily has invited us to visit her until school resumes after New Years. Don't know yet whether I can go or not, but the Family has it under consideration. I saw a very interesting boy in New London the other day. Mother and I had been shopping and were taking the train to Mystic, instead of the trolley. This boy wasn't handsome, but very self possessed. I named him Maxwell Griffith, not because I particularly like the name, but because it flashed thru my mind.

<u>Dec. 25</u> - A very nice Christmas. Grandma gave me a cameo lavaliere and I had a number of books, a bracelet and a flask of perfume etc. The tree looked gorgeous although rather straggly at the base. As usual Ase waited until the last minute before ordering it and was indignant because they didn't send a perfect one.

Went to S.S. where I found everyone pleasantly excited and properly devout. Walked up to Priscilla's in the afternoon. Marion home and very entertaining. There was an abundance of candy, nuts and fruit, and when it grew dark we lighted the bay berry candles and sat cross legged on the hearth. Norman brought root beer from the cellar and we were too blissfully content to move; however we had to because we had promised

Elizabeth and Alice Colby that we would go to the Methodist entertainment with them. It was very boresome, but the long cold walk made up for it.

Last night the C.H. had its' Christmas Tree Program and for a week the huge outdoor tree is to be strung with colored lights. As we hurried home over the hard ground with the sharp cold air stiffening our faces, I really <u>felt</u> "peace on earth, goodwill toward men."

1922

January 5, 1922

Back from Norwich with so much to write! Priscilla and I left on the morning of December thirty-first, taking the trolley car to Groton and the train from there to Norwich where we were met by Junior and Mrs. Gallup who drove us out to Laurel Hill.

Emily greeted us at the door with the three cats, David, Pat and Judith winding themselves about her legs.

I like Mrs. Gallup and am especially fond of Mr. Gallup. In appearance he is a small, wizened farmer, but he has quite a good income and comes from an old family, Grandma says, though not as old as ours. Being fond of music he has a fine victrola and more records than I dreamed any one person could possess. I like the operas because of their stories, but instrumental music is my favorite. One of the records I loved best was Mischa Elman's "Spanish Dance" which is one of his favorites too and made us very congenial. We listened to records for hours on end. He would say, "see what you think of this", or "you'll like that," one leading to another or serving to remind him of something else, until he had Junior who looked very disgruntled, hunting for old records put away on a high shelf. Emily plays the piano much better than I do, but Junior plainly suffers and is completely unmusical.

Mr. Gallup discovered I liked old books and had some in the family, so he showed me a very old book bound between wooden covers laced together by deer throngs. I was thrilled. He asked "why?" and waited for me to answer. I wasn't exactly coherent on the spur of the moment, but I said think of a deer standing alone in a clearing on a lovely day years and years ago; of a hunter's bullet from an old muzzle loader like the one in the attic, shattering the stillness, of the curing of the hide and cutting it in strips and binding the covers so cleverly they have never come apart though hundreds upon hundreds of hands have handled it. He nodded his head like the old Mandarin in the fairy tale and seemed pleased. Emily hooted derisively and said, "Well Pa, at last you've found someone like you."

Mrs. Gallup showed me an old willow-ware platter which is cracked and seamed and altogether lovely. They have an old desk like ours mahogany instead of curly maple, and theirs has a secret drawer! I must look again.

One of the most interesting things is the Insane Asylum which is quite near. Emily and Junior had a great many stories to tell and racked their brains for more. Junior says crazy people hate water and simply scratch when given a bath. And he said very solemnly that when water touched them they hollered "fire." Living with Ase has made me cautious about accepting things out of hand. Emily says when the wind is right and the windows open at night you can hear them wailing, wailing and always when there is a moon. I can believe <u>that</u> because of Jimmie and his violin.

There is a Dr. Wilcox who believes the hopelessly insane should be mercifully put to death. I think it a very humane idea, but of course there are a lot of things to be considered. Many people are shocked at the idea and it is a sure fire topic for an argument.

On New Year's Eve, Emily gave a small party at which we had a very good time. There was a girl named Marion Royce for whom Cill seemed to take a liking. I didn't like her at sight and still don't. She is plain and coarse.

<u>Sunday afternoon:</u> This account is moving forward in hitches. Where was I? Oh, how Priscilla can even pretend to like that girl is more than I can fathom. I have heard her criticize girls severely who weren't any more common. Bob use to like Marion (she <u>does</u> have a way with boys,) and all last summer Cill hated her, but <u>now</u> she falls all over her. This Marion can play the piano a little and sing worse, both of which she does a great deal without being asked. Her hair is dull, her complexion muddy, her teeth an off white and her hands grubby. She <u>has</u> interesting eyes, grey, almost luminous, rather weird; when you look into them you find yourself forgetting her many imperfections.

The boys like her, even Junior who either does or pretends to because he doesn't want the other boys to think he is missing anything. All of which gave me a very peculiar feeling. When I first saw her I felt rather sorry for her as you do for a girl who is not pretty or has no nice clothes to help her out. My experience has been that such a one is usually meek and apt to think I am sort of wonderful. Well, this Marion didn't think so at all. In fact, she acted as if she was a raving beauty gowned in something from Paris and I was a nobody from the back woods in a gingham dress. I was so surprized I let her grab Junior away from right under my nose, not because she likes him, but just to show she could. Although I felt - well, <u>vexed,</u> I had sense enough not to show it and I got to work on Junior myself in a manner of speaking. Before the party was over she was regarding me with respect at least, and satisfying resentment when Charlie showed signs of liking me.

Sunday, we went to Sunday School. Several boys asked Junior to introduce them to me, he told me later. "Well, why didn't you?" I demanded indignantly." Haven't you any manners?"

"I've got sense," he growled. Darn him! Some of them were good looking too.

Emily says she believes I have a crush on her father instead of on her brother and she is not far wrong. <u>Why</u> can't Junior be like his Father! I don't believe that boy possesses a single even half way cultivated taste.

Mr. Gallup and I discussed books and music in the most satisfying manner. We have both read *"If Winter Comes"* by Hutchinson. As a rule Mr. Gallup doesn't care for modern authors, but he found something in this novel he liked. He asked if I knew "Ode To The West Wind" from which Hutchinson took the title: "Oh wind, If Winter Comes can spring be far behind." I said I had read it but not memorized it, and so he got Shelly from the bookshelves and read it over and over. Junior acted as if it were really more than he could bear. He has no poetry in his system at all.

Jan. 13 There was Minstrel practice after school and after that, Mary and I stopped to watch the basket-ball game. How I envy girls who are good at sports, for I am not good at games of any kind. Even as a child a hard game of Hide-and-Seek or Snap-the-Whip would give me a blinding headache.

When we left the hall, there was no trolley car in sight, so we started to walk toward Mystic. It was cold, clear and invigorating. When we passed the ice pond we were tempted to stop, but didn't. Presently, Billy came along in his old delivery truck already crowded with boys and girls he had picked up along the way. Leila, Pat, and Florence were in front with Billy, so it was quite a problem where to put us. Finally, Mary sat in Florence's lap and I sat on the floor with the door open and my feet on the running board with Jack standing on the running board more or less fencing me in with his legs. Fortunately I could see out a little to one side of him, for the sky was golden with bands of amethyst much too wonderful to have missed. I loved the fields stretching brown and bare, the hills dark with pine and cedar and the cold blue flat endless sea so much I shivered. And when the lights twinkled in the windows and I saw the evening star I felt as if violins were playing. All of which was very wonderful in the midst of laughter, shrieks and the rattling truck. I was so quiet Billy, who was too hemmed in to see me, asked if I had fallen out along the way. It is not often that I can detach myself from noisy sound and simply float, which is a delicately, beautiful sensation.

I am thrilled to the very depth of me! At last I have seen "The Shiek" - and Rudolph Valentino is a creature far, far beyond my dreams.

Everyone, simply everyone has read the book except me, I verily believe: people on the trolley cars, even the teachers at school, but as Ase would not allow me to buy it and it was impossible to borrow a copy for more than a few minutes, I knew nothing beyond what the girls fortunate enough to have read it, cared to divulge which was naturally just enough to whet one's curiosity.

Ase didn't even want me to see the movie! If I hadn't I should never have forgiven him.

Well, last night Leona, Alice and I saw it and have talked of nothing else since. Of course we had been tingling with keenest anticipation for ages due to the posters, leaflets and masses of advertizing, but if I live to advanced years I shall never experience a greater thrill than when he flashed on the screen. His eyes so slumbrous yet burning, his patent leather hair, his lips - words fail me.

When he kissed Agnes Ayes, who was Lady Diana, I felt faint. How could she have resisted him for a moment? I should be almost afraid to meet him, because of the terrific strain it would bring to bear upon my moral scruples which as yet have not been under any strain.

Grandmother and Mother saw the matinee, and Grandmother instead of being shocked as one might expect said right out she didn't know when she had enjoyed a movie so much which completely took the wind out of Ase's sails.

I am certain the effects of this movie will be felt by every woman in America.

Jan. 15 - Isn't anything exciting ever going to happen to me? You'd think something might. Even my social life is dull as ditch water. May's party was no fun at all, the boys simply pills. One can well imagine when I say Marcus was by far the most attractive boy there. He may be stupid, but not so stupid he didn't realize it - I in turn acted indifferent, not deigning to notice him until I found myself paired with a boy I dislike, when finding the situation intolerable, I cast my eyes around for a way out. Marcus was pretending an interest in Myra which was down right ridiculous.

"Marcus," I said quickly, "I have something I must tell you. Jim will amuse Myra for a few minutes, I am sure."

So, before anyone recovered their senses I walked off with him out of the room and closed the door. Then, finding a seat on the back stairs, I laughed at his scowling face.

"Well! What is it?" he demanded rudely.

"Why, nothing of course," I said. "Do sit down and stop glowering at me. You know perfectly well you'd rather be with me than with Myra."

To my surprize he didn't sit down, and for a moment I thought he was actually going to walk away, but instead he lost his temper and waxed most fluent.

"Don't be idiotic," I said, patiently.

You wouldn't look at me if there was anyone here you liked better," he flared accusingly.

"If I like some one better, why should I?" I demanded.

He raged on and on until I snapped, "Oh be quiet! Anyone would think I'd done you a violent injury. You're always wanting to be with me, so why not make the best of it."

At last he began to show signs of running down, and heaving a shivery sigh he sat down beside me.

Helen," he said. "how can you be so -."

"So what?"

"Lord, I dunno," he said feebly.

"Marcus," I explained patiently. "I don't like being with Jim. You should have rescued me in the first place and I'd not have had to be so high handed. It was mean of you to let me get in such a fix. You don't care a red cent for Myra, a girl who is double-jointed and always cracking her knuckles to be funny! I though I was doing both of us a favor, but maybe it was a bit high handed. Of course I wouldn't have done it if I hadn't thought you'd be glad. I never thought perhaps you didn't want me. Would you rather be with Myra after all?"

He didn't answer at once and to my surprize I felt a pang that must have been jealousy. Imagine!

"If I'd known how you felt about her I wouldn't have done it," I said sadly. "I guess you'll have to forgive me for old times sake. I've just got the habit of turning to you Marcus, you've always been so good."

"Oh gosh, Helen," he said. "You know I don't care a hoot for anyone but you. I try to and I can't, the minute I see you it starts all over again."

"I guess if you went away you'd forget about me," I sniffed. "Men are like that."

"I'm not. If I went away for ninety years and came back I'd feel that way all over again."

Then he put his arms around me and asked very seriously, "<u>Do</u> you care a darn if I like Myra or anyone, or is this just one of your games?"

"Well," I answered honestly. "I guess I am a little jealous."

And as proof that I must be really bad at heart I confess with shame that when he doesn't talk and concentrates on kissing me I am a little thrilled, because he is strong and gentle (but not too gentle), and respectful, and he is likewise big and clean and nice. If only he weren't so stupid! I should like to feel the same about him ten minutes running, but I can't. He could be magnificent with his smooth dark skin, black hair and eyes, and he isn't nor ever shall be.

Sometimes I wonder what devil has gotten under my skin. I find myself doing silly things almost in spite of my Inner Self, things I writhe away from when I have a wakeful night. I frequently instigate a reform which lasts for a few days during which I am unaturally quiet and subdued to everyone's wonder. I read and think and behave like the girls in the Anne or the Little Colonel books, but sooner or later I burst out.

Even if this isn't precisely the fun I want, it is all there is.

I forgot to record that at last I have read *"The Shiek"* and was somewhat shocked although already more or less conversant with the hot parts. Somehow reading it alone with no one to make jokes, I was shocked and my ears rang. I have written a poem.

I hear the crying of the gulls
And go because I cannot stay
I go without a backward glance
Though woods are sweet in May.
When Spring comes round, I'll think of earth
new turned so what if I pine a bit?
With a white sailed ship a part of me
And I a part of it!

An Account of My Life

<u>Jan. 20</u> Sometimes I wish Ase had more conventional friends. No wonder I inadvertently use words and phrases shocking to some. Kirk and Dr. Lew are bad enough, but Peter Marcus the artist is infinitely worse. I have heard that he is a Jew, but I don't know. Ase says, "What to hell if he is!" Well, I just wondered. He is too <u>something</u>, I don't know what to be Yankee, though the idea that a Yankee has to be a tight, dry, thin lipped individual is laughable; however there is a difference.

Peter could be interesting if he looked more like an artist and less like a prize fighter. He is nearly always bare headed, wears flannel shirts and baggy tweeds and being rich doesn't give a damn. I should very much like to be rich.

I don't mind the stories about his drinking parties - wicked though I may be, they sound like fun, but the things he says are far too Elizabethan. His stories are funny, but can't be written down because of the vulgar words he uses. He hates la-de-dah women and one of his worst and funniest stories is about such a person and the beautiful Persian jar in his studio.

One time I said, "In Shakespeare's day, the chamber maids threw the slops from the bed room windows into the street below sometimes splashing people. <u>Plumbing</u> has improved since then."

"But not the excrement," he said and roared with laughter.

He is not well bred. But then, look at Shakespeare? Oh dear, it's <u>so</u> hard to know. According to Peter a prude is the most vulgar thing imaginable. I am not a prude - at least I don't <u>think</u> I am, but I do find many ordinary things make me sick when rudely brought to mind.

<u>Jan. 24</u> - Mid-year exams. Got 92% in English. Letter from Junior. If I knew for a <u>certainty</u> I was destined to live an exciting life I might bear the present monotony with patience. Perhaps I am, but it is awfully slow getting under way.

<u>Fri.</u> - Exams over. Marks 99, 98, 92, 90 and 84. Part of the Latin was a retake so that doesn't count. If I could keep it up for any length of time I should be quite brilliant, but just about the time I get the name for it I come up against something I don't like or don't understand, or a teacher with whom I am in not in tune, or for no apparent reason, I go into a fuzzy period and decline with startling rapidity.

Kirk does not think it matters. He was consistently brilliant as a youth until having been forced on and on by his family, his ambition completely deserted him. He left a brilliant future as a New York surgeon to come back here to live on his income and for his hobbies. He says he is completely "burned out." Nothing makes him so furious as to hear of anyone "pushing" a boy or a girl. When he discovered Mrs. Morgan wanted Toby to lead his classes and made his life miserable because he couldn't, he gave her a terrible talking to she says. He declared Toby was just an ordinary, an agily bright boy and she was only feeding her vanity by her insistence. He shocked her still more by denouncing women who feed on their young; but she felt better when he said if let alone and allowed to develop along his own lines Toby would have a better life than the more brilliant ones ever know.

"Look at me!" he roared. And she did.

He ought to know," she told Mother. "If ever a man wasted talents. What an odd stick he is!

He is something of an artist, he writes books and magazine articles on fishing, besides being a very able surgeon, and here he sits in Mystic when everyone had him marked for a great career. Doesn't marry, hates women, all that brain plain going to waste. And he is queer as Dick's hat band. The other day he walked into the parlor and without a word sat down at the piano and played and improvised for a solid hour, then he got up and walked out. I found out later he fancied his piano slightly out of tune, and feeling the need of one he used mine! Always said he liked the tone!

There was the time he brought us some trout. He walked in, put it in the ice box and walked out without a word. No one saw him or knew anything about it until Mother went to the ice box for something and found the trout.

Ase told Kirk that he wished he knew from one month to the next if I would lead the class or flunk out. It _is_ hard on him, because just about the time he starts bragging about me, I go flat; and when he becomes convinced I am down never to rise again, I shoot up. I shall never forget the year at the Academy when I led the class for months getting such high marks people stopped to congratulate Ase. After maintaining an average of 98% consistently I started down hill again until I was among the lowest. The teacher was bewildered, Ase frantic, and I chittering with nerves. Nothing did any good, and the more I forced myself the fuzzier my head became. Finally, after suffering tortures I began to shoot up again - not so high, but decently so. What makes me like this? How wonderful it would be to have a well regulated brain!

Jan.-- Perhaps I am not really in love with Rudolph Valentino, but I might as well be; all the boys look _so_ homely.

"The Old Oaken Bucket," a moving picture produced by a company called the Lithograph Co. was shown in the Mystic Theatre last night. It was of particular interest to us because the scenes were taken at Danny Brown's and Deans Mills. Mary and I are very fond of Danny's place, in fact it is one of our milestones so to speak. We often say "as far as Danny's, or a little beyond Danny Brown's."

It was exciting to see the old house and barn and well on the screen. Both Danny and his wife had small parts. They came to the matinee performance as the guests of the management. Besides the Company paid them $300 and they need the money.

I am pleased that they could have such a stroke of luck. I guess it is the easiest money Old Danny every earned.

The movie itself was silly.

An Account of My Life

<u>Feb. 15</u> - Sunday afternoon. Mary and I walked to Fort Hill after we had had our Sunday dinners. The Lake of Shining Waters was cold and grey in the winter light. It isn't a lake of course, but I wanted one like Anne. In summer cardinal flowers grow along its banks and the waxy flowers or arrow root lift their heads.

We passed Danny Brown's house which reveals itself almost paintless now that it is stripped of vines and flowers. The back yard is sharp cut with frozen wagon ruts, and everything looks sad and drear.

<u>Feb. 20</u> - Gladys and I saw Richard Barthlenuss in "Way Down East." Oh, but it was lovely and sad - the sort of sadness you can enjoy. I <u>love</u> Lillian Gish.

An awful thing has happened; the dirigible "*Roma*" blew up somewhere over Virginia and a great many were killed.

<u>Feb. 25</u> - Constance is starting a Diary. I guess it is in our blood.

<u>Mar 11</u> - Mary, Althea and I went for pussy-willows this afternoon. We found a lot of them in the swampy place where they grow large and plump with a lovely faint rose showing thru the silvery fur. I shall send Elizabeth a tiny twig of them to show her spring is here as I have done before. She says she starts counting the days until she'll be here, when the pussy-willows drop out of the envelope.

The ponds are spilling full from the thawy days and there is the haunting smell of moist, dark earth.

On the way home we stopped at Danny's well for a drink and discovered that he is going to have his house painted. I am glad!

I used rouge for the first time today - but very sparingly and Mother never noticed.

<u>Mar. 20</u> - Sheets of rain and now, a blanket of fog. I didn't realize how funny that was going to sound! I love little feathery wisps of fog creeping over the marshes, but this suffocating white wall is depressing.

Mary thinks I am awful because I don't even pretend to like babies in their early age. No beautiful glow of in-born mother love wells up in me. Either the books are wrong, or I am.

<u>Mar. 22</u> - Back from Norwich and a wonderful time as always.

Junior gave me a book on operas, but it was his father who suggested it. Junior is silly. No, that isn't fair or entirely true, but then, what <u>is</u> completely anything? If I liked him as much as he wants me to, I might be embarrassed by his affection, but I shouldn't think it silly. When he gets cross I am not at all bothered. I simply leave him alone until he gets over it. It gives one a lot of power, but what is the good of it if one does not feel like using it, except maybe occasionally?

Our moods never fit. For instance I was glad to see him at the station; he looked almost good looking and I always feel fondest of him when I haven't seen him too recently. I smiled expecting him to act glad to see me, but he looked away, grunted out something about "train's late" and picked up our bags. He might have been meeting anyone and not too gladly at that! What small talk he managed was either general or addressed to Cill. I didn't <u>care</u>, neither did I like it.

After supper I sat on the couch with the "Norwich Bulletin" spread out on it when he came striding across the room, and sat down heavily, rumpling the paper badly.

When I sputtered indignantly, he wadded it up and dumped it on the floor. And then he reached for my hand. I thought for a moment he was going to kiss it and thrilled, but he only glared at it. I pulled it away, only to find his arm around me. It occurred to me that if I objected to one thing he immediately did something a little worse - or maybe I should say, <u>advanced</u>, and so purely from curiosity I objected. He kissed me.

Emily and Priscilla hooted at him, only laughing harder when he told them where to go. At that point Mr. Gallup entered the room and we played victrola records much to Junior's disgust.

When I feel in the mood to be noticed he is as likely as not talking about machinery or showing me something in a "Popular Mechanics" magazine, and if I feel like being left alone he is sure to act silly. He hasn't an iota of poetry in his system and less than no understanding of women. When Emily, Cill and I talk about Rudolph he becomes sarcastic at once and asks "What do you see in that slimey Wop that's so wonderful?"

Emily replied sweetly, "Little Brother, <u>you'll</u> never know."

Cill said he was jealous, at which he yelled furiously that he wouldn't be a "grease ball" for anything. That was too much to be born in silence and I told him indignantly, that if women were fascinated by him, it was because there was a dearth of Romance in their lives. "I bet you got that out of a movie magazine," he said scornfully, but he looked at me in such a thoughtful, considering sort of way, I regretted my outburst.

"Romance" I said feebly, "is <u>not</u> squeezing the breath out of a person!"

<u>March 29</u> An article in a movie magazine has started me to thinking on a serious subject. According to Rudolph Valentino, the English speaking race is too cold and too given to senseless formalities. He says there are many beautiful things about passion and that it is not a low form of love. I wonder? I am not aware of having a passionate nature, but one can't tell what is lying dormant in one.

Marriage seems harsh on Romance to me, but the other way is wrong of course. I shall marry of course, but I never dream of white satin and wedding veils as girls are supposed to do - in fact all that fuss almost discourages me to start with. I think, wicked though it may be, that Experiences must be interesting and illuminating. Marriage, unless one does it three or four times, limits one so dreadfully. What sweet maiden fancies I do have! Imagine Anne thinking such terrible things.

Cill and Katherine saw him in "The Four Horseman of the Apocalypse" from the novel by Ibanez in New London, and they say he is even more wonderful, if possible. Kat says she would go to the ends of the earth with him. Well, it would be easier for her than for me, as her Mother is a French Creole her father brought back from Louisiana on one of his voyages.

<u>April 4</u> - I am reading Schopenhauer's Essays, but without enthusiasm.

I asked Kirk if he had any thing by Dostoievsky and he said, "Wouldn't tell you if I did. In God's name, what started you of on that tack?" So I read him what Nietzche says about "the scum and dross of society, diseases of the nerves, childish imbecility seems to have given each other rendezvous... a proper material for the pen of Dostoievsky."

He puffed his pipe surveying me as he would something under a microscope.

<u>April 20</u> - A crowd of us walked to Porters Rock today. I prefer its other name Lovers Leap secretly, though Marcus makes it sound plain silly.

Capt. John Mason and his men camped out at Porters Rock the night before they attacked the Pequot Village. Even on a nice day there is something strange about the place, or maybe I imagine it. Perhaps Capt. Mason thought his awful act necessary but I should not want it on my conscience, and though I am descended from him I never look at his monument without wanting to spit at it.

1922

Latham Avery's grave in the Burrows Cemetery Top of Fort Hill, Groton

Capt. John Mason statue where it stood on Pequot Hill

Constance dressed as a Dutch girl

Helen (left) and Constance

An Account of My Life

<u>May 16</u> -What a relief to have a real journal again ! I have been waiting for my Liberty Loan money, my allowance being accounted for and the Family not in a giving mood.

One night last week when Mary, Jerry, Jack and I were walking home from Stonington a beautiful red Stuz roadster came into sight and Jerry hailed it for a ride.

He did it entirely for deviltry not expecting anyone with such an expensive car to bother with school kids - trucks and flivers are usually our lot; however the man actually stopped and let us squeeze in and all over him. Jerry was so surprized he never let a peep out all the way home. Such luxury! How I should love to be rich.

It is queer but I remember seeing Rudolph in "Camille". Cill says she remembers that I spoke of the slim, dark fascinating man who played with Nazimova although he looked much younger than she. He was unknown then and while I hoped I should see him again sometime, I had more or less forgotten him until the Shiek. Cill envies me. She says its almost like having known him as a boy.

I have a swell picture of him and Nazimova embracing. We sat looking at it and sighing.

Cill said, "Can you imagine any of the boys we know -"

And I said "no" promptly.

After a few seconds she asked, "Would you like any of them to hold you like that, looking down at you like that?"

"I'd burst out laughing," I said. And we laughed and laughed at the thought.

But with Rudolph!" she signed.

"Oh, well!" I exclaimed and we sighed together.

"Would you be frightened?" she asked. "I guess I should - a little."

I said I didn't think so and she said, "Aren't you afraid - you know?"

"I don't know what you mean," I said slowly. "I don't see why one should be afraid of a man. Of course if you saw a Bill Sykes you'd be afraid of a black eye or a beating, but you'd be afraid of a strong cruel woman the same way. Being afraid of - love, I can't imagine that."

"Not even the first night?" Cill was embarrassed, but curious.

"Well," I said honestly. "It seems to me I'd be more interested than anything else."

"You don't think its horrid the way the old folks think?"

"Not after seeing Rudolph," I said. "Do you?"

"But suppose we never meet Rudolph or anyone like him? Suppose its just some ordinary man?"

I shuddered. "That," I said. "Would be awful."

Cill and I talked on serious subjects quite often. Its not like talking with Mary who always leaves one feeling sick and disgusted.

Cill said: "When you hear about girls - well like Marion, doesn't it make you wonder how she <u>could</u>? I mean he is such a pill and they never acted in love, only silly and mushy. She isn't - I mean she wasn't like those girls who are always doing awful things. We've known her for years and never noticed anything, she was a good kid. It just seemed to happen. We never even knew she thought of such things."

"Well," I said. "Maybe she didn't. Maybe as you say, it just happened."

"But don't you see!" Cill looked frightened. "It could happen to anyone - even to us."

Well," I said. "If I ever feel such a fit coming on I shall think of Grandmother and that will scare it out of me." She often says she would rather see me dead at her feet than in trouble. She means it, too. Well I'd just as soon be dead.

The wisteria is especially thick with bloom this year and when I breathe in its fragrance I can feel my toes curl up with estacy. I do my studying under the apple trees and sometimes when I open my books in class I find pink petals hiding away between the pages.

I sit there long after it is too dark to see the print, watching the lighthouse wink its yellow eye.

<u>May 17</u> Rudolph is married to Winifred Hudnut the perfume man's daughter. Well, I don't care - much. If I don't see him and get started all over again. Some of the girls are broken hearted.

I should like to fall in love - but with whom? Sometimes I wonder if there is anything wrong with my nature. I don't think there has <u>ever</u> been one in the Family - an old maid, I mean.

The kitchen is being painted and the living-room papered. All I can hear is the slap of brushes and the crackle of wall paper while every one of the three men is whistling a different tune.

Guess I'll take DeQuincy's "Confessions of an Opium Eater" and read under the trees.

<u>Sunday</u> Feel very despondent. I long for something. I don't know what, exactly. My room is being done over and I am staying at Grandmother's. I feel like crawling off somewhere and having a good cry.

<u>June --</u> Junior and Emily down. Junior was here when I got back from the library. We decided to go up to his Grandmother's for the day. I was glad to see him and for a wonder he didn't rub me the wrong way.

On July 2nd we have the installation of B.Y.P.U. officers with the usual speeches. The church service is omitted for that evening. Emily and Junior are coming down for it and we, Cill and I, are going back with them to stay over the 4th.

I have a speech - quite a long one. Boat Race Day - Yale won, Didn't get over although I wanted to.

<u>June 29</u> - I wish a good big circus would come to town. You have to go to New London if you want anything more than a traveling show with a

An Account of My Life

mangy lion. I'm not allowed to go to New London alone and the Family can think up a dozen reasons for not going. Daddy loved circuses.

I am reading Keats: almost too beautiful.

July 9 - Back from Norwich with such a lot to write! Sunday, July 2nd, Emily, Wallace and Junior spent the afternoon with us and attended the installation at church. We drove to Norwich directly after the meeting. I should have enjoyed the drive if let alone but with Wallace at the wheel, Junior was free to lavish his attention on me. We hadn't been a mile before I was sick to death of him.

Oh, I don't understand myself! I <u>like</u> Junior, but I don't like to have him kiss me. He <u>knows</u> I don't, but acts as if he thought I didn't know my own mind!

Mr. & Mrs. G. are very strict and old fashioned although they think themselves unusually broad minded and understanding. I think my offishness with Junior pleases them. I think he is getting too old to be managed so much, but Grandma says <u>not</u> as they figure ages. She says neither of them was young when they married, which explains why Mr. G is an old man, more like a Grandfather than a father. None of them Gallups <u>or</u> Slacks were ever known to do anything rash except possibly Jr's Uncle Will who sometimes drinks too much cider after it is hard.

Mrs. G. dislikes "bold girls" - that is why she doesn't approve of Marion R., who as she puts it, "leads the boys on." Well, she doesn't have to complain about me on that score as I spend my time saying "no" and "don't."

When we arrived I drew a breath of relief. Shortly after, we drove Wallace home as he lives six miles away and the trolley cars do not run that late at night. In the many times we traversed the road I noticed several interesting land marks. One an old house (buil[t] in 1659, I think). Mr. G was pleased when I spoke of it; he says I keep my eyes open. He says sometime he and I will make a day of it, Indian Reservation and everything. <u>Why</u> can't Junior be like him!

<u>Monday</u> - Rained much to our dismay. I read one of Mr. G's old books called *"Paul and Virginia"* and played records on the victrola. A rainy day with Junior is enough to drive one crazy. He doesn't care about anything in the world but machinery and me. I remember reading in a column somewhere, advice on how to act in order to be popular with the other sex. You were supposed to be flattering and interested in whatever the man was interested in - and all that sort of thing. I break every one of those rules with <u>abandon</u> and he keeps getting crazier and crazier about me.

Emily says he never acted so before and that he acts like all possessed.

<u>He</u> says I'm mean to him.

1922

One day, can't remember which, Mr. G took snapshots of us, and just because I wouldn't be silly enough to pose in a sentimental attitude, he sulked! Mr. G told him not to.

I wonder if I am always going to feel so at cross purposes? Honestly, he is words fail me. If I'm anywhere near him his arms go around me; if I look at him as I have to because he is so tall, he kisses me: I can't even fold my hands in my lap but he reaches for them.

Emily will say, "Quit pestering her, for heavens sake! Can't you let her alone a <u>minute</u>?" Of course he is more restrained in front of his parents, although once while Mr. G and I were talking he sat down beside me and quite <u>shamelessly</u> slid his arm around me. He told Charlie, Cill says, that I had more red peppers in me than in chili-con-carn[e] (the Mexican dish). Such a thing to say! And he told me my lips felt just the way they looked. There is something wrong with the few compliments he pays - if they <u>are</u> compliments. One day he held my head in the crook of his arm and scrubbed my lips with his handkerchief. I was furious. He simply said he wanted to see if they were really red! I told him he was a big brute and when I wanted to use lip rouge I should.

"I don't like it," he said, as if I cared!

Emily and the rest were shrieking with laughter and kidding us unmercifully. Of course we were joking, but I was angry too.

Wallace said: "Now's the time to tame that wild woman of yours, Jake. If you can!"

And Jr. caught both my wrists in one hand like a hand cuff. I guess I never realized how strong a boy can be because I couldn't even begin to break his grip. It gave me a queer, weak, helpless feeling and made me madder than ever. Quick as a flash I bent my head and bit him.

"Why you little devil!" he said in amazement.

By that time the others had laughed themselves into the state where they could only squeal and hold their sides.

Mr. G. has a very old copy of *"Plutarch's Lives"* and he told me a lot about books and bindings. I didn't know books had even been bound in <u>human</u> skin. It makes me sick. He says I know how to hold books, that most people don't

If Daddy were alive he'd be an old, old man, much older than Mr. G. but they seem in the same age group. I almost love Mr. G. in memory of Daddy.

There was one time, however, when he seemed lacking in understanding, but not with me. It was an evening. Wednesday (?), when a friend dropped in to see him. After the usual remarks the man said to Junior: "What's the matter with you, Boy? You look like a half starved hound dog. Don't they feed you enough?"

Junior <u>is</u> as bony as the last run of shad, but he is meant to be bony.

He laughed good naturedly as he said it, but Junior said gruffly, "I'm alright." And stalked out of the room. Mr. What's-His-Name looked at Mr. G. inquiringly and Mr. G. said, "He's alright. Got it bad, that's all."

"So that's it," Mr. So-and-So looked amused. "Well he's a good lad and not the first to go down before a pair of eyes. You've kept him reined in pretty well you know."

"Pat!" said Mr. G.

The other laughed and added, "It <u>can</u> be Hell."

With everyone laughing and talking I suppose they thought their low voices would not be heard. I felt prickly cross, but very thoughtful. The rest were busy and Junior hadn't returned, so I went out on the veranda and sat down on the step. I tried to imagine how it would be if I were crazy over him and he didn't care a cent for me. I felt quite touched until it came to me that if it <u>were</u> the case, Junior would be much less kind to me than I am to him. Emily teases him about a girl who likes him and he is rude and sarcastic about her. <u>He</u> hasn't any intentions of being pestered! Its a man's world alright.

The screen door slammed and he came out and sat beside me. He just sat without saying a word. It was restful, but after a time I began to wonder. I don't like to be pestered, but neither do I enjoy being ignored. He looked rather attractive in the light from the open door and I felt fond of him, although I knew it couldn't last. Shrieks of laughter came from the house.

"Shall we go in?" I asked.

"No," he said.

So we sat in silence. Probably because he left me alone, I found myself thinking devilish thoughts. I wondered what would happen if I kissed him quickly and then ran as fast as I could, but I knew what would happen, besides I have never kissed a boy and don't intend to start in. I was getting bored when it occurred to me that the full skirt of my black and white checked dress made a good checker board.

"Get the dark and light jelly beans from the bag on the table in back of you and we'll play checkers," I suggested.

"You think of the darndest things," he said, reaching for the bag.

"Have one?" And not waiting for my answer popped one in his mouth morosely.

"Your manners are terrible," I told him crossly, and spread my skirt flat on the veranda floor. "Well?"

So we played for awhile but his heart wasn't in it.

"I don't know why I should try to amuse you," I said gloomily, pulling my skirt into shape and eating the jelly beans. "I'm going in where there's fun."

"No, don't. Let's sit in the car."

I must explain that it was parked in the driveway waiting to be driven into the garage, or rather the barn.

"Well, alright," I agreed rather reluctantly. So we sat in the back and he dragged me across his knees saying sternly. "What's the matter with you anyway?"

"Nothing. What's the matter with you?" I retorted.

He sort of scooped me up and kissed me practically continuously. My arm was cramped so I slid it around his shoulders, because I figured I might as well be comfortable. Well - I don't know why I wasn't angry with him, I've given up trying to understand my reactions, but it was as if he couldn't help it - being so sort of crazy.

Finally I said: "You stop it! You know better. I'll never go with you anywhere if <u>this</u> is how you are going to behave."

I think he was a little shocked at himself, because he let me sit up and he said "Oh damn it!"

And then: "Sorry Helen. I couldn't help it."

At the moment we became aware of voices and saw others coming out of the door.

"Where are they?" Cill asked. And Emily said: "We'll find out. There's been a gleam in Little Brother's eye."

Of course they laughed at that.

"Keep quiet," Jr. whispered slapping one large hand over my mouth.

They nearly got by when Emily cried: "I'll bet they're in the car! I wondered why Junior left it out. Here they are, the little devils. Move over children."

"We wondered why you didn't come out, Emily," I said sweetly. "It's very pleasant out here."

"It was," Junior said pointedly.

<u>July 4th</u> - Rained. Wallace, Bob, Charlie and Marion spent the day with us. I do <u>not</u> like that girl! Her nails are grubby and she needs a good holy stoning. We went to the city to buy fireworks and the way she called attention to herself was awful.

In the afternoon we drove to Eastern Point and as Junior was at the wheel and couldn't pester me too much I enjoyed it.

We drove by Mr. Morton Plant's wonderful estate - It's another world - and why wasn't I born rich?

Junior thinks all millionaires are rakes - at least when they are young.

I said: "Why? Because they are the ones who get into the headlines?"

He said: "It stands to reason."

I asked why? "Would <u>he</u> be a rake if he were a millionaire's son?"

Emily snorted at that and said he'd never be anything that cost any money, being too stingy. She is always razzing him because he is so miserly.

I said if he had millions he couldn't be so saving, and she said, "Don't you believe it! If he had a million he'd want two and so on. And if you wonder why he looks like a rag bag its because he saved the money Pa gave him for a suit."

"Don't forget the hat," Wallace put in, whereupon they laughed and laughed.

An Account of My Life

It seems that Junior bought one thing: a straw hat.

"Ma won't let him wear it," Emily explained. "It doesn't fit him and suit him and he's a sight in it."

<u>None</u> of the boys wear straw hats now, and I was just going to say "Why in the world, Junior - -" when I noticed the expression on his face.

"I think its splendid of him to be putting money in the bank," I said. "My Grandfather had a bank account by the time he was twenty-five and never after was he without one."

Emily looked dazed. "Do you think it's love?" she asked the others.

Marion purred. "It must be."

"You've got more sense than most girls," Junior said to me, ignoring the others. Cill simply shrieked at that and began to list my extravagances and careless ways with money - which were all too true. I <u>haven't</u> any money sense - its the Clarke in me.

"Well," said Junior. "I guess she can learn."

There was something so grim and final about his tone, I shivered inwardly and experienced one of my lightning changes, I no longer liked him.

"So can you," I said, equally grim. Wallace and Em, Bob and Cill, Marion and Charlie laughed themselves sick.

Honestly, Junior is so narrow he's an anachronism. One expects it in the older people - such rigid thinking I mean, but it's terrible in one's own generation.

He doesn't approve of rouge, he doesn't care for dancing, he thinks any girl who smokes everlastingly damned, and a Hester Prynne could never be clean again in his eyes. Yet he's not the stick that makes him seem. What <u>he</u> can do is something again! And he has a way of saying not very nice things in a dry way that is almost funny.

We stopped at someone's house in Groton - friends of Mr. & Mrs. G's. There was a hammock under the trees and Junior led me to it. The thing was wringing wet and broke, letting us down ker-plunk.

Partly because I didn't like Junior at the moment and partly because I felt mischievous, I decided to play the part of a goody-goody girl.

I acted shocked at nearly everything he said and I acted shy and bashful dropping my eyes shly whenever he looked at me. I wished I could blush at will but that was beyond me. At first Junior was bewildered. he couldn't think what had come over me. The girls caught on and snickered. The elderly people we met were favorably impressed by my girlish modesty.

Junior thought it would wear off on the way home, but when I continued to shrink he lost his patience. "What the hell is the matter with you?" he demanded.

"He swore!" I said to the others, my lips trembling.

"Junior." Emily spoke sternly. "Apologize at once! A gentleman never swears in the presence of a lady."

"Ladies," Cill hissed.

"Sir!" Marion said, rather neatly, "You forget yourself!"

I was sorry I hadn't thought of it myself.

All I could think of was "unhand me wretch!" and he wasn't doing anything at the moment.

Junior pulled the car over to the side of the road and shut off the motor.

"What," he demanded, "Is the big idea?"

At that we all burst out laughing, laughing until we squealed helplessly.

"Cut it out," he ordered crossly.

"Don't be uncouth." I said. "Have you no respect for our unsullied woman-hood?"

He hooked an arm around my neck half strangling me.

"Going to cut it out?" he asked threateningly.

I said "yes" meekly and he let me go.

We set off the fireworks from the veranda because it was still raining a little. It was really pleasanter indoors, so we made candy in the kitchen. At first we had heaps of fun laughing until we were limp. The boys wore aprons too and Bob made paper hats for them. We had a battle with sticky spoons managing to give one another gummy swipes. Bob dabbed a bit of chocolate on my nose and then wiped it off with his handkerchief.

"Now blow your nose," he ordered paternally, pinching my nostrils so I couldn't. It seemed funny then, and I guess that's where the trouble started. Anyway he kept on joking and teasing me until I saw a glint in Cill's eye. It was really so silly, because he is terribly gone on her, but I tried to keep away from him, which only made him worse. Still it was no more than a trifling incident until Junior stepped in with both feet.

He told Bob to leave me alone in such a rude way as to make it practically impossible for Bob to do so without losing face.

"Regular baby vamp," Marion observed sweetly, to which <u>catty</u> observation Cill added a few mean remarks.

Charlie said good naturedly. "Oh lay off the Kid!"

If looks could kill Marion would have finished him then and there.

In fact it was so venomous even the boys acted uneasy. And then, heaven knows why! Wallace, who had kept out of it up to that point, said: "What's the matter with everyone? Why are you so sore at Helen? She can't help it if these two nuts exchange dirty looks."

I gave him a small smile of gratitude, wondering if he thought he was helping me any. Well, without doing anything everything seemed to roll up.

Junior said: "I'm not sore at Helen."

And Marion put in, "Oh <u>no</u>, of <u>course</u> not!"

"Well, I'm not!" Junior snapped. "Its that guy crowding in where he's not wanted!"

Bob came back with a mean remark promptly.

It was so darn silly! Bob was sick of it all - he hadn't meant anything anyway!

Fortunately, Mr. & Mrs. G. came home at that point and the tension eased.

I never liked a girl as <u>little</u> as that Marion person!

<u>Thursday, July 6</u> We were introduced to Mrs. Harbeck, Wallace's Mother, who is a widow, her husband having died when Wallace was small. Besides him there is Unabelle who is a younger than I. I hadn't thought of it, but I suppose they are quite poor. Junior's Mother said something about it, but I didn't pay any attention at the time. However the fuss Unabelle made over my dress and wrist-watch and things like that brought it to my attention. Mrs. Harbeck is paid by the City or the State to care for sick babies of unfortunate parentage. There were only a few there at the time, and one of them and by far the sweetest, was a little Indian-Negro baby named Stirling Silver. The Mother, an Indian, is dying of tuberculosis, while the father has run away not caring what becomes of her. It is odd how words suddenly take on meaning: sin and misery for example. Grandmother quite often says someone or something "looks like sin and misery," not meaning that at all. Mrs. H. said little Stirling Silver was nothing but a bundle of rags and filth when she first saw him, and now he is sweet, clean and nearly well.

Wallace looks like her both being red cheeked brunettes, but Unabelle's hair is brown and her skin pale. They all said we looked alike, except Junior who insisted we didn't. As a matter of fact, we <u>do</u> and we are of much the same build. Unabelle is better looking than I, but I shouldn't say she was as well made.

However, this is the funny side of it: Unabelle is the girl Emily teases Junior about! Its plain to see he likes the type, but what I can't understand is why he doesn't like her as well as he does me. Of course we are not <u>really</u> alike, but Junior isn't concerned with internal things. Grandma frequently says "Men are contrary critters" and after this I shall believe it. There she is only a few miles away and Wallace's sister - and he doesn't care a cent for her. And on top of it she likes him and would be far nicer to him. Besides that she has to do a lot of the homework and help with the babies which makes her the domestic kind he should admire. She doesn't care for books and she is either interested or pretends to be, in Ford engines and the like. Wallace is good at that sort of thing and she has picked up the mechanical terms. It is beyond understanding.

Emily and Priscilla held babies and cooed over them while discussing their respective merits, but I felt no desire to hold one. Lacking proper feeling in that respect, I won't pretend.

Junior, who is really paternal or something, picked one out and thrust it into my more or less reluctant arms and stood smiling down at me. I held it rather gingerly and then thrust it back in his arms, at which he gave me a disapproving look and sat down with it in his lap looking too funny for

1922

words, if he had only known it, with his long legs sticking out in front of him. The pained expression on his face made me feel a monster - which I may be, for all I know.

"Don't you like babies?" he asked, as if such an idea had never entered his head.

"Not much," I said coldly. "And only when house broken."

"I thought all women did."

"Some do and some pretend," I replied shortly.

"It's what you were created for," he spoke solemnly.

I turned upon him with exasperation. "Don't be so darn biblical!" I snapped.

Well he _is_! Even his name Jacob is just the sort of name to have a string of "begats" a mile long after it.

We played croquet until dark and then rowed out on a little pond. It was moonlit and beautiful. Why, _why_ should such a perfect night be wasted on Junior!

After we had gone to bed Cill kept me awake raving about Bob. I stood it as long as I could and then I said crossly, "Oh _do_ go to sleep."

Why can't I feel starry eyed when a boy kisses me? Cill can't believe me when I say I don't get the least kick out of it and never, never have. It's true though; it can be pleasant, or it can be unpleasant, but I literally don't know what a thrill is, unless it is the sort of feeling I had when I saw "The Shiek." It makes me feel sort of null and void.

July 7 - Friday evening we walked as far as the Drawbridge. Another perfect moonlight night wasted. We went out on the river and drifted about while the dance music from the Happyland Dance Hall came over the water setting me to tingling. I thought it would be fun to go there, but Emily said in that patronizing older sister way of hers, "Why Kiddie! No one goes there!" And Junior, agreeing with her for once in his life, added carelessly, "Nothing but cheap Janes."

Wallace murmured, "I wonder how you know, Jake." And Jr. said, "Shut up."

"I still think it would be fun." I insisted, tossing my head. "What harm would it be?"

"You don't know anything about such places and you're not going to." Junior said flatly.

"Is it a bad place?" I asked partly to be preverse, but partly because I was interested.

"No, it's not a `bad place'". Junior mocked. "Its cheap and thats that."

Bob said slyly. "Some fellow might look at you, Helen, and Junior'd burst a blood vessel." Junior got really angry at that, and being a guest after all, I recalled my manners and changed the subject.

After a time, we landed and walked thru a pine grove, smooth needles slipping under foot, moonlight falling slantingly, shadows sharp cut and black. I hardly realized when the pairing off began until I felt

An Account of My Life

Junior's arms going around me. I thought I had never known a night so meet for Romance. He drew me to him. How often have I read those words and closed my eyes in anticipatory bliss! How different in reality.

After I had had all I could endure for <u>one</u> spell, I pulled away from him so sharply and determinedly I lost my footing on the slope of slippery pine needles. He steadied me quickly and then almost with the same movement he lowered me to the ground throwing himself beside me. I looked up at him, not angry, not anything. His hand closed around my throat as if he meant to choke me, then it loosened and he began to stroke it very gently from my chin down the deep V of my dress. I didn't object to it really, but I felt uneasy. Somehow, it didn't seem at all horrid, I mean he was sort of decent and clean - not at all nasty. He kissed me and I didn't turn my head, but I looked into his eyes and then, as if someone had jerked me upright I found myself sitting bolt upright looking down at him.

"Junior!" I said.

"I know," he answered.

I surveyed him silently, somehow feeling a sort of - it can't be respect but something like it - for him.

I heard the others coming and stood up, but he lay there making no move, still breathing hard.

"Get up," I ordered sternly.

We were very quiet as we walked home along a road so bright with moonlight one could distinguish the spears of grass by the wayside. Never have I seen such moonlight: the most ordinary things were wrapped in white majic. It was late and there were only the night sounds and the gritting of our footsteps in the dirt. The others were a little ahead, Emily looking back once in a while.

I slipped my hand into his, and after a second of surprize, for I am not given to acts of affection, his hand closed around mine tightly and we walked along that way hand in hand.

Once we paused for a minute to look over the moon drenched fields. For the first time since we had left the grove, he put his arms around me. I looked up at him and he said, "Helen" and stopped short as if something choked him. "I'm sorry, really - which is a damn lie. Do you know what I mean?"

"I guess so," I said.

He placed his cheek against my hair, but he didn't kiss me, and then we walked on. I liked him.

<u>Saturday, July 8</u> - We raised the devil all day! Mrs. G. said she couldn't get anything done for laughing at us. Even the cleaning woman laughed. I don't remember exactly what we did or said, but we were all in wild spirits.

Later, Donald Gildersleeve came over and while he is older - in his twenties - I like him because he treats one as if of no particular age. He plays the violin, talks books and music and pets the cats. He seems to be exactly the sort of son Mr. G. would have enjoyed.

I like his half sister, Dorothy too, whom I met in S.S class. She isn't pretty, but she is nice looking in an immaculate, sweetly mannered sort of a way.

I told Junior she was much better suited to him than I, and asked why he didn't see it, to which he answered, rather strangely for him, "Why do people drink wine instead of water?"

"They don't," I said promptly, "If they know what's good for them."

"I guess they don't stop to think of that."

"You don't approve of drinking wine," I reminded him, and after a pause, "You don't approve of me either, do you?"

He looked angry. "I wish you'd be more sensible and not so - so frivolous," he said.

"But then I wouldn't me," I teased. "I'd be more like Dorothy and Unabelle and all the girls you should like and don't!"

"I know it," he groaned.

When he isn't making me cross I feel sorry for him and rather tender toward him.

I love old Norwich Town. Mr. Gallup pointed out historical spots and I enjoyed it all thoroughly. We talked about the Pequot Indians and he thinks just as Ase does that the massacre under Capt. John Mason [was] a shameful thing. I am not a bit proud of being a descendant of his, and when I sit on the base of his monument or walk in Cliff Woods I sometimes think of the screams and the burned bodies.

Junior has no patience with us. He says Mason had a job to do and he did it with completeness and dispatch and that he'd have done the same if he had been in his boots.

We sat up until Mrs Gallup almost shoved us off to bed. Emily decided to sleep with us for the fun of trying three in a bed, but she also, is fairly sizable. They put me in the middle because I am the smallest and therefor the most likely to be pushed out. I felt like the filling in a sandwich and said so. That set us to trying to decide what kind of a filling and after giggling awhile Emily said she had talked herself into an appetite, let's raid the icebox. We slid into kimonas and slippers and and crept down to the kitchen which seemed very clean and lonesome and as if surprized to see us. Emily had her head in the ice-box when we heard a sound and looked up to see Junior in the doorway looking very tall and gaunt, his hair towsled like a little boy's.

"Think you're smart!" he jeered. "Heard you plain as plain. Make mine ham, thick with plenty of mustard and a glass of milk. Also a hunk of apple pie. Any cheese left?"

"Who do you think you are ordering around?" Emily said crossly, for we had been talking quite intimately and we wondered how much he had heard.

An Account of My Life

Not having a brother, I am not accustomed to having a boy looking upon me in deshai-bille and envied Cill and Emily their absolute sang froid. Still, he wasn't looking at them any more than at the kitchen stove, while he was certainly looking at me. It made me uncomfortable.

After we had finished our snack we rinsed the glasses and swept up the crumbs. As we were about to go up the stairs Junior bent down and kissed me.

"March!" Emily snapped, and to my relief he did.

I guess I am fickle, for I find myself growing tired of the Rudolph type. <u>This</u> man is now my favorite type. [Photo of an unidentified man] If the Marcus I know could be like this Marcus how heavenly it could be! I didn't care a great deal for the book, but I do think him absolutely the most wonderful man - and the illustration fits him so perfectly which seldom happens. Or if Junior could just <u>remotely</u> resemble him I should have no trouble being completely crazy about him. And it is <u>not</u> the uniform alone; its his face.

Maybe this is silly of me, but I can't help it if I feel this way. It is so <u>easy</u> to fall in love with a man in a movie or in a book and <u>so</u> hard to even tolerate the boys I know. I was frankly jealous of Hesper.

The morning after the raid on the ice-box, Junior was a few minutes late for breakfast thus earning a dark look from Mr. Gallup who is punctual about everything. He looked sleepy, self conscious and rather nice. I smiled at him, a nice friendly smile, but not one calculated to make him upset the cream pitcher which he did. Mrs. Gallup scolded and sopped up the spreading pool, while Emily giggled. He looked so big, so awkward and uncomfortable I wanted to be nice to him and make everything all right for him.

"I want you to go to the little store, Junior," Mrs. Gallup said, as we left the table. "I've a list ready."

"Will you come with me?" he turned to me.

"No, she won't," Emily said firmly. "We've plans."

Junior ignored her still looking down at me. I didn't particularly want to, but his day hadn't started very pleasantly, so I said,

"I think I will, Emily, if you don't mind. It's a pleasant walk."

So, we started out, he suiting his long Abraham Lincolnish stride to mine. We had a good time. I like the little store and the old woman who runs it. She has known Emily and Junior all their lives and feels free to tease Junior if she likes. He didn't seem to mind, and oddly enough I didn't feel cross either.

"I wish you didn't have to go home, ever," he said on the way back.

"If I never left how could I come back?" I laughed. "And I do love coming here."

"Do you honest?"

"Yes," I told him. "I do."

There being no one in sight I let him kiss me once. I like him so much I wish I could like him more.

1922

Sunday - July 9 Church and Sunday School in the morning. Donald plays for the choir. After dinner we went for a drive Hartford way. I love the hills and sloping fields and grazing cows. Back home I take it for granted I guess. The sky was a fair blue curdled with little clouds. Back in time for evening service. I liked Jr. to-day - he was nice.

Mon. July 10 - Matinee in the afternoon. Bought bittersweet chocolates and listened to countless victrola records in a music store finally buying one.
That evening they drove us home which was nice of them, although I get a kick from riding on a train even so short a distance. Junior very gloomy. He said gloomily that he was pretty crazy over me. Well, I don't know what to do about it. Thank heavens he doesn't live in Mystic. I was sorry to go - I always feel sorry because we have so much fun and I like them all so much (except that Marion R.), but I need a rest from Junior who is too <u>devouring</u>.

Tuesday - Mother and I have been shopping in Westerly. It must be wonderful to have a long, dark automobile and a chauffeur. I no longer enjoy trolley cars. I have become quite interested in Theosophy. Mother thinks I am abnormal or something because she "never delved in such stuff."
Ase laughs and gives me money for the booklets: "Do the Dead Live?" "The Occult Side of Christianity," "The Laws of Human Destiny" and "Do We Live on Earth Again." Moonlight. I am sitting by the hall window looking out to sea. A motorboat is put-putting down the River leaving a trail of froth in its wake, shivering the moonglade. The Stonington Light flashes a bright eye and the Noank beacon glows every 20 seconds or so. On Mason's Island is a camp fire and the white spots that are tents. Everything is so beautiful I want to cry.
The Sunday School Picnic wasn't held at Atlantic Beach as is the custom, because of infantile paralysis in Rhode Island; it was held at Happy Land.
It would have been impossible not to have a good time because Roland Coleman was there, a little browner and better looking than before. I grant that he is conceited, but as Cill points out quite logically, hasn't he a right to be?
Capt. Rowl is the only one who doesn't spoil him consequently he thinks his Grandfather doesn't like him. He is just back from Camp and is going to Canada late in the summer. If he were stupid I could dislike him easily, but he is clever, well read and interesting.
Juliet Haley was there in her Caddilac [Cadillac] and she asked us to ride back with her. We were delighted - a Caddilac is certainly preferable to the picnic truck and I'd ride with Juliet in an oxcart and deem it an honor.

An Account of My Life

However when Miss Hattie learned of the arrangement she asked us to stay with the others, saying we had come together and she didn't think privileges should be granted a few. A Christian woman, but how I hate trucks!

Rowland said: "You're not going to pay any attention to <u>that</u> are you. She can't make you."

Cill and I looked at each other. "Well," she said. "If she wants us to stay I guess we ought to."

Rowland looked very haughty and arrogant. "You <u>are</u> a pair of sillies." he said.

But Juliet smiled and put an arm around each of us. "They're not," she told him. "They are sweet kids. I'll take you some other time."

"Does that mean you don't want me?" he asked, looking downcast.

She laughed and called him her 'Lad With An Opulent Air.'

"Come along," she told him. "You amuse me."

"She's the sweetest thing in the world," I said to Cill as Juliet slid behind the wheel.

"She probably wouldn't bother if he weren't handsome," she retorted cynically. "She's old enough to be his mother."

We had a scrap then and there. I <u>adore</u> Juliet Haley, always have and always will. I'd rather be like her than anyone in the world: she <u>couldn't</u> be more perfect. As for her age - while other women her age marry and have babies and become fat and dowdy she remains the same year after year like something set apart and beyond the ravages of time.

Cill said she should have told Junior we'd be there and he would have managed to get down. Heaven forbid. I can imagine how well he'd like Rowland.

<u>Aug. 20</u> - Emily and Junior down for the day. Attended B.Y.P.U. together. Marcus and Junior still eye each other with keen dislike.

Ase swearing at President Harding. I shall never like politics because I have been brought up on <u>Discussions</u>. He says he is a poor damn fool and Mrs. Harding is a b---.

<u>Aug. 25</u> - Started Carlyle's "*French Revolution*," which is too hot for summer reading Ase says wait until snow flies.

<u>Aug. 26</u> - Wrote to a Photoplay Company for an imagination test for scenario writing. I did very well. The course of study is only ten dollars a month for ten months, but the Family turns thumbs down definitely. In no time I could be earning money.

<u>Aug. 30</u> - Sent a children's poem to "Little Folk." It wasn't accepted but the editor said it was interesting whatever that means.

1922

<u>Sept. 1</u> - Everyone migrating as usual, every week finds fewer here. Must I always be left? And Elizabeth envies me: she says we have more fun here than she does in New York!

<u>Sept. 2</u> - There are so <u>many</u> things to do - to see - to be, I am crazy with restlessness. I never knew before that Johnnie's Grandmother was Spanish. A sea Captain brought her here after her parents were killed in an earthquake.

<u>Sept. 17</u> Seventeen years old today. I hope this year brings me to some of the things I want to do.

Emily and Junior were down today. Emily gave me a silver pin she made in jewelry class and Junior gave me a very pretty vanity case. I was surprised at his choice and his taste until Em explained that she had selected it. "Heaven knows what he'd have picked out!" she told me. "And seeing he felt like spending money for once in his life I thought I might as well have a hand in it."

Walter told Junior that I had been his girl for years and he told Mr. Bishop the same. Mr. Bishop has had my photograph in his studio window for quite a while. I don't know why because it isn't a very good one - and Walter went in and told Mr. Bishop that! As if he cared! Honestly, Walter is a dim-wit. He is a soldier now. I mean he joined the army and is in uniform. It ought to help but he simply looks like an overgrown Boy Scout. As Grandmother would say, "it takes more than regimentals to make a man."

He told Junior some ridiculous story about having saved my life. I fell off my bicycle and he untangled me - if that is what he means.

Junior very sulky about it, also wants my picture "out of that window."

I told him not to worry it probably was pretty fly speckled by now and would be replaced by someone else. Honestly, he acts as if he owned me!

<u>Sept. 18</u> - This Halls-Mills murder is a horrible mess. Mother doesn't like me to read about it, but Ase says, "You can't keep the girl wrapped in cotton all her life! She's seventeen, damn it."

And Mother answers that she sees no need for me to read about unpleasant things. He is getting a big kick out of Grandmother's recently acquired taste for tabloids. She use to say they weren't fit to be handled without tongs, but of late she has developed an interest in them. Of course she doesn't buy them, she asks Ase if he happens to "have one of those things laying around." He buys them purposely for her and she tucks them out of sight when she sees me approaching.

He hasn't been so amused since the time he gave her a little hard cider. She drank a glass slowly, caught herself smiling, and got to her feet.

"Ase Clarke," she said sternly. "You're trying to get me drunk."

An Account of My Life

And without another word she marched out of the door and up the path to her house.

<u>Oct. 23</u> - Junior down yesterday. I guess he intends to marry me someday. Well, I suppose I must marry someone and as I seem to be incapable of falling in love it may as well be he. I can't see why anyone should be in a hurry to get married.

We drove up to Charles Q's museum. He is a relation of some sort - don't think the Eldredge line comes in except by marriage, (his brother John married great Grandmother's sister Abby Bennett) but he shipped as cabin boy under Great Grandfather Capt. Rhodes and has been everywhere and done everything. He has made fortunes and lost them and made them again. He built the mansion on the River, bought yachts and fine horses. He has been married twice or more and his son shot himself in a hunting lodge on Lovers Leap, on account of a chorus girl.

Grandmother doesn't approve of him, but she is rather proud of him in an off-hand way. He is really an extraordinary person. I should be up there half the time but for one thing. It's like this - as a relative and a friend of Capt. Rhodes it seems perfectly proper for him to act affectionate, but he isn't affectionate in a proper way, he likes to pet me. He isn't in his second childhood although ninety I guess, and his mind is as sharp as a knife, but well, he is like that. Mother says he always acted silly over women and there's no fool like an old fool.

Well, Junior took charge without hestitation, managing to keep between Charles Q. and me in such a way that I could really see and enjoy the curios. It gave me a comfortable feeling and I told him so.

"You need looking after," he grunted. "If he wasn't so old I'd pop him one on the jaw."

"He doesn't mean any harm," I sighed, rather embarrassed.

"Not much!"

"I'm sorry for him," I said. "Though he's had a wonderful life, maybe better than I shall ever have. After so much living it must be hard to dry up. Its as if he were trying to warm his hands."

It doesn't do to think out loud before Junior, as I well know and realized anew in the shocked pause that followed.

And then I made it worse by saying defensively: "You don't have to be so darn literal, do you?"

I <u>had</u> to say goodby to him because he asked about "Mill" (Grandmother) and how was Allie and about a lot of old people.

I said, "yes, yes...I'll tell her...she's very well, thank you...us they haven't been here for several summers...no, I don't remember that...oh she's a big girl now...yes, I remember...and so on while he held my hand and stoked my arm and started that crowding act of his - and all the time so moist and drippy and <u>old</u> I felt sick.

"Don't say it!" I told Junior warningly as we got into the car. "He's a connection of mine."

"Connection be damned!" Junior gritted out. "You stay away from that place."

"I do," I said stiffly. "<u>You</u> wanted to see the carcass of the whale."

<u>Sunday morning</u> Halloween festivities. Friday night a social at the church. Played all the usual games - bobbing for apples etc. and we threw apple parings over our shoulders to see what letter they'd form. Mine didn't look like anything. The basement was very attractive with corn husks and pumpkins in profusion.

Saturday I cut dozens of goggle eyed pumpkins from crepe paper for Constance's costume. And in the evening I went on a straw ride to Lantern Hill with Howard of all people! [*Ed.note: not Howard Duell*]

I don't like him and I knew what to expect more or less, but it happened like this. The Congregational Church was giving it and Ernestine was selling tickets. When she approached Howard, he simply grinned and waved her aside. Of course she tried to sell him one anyway and finally he said looking at me: "OK, if Helen will go with me."

I simply wrinkled my nose at him and opened my book. But Ernestine who is frightfully determined pounced on me. To hear her you'd think I was seriously holding up the sale of tickets and behaving like a pig.

"Even if you <u>are</u> a Baptist," she said. "You might help out a Congregationalist. I've been to all kinds of things at your church, but I'll never buy another ticket."

I still shook my head and she added, "Even if you don't like him I guess it won't kill you for once! Uncas Lodge is swell and it will be fun!"

"Ouch!" said Howard. "Who ever called it the `gentler sex' was nuts! Don't pull your punches any, ladies."

"Well, its your own fault," she told him. "You know how you act and so does everyone. I wouldn't blame her if she didn't go some places with you, but a church straw ride with chaperones! Come on Helen, be a sport."

Well, it did seem silly - and Ernestine is persistent as the [dickens], so I gave in.

"You'll see how you've misjudged me," Howard said virtuously - and grinned.

"Yah!" I retorted.

Well, at least you know what to expect with someone like Howard, and act accordingly.

It was a marvellous night and one that simply beggared descriptions: a moon, myriad stars, crisp air, rustling leaves and stillness.

Uncas Lodge, which belongs to the Twin Lake girls, is very attractive; rustic of course, with a wide veranda over the lake. Inside a fire blazed in the rough stone fireplace and there were comfortable chairs and a victrola. The room was lighted by the flames and the grinning pumpkin moonshines peering from a bank of russet oak leaves on the mantle.

It was a good crowd, the food was swell and the cider excellent - but Howard, is Howard. He thinks the only virtuous woman is a dead woman.

However he is amusing, witty and rather likeable. Mother says his father was like that before him.

We danced on the veranda, drank coffee and ate great platters full of crisp, golden doughnuts. After Howard got some of the ideas out of his head we got along very well. I like his sense of humor.

Oct. 30 - The Gallups came down yesterday afternoon. Emily says Junior might as well move down and be done with it, he is either planning to come or fretting because he can't, all the life long time. It takes some one like Howard to make me appreciate Junior I guess, because I was really glad to see him. Besides he has improved lately - I mean he acts like a man and not like an ungainly school boy playing practical jokes. In fact he acts too much like a man. Is there no pleasing me? I mean I don't like a boy to be too serious - flirting is so much more fun. Junior has no light or frivolous moods. He doesn't pay compliments or say pretty things, he doesn't know the meaning of being gallant. The plain truth is, he isn't romantic. I like him but I just <u>can't</u> fall in love with him. Why, he has never said he loved me in so many words! He is as chary of the word as Grandmother - and he is so stern and rocky! There isn't any <u>give</u> to him. Strength is a good thing, but not when it imprisons one like a prison wall. He'd start in where Grandmother left off: I'd have to fight to call my soul my own. And yet I like him and feel sort of proud of him!

One thing, he doesn't act so crazy any more. It's as if he were waiting patiently. Somehow it gives me the shivers. What nonesense I have written.

It has just come over me that he <u>is</u> a man practically - he must be going on twenty. I forget he is older than I and naturally ages year by year.

Nov. 5 - The most wonderful time! At last I have met someone who really interests me. He came home with me from the party and is meeting me tonight at the church. Mother says she never knew me to go out of my head over a <u>boy</u> before and who <u>is</u> this Joe person? I had about given up all hope of ever meeting anyone who <u>mattered</u> and practically resigned myself to a life of alternate saps and pigs - and now this!

There was a surprize party - and I almost didn't go. Suppose I hadn't? But Fate saw to it. There was a large crowd and an unusual number of strange boys, which promised to be interesting from the start and certainly was. One from Groton was nice and if it hadn't been for Joe - My pen is simply racing, yet I don't seem to get anywhere at all! I guess my thoughts might be called chaotic.

Well, there was an orchestra and we danced when we weren't playing games. I noted with satisfaction that it was <u>not</u> a kid party as none were younger than I and most were much older. Now, referring to the Fortune I tore off at the Halloween Social it <u>would</u> seem like Fate that I should meet Joe at the very first party I attended after the Social. It is positively awesome and restores my belief that such things <u>can</u> happen.

1922

Abby said I'd meet him probably as no large party was a party without him. I asked "Why? Is he so much fun?", and she said, "no, he isn't the life of the party kind, in fact he is quiet and rather moody."

"Well, what's so wonderful about him, then?" I asked. "Why do you all say his name that certain way?"

Abby giggled and said, "Oh, he dances divinely, kisses like Rudolph and is absolutely fickle. He has a terrible temper and doesn't care what he says or does, and surely you have heard he has a Reputation!"

I looked interested, so she whispered some things I shall not set down here.

"Where'd you meet him?" I asked directly. She said at Columbus Hall.

I wouldn't admit it, but I felt rather out of it, not having met him. Of course, I had heard his name with one girl or another, but never anyone of my set.

Well, when Abby introduced him I thought he seemed conceited and in need of being taken down a peg or two, so I was distinctly cool. Abby, either from fun or sheer mischief said, "She says you are just another Shiek, Joe!"

He looked straight into my eyes and I knew that he knew I had had no experience with any kind of Shiek, and that he dared to mock me with his one sided smile. He didn't say a word and even seemed a bit bored. Fortunately, the Groton boy, whose name doesn't matter now, was at my elbow and I ignored Joe while seething with resentment. It is hard to describe the mixture of interest and annoyance he aroused in me.

Abby came up to quizz me until I was forced to admit he was good-looking and different, but I added airly that I wasn't sure I liked the difference. "He seems," I told her savagely, "he seems to think he is the answer to a maiden's prayer."

"Well, isn't he?" she laughed.

No wonder he is completely spoiled!

When I had to give out forfeits I saw him looking at me with the sort of smile you long to slap, so I sent him out of the room with the one girl I was pretty sure he wouldn't choose to be alone with. From what I had gathered, she was an old flame of his and still simply gone on him. It struck me as a nice fiendish way to annoy him.

However, when he returned he smiled mockingly and bowed low. I knew then that he knew why I sent him out which was the same as admitting he had mattered to me! I prickled all over. His hair shone like Rudolph's in the lamplight and he showed absolutely no signs of annoyance. I wondered if I had been right after all: maybe he still liked the girl. There were two other girls in particular who seemed to be his Harem Favorites and they spent their time pleasantly sticking pins into one another, figuratively speaking of course. He was perfectly aware of it and completely indifferent. Most boys hate to have two girls scrapping over them - publicly at least, but Joe acted used to it and rather bored.

Abby had said he was seventeen, but I found it hard to believe: he seemed years older.

Both girls were pretty and blonde. As a brunette I admire and detest blondes! Then too, they were far prettier than I with that very real prettiness about which there can be no dispute.

I was wearing my blue taffeta with the little pink rosebuds and I needed it with the competition so fierce. It was prettier than either worn by the Harem Favorites, and I caught them eyeing it covetously.

We played Post Office eventually. After a few minutes I knew his number and carefully refrained from calling it, but it was in the nature of an insult to discover he apparently had no idea of calling mine! It honestly came as a stunning blow to my pride. In due time he had called every attractive girl but me and toward the very end when the game was beginning to lag, he actually called mine. I was seething! Instead of being first or among the first, I was at the end - an afterthought. Of course pride kept me from showing any resentment even though I burned.

When Cliff closed the door on us I faced him in no very pleasant frame of mind. There he stood calmly making no effort to kiss me. Honestly, I wanted to march straight out without a word, but as it was my place to remain and call a number, my appearance would have called forth jeers and demands for an explanation. Besides, I wanted to see what would happen.

So I said sweetly. "Wouldn't it have been better if you had made up your mind before you called my number?"

At that he put his arms around me casually as if it were hardly worth the effort, and then he lifted my chin and kissed me lightly. Thinking that was all and he had been <u>greatly</u> over rated, I drew away - or tried to.

"Keep still," he said. "I'm not thru yet."

I literally <u>gasped</u> at his audacity. His mouth came against mine and remained a long time, for even as I turned my head from side to side his followed mine.

"Like that better?" he laughed, still holding me.

I <u>had</u> liked it which made me more furious than I had ever been in my life.

With a great effort I rallied my senses. "All you need is practice," I said, "And you'll be almost as much of a Shiek as you think you are!"

He took his arms away then - in fact he all but shoved me, but his voice came steady and mocking.

"Know that thing the kids say? `Open your mouth and shut your eyes, And I will give you something to make you wise?' Well, do it the next time."

Then he walked out and I most certainly <u>didn't</u> call his number, as he <u>may</u> in his vanity have thought I would.

1922

Time elapsed. The Groton boy - Ralph (any other time I should have liked him very much) had to leave the party before it was over and he asked me if he could take me home.

I told him rather regretfully that I rather wanted to finish the Party, so he left. All things must come to an end and shortly before twelve Joe came over to me and announced that h<u>e</u> was taking me home. I looked at the Harem Favorites who were glowering, and back at him.

"Well?" he lifted an eyebrow, oh so sure of himself.

"It will make quite a procession won't it?" I asked.

"No," he gave a twisty smile, "Just you and me. They've rowed with each other and with me."

"And am I next prettiest?" I asked poisonously.

It didn't floor him at all, he simply looked amused.

"No." he said, looking me over critically. "I don't think you are, but you'll do."

Before I could expell a breath of sheer fury, he added "That guy couldn't have been making the hit he thought he was. I notice you didn't go with him."

"I wish to Lord I had!"

"No, you don't." he spoke as if to a child. "You wanted me to ask you."

I have not been rendered speechless many times in my life, but I was this time; my mouth opened and shut and nothing came out. The sheer nerve and affrontery of it took the wind out of my sails, and besides I knew he spoke the truth and would only mock me with a smile if I issued a passionate denial. I found myself being slid into my coat very expertly.

"Ready?" he asked, and smiled a smile that made something turn completely over in me. But I was not completely vanquished. As we went out, Abby said indignantly, "And I believed you!"

"I <u>don't</u> like him," I told her emphatically.

"Who, me?" he grinned.

"Oh, no," I drew a deep breath. "Just a fresh show-off who thinks he knows all about women."

Abby gasped. Joe looked a bit startled for a moment, and then he laughed.

Well, he <u>is</u> fascinating, although I shall die before I let him know I think so. He doesn't belong to my set, they say his family is common and there are simply dozens in it, and he is not of our race or religion. However, I shall say this for him, he doesn't make vulgar remarks as I imagined a fellow of his class would, and his surface manners are good in a smooth, insolent way. And poise! I never saw such poise! I tried to break it down again and again only to catch at my own as I felt it slipping away.

At the door, he kissed me. I must confess he knows how to do it. I didn't know kissing <u>could</u> be like that - like rockets and pin wheels, etc. He looked a bit surprized himself. It was the first time in my life when, though I pretended otherwise, I welcomed a kiss. It's a relief to find I am normal after all - I was beginning to wonder.

"Want me to meet you somewhere tomorrow night?" he asked.

<u>What</u> a way to express it!

"I attend the evening service at the Baptist Church," I said, my chin in the air.

"You may meet me there if you like. Don't get the idea you are conferring an honor, because you are not."

"And don't think you are either, Lady Astorbilt," he laughed. "I may be there or I may be not."

"Purely a matter of indifference to me either way," I answered coldly. And so we parted.

<u>Sunday Night</u> - Tonight he met me outside church. After sober reflection I had decided to put no faith in him, for from what I had heard it seemed likely that he might not show up. It seems he has a reputation for leaving girls hanging mid-air. And there was the chance he had patched up - or the Harem Favorites had patched up their troubles.

When I first came out I didn't see him at all, and Marcus evidently thinking me about to go home alone, stepped forward just as Joe stepped from the shadows of the building. They looked at each other. and Marcus being used to that sort of thing, stepped back.

"Well, Sherlock!" I greeted Joe. "Are you sleuthing - or does the light hurt your eyes?".

1922

Dean's Mill was a popular picnicking spot

The Community House was located on Holmes Street

Helen's first job was at the Rossie Velvet Mill

"Say, didn't I tell you I'd be around?" he demanded angrily. "What do you think you're pulling anyway?"

"Here you are and here I am. What a coincidence!" I said brightly, enjoying myself.

"Whats that goof here for?"

"Oh, he's always about - more or less. Don't you like competition?"

"If you think you can make a monkey out of me -" he began, when I interrupted to ask sweetly, "Why should I make a monkey out of a first class jackass?"

"Say!" he exploded - and then he laughed. "I like your nerve!" And as I said nothing, added, "You've got a wicked line."

We went for a walk and never, never, never have I spent such a bewildering evening. Whatever he is, he's never boring.

First of all he asked calmly if I was "after thrills like the rest of them."

"How do you expect me to answer a question like that!" I said indignantly, stopping short in my tracks.

"Why not say `yes' or `no'." he suggested. "Or maybe you don't know what a thrill is?"

"How could that be! You forget you have kissed me."

He laughed. "I haven't forgotten - that's why I asked."

"Let's start all over again," I begged. "We're talking criss-cross. You can't be as awful as you seem to be."

He met that with a short laugh and a "You can't be as dumb as you make out, either. You were willing enough to come with me tonight."

"They said you'd try to get fresh," I told him coldly. "But I didn't altogether believe it. You weren't the last time and I know the type of girl who says things like that usually likes it. I was curious, that's all."

"OK," he shrugged. "I asked to be sure. You don't have to pull the high and mighty stuff. Want to go home?"

"Of course," I said coldly, and we walked along thru a thick, black silence.

I looked at him curiously under every street light, until he grinned and said, "You ought to know me next time you see me."

The jeering tone stung me - but I _had_ examined him minutely, so to speak.

"Are you always like this?" I asked, stopping short.

"Not always," he said with that tinsly smile that makes something turn over in me.

I fumed inwardly, but for all the smart and sting and distaste, I know I like him. It sounds ridiculous, but its so. I don't see how I can; but I do.

"You're going to be mad if I kiss you and madder if I don't," he said as we reached the door.

I let out a gasp of rage.

He laughed and kissed me.

I banged the door.

1922

Monday - Nov. 6 - Joe just telephoned. Ase answered and nearly took his head off. If I hadn't been there to take it he would have slammed the receiver on its hook. Just because he didn't recognize or like the tone of his voice! I don't like Joe on the telephone, but I'm going to a movie with him tomorrow night. I wanted to say `no' - oh how I wanted to say it! And I said `yes.' I made it casual, but I said it. I guess I'm crazy.

Grandmother has told me about the man who said something improper to Great-Aunt Mary Jane and was immediately ordered from the house by her. She never spoke to him again Either she had an awful lot of character or she didn't like him anyway.

I have heard - not from Grandmother directly, of course, but from conversation, that Great Aunt Mary Jane raised Ned on her wedding night.

Grandmother, I guess, doesn't quite approve of that, because she believes when you make a bargain it's up to you to see it thru, but I think she's rather proud of Mary Jane's sensibilities. Well she may have been very pure, but now she cackles and pries, showing a very horrid curiosity about such things. I feel rather sorry for Great Uncle Phillip, personally.

Tuesday, Nov. 7 - I met him at the door just before Ase exploded.

He acted rather peeved and I couldn't blame him. After the show he decided a dance would be more fun than walking. There was a Public Dance at Noank, he said. I told him I wasn't allowed to go such dances unless a party of us went together. Ase knows all of Noank and - oh it was simply impossible.

"I'm going," he said stubbornly.

We walked along in silence until we were at my door.

"Last call," he reminded me. "Changed your mind?"

"No." I said distinctly. "I'm sorry. Thanks for a pleasant evening."

"You can't stop me from going," he sounded positively belligerent.

"I'm not trying to stop you. I don't care!" I told him flatly.

My anger bolstered me up until I was in my room.

Friday - Tonight he telephoned. Wanted to go somewhere.

"Go on," I said crossly.

"You know you want to go." he told me confidently.

"The loud sound you don't [hear] is me clapping my little paws together with glee."

"Don't we get along just jim-dandy!" he observed as I hung up.

I was almost crying with rage at him and myself.

I've never known anyone who could reduce me to a pulpy rage.

Nov. 11- Joe phoned again. I wondered if he would.

"There's a good moon tonight," he suggested.

"Is there?" I asked trying to sound cool.

"You make me mad as Hell," he snapped. "Do you think you're the only pebble on the beach!"

I felt a thrill of deep pleasure as I realized I had managed to get his goat. Evidently he took my silence to mean I was hurt because he returned to his confident conquering male manner and said: "How about it?"

"You don't exactly hate yourself do you?" I murmured.

"Quit the kidding! I'll meet you at Kretzers."

"You will not," I said, "You'll call for me." And I hung up.

Ase was looking at me and as he caught my eye he shook his head sadly.

"So that's how it's done," he grunted. "The God damned smart Alec wants to pick you up on a street corner."

"I'm not _that_ dumb," I told him briefly.

Later, as I dressed, Mother asked, "I suppose it's the same one - that Joe?"

I nodded.

"Aren't there enough nice boys for you to go around with?" she complained. "A Catholic too! Your Grandmother will have plenty to say."

Well, we went and enjoyed ourselves. On the way home we began to squabble. "We're getting to your house too fast," he objected. "Let's sit down and fight this out."

I didn't care so we sat on a wall and plunged into an argument.

"Now," he said. "I want to know why you don't take me serious."

"What?"

"This! Me! What do you think I'm phoning you for and taking you out and all that?"

"I'll bite. Why?"

"I'm crazy over you, that's why."

"Yes, you are!" I said derisively.

"I want to know why you haven't given me a ring on the phone?"

"Why should I?" I asked in surprize.

He whistled a bar of a popular song, breaking off abruptly.

"Say that again," he demanded. "I didn't hear right."

"Yes, you did."

He sighed. "Girls are always phoning me."

"My, my!" I said sweetly.

"No one," he went on sadly. "Hardly no one believes I have dates with you."

"That is just too bad," I told him coldly. "If you think my scalp is going to dangle along side your telephone with the other specimens, you are sadly mistaken."

"For crying out loud!" he burst out laughing. "You're the limit! Little dumbell, don't you know I'm nuts about you?"

Then in answer to my derisive sniff, asked softly, "Like me?"

I could feel that darn charm of his spreading over me.

And then he caught me in his arms bending me back while he gave me the longest kiss I have ever experienced. To my surprize it took all the stiffening out of me.

"Like me?" he insisted.
"A little," I admitted.
And we laughed for no particular reason.

<u>Nov. 12</u> - When Joe met me after church tonight my heart flopped over.

"Someday, someone will accuse you of being true to me," I mocked. "Think how that will damage your reputation, O Shiek!"

"Don't matter," he shrugged. "The guys are razzing me already."

"Why do you come?"

"If I don't some one else will, that's why!"

"So?"

"You're my girl," he said crossly.

Instead of flinching away as I have when others have said that, a pleasant glow spread over me and I gave a little laugh.

His arms went around me and he kissed me hard.

He is marvellous!

<u>Nov. 14</u> - Movies to-night.

The Family has donned war paint and is splintering the air with their war [w]hoops. Ase says he has it on good authority the boy is no damn good.

<u>Saturday</u> - I am writing this at one o'clock in the morning, hoping no one will see my light and ask if I am unwell. I'm tired, but a thousand miles from being sleepy. There is music going around in my head, and voices, snatches of talk and laughter.

When Joe stood in the hall removing his coat our eyes met and a strange tingle went thru me. All that mocking look was gone and his eyes were shining. He came over to me swiftly and we looked at one another like idiots, not saying a word. I think this is the first time in my life I have ever been blind to every boy but one. We danced, not speaking, as if lost in enchantment. Once he brushed the tip of my eyebrow with his lips.

We sat on the hall stairs away from the others who were giggling and wise cracking.

"What's going on up there?" Pat called up, and the teasing remarks came thick and fast. Only Marcus was silent. I am sorry he minds so terribly, but I can't help it.

Someone changed the victrola record and "A Kiss In the Dark" came floating up the stair well. Joe hummed it, his head bent over mine: he has a very good voice.

"I like the words, too," I said softly.

"Yeah, they're swell," he agreed.

I ran my hand over his sleek head. I've been longing to do it, and then I pulled away, hurt and surprized that he should jerk away from me.

"I'm sorry," I said.

An Account of My Life

  He made no answer, seeming to withdraw deep inside himself, like a snail or a turtle. He was oddly remote from then on, until upon leaving he bunched the fur collar of my coat up around my face and held it so. I looked up at him and he was smiling - a strange sweet smile, I thought. Maybe boys can't smile that way, I only know it seemed so to me. His face grew sober for a moment, then it broke into a grin.

  "You're a funny girl," he said, letting go of my coat collar.

  We stopped under the trees to say good night, because though it was late, and though it had been a strange, unsatisfactory evening, we hated to bring it to an end.

  I am all at sea with him, I don't think I understand him at all. He is never shy or ill at ease and when he is silent you know it is from choice, not from bashfulness.

  "Do you want me to kiss you?" he asked, thereby embarrassing me.

  "Don't you want to?" I parried.

  "Sure," he said. "I'm asking you."

  "Why all the ceremony?" I was cross by that time.

  So he held me tight against him, kissing me not once as I had expected, but over and over again, harder and harder. His hand slid in under my coat and his lips forced mine apart. I pulled away from him and started for the door. He made no effort to stop me. I shut the door, and here I am writing, more awake than ever before in my life.

  <u>Nov. 22</u> - Something funny happen to-day. Oh it was rather embarassing too, but I can't help laughing. I had stopped at the C.H. for a few minutes after school and Joe was walking over town with me when we encountered Deacon Elias Wilcox. If I could have avoided it I should have done so, but before I realized it his beard was wagging cheery greetings and there was an inquisitiive and acquisitive gleam in his eyes. After calling me his dear child and touching upon the subject of the weather he looked at Joe so pointedly there was nothing to do but introduce him which I did. Well before many sentences had rolled out he was taking Joe to his scriptural heart and I was fighting a desire to laugh while silently praying Joe wouldn't disgrace himself.

  "Oh, a newcomer, I presume," Capt. Elias said benignantly. "This little girl doesn't let any grass grow under her feet, a popular young lady, yes. And quite a poetess too."

  This was news to me.

  "She wrote all the lines for the little bags at the Penny Social. They were appropriate - yes. I thought them very appropriate. She told Mrs. Wilcox she'd rather do that than make the darn bags."

  Here he chuckled, remarking that I was more at home with a pen than a needle.

  "I told Asy you were a bright young lady."

  Joe was regarding me with suspicion.

  Then suddenly he pounced - I mean Capt. Elias pounced on Joe.

"Did you say you had lived here long, my boy?"

Recognizing his tactics I hastened to say, "Oh yes, Deacon Elias, he isn't a newcomer at all! He -"

But Deacon Elias rolled on. "Strange I haven't met you before," he beamed. "however, I don't get around as much as I use to except to church. As you may know, I have a large Bible class, a fine lot of Christian young men. Perhaps you are acquainted with Evans Morgan - - - - here he went on to name half a dozen or so.

"The class is augmented in the summer by young me from the summer colony. I am afraid it seems very quiet after they go. I think you'd like us, my boy. Why not give us a try?"

And becoming more benign by the minute he turned to me. "I guess I can count on Helen to bring you within our fold."

"I am Catholic," Joe said flatly.

And I thought: may the Lord keep me from laughing!

Having assured himself we were not indulging in a very bad joke, Deacon Elias said calmly: "In that case you are well looked out for, my boy."

For the first time in my life I was consciously proud of Elias Wilcox, with Popery ever a stench in his nostrils, he was a gentleman. Even harder for one of his dignity was the sure knowledge that this impulse had made him look rather foolish for a moment.

"I must be getting along," he said calmly. "The air is chilly. Winter is almost upon us. Gooday, my children."

"Gooday Deacon Elias," I said gravely.

Well, we walked the length of the street, Joe so omniously calm I couldn't keep back a spurt of laughter.

Joe, looking more or less like a thunder cloud, regarded me silently.

"He is proud of his class and is always looking for new members," I said placatingly. "He didn't know. You saw how impossible it was to break in on him. You can't rudely interupt a Deacon who knew your Grandmother as a girl, can you?"

"The old goat," he scowled.

I was angry instantly, at the same time wanting to laugh, because I have secretly thought the Deacon does look like a goat with his beard wagging up and down.

"He has known me all my life," I said calmly. "and never before seen me with a Catholic. A natural mistake to make, I think."

He received that in stormy eyed silence. "Who are all these summer people?" he scowled.

"Why, just the usual ones, you know."

"I don't."

"Oh well," I sighed, making an effort. "Practically the same ones every year. Celia Laurence's brother, Elizabeth's brother, Teddy Mosher"

"The sap with buck teeth and million dollar clothes?"

"Yes," I admitted the accuracy of his description, while resenting it.

"Then there is Maurice Burrows, a relation and he's older and Rowland Coleman etc."

"Does <u>he</u> go to your church?"

"Are you being funny?" I glared. "You must know perfectly well that Deacon Elias is his uncle and Capt. Rowland his grandfather. Of course he does, when he is in town."

"Go on."

"I can't think of any others off hand - unless it's DeWitt St. John ..."

"No one," he interupted firml[y]. "No one alive ever had a handle like that."

"Well, <u>he</u> has," I laughed at the expression of disgust on his face. I don't imagine he likes it any better than you do. The boys were prejudiced at the start. They could swallow the limousine and the chauffeur and Mrs. St. John, but the DeWitt business stuck in their crops. Toby told me they liked him after they got to know him. All the swank was on the surface and not his fault, if you know what I mean. Johnnie says he'd be alright if he lived here the year round."

"I suppose <u>you</u> think he is swell," Joe muttered.

"He is a good kid."

"I'll bet!" fairly dripping sarcasm. "What kind of a class does the old boy have, for Pete's sake!"

"What makes you so cussed," I snapped, tired and exasperated.

He gave me glare for glare and taunted, "I suppose this is the off season. When <u>they</u> are in town you go around with them."

"I wish you'd take that expression off your face," I told him. "Anyone can tell you're mad a mile away."

"I'll take my face away, that's better," he snapped, and walked away.

You'd think we could walk thru Main Street without trouble, but it seems we can't, of all the <u>unreasonable</u> people!

<u>Nov. 24</u> - A row with Joe. I told him I wasn't going to the C.H. dance and I wasn't but at the last minute I went with my crowd. He seldom goes to what he calls stuffy dances, so I didn't expect him to be there. He was. We fought every step of the way home and parted in fury. Now <u>that's</u> over. I should have known.

<u>Nov. 26</u> - Sunday. Felt listless and tired this morning. When I came home from S.S. I asked if anyone had telephoned, whereupon Mother looked daggers at me and said `no.' I was already for a miserable afternoon when Junior popped in. He didn't pay me a single compliment, but acted very contented. We went up to his Grandmother's later, and while we were there the phone rang. Jr. answered and told me with a scowl that some guy wanted me. It was Joe!

"How'd you know where to find me?" I asked crossly.

"Oh," he said cheerfully. "After I'd called your house enough times someone told me and hung up fast. Seemed to think I was poison ivy or something."

"Well?" I asked, keeping a weather eye on Jr. who was looking distinctly unpleasant.

"I'll be up this evening." Joe said. "Thought I'd let you know."

"Don't bother, it won't be necessary," I told him coldly and hung up.

The nerve of him! And yet I wanted to laugh too.

"It's just too darn bad!" Junior said with considerable sarcasm. "But I'm staying for church this evening myself."

"That's swell," I smiled. He didn't look convinced.

Well, Junior and Marcus are not exactly friendly, but they would band together against Joe in a minute. When one of the girls said she'd seen Joe downtown and he had told her to tell me he was coming up whether I liked it or not, I began to see unpleasant complications arising. Marcus is easily managed, but Junior is not the kind to step back easily. Besides I didn't want to hurt his feelings, because he had come all the way to see me. Then too, Joe was blissfully unaware of Junior. Fortunately it was getting late and after B.Y.P.U. Jr., who is really afraid of his father, said if he stayed to church service he'd be so late getting home his father would raise the roof.

"I don't care about that," he told me. "but he will be mean about letting me come down next time."

I agreed with him and by dint of being unusually nice to him, thereby bewildering him, I managed to get him off.

I had no idea of going to church, myself.

Joe appeared as he had threatened.

"I smell a nice big rat," he announced cheerfully.

"It's not a rat and it's on its way home," I said feeling the strain.

He was just as nice as though there had been no awful battle and I was too tired to throw the gauntlet.

"Like me?" he asked, presently.

"So-so." I admitted cautiously.

"What were you doing [at] that place I called?"

"A quiet Sunday afternoon with friends," I said vaguely.

"Was that the friend driving off?"

"Yes," I said meekly.

"Well, he's wasting his time," he told me complacently.

I remarked that I didn't think him very flattering!

"Crazy little nut," he laughed and kissed me.

Dec. 1 - They have opened an ancient tomb in the Valley of the Kings in Egypt and are finding many marvellous things. Archeology thrills me and chills me at the same time.

<u>Dec. 3</u> Church as usual. Parts have been assigned for the Christmas Pageant. I am to be the Spirit of Love. It is the longest part of all and I am on the stage thru more than half of it - and I can't think when I shall find time to memorize the lines. The Rev. Osborne gave me the part although his wife wanted someone "less frivolous." Oh I'm not at all happy underneath, but I can't be anything but gay; I feel like a spinning top.

Joe tonight. Some of the girls cattily reminded me of his family. They'd forget it quickly enough if he looked at them.

<u>Dec. 8</u> - School Dance. I told Joe that I wanted to go and <u>he</u> wanted to know why I wanted to go to the silly thing when he knew where there was a <u>real</u> dance. The usual squabble. I went just the same and wore my new rose dress, but I only punished myself. Bob T., a man, hangs around a lot and I don't like him. Al is rather nice, but Arno really interests me. He is a shock headed peasant, frightfully ugly and extremely brilliant, never looks at girls except at me - just studies. He has two classes with me and is a big help when it comes to experiments. On the other hand I am much better in English than he. He likes me best when I act dumb and helpless. Tonight he told me all about himself and wanted to take me home, however, he was on the Committee and couldn't leave until the last gun was fired and I was too tired to wait. Bob took me home. Hope he doesn't become a nuisance.

<u>Dec. 11</u> - Monday - Joe, last night, very indignant. Said if he'd known I really wanted to go he'd have taken me. And he bet I had done it on purpose. Didn't I know better than go around with a man Bob T's age? Besides he had a punk time at his dance and it was all my fault.

"There doesn't seem to be much fun in going seperate ways, does there?" I asked ruefully.

"If you had as punk a time as I did, I'm satisfied," he grinned.

I have always thought kissing greatly over rated, but it isn't. Most boys either peck - or like Junior, quite brutally break ones neck, but Joe - well! He has a very expressionless face and his eyes so grey and moody. I told him he had a lovely nose and when he felt of it wonderingly, I laughed, whereupon he called me a "cute little devil." He is so utterly <u>different</u>.

<u>Dec. 14</u> - Sunday. Another party last night and I had a wonderful time!

I wore my peach dress and had a spell of looking actually pretty.

Joe and I couldn't look at one another without dissolving in one anothers eyes and though he is touchy and quick tempered, he only grinned when the boys kidded him.

All of a sudden I felt too old for party games and the thoughts of playing Post Office positively nauseated me. When those of us who didn't care to play began to pair off, Joe and I went out into the hall. It was unheated and I protested shiveringly, but he drew me toward a seat of some kind in the inky darkness.

"You've either been here with some other girl, or you have eyes like a cat's," I said accusingly.

"I spotted this when I came in," he answered serenely. "Will you stop shivering!"

"I can't," I chattered. "If you had a thin party dress on -"

"Don't move!" he ordered and left me while he dug into a coat closet and came back with an armful of wraps which he wrapped around us until we were half buried beneath their weight.

"Warm?" he asked, and I purred, a specialty of my own which intrigues him. After a time we stopped laughing and wisecracking - he was serious and awfully dear. He tipped my head back and whispered, "Kiss me."

I didn't stop to think - I just did and we both felt drunk.

"Holy Smoke, kid," he said jerkily. "If that's the way you kiss, don't do it very often." And his hand was hot and dry under my chin.

"No," I promised. "I won't. I never kissed anyone else and I'm just as surprized as you are."

"You honestly never kissed any other fellow?" he asked in awed tones.

"Cross my heart."

"Well," he said. "You're probably lying, but I think I'm going to believe you. You are a surprize package if there ever was one."

To my surprize he began to unwrap us and when we were uncovered he kissed me hard. "We're going back in," he said in answer to my question.

"Why?"

"Because, you nut, the lights are on and there are people."

When we opened the door, Lee said - sort of spontaneiously- "Helen, you're the prettiest thing!"

Surprized and pleased I looked at Joe with a little laugh. He smiled that slow smile of his looking into my eyes until everything else became misty shapes.

"She's - she's more than that," he said, as though he didn't have much idea of what he was saying.

I heard a girl ask laughingly, "When are you going to put him back in circulation, Helen?"

And a man's voice, "What eyes the girl's got!"

On the way home we stopped once and looked at each other until he drew me to him slowly, yet roughly. I pulled my bare hand from my pocket and traced his lips with my forefinger. He shivered and pressed his lips against the inside of my wrist.

If we could keep this majic, just as it is forever.

Dec. 18 - Saw Joe at the C.H., this afternoon. Last night was as full of majic as was Saturday, but today there was a slight rift.

An Account of My Life

"You might want to phone me sometime, you never can tell," he grinned.

"Here's the number on a piece of paper. Tuck it in your pocket. I'm there a lot, but if I'm not the boys will either know where I am or give me the message when I come in."

I looked at the slip of paper, idly, and then said in surprize.

"Why this is a Public Garage, Joe!"

"Sure," he admitted. "It's handy and I hang around there a lot."

"I'd rather not call a place like that," I said slowly, handing the slip back to him. "It isn't necessary anyway when we see each other almost every day and you can always phone me.

He tore the paper up without a word. It's little things like that -

<u>Dec. 19</u> - Tuesday. My pride is in shreds. It all started when Joe began to chuckle to himself.

"Tell me the joke?" I asked curiously.

"It's on me," he said - And I felt glad that he <u>could</u> see a joke on himself, for he is as conspicuous for his lack of humor as he is for his fighting abilities.

"Remember the Party where we met?" he began. "Well, I went home with you just to see if I could. You acted like you were better - I mean that high hat stuff gets my goat - the snooty kind aways does, specially as they can usually be made. I didn't know you were so green and you sure had me guessing. Some of the guys wouldn't believe it when I said I'd taken you home. A few of them came up the next night. Sunday, you know, just to for the devil of it. They were around the corner."

"So that's why you were cross about Marcus," I said in a small voice. "He almost spoiled your fun, didn't he?"

It seemed he <u>must</u> feel the hurt I was weltering in, but he laughed and admitted, "For a few minutes. I thought you'd two-timed me."

"Go on," I urged. "There's more to this, isn't there?"

"You know the first time I took you to the movies? Well, I didn't make that date on the phone."

"No?"

"No, one of the gang did it for a joke figuring you'd never heard my voice over the phone. They didn't tell me until that very night and maybe I wasn't sore! There I was all set to go to a dance, remember? You see I wasn't going to date you anymore, <u>not</u> that I was mad, but you'd made it pretty plain what you thought of me, and I was sort of sore about it. I never figured out why I threw over a dance and another girl and took you to a movie I'd already seen. It wasn't <u>my</u> fault if the fellows made a date using my name, it didn't make <u>me</u> responsible, and I passed up a good chance to pay you out for some of the mean cracks you'd made. Well we went and you seemed more interested in the movie than in me, and all of a sudden it came to me, why not take you to the dance? The more I thought of it the better I liked it. And you turned me down flat! Believe me I called you

248

plain and fancy names to myself. Just the same I sort of thought you'd phone me the next day.

I couldn't get you sized up at all, but I felt you'd make some sign.

You see I was pretty sure that you'd never have had any dates with me unless you liked me. I knew at that first party, and so did you.

When you didn't call, or write or try to see me anywhere and the fellows razzed me, saying you'd had a good time with me and that it served me right for getting into that set. I _had_ to find out, and it knocked me for a loop when you said you hadn't any idea of calling me - "

"You said something about a joke on you. You meant on _me_, didn't you? I asked coldly.

"Don't you get it?" he asked impatiently. "I thought it was - well I expected to walk out when I wanted to - I didn't guess I wouldn't want to drop you. It's a swell joke on me."

I received that without comment.

"Are you peeved?" he asked, amazed.

"You must think I enjoy being made a fool of," I told him coldly.

"Holy Moses, what makes you so thick!" he raved. "I fell for you, so the laughs on me, isn't it?"

"There's no use trying to make you understand," I said tonelessly.

"Listen you, what's gotten into you anyway! You're the darndest - What am I supposed to do, eat dirt!"

"That night," I said slowly. "That Sunday night. You met your friends after you left me, I suppose. They asked questions and snickered, didn't they? Maybe they said dirty things." I dug my nails in deeper. "Did you laugh too, and say things? Did you?"

"No," he seemed rather taken back. "No, I didn't. As a matter of fact I told them to lay off and not get funny ideas. I said you were a nice kid, but not my type.

"Thanks," I said dryly.

He gave an impatient shake. "You've done everything but bawl," he told me brutally. "If you're going to, get it over with. I should have kept my mouth shut, knowing you can't talk to a woman."

"You'll never see me cry, no matter what you do," I said, my head high.

"Proud?"

"Maybe," and then deliberately, "Maybe you don't mean enough to me."

He digested that, not liking it very well.

"O.K." he said at length. "I won't make you sore again if I can find out its going to make you sore in time to keep from doing it."

I laughed shortly.

It ended there, but I writhe when I think of it.

Dec. 21 Thur. Had a rather wearing experience with Marcus. I told Joe not to meet me after rehearsal because I had no idea when it would be over. Its too cold to wait outside and he wouldn't come in.

Well, Marcus wanted to take me home and it didn't seem to matter. I was tired, and it was late and I like him well enough.

Just as we were saying goodnight in front of the house I saw Ase coming up the street. He has been very sarcastic about keeping Marcus on the string and I knew he'd say something embarassing if not actually devilish. I had time to get into the house, but he and Marcus would meet face to face, so without thinking, I grabbed Marcus' hand and ran up the path to Grandmother's. I knew it would be safe under the apple trees and planned to stay only long enough for Ase to get in. I hadn't time to explain and to say Marcus was surprized is to put it mildly. However, if I should say, "Come, let's sit in a tub of boiling water," he'd do it. Between laughing and breathing hard from the up hill run, I told him that it was the only thing I could have done unless I wanted to be marched in by the ear, figuratively speaking, at least.

"Are you going to let me kiss you?" he asked, and sounded so wistful I was touched. Besides it was an amusing contrast to Joe. And to be honest, there are times, unfortunately, when I like Marcus. I like the sleekness of his hair and the smooth leaness of his cheek.

"I don't care," I told him, and when he put his arms around me I liked it, and when he would have lifted his head, I held his mouth to mine. I knew the devil was in me and didn't care. Beside I didn't know he had it in him. Candidly, I enjoyed it, until he said in a queer, agonized way, "Helen, I want you so!"

Well, I was embarassed. Joe never says that - he may imply it and act it - he expects me to have sense enough to know it, but he never says it.

I pulled away, stepping back a few paces, whereupon he took a stride toward me, and put his arms around me.

"I didn't mean to scare you," he said.

Human nature is a most peculiar thing, for while I never doubted my ability to handle the situation, and I really appreciated his goodness at the same his remark struck me as both pathetic and amusing.

Then he went on to say - oh all manner of things, simply pouring the words out. I felt as if I had turned on a faucet for a little drink only to be lost in a deluge of water. I wanted to be clear of it all but was too near drowned to reach the spigot.

"Doesn't this mean a thing to you?" he pleaded. "It must, Helen."

"It means no more than it ever did," I said desperately.

"You never kissed me before," he answered. "Only let me kiss you."

I writhed, finding nothing at all to say.

Lifting me to the level of his face he half demanded, half pled:

"You're not going to see Joe anymore!"

"Yes, Marcus," I said. "I am." And feeling weak in the knees as he released me I sat down on a stone step in miserable silence.

1922

Anything he might have called me I called myself as I sat there shivering with nerves and tiredness and cold.

When I looked at him again he was leaning against the Baldwin tree his back to me and he was crying.

I put my head down on my knees and thought, if it were a hurt animal I should help it with tears running down my face, and here I sit doing nothing, dry eyed because I don't know how to comfort him without telling lies. I've always known he cared for me and have taken shameful advantage of it, but I honestly never realised how much he cared.

At last I spoke, not daring to touch him: "I'm sorry, Marcus, I didn't know. I'll never flirt with you again, now I know."

"I'm a fool," he said thickly. "the biggest in the U.S.A. And you fall for that guy! Already you've learned plenty. I might of known! I bet you were wishing it was him all the time, and I thought at last, at last you understood how I felt about you, how I always felt about you and always will, and that you felt something for me!"

"Listen Marcus," I said. "I was not thinking of him. Such as it was it belonged to you."

And that was that.

Dec. 22 - Life becomes more difficult day by day. Way down deep inside me I know Ase, Marcus and the others, are partly right about Joe, but inspite of it all he fills my thoughts completely.

One night - which I didn't record because I smarted so much from the humiliation - one night he took me to a C.H. dance and after dancing with me disappeared, just simply disappeared.

It was largely my crowd, and the boys were sweet to me, but every cat of a girl asked, "Is that the way the Greenmanville gang does it?" or something of that nature. Cill didn't spare me either. My eyes burned, my hands and feet were ice, but I would not haul down my flag.

At the end just as I was about to accept Frankie as an escort, Joe showed up smiling as if nothing was in the least out of the way.

"I'm taking you home," he said, favoring Frankie with a brief glance.

"Are you indeed?" I asked icily.

"I brought you."

"Did you? I thought it must have been another girl?"

At this point Frankie said `goodnight' and left in a hurry.

"Kind of you to come back, just for me," I remarked.

"I don't go for sarcasm," he said, "so shut up. I can't go those damn dances and you know it. You wanted to go, I took you. Nothing to say I can't step out for awhile. I'm back in time to get you."

"Where have you been?"

"That's my business," he told me in an ugly tone.

"Don't you think you own me an explanation?"

"I gave it to you."

I shrugged.

"Listen here!" he was furious. "I didn't hang around because I didn't want to - see? I won't dance with every pill because she's some fond mama's daughter. I'm here in time to take you home. What are you squawking about? I won't be bossed by you or any other female - see?"

"Oh perfectly," I said. "Do forgive me for daring to object! I am rather tired of having your lack of ordinary good manners flung in my face. Such a pity to show yourself up before them all. They may even think you don't know any better."

I meant to be poisonous and I was. If he had dared he would have slapped me, but I wasn't afraid and he knew it.

"I'm fed up," he said at last. "You want to keep me at you elbow all evening. You get a kick out of digging up some girl no one else will have and expecting me to dance with her. Lot you care whether I enjoy myself! Why if I dance with a pretty one of my own choosing you're mad and polite for an hour after. Who to hell do you think you are, anyway? All you want to do is show off and keep me on a leash. I can dance, and I'm good looking and you feel brave as hell to be seen with me. You're not going to boss me and you might as well know it."

"You," I told me, stiff with fury," are nothing but a damn, imitation Shiek on the prowl."

The next day he was so sweet and attentive the cats were unable to condole with me. And all he ever said was,"You've got the devil's own temper." Not sorry he had behaved badly or admitting that he had! He added that he could have had a drink or two and didn't because of me. "I might as well have," he concluded bitterly. "You couldn't have dished out any more hell if I'd been soused."

Dec. 23 - Christmas all but upon us and there's so much still to be done!

I've had an invitation from Emily for the holidays. Mother is anxious for me to accept it for obvious reasons, but for the first time in my life I don't want to go to Norwich and intend to get out of it as diplomatically as possible.

Friday was a busy day. School closed at noon for the Christmas vacation and from there I went to the church where we rehearsed for the Pageant all afternoon. At 4:30 or 5 we had to get ready for the Christian Endeavor Social and Christmas Tree that very evening. There were dozens of things needing to be done at the same time, and while the boys helped us, they hindered with their tom-foolery until we girls were frantic. The worst of it was they were funny and we couldn't help laughing which of course encouraged them. Boys are such children!

Cill and I raced up to Mrs. Wolf's for the tableclothes and of course she gave us the oldest and the most darned. You'd think we weren't old enough to eat without splashing our food and drink. She loves being a Stewardess. How we accomplished as much as we did I don't know, but somehow the tree was trimmed, the greens hung and the tables made ready, all in the basement.

At 6 o'clock I ran home, dressed, grabbed a pan of escalloped potatoes Mother had ready for me, and seized a present for the tree and raced back to church hoping to get a seat at the first table as I hadn't eaten anything but candy since breakfast. Well, I didn't sit down for <u>hours</u>. One of the girls supposed to wait on table didn't show up and I was pressed into service.

The Program was quite good. That boy Dorence Grimes played the violin.

We were washing dishes in the kitchen at 11:30. Toby and Jack helped us clean up the lamps.

At seven the next morning - <u>this</u> morning, Cill, Glad, Jack, Harold and I went for greens. I think we walked at least five miles before we found enough to satisfy us, and we sat in the snow digging leaves and ice away from the Princess Pine, laughing until we were sore all over. I don't know if we were funnier than usual, or simply sillier. Anyway it was fun - even dragging the sacks of greens home. And now I have a costume to help finish, a rehearsal this afternoon and the trim to be churched. I mean of course the church to be trimmed. Told Joe I couldn't possible be seen - possible see him, I mean before tomorrow night.

<u>Dec. 24</u> - The Pageant was a great success! Everyone did well which was something none of us really expected after that last awful rehearsal. Rev. Osborne said I was pretty as a picture, but his wife asked me if I had <u>enough</u> on under the cheesecloth. The very idea! Of course I did. Ase thought the Grecian robe effect was very funny, but at least it was becoming. Some of the girls, less fortunate in their Mothers, had a swaddled look which I <u>presume</u> Mrs. Osborne preferred. I can assure her I had on the proper underpinning.

The Family attended the Pageant en masse. So did Joe: the first time he has been in my church. I saw Mother looking at him coldly, but apprehensively as if she had hoped he wouldn't prove as good looking. Grandmother had her I've-done-all-I-can-it's-up-to-the-Lord expression very much in evidence. She often remarks that she has known a number of scamps in her day (although not intimately of course) none of whom were homely, for the Devil is notoriously good to his own.

Fortunately the Family didn't wait for me to change my clothes, Grandmother not use to being out late in the night air, so I was able to meet Joe after it was over.

"It was nice of you to come," I smiled

"Oh that's all right," he said airily. "Had to see what kind of a Spirit of Love you'd make didn't I?"

"Well?"

"Swell. You're it."

I was rather doubtful. "I wasn't meant to be <u>that</u> kind of Love," I told him.

"Then, they picked the wrong one for the part," he grinned.

"Didn't I look a bit holy?" I persisted, a bit worried.

He hooted at that. Well, of course, I am not the spirituelle type.

I had been eyeing the enormous box of candy he was carrying and he took that time to present it and to lecture me about Marcus coming home with me.

"How'd you find out?" I asked resignedly.

Honestly, it is amazing how he hears everything. He was only a little cross, because it would be dumb of him to be jealous of Marcus.

I love the way he tips my head back and looks at me for minutes it seems, before he bends his head to kiss me, and I love the slow, lingering way he does it, and the way he suddenly becomes hard and steely, and his kisses begin to come so hard they hurt.

Dec. 25 - Junior sent a huge box of writing paper - not candy, thank God!

The Family sniffed at Joe's candy, but I notice all hands are in the box.

Grandmother gave me a lovely fur piece, and Mother gave me soft wine red wool for a dress. I have always taken clothes more or less for granted and feel faintly surprized with a Summer Person exclaims, "What an enchanting little frock!"; but Joe has made me clothes conscious almost over night. None of the boys, except Reynolds who is like that, know what a girl wears, but Joe has a quick appraising glance that misses nothing.

He says homely, dowdy girls make him positively sick. Mother wonders why I never wear a certain lavendar dress with green embroidery. Joe told me frankly he didn't like it.

"I know lavendar isn't good on me," I confessed, "but I thought I could get away with it for once."

"You're not pretty enough for that," he returned bluntly. But when I wear the peach colored party dress with its square low neck and short sleeves and flat turquoise velvet bow, his approval is very evident. And the creamy, tan crepe with its braided girdle of jade green taffeta is a favorite of his. I like it too, although he makes me feel positively unclothed when he points out there isn't more than half a tone's difference between the material and my skin, especially as the darn stuff clings sort of unexpectedly.

The taffeta bouffant makes me "look too much like a doll" according to him. I explained that Mother was always ruffling and flaring things to hid my thinness.

"Don't let her," he advised. "What you've got is good, so why hide it?"

It's fun dressing for someone like Joe!

He has decided to go to High School. He claims he started once before and quit because it bored him, but I don't remember seeing him. The girls think its my idea, but I never suggested any such thing. He said he'd planned to go to Detroit or some such place and work in an automobile factory, but meeting me had upset everything. It shows the very strangeness of our relationship that until today I never knew what he did with himself days. It seems he has been working off and on in the mill.

I thought he seemed to have plenty of spending money.

I asked if he had to earn his own living at such an early age and he laughed and said, "The old man don't care what I do. I can go to school if I want to."

Apparently they are not horribly poor, at any rate.

I looked at him speculatively. "I expect you are quite smart, aren't you?"

"I can learn if I want to," he said.

If he is intelligent and his father can afford to send him to school, why should he work in a mill?

I guess I know the answer if I am honest. In order to have money to spend on girls.

1923

January 1923

Jan.-- - Johnnie, Roland P, Mary and I went sliding on Three Hills in the moonlight. The sleds flew over the hard packed snow and the air was so keen the boys steered blindly with tear filled eyes.

As the moon whitened the stone in the burying ground I thought of Them sliding down these very hills when the tall dark pines were young.

We had several bad spills and laughed until we were to weak to walk.

Jan. 10 It amazes me to discover how unfamiliar Joe is with the Mystic the rest of us know. This evening we walked up Spicer Street and down Burrows Street where every house was strange to him and he had never heard of Capt. Spicer or clipper ships.

I pointed out great Grandfather Capt. Rhodes Burrows house, remembering that he had sold the back lots to Mr. Partridge who in turn sold it to Capt. Spicer for the building of the Library. There use to be a deer park on the grounds, a hot house and a fountain, but now that Capt. Spicer is dead and Miss Annie lives alone, the deer park and green houses have been abandoned and the fountain never plays.

Joe had heard of Mr. Lathrop, of course, because of the Lathrop Engine Co. or whatever it is called - everyone around here just calls it Lathrop's and lets it go at that - but he didn't know Mr. Lathrop had one of the first if not the first automobile in Mystic and use to drive all around Robin Hood's barn to avoid the hills.

He asked questions which I answered as best I could, relating little stories about this and that which made him laugh more than once. It was, he said a new experience for him to be carrying on a regular conversation with a girl, but darned if I wasn't kind of interesting to listen to.

Of course we eventually hit a reef in the always perilous sea of understanding. While speaking of Mr. Lathrop he asked if "that little stuck-up monkey" was his son.

I said," Jimmie? No, grandson. Heavens, he is younger than we!"

At which Joe snorted and observed," Old duffers have been known to get kids, you know. That Jimmie needs a swift kick where it will do the most good, if you ask me!"

"He is spoiled," I admitted. "Being Motherless they try to make it up to him. Besides Elsie was their only daughter and they all but worshipped her."

"He's worse than spoiled," he grunted. "Go on with this sightseeing tour."

"This is Burrows Street" I announced.

"Got a street and everything!" he jeered.

"Why not?" I said shortly. "We've always been here. My great grandfather walked here and his father knew it before it was a street and before that all that you can see and much more was his land. My great grandfather was born, married and died here. He and his father sailed the seas, worked the land and were buried in that burying ground. As long as any of us are alive they are alive. If thats being stuck-up make what you like of it."

After a pause he said cynically. "You'd be surprized how many can't put a name to their grandfather and think they are doing darn well to name their father. Ever think of that?"

"No" I admitted slowly. "I don't suppose I have."

"Tell me about the old dame in this house here. She's a hundred they say and rich as mud. Her name isn't Burrows and she's too old to be very near and dear to you."

"She is a Burrows, she married Uncle Tom Packer."

"She's stinking rich isn't she?"

"She's well to do," I admitted, rather stiffly.

"Is she really a hundred?"

"Of course not, but she is well along in her nineties I guess."

"What's she to you?"

"Great-great Aunt."

That struck him funny. "How do you figure it?" he wanted to know.

"Aunt Jane is one of my great grandfather's sisters. She is Aunt to Grandmother, Great Aunt to Mother, and Great-Great Aunt to me."

"My God," he said fervently. "What's she like?"

"Old and frail and wrapped in cotton batting, a nurse in attendance."

"I don't believe she was ever young," he stated firmly.

"Well," I said thoughtfully. "She couldn't have been much older than I when she married Uncle Tom."

"It gives me the willies," he shivered. "Let's not get that old."

At which point we kissed and left the ancestors to themselves.

Jan. 12 - I don't know why we quarrel so much! This time the starting point was chewing gum. A lot of dignity and romance to that! He was chewing it and I drew back when he tried to kiss me, which touched his pride and so we fought, not stopping until we were mentally and spiritually in tatters. After we had completely exhausted our vocabularies we sat down to recover, for neither of us were mad any longer.

It was then that he did something I could not allow. To be exact he put his hand on my ankle and stroked it gently. I shook it off after a moment, angry that it should be so pleasant.

"Quit it!" I said curtly.

"Alright, Miss Touch-Me-Not," he answered good naturedly, but he didn't, and his hand was on my knee.

I put an end to it, by jumping to my feet.

"Don't you like it? You've got swell legs," he said lazily, making no effort to move.

"What's that got to do with it?" I demanded, glaring down at him angrily.

"Plenty," he said calmly. "Don't you like it?"

"No."

He seemed to accept that and I considered the matter closed, until he asked, "Are you being a good girl, or don't you want to?"

"I don't want to."

"Why not? How do you know? You think about it don't you?"

"No."

"Oh baloney!" he jeered rudely. "Tell it the Marines!"

"It is immaterial to me whether you believe it or not," I said coldly. "It happens to be true."

After a silence during which he seemed to be undergoing some sort of mental struggle, he burst out: " How do you get that way?"

"I don't let myself."

"My God!" he said simply. "Maybe that kind of dumbness went alright in the old days, I dunno. Girls stayed at home - the nice ones - and waited for some guy to ask poppa, didn't they? This is 1923 and you're not sitting in a parlor or trailing a chaperone. We didn't come out here to talk books or the price of beef. What do you think I'm made of?"

"Green cheese, maybe, like the moon," I answered lightly, not giving any thought to what I said in an effort to divert him.

He was on his feet in a flash. "Think so?" he asked hotly, pulling me against him so hard it all but knocked the breath out of me.

I convinced him, I guess, because he let me go.

"You act as if you meant it," he said in amazement.

"I do," I told him.

"Well," he said, breathing unevenly. "That's enough for <u>one</u> night. You're going home."

<u>Friday 19th</u> - We were in Catherine's little store ordering hot dogs and chocolate this noon when Joe and a crowd of boys came in shouting for food. Little by little he wormed his way thru the jam until we were side by side at the counter.

"Hey, Catherine, the same for me," he ordered, watching me bite into my hot dog with a juicy plop. Somehow he always gets service and Catherine who is fat and fond of him, heard him in all that din.

"Friday, Joe," she reminded him.

He groaned," And I could eat a horse! Bring me something, Kate."

"A nice tuna fish salad sandwich," she promised, heading for the kitchen.

"With a little more filling <u>and</u> an extra pickle. What is this power you have over women, Handsome?" I asked sweetly.

"You ought to know," Henry butted in, sure of the laugh it would bring.

"Who, me?" I asked innocently. "I never saw the man before."

"Lay off," Joe said laconically. "I can't laugh on an empty stomach. I'm funny that way."

Somehow it had never occurred to me that he didn't eat meat on Fridays, and I thought about it as I finished my dog and finding a dime in my pocket ordered another.

"You'll be fat the way you eat," Joe said, eyeing me severely.

"See any signs of it?" I asked impeturably.

Catherine slid his sandwich in front of him. "Don't that look good?" she smiled.

"Sure. Thanks," he said morosely. "Only I don't like tuna fish."

As we ate I reflected upon a religion that could make a person of his type abide by it so strictly. I have never known any Catholics intimately and I have never asked Joe questions because it seemed wiser to let that topic alone.

Daddy had a book on Popery that use to bring me to a boil, but somehow I could believe it only as long as I read it; it didn't seem to have any connection with the Catholics around town. And there are some yellowed clippings in another book, telling about the Pope and his aims and Catholic nurses converting Protestant children and all that sort of thing. I've always expected a Catholic to at least try it, but no one ever has - Imagine Connie Costello!

There must be something in a religion. I mean, anything that can make Joe get up for Mass, dead for sleep after being out late, has a tremendous pull. The only thing is, I can't see where it has any effect on his behaviour. He goes to confession and starts in all over again. Grandmother's Conscience is much worse, because it must bear whatever lies upon it. Confessing doesn't bring relief to people like us - even if we could bring ourselves to lay our hearts bare. Of course some people talk with their minister, but only in extreme cases. When we do wrong we have to bear the weight of it. The Roger Williams-John Clarke ancestors of mine with the hundreds of years of Protestant faith in back of me, make the Catholic religion completely foreign to me.

I looked up to find his eyes on me. Our eyes held - and we laughed for no reason at all.

"Cripes!" said Henry. "You two've got it bad."

It burns him up that I won't as he puts it, take him seriously, and I have found quite by accident that a certain poem by Herrick from The Golden Treasury which we have in English, annoys him decidedly when recited in a mocking sing-sing way. I have only to start:

"Bid me to live, and I will live
Thy Protestant to be
Or bid me love, and I will give
A loving heart to thee."

to get his goat. The stanzas beginning: "Bid that heart stay and it will stay" and "Bid me weep, and I will weep" and "Bid me despair, and I'll despair" - when he permits me to get that far, really rile him, while the last stanza, "Thou art my life, my love, my heart, The very eyes of me. And hast command of every part, To live and die for thee." brings him to a boil.

"Its the way you say it," he growled. "You don't take anything serious."

Thats all he knows!

I love going into the Greek's with him. Everyone looks up, calls out a gay greeting, and the girls say things to one another in an undertone. How anyone as quiet as Joe can make himself so evident is something I've never fully understood. It must be sheer charm and personality! He can be fun, for he has an occassional light mood when he is amusing and at such times he and I have the others in stitches, but often as not he is quiet and, withdrawn, and then again he can be sullen or even in a fighting mood. I mean <u>actually</u>, a fighting mood, he likes nothing better than a good fight. The boys say he fights until he drops, his face white as a sheet and shut tight. From what Warren told me, I gather there have been some classic rows.

Unless a boy is itching for a scrap he seldom runs the risk of getting Joe's goat.

4:00 P.M. - Late afternoon and so dark the lights are burning. Joe and I quarrelling again. <u>He</u> is, I'm not. Said he was tired of having Marcus around every corner. I told him he must be hard up for something to quarrel about.

Letter from Junior who writes <u>so</u> regularly. This crazy thing - whatever it is, between Joe and myself is making me hard and selfish. Perhaps that is proof that it isn't love, because love is supposed to be enobling. Its a strain knowing anyone like Joe, for there are so many things involved: clothes, and one's popularity with the need of being amusing or appealing and care not to show too much liking and things like that.

I know Junior was hurt that I did not spend the holidays in Norwich, I know he counted on them. Well, I didn't want to leave, and I knew I'd be stiff with him, my mind continually on Joe. Yet I feel a strange mixture of regret and shame.

For all its not what I imagined love to be, it is very real and definite. I find myself thinking of every word he has said, of every lift of his eyebrows, every quirk of his lips. On the other hand I have no longing to do wonderful, sacrificial things for him, or any desire to be submerged in him. I guess it is sort of unique, this feeling.

"Do you think the old fashioned way was best?" I asked him.

He snorted contemptuously: "Hand holding? Keeping locks of hair? Writing mushy notes? Sleeping with a picture of the loved one under your pillow? Nuts. I don't want you <u>under</u> my pillow."

"Shut up," I said firmly. "Maybe there is something in the old way. They had things neatly docketed: friendship, courtship, love, marriage."

"Fuss and feathers," he shrugged. "Must have been tough on the poor devils."

"They played according to rules!"

"They took the long way around, if you ask me! And I bet they took short cuts."

"Do you believe that love is ninety-nine percent passion and one little soupcon of jealousy?" I asked with interest.

"What the hell," he looked at me suspiciously. "Where'd you get that from and what does it mean?"

"'This Side of Paradise' by Scott Fitzgerald. Soupcon is French for touch - a touch of jealousy, or a drop of jealousy. Don't you read <u>anything</u> but stories of the great Northwest? You ought to read it."

"Why?"

I stared at him. "Everyone has."

"Well, that's one way to learn," he remarked with sarcasm.

<u>Jan. 21</u> Sunday. Last night there was a party - Joe's friends - and when he asked me to go I felt I couldn't refuse, and besides I wanted to see for myself. They were quite friendly, but they talked of too personal things, petted rather brazenly and were too unrestrained. They didn't seem to have any manners at all. Most of them were older, some quite a lot older. The only way to have a good time was to act like them and I couldn't. They knew Joe so well I felt I didn't know him at all, and likewise gave me an inkling of how he feels with my crowd. I couldn't help seeing that they were kinder than my own, generally speaking.

He was different too: his manner, his speech. There were nick-names and catch phrases that meant nothing to me and jokes whose points I missed. After awhile they left me pretty much to him and I was glad. That was one party where I felt no desire to be popular, which was just as well, as Joe was awfully possessive. One man was rather bold until Joe fixed him with an angry glare. He had had a little to drink, and he turned that furious white glare on any one who showed the least interest in me. I thought liquor made men red faced and inclined to be silly. One man seemed rather taken back and amused because he said, "OK, boy, if that's the way you feel about the little lady."

Joe, who was watching my face said rather anxiously, "Having a punk time, aren't you?"

I said, "Oh no."

"They don't matter," he smiled. "We won't let them bother us, and its better than freezing to death outdoors."

So far I haven't been simple enough to tell him what that smile does to me. If he knew how something tightens, twists, and turns over in me - Oh, its not the very ordinary things he says! - but when he lifts one eyebrow slantingly and gives that lopsided smile of his, I wonder how I can feel so marvellous and not burst into a thousand minute fragments.

He was right in saying the others didn't matter - the whole crowded room full of them receded more and more, and of all the voices piling one on top of the other, I heard only his.

"You're so soft and little without that damn coat," he said. "You smell sweet too, like spring flowers."

Oh it was so strange and dream-like! I kept saying to myself, this is I, this is Helen, but it didn't mean anything.

A boy and a girl passed by closely, and as they did so, the boy deliberately ran his fingers up the nape of my neck. I jerked away, instinctively. And then the amazing thing happened. Joe jumped to his feet with the devil in his eyes - and even in my bewilderment the thought flashed thru my mind, that no other boy moved in quite that springy way. He yanked the girl toward him and kissed her on the mouth. It took only a few seconds and he was beside me again.

"Now I've warmed her up for him, he can leave my girl alone," he grinned, tossing a lock of hair off his forehead.

He interpreted the expression on my face as fear, "Scared?" he asked. "He don't care about her and he knows I can lick him."

I didn't feel much of anything, or think it even. He was gentle with me and when his fingers ran over my face and into the little hollow at the base of my throat I felt enchanted.

Someone put the lights out and before the exclamations, questions and laughter had more than begun, he was forcing me back against the cushions. I pushed against him, but the lounge was squashy and the will was weak.

It was only a few minutes before the lights flashed on and he pulled me upright.

"We'll get out of this as quick as we can," he whispered. "I know where we can go."

Voices, music seem to come from an immense distance, and when he held my coat I slipped into it obediently, leaning back against him for a moment.

When the cold air struck against my hot face and the sounds of the party were shut in by the street door, my damn head began to clear. I've heard of girls who said they didn't know what they were doing, but theres something in me apparently that won't let go. Like crockery smashing came the realization of what it meant: a party, vulgar, cheap, scummy - and I slipping out like a half-baked girl at a Camp Meeting. In short, I was myself again, or as nearly so as one can be after such an upsetting experience.

"We're crazy, Joe," I said. "Take me home please."

He did, but not until he had said a great deal. I didn't agree, because my sympathies were more or less with him. <u>Why</u> can't I react to things in an orthodox manner?

1923

According to all I have learned I should prefer these regrets to the ones I should be feeling if we had acted different - at least I think so, but how can anyone know?

I knew he wouldn't be up tonight, and when I think that he may be, that he probably is, with someone else, I could die.

Jan. 23 - I can't read by the hour as I use to do , all my life I have read and now I can't. The Red Queen has hold of my hand and is crying "Faster! Faster!"

Jan. 27 - Went to the Radio Dance with William last night. Didn't want to go, but the Family said I must because he is such a nice boy and never seen in a pool-room. Even Ase shook hands with him man to man instead of grunting something over the top of his newspaper.

William was very grave, dignified and courteous. One knew when we went out of the door that I would be returned safely without a hair ruffled, at the proper time. I like all that in moderation, but I don't see any need for a man to spread his cloak when there are no puddles to cover.

I was bored, merciful heavens, was I bored!

Jan. 29 - Joe not at all disturbed by William - in fact he grinned.

"I guess that hurt you more than it did me," he observed. "I hope you'll appreciate me now."

He has found out about Junior, too. He says the least I can do to make amends is to give him my photograph. I'm not too keen about it, because I take a terrible picture - look stuffed and set. Ase says I have such a vivacious face no one pose looks like me.

I could tell from his manner he had something on his mind and tried to hold it off as long as possible. We use to have fun, and now I never can tell when he'll turn serious. After we had gazed at the lighthouse for a long time I sighed heavily.

"Tired?" he asked.

"No, bored."

"With me?"

"With everything," I said glumly.

More silence so lengthy and prolonged I said meekly. "Please take me home, or pay some attention to me. I'm so neglected."

"I'm thinking," he told me. And continued to ignore me until my patience snapped.

"Why didn't you stay at home? I don't like you."

"Quit kidding," he said.

"Well," I amended, "I don't like you as much as usual."

"Will you come home with me sometime?" he asked.

"Will I what?"

"Come home with me. I live in a house same as anyone else."

"But <u>why</u>, Joe?" You know we've sort of an unspoken agreement - I mean there'd be all sorts of trouble if we let the families in on our affairs."

"I want you to meet my Mother," he said flatly.

"Does she want to see me?" I asked timidly.

"She has seen you."

"But where? I never -"

"You go to the Morgan's a lot, don't you? Well, we live nearby. You know the neighbourhood isn't what it use to be!"

"Oh," I said feebly.

"Don't like the idea very well, do you?" he asked keenly.

I didn't, because all of a sudden I remembered seeing her. Mama and I were in the yard and old Mrs. Stillman asked us over to see her plants. As we crossed the lane way, a woman passed on her way to the little houses at the end. Mama who speaks to everyone said "hello" and we walked on. It didn't <u>have</u> to be his Mother, but somehow I felt sure it was. She looked at me with considerable curiosity, I thought.

"I'll see what I can do," I promised, after a moments silence. "But I think she'd better ask me herself."

"Do they know when you're out with me?" he asked suddenly.

"Naturally, when we go to the movies, and they know you meet me at church."

"How about the other times? Sneak out?"

I flushed angrily. "I don't like that word! They know when I go to the C.H. - they know all my crowd goes there, and I suppose they think I stay there. There are a number of ways -"

"Without once telling a whopping lie."

I stared at him angily, uncertainly.

"Then as far as they know it amounts to a movie now and then, a soda at the drug store, meeting you Sunday nights after church. And they fuss over that!"

"They don't like it and they are sarcastic, but they don't prevent it," I said coldly. He fished a cigarette out of a limp deck looking at me in the glow of the match.

"I didn't know all this," he said briefly.

"I've told you they were difficult time and again," I protested.

"Sure. I didn't take it in maybe."

"But what made you think they'd let me meet you here and there, when they won't have you at the house? You must have seen that didn't make sense!"

"I wondered," he said laconically. "Did they know about that last party?"

"They knew I was going to a party, but they supposed I knew the people. Mother's always saying she can't keep track of my acquaintances any longer. And they supposed my crowd was going."

"Did you say so?"

"I didn't say they weren't."

"Its alright for you to go anywhere if your crowd goes, is that it?"

"There are places," I said stiffly, "Like the German Club and Public Dances where we can't go unless we make up a party and stick with it."

"Well," he said. "I have to hand it to you."

I moved uneasily. "It's the only way it could go on," I muttered.

"And the lid will blow off if you get pally with my folks?"

I said nothing, but he took my silence for an answer.

"OK. Forget it," he spoke abruptly.

"I'm sorry Joe, " I told him softly. "I should like to meet your Mother."

"Sure, I know. Forget it."

Feb. 1 - The Principal has become very sex conscious all of a sudden, some one has been filling him full of impure thoughts, apparently, because today we were herded into Assembly - (girls only, boys to be dealt with later) - and given a talking-to by a silly, fool of a teacher, with frizzled hair and skirts up to her knees. Betty and I linked arms as we went in together.

"The facts of life, at last!" Betty prophesized gloomily.

Well, it seems that our short skirts and rolled stockings are inciting the boys to improper thoughts. Teacher says that when they stand on a lower floor and look up -

"Do you supposed they've complained?" I whispered gravely which caused Betty to give a little snort of laughter.

Well, the Instructor of the Young cast an icy glance in our direction and began to paste certain incidents upon certain ones of us, without actually calling names. She really should conduct a gossip column in a newspaper. If she herself didn't act silly over every good looking boy it might have had more weight.

It was awful going back into class room because the boys had got wind of it and were sickening or funny according to their natures.

"Hey, Helen," Bill called cheerfully. "Ain't we the sinners!"

I don't suppose that old Has-Been would believe it, but I never thought of inciting anyone with short skirts etc. It's the style, that's all!

All the utter pills listened intently with mouths ajar, for to quote Betty, she put ideas into heads where never a one was found before.

I asked Henry point-blank if he thought our style of dress improper. He looked up, indignation all over his freckled face. "Do you think I'm an old man to get het up at the sight of bare knees? I've seen thousands." And as an afterthought: "Generally speaking they aren't much to look at."

"Dear Henry," I said gratefully.

Helen attended high school in Stonington Borough

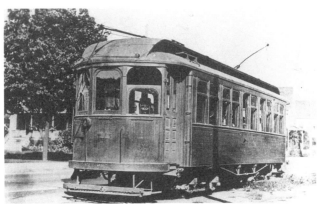
One of the trolley cars that ran through Mystic

Broadway School in Mystic

1923

Feb. 8 - Walked into the living room where Ase and Kirk were deep in a discussion of post war youth. Everyone is shrieking about flappers and the jazz age. You'd think this generation had invented red! These newspaper and magazine articles make me sick and I'm tired of having Ase shove them under my nose with a demand for an explanation. If the ministers and priests would shut up about sex for a few minutes maybe we wouldn't think about it so much.

Tonight Kirk waved his pipe at me, observing, "The product of our times: a flapper."

And then to me: "How are your morals?"

"Fine, thank you! How are yours?" I retorted.

Kirk seldom does more than chuckle but this time he roared with laughter.

Feb. 11 - Joe was dear tonight; said he wanted to kiss me under my chin and did I think I'd like it? I told him I couldn't tell never having been kissed there. So he did.

"Very nice," he decided. "That's my special spot."

"Would you feel bad if I died?" he asked for no apparent reason.

"Oh no!" I assured him cheerfully. "It would give me great pleasure my Melancholy Man." And then in superstitious fear, "Don't you feel well?"

"Guess I'll hang on for awhile," he grinned, putting his arms around my waist. I was sitting on a wall looking down into his face. The street light shone on us, but no house was near and everyone was indoors. I placed my hands on his shoulders and said gravely: "Joe, if you were any better looking I simply couldn't bear it."

There was a catch in my throat and when he suddenly buried his face between my throat and the fur collar, I felt an actual pain.

Well, presently he swung up beside me and there we sat wrapped in thoughts, for we know each other well enough to do without continual chatter. Besides Joe, except when he's in a temper is rather a quiet person.

I was looking out to sea when he kissed me so roughly and unexpectedly he had to grab me to keep from falling off the wall.

"There!" I spluttered. "Is a perfectly good mood shot to thunder and probably a pair of silk stockings, not to mention yards of skin from my anatomy. Are you subject to fits, or what?"

"Have I got to blow a whistle before I kiss you?" he demanded.

"Oh Joe! Think of the hidious tooting," I cried, tickled by the thought.

He quirked one eyebrow at me: "Modest little thing aren't you? Toot-toot here I come."

And so what with laughing and kissing we both fell off the wall.

"Want to go to the movies tomorrow? I've got the price?" he asked cheerfully helping me to my feet.

"I guess so."

"I don't know why I take you," he complained. "It's a waste of money, because you won't pet. You are the only girl I ever knew who wouldn't pet in the movies."

"I'd just as soon eat my dinner in the middle of Main Street."

He thought it over.

"Well, have it your way," he shrugged. "You make a guy work for what he gets, but I like the work."

Feb. 12 - Joe knew about Jr. in a dim sort of a way, but never showed any jealousy until some malicious person - he won't say who - told him a lot of stuff. Whoever it was said Jr. belonged to an old and well-to-do family; that he was going to college; that his father owned three automobiles; that he was six feet tall and crazy about me; that I visited there - and oh! I don't know what else. Not having thought of Jr. like that, I was surprized at how good he sounded! I floundered a bit in search of suitable replies, because while Jr. certainly won't go to college, not possessing that kind of mental equipment, the description was, in the main, perfectly true.

Joe seemed to resent Jr's height more than anything, because he himself is not tall and to judge by his father, never will be. He wanted to know if it was true that I visited his family weeks at a time. I explained that Emily his sister was one of my best friends.

Joe said he had sisters, but he never noticed me making friends with them! I was so reasonable and patient with him he calmed down a little, and I turned the tide by telling him I had been asked for the holidays and hadn't gone.

"Why not?" he asked woodenly.

"I should think you'd know." I sniffed.

"You mean on account of me?"

"Yes," I said. "On account of you."

He didn't say anything for a minute, and then he tipped my chin up until my eyes were looking into his.

"Oh you little thing!" he whispered. "Haven't you any sense at all?"

I guess I looked bewildered because he laughed and kissed me tenderly. He is so darned good looking, and dear! Or is it just my state of mind? No, it can't be - how about all the other girls who think him practically irrisistable? I'll confess to these fair pages that I've got it bad for the first time in my life!

Feb. 15 A new girl came to school to-day and she hadn't been there many hours before she noticed Joe. The female eye just naturally hunts him out.

I saw the mocking, insolent once over he gives and knew that although she tossed her head and said "Fresh!" she was really flattered. She was sizing me up before the day was over, so I knew she had made inqueries, and as she didn't seem at all set back I imagine she thinks she can hold her own with me. I wonder if I shall ever see a pretty girl without that quickening fear that someday he will see someone -

Feb. 16 - He just <u>dared</u> me to mention the new girl, but I wouldn't, so he grinned and admitted he didn't think much of her legs, adding that the seams in her stockings were crooked.

Ase told me this evening: "This damn foolishness is lasting too long. I gave you credit for enough sense to bring you out of this infatuation. The boy's no damn good! I don't care a God dam if he's Catholic or Moslem - the women can fight that out with you. The little squirt's not worth the powder to blow him to hell!"

Oh it went on and on with me getting more mulish by the minute.

I suppose he has been discussing modern youth with Kirk again. Why can't he leave me alone? Does he honestly believe his howling does any good? It's my life and I've got to live it. It's getting so I never know what will set him off. Take the song "Hot Lips." I can't sing, so while he has heard me play it and mildly cursed, he never knew the words until the other day when he heard some kids singing it. Well, the man was shocked pink! He ran thru my popular music, old and new, exploding at every title. "Ain't We Got Fun" brought forth lurid remarks. The poor man reads the worse tripe about the jazz age, works himself into a lather, demands that I explain certain things and finally dissolves in shame.

And in this state he has <u>no</u> sense of humor. The silliest slang expressions burn him up "you're the cats whiskers," or "the cats meow" or "the cats pajamas," while "it's a thrill," "bees knees" and "hot and bothered" practically shock the pants off him. He sees dirt where I honestly never saw it. The older ones may have been pure in practice, but they must have had dirty minds. At <u>least</u> we are honest.

I thank the Lord Mother is easy to get along with. She expects me to behave myself and I do. Most of the girls I know draw the line at certain things, but Ase apparently thinks I'm toboganning straight to Hell. If I can't play "Hot Lips" without - oh what's the use!

He raves about dancing cheek to cheek, as though it were unmitigated, unholy pleasure! Nine times out of ten I hate it, but does he expect me to do a polka all by myself? It's only with Joe that I like it.

Feb. 17 - I am just <u>worn</u> out by the Family! Gandmother got hold of me to-day. If she had been dictatorial I could have fought, but she was patient, thus cutting the ground from under my feet. She said she knew I didn't realize the unhappiness I might be storing up for myself and Family by going with Joe.

I cried out in exasperation that there was no <u>need</u> to take things so seriously when it wasn't a question of marrying or anything but having a good time!

"I know that story," she said grimly, and after a pause. "You like stories so well, ever think of Ellen Holmes? Married George Costello. <u>They</u>

started out young. The Holmeses must have spent the better part of twenty years trying to break that up. They kept them from marrying, but they couldn't keep them apart. They had a meeting place somewhere. The Holmeses wouldn't have George there and Ellen couldn't have enjoyed going to George's. Old Mike, George's father, was nothing but a drunken Irishman reeling around town, a lazy, good natured sot. George's mother was a good woman, the boys must have taken after her, but she was just the Mallory's Irish cook."

"Ellen and George were well along before it was so that they could marry. They'd been true to each other for years, no one begrudged them their happiness. Besides George was fair in that he never asked Ellen to turn Catholic, knowing it wasn't in her to do so. Sentimental folks say they were made for one another, but with years and years of heart break for all hands they paid a high price for each other. Only they know if it was too high."

I understood as I could never have understood a short while ago. A meeting place - we know how hard that is, and I know how Ellen must have felt about Old Mike, how she may have loved George's Mother never feeling the least kinship or understanding. And heaven knows, I've had a taste of the incessant quarrels that must have been their lot.

"They loved each other," I said. "I am not in love, nor he with me. Can't we just be let alone?"

Grandmother flinched away from my brazen use of the word `love,' and shot me a glance.

"Why do you choose them?" I fired. "How about Bud's father marrying a Catholic when <u>his</u> father was a minister? How about Constance MacDonald's mother marrying Catholic?"

"They married out of their religion," she said. "Which makes enough unhappiness, but they didn't marry out of their class. When you marry out of both - well, you go down to that level. I've seen it time and again."

"Ellen Holmes hasn't," I said defensively.

"They are out of the common run," she answered. "If they'd married young who knows? Women just as well bred as Ellen have married for love, seen it go, known poverty, had a raft of children, and slipped little by little, too tired to hold their heads up. But they had to wait, and any feeling strong enough to last all those years under those conditions is good. He's better for having known her and he has had to climb up to keep from sinking. She went to meet him someway.

"You remember old Adeline, don't you? She married a Protestant and a good man, but common. Your Great Uncle Aborn knew her when she was a high spirited, handsome girl. One time when he was home from Washington, he saw her - she'd been married some time by then.

" 'Well, Millie,' he said to me, 'Adeline couldn't raise Levi to her level so she's slipping down to his.' "

"He was right. It had been so gradual like I hadn't noticed, but he coming from away, saw it at once. "

1923

"You think this talk of marrying is foolery and so it is at your age. But I've seen lives spoiled that started in just such a way as you have willfully set your feet. You've seen plenty of cases around town where respected names belong to trashy families A family can breed so true it will peter out, I know, on the other hand nine times out of ten when you seen a slovenly house, or slattern of a woman and a pack of gormy children you'll find that somewhere along the line two young fools with no heed to anything but the night's pleasures bred wrong and thoughtlessly. I don't say our kind is everything to go by, but if you are born and bred a certain way its best to live by those rules. Now go away, I'm tired. Someday you may thank me for this, I don't know."

She <u>looked</u> tired - and old. I bent with a quick rush to kiss her.

This morning I went downtown on various errands. Mrs. Lib Rathbun was in Dennison's Store and we walked over town together until she remembered a silk sample she had to match. I knew I'd be in and out of every store in town and chatting with everyone if I stayed with her, so I made my excuses and went my way. I had taken but a few steps when I heard a familiar voice asking:

"What's the rush?" - and swung around to face Joe.

"Where'd you pop from?" I smiled, trying not to look <u>too</u> pleased.

"Right in back of you," he said. "Thought you'd never shake the old hen."

I was silent a minute and then I told him I didn't want to sound fault finding but I <u>did</u> wish he'd speak of my friends with the respect due them.

"You mean that old snob?" he asked in amazement.

I just stared at him. "Mrs. Lib?" I spoke increduously." Why she's easy as an old shoe.

"I'm not the only one in town who thinks so," he said mulishly. "She's always looking down her nose at me."

I don't believe Mrs. Lib ever saw him to know him in her life, but I couldn't say that very well.

"Well, for heavens sake," I sighed helplessly. "Let's talk about something else."

I guess I've read too much poetry for my own good - "Locksley Hall" for instance.

"......... thou art mated with a clown, and the grossness of his nature will have weight to drag thee down." Oh this is <u>absurd</u>. Who is <u>going</u> to get married! And anyway it doesn't have to be true. Besides he isn't a clown and he isn't really gross.

<u>Feb. 19</u> - He didn't come to school today consequently everything is flat, flat, flat. Bud says he has a bad cold.

<u>Feb. 22</u> - He was at school today. I was late for class and simply racing down the corridor when I slammed smack into him. I said, "Oh, I'm sorry! Oh its <u>you</u>! "

271

"Glad to see me?" he asked, laughing at me.

I nodded and went on my way with little lanterns lighted in me.

Later: Just back from the C.H. I'm usually stingy with compliments, but I burst out with: "You're a fascinating devil, Joe."

"Yeah?" he smiled. "Same to you."

<u>Sunday. Feb. 26</u> - Everything is getting so difficult - getting?; it <u>is</u>. Theres a lot to write and its hard to get it out with this turmoil in me.

Joe came to church with me tonight - I mean the regular service. I've never asked him to and we have avoided the question of religion and the Klu-Klux-Klan. It was nice of him, because the old timers stare at him and I'll swear Capt. Elias looked at me with awe in his eyes!

Ase loathes the Klan and all it stand for. He says its made up of morons getting a thrill parading around in sheets, their stupid faces safely hidden. As usual his opinions aren't popular. He knows the priest, enjoys talking with him - and to hell with anyone who doesn't like it!

Joe expects me to come to his church in return which is only fair. It would be an interesting experience, but oh Lordy I dread the disapproval and catty talk and conjectures. Betty went with Bud so I know what to expect. And Bud is only half Catholic, his grandfather was a Congregational minister. Betty said indignantly that the priest wouldn't take her seriously and all but spanked her bottom and sent her home. He was right to do so: Betty is capable of turning Mohammedan if she thought it would give her a thrill.

That's <u>one</u> thing - and here's another. Joe's sisters are stiff, sulky and rather poisonous. In fact they are so sure I'll snub them they snub me first. Unfortunately I have seen them at the C.H. any number of times and never until I knew Joe had any reason (or desire) to speak to them. They have their set and I have mine.

Now that Joe's friends have become convinced that we are really going together I am included in invitations I couldn't accept if I wanted to, and Lord knows I don't! A fifteen minute talk with his best friend's girl convinced me of that. Of all the coarse, vulgar - well that's enough. Naturally I don't say such things to Joe, but he knows and is uncomfortable. Being uncomfortable and being Joe, he takes it out on me, becoming sullen and sarcastic.

They don't like me and I don't like them. Joe and I argue back and forth without getting anywhere. He couldn't deny that his sisters dislike me, its all too evident.

"They say you are having a good time with me and maybe they are right," he said sullenly. "What's all this leading to, that's what I want to know?"

"Oh Joe," I spoke helplessly. "Can't we go together, until we quarrel or get sick of it? Does it have to be any more than that?"

"Yes," he shouted. "You flirt like the devil! If I act like a saint you're not happy till you've got me started. Girls like you give me a pain!"

Then he hunched his shoulders and asked: "You want to get married?"

"Are you <u>serious</u>? I gasped.

"Wouldn't say it if I wasn't, would I?"

"Listen," I said gently. "You don't want to get married."

"Who says I don't!"

"Well, you don't and they'd annul it anyway. Besides I couldn't be married by a priest."

"You could," he retorted bitterly. "You could and you would and our kids would grow up in the faith!"

"I wouldn't," I said grimly. "And maybe there wouldn't be any children."

"There would," he answered promptly. "Look at my family!"

I shuddered inwardly.

"A Protestant I am and a Protestant I stay," I told him grimly.

"Didn't know you were religious?" he mocked.

"I'm not: I'm a Protestant. As for children if any, they ought to decide for themselves."

He was coldly furious. "You don't know what you're talking about!"

"Of all the <u>intolerant</u> -" I began and bit it back, drawing a deep breath.

"I don't care what you are why should you care what I am? I've always despised people who changed religions."

"If you love a person enough," he muttered. "You want to -"

"Would you change yours for the love of any woman?" I broke in.

The shut look came over his face.

"This is silly," I decided. "Marrying is definitely out."

"Alright!" he snapped. "If we get any crazier - In the first place we've had time to get sick of each other if we were going to, and we haven't. Rows don't mean a thing to us the making up is so swell. What's all this leading to?"

I didn't say anything for several minutes. "Joe," I asked hurriedly. "Do you honestly think its because I'm scared?"

"What else? You're not cold."

I let it go at that. What's the use trying to explain?

"Go to the devil," I told him concisely, jumping down from the wall.

As we said goodnight he tipped my face up with his forefinger and kissed me one very seriously and gently. I started for the door, then turned as if he had spoken my name. He came up to me.

"Helen, don't go in - yet," he whispered.

"But I must."

"Don't go in," he went on rapidly. "Come with me Helen, just for a little while - please."

"But where? I can't, it's too late. If Ase hears us - I'll see you tomorrow night if I can."

"No," he said. "Tonight."

And I couldn't say anything because his arms were tightening the breath out of me and his mouth was pressing hard against mine. We seemed so melted together I wonder if we could ever become separate again.

He was talking to me. "You've got to. I've done pretty much what you wanted, haven't I? I've waited long enough. Just for a little while, Helen, Please!"

"No," I said dully. "I can't. Don't you know I can't."

"You mean that?" he asked, as if he couldn't believe his ears.

"I must mean it," I said desperately.

"Alright," he said, after a moments silence. "Goodnight."

Mon. Feb. 24 - I have been unhappy before, but never like this.

At school today . . . everyone asked me why I had thrown Joe over. I simply looked stony and waited.

"He says you did." one girl insisted. "Did he get fresh or something?"

I'm not feeling much now but numbness. I didn't know he intended to make a clean break. Why, he didn't say "goodbye," just the usual "good night."

Well, it must be born - somehow.

Feb. 28 - It sounds maudlin and I'm trying hard to be composed and sensible, but I can't help wondering what the days will be without his slow smile and the flickering light in his eyes.

He is right, it had to end, but I didn't want it to come to an end. I knew it couldn't last from the start, but I was counting on getting tired of him.

No one can tell how he is taking anything, with that poker face of his, but the devils in him seem to be quiet and there is a set look to his mouth that warns the inquisitive to leave him alone. We meet because we can't very well help it, but neither of us can act casual or friendly. We look at one another coldly - or try to. When I think that a smile from me or a glance would end this agony, I feel torn in two. No. He'd hate me if I should mend the break and then expect things to go on as they were before.

Did Marcus feel like this? Oh no! But if he did I am sorry. I'm skinned alive and the very air makes me smart and writhe.

Feb. 29 Nothing matters any more - clothes - or dates - or anything. Nights are terrible. The tears roll down my face and there is no use wiping them away. They trickle into the corners of my mouth and are salt as the sea. The sea! I could bear this better if I had the sea. I've never cried like this before: it is very strange. I've sobbed and moaned and twisted, but I've never kept so still, hardly breathing, not moving with the tears wetting the pillow until I turn it over. I try to make myself small, so that I won't hurt so much.

I tell myself he isn't worth it, but whether he is or not, it makes no difference. And I'm seeing myself with new eyes, not liking what I see.

Funny - the little things you store up in your mind - such silly little things. Its awful seeing him and pretending I don't care. I don't think any one guesses how I feel and my attitude of cold indifference adds strength to his statement that I brought it to an end. Maybe I did, but I didn't realize. I get up - and go to bed with one thought uppermost in my mind: no <u>one</u> must know how I feel - I've thought of him so much I can't stop all at once. These past entries are so many knives. <u>Does he</u> feel like this? I won't lift a finger to call him back, if it kills me!

One of the girls asked me if I knew that the priest spoke to him about coming to my church - and of other things. I don't know whether its true or not - she swears it is - but Joe never told me anything about it.

Four months ago when I put on my blue taffeta and went to a Party I never guessed I should be feeling like this now.

The Family is enormously relieved. They <u>knew</u> I'd come to my senses! Ase, curiously enough, seems to have an inkling of the truth, for along with the satisfied look in his eyes there is a gleam of something like compassion. I don't want compassion - or pity. I don't want anything, but the will to live this out day by day.

When Kirk dropped in this evening I slipped out the back door and ran up to Grandmother's. I didn't go in because I knew she'd want to go to bed and would send me home. I had to walk to keep warm and I kept thinking of Joe and wondering what Ase was telling Kirk. I couldn't stay out long or Mother would worry, so after awhile I went back and in the kitchen door.

Mother must have been listening for me because she called "That you, Helen." I said yes and walked in. Ase and Kirk just glanced at me and went on talking and I found my book and went into the little room where Mother sat sewing. I tried to read and managed to cover many pages without any of it sinking in.

"The cat's yowling to get in, Helen," Ase called in, and I got up and let it in without a word.

"There's a last month's "Atlantic" you can have if you want it," Kirk said. I thanked him.

They are both very kind to me - each in his own way.

<u>March 2</u> -Dorrance Grimes played at our church social last night and became aware of me for the first time. He <u>would</u>, now, when I can think of no one but Joe.

I had forgotten about him until one Sunday not long ago when several of us attended evening service at the Congregational church. He came in with a crowd of boys and I was amazed to see how tall he had grown and how very good looking too. The light shown on the crisp golden brown waves of his hair and Alice Colby fell for him like a ton of bricks. I rather resented it as I discovered him ages ago.

Well, Alice who was on the Social Committee said she was going to ask him to play at the next social. This was it.

I have had a most unpleasant letter from Junior. Of course I have spoken of Joe briefly, because I never have made a secret of going around with other boys. Why should I? He has never seemed to care particularly so long as the deck was clear when he came down. Seems Cill told Emily a lot about Joe, also that he is a Catholic all of which burns Junior up. Such narrowness! Well he ought to be happy now. I shan't tell him its over and done with until I feel like it. Let him squirm.

Mar. 9 Today in Study Hall Dorrance asked me to go to a party with him a week from now. I'd forgotten about that social and when he sat with me in Study Hall I thought at first it must be accidental. Well, its taken an awful long time to get him started!

I've always wondered how people with broken hearts kept on living, but I know now that life goes on pretty much the same except for a dull ache and a flat taste. Joe is so mixed up with everything I can't get thru a day without a thousand twinges.

My school marks should be suffering from all this boy stuff, but they are not. My brain seems to be hitting on all cylinders and even Ase doesn't complain. Lord how I hate that place! Yet I can no more explain the feeling than I could at the beginning.

Boys - well they are tangible.

Ase on the warpath again. I knew something was up when I heard him talking to Mother in a low shocked tone.

"I don't believe it," Mother said flatly.

Presently he charged into the little room where I sat reading.

"Helen," he said ponderously. "I have heard a terrible thing about a girl we know, a girl of good family."

My first thought was, someone's got caught, who?

"They are saying around town that this girl went out with a boy - stark naked."

I made no answer.

"Well?"

"She wore a long coat buttoned from top to bottom. She claimed the boy was such a pill he'd never know. He didn't."

Ase turned purple and asked how the story got out.

"Why she told it herself," I explained. "It was a joke you see. This boy rather fancies himself - thinks he's hot and all that. To hear him talk you'd think no woman safe with him. She showed him up, that's all."

Well, he swore, ranted and raved. His horror was genuine and pathetic.

"If you ever get yourself talked about," he shouted.

"I could have lied to you," I pointed out. "Most of us have found that its no use telling your generation anything."

"No shame!" he raved. "No morals, damn little strumpets!"

If he had let it go at that, but he kept on and on and on.

1923

Finally, knowing full well that it would goad him anew I used an explanatory phrase popular with the crowd and good for a laugh when used certain ways.

"C'est le guerre!" I shrugged.

He practically burst into bits. What a sap I've been to bank on his intelligence and broad mindedness. Oh he is broad minded enough except where I am concerned.

Grandmother, bless her, takes it more or less in her stride!

Bobbed hair and short skirts don't bother her a bit, although she does fuss about our scanty underclothes and says I'll catch my death.

Ase has lost all faith in her since she enjoyed the movie, "The Shiek" and took to reading tabloids on the sly.

Mar. 10 - Several of us were talking about [sex appeal] this afternoon, remarking that this one and that had `It' in varying degrees. I'd be a hyprocrite if I didn't admit I possess a fair amount, but as I said to Cill, my hat is off to Mary Holdrege, <u>that</u> girl is nothing but!

Cill sighed in agreement, "What <u>is</u> it about her?" she asked, not expecting an answer.

"She is rather pretty," Glad offered, adding, "Even with that blotchy skin."

"It isn't that," I objected. "She isn't any more than good looking. The girl doesn't do a thing; she just is. She goes with what ever boy rushes her the hardest. If you ask me she hasn't any preference. Boys and men go for her without fail."

I don't think any of us like her - or dislike her. As far as we can see she is a negative personality, but it has been forced upon us that she has a strange inexplicable charm. She is stupid, really stupid and she never said an amusing thing in her life. If any other girl acted as dull, heavy, lothargic as she the boys would call her a lemon, a pill, a wash out, and be bored. I've tried again and again to catch her at it. She <u>must</u> do something, but she doesn't. She sits, smiling pleasantly and the boys go to her as if drawn by an invisible force.

Tetia asked doubtfully. "Do you suppose she's - you know."

"No" I denied flatly. "Not from choice, anyway. She is sluggish as a slug, unless she is the greatest actress of all times. Besides we'd be bound to hear things."

"Well," Tetia offered. "Some of the great charmers and courtesans weren't as good looking as she."

"Where does she fit?" I demanded. "She hasn't the intellect of a Madame Whats-her-Name, nor the curves and lusty look of a Nell Gwinne. She hasn't any more animal spirits than a stuffed cat; she's about as spiritual as a piece of furniture. She isn't the sweet girl type; she isn't the wholesome Sunday School type; she isn't hot stuff. What <u>is</u> she?"

"One hundred percent sex appeal, that's all," Tetia said dryly.

Perhaps she wears [a] Venus embroidered girdle - a cestus wasn't it called?

<u>Mar 15</u> Joe and I don't speak, but he is as aware of me as I am of him. I can feel when he comes anywhere near. I know he is there before I see him. Something seems to reach out and surround me.

All interest in us has died out, thank the Lord. As long as they suspected a quarrel and thought we'd tell stories about one another, they were interested, but two people who won't say a word give them a pain. So far, he hasn't noticed any other girl. I shall know quickly enough when he does as my <u>dear</u> friends are just waiting to tell me. Well, <u>they</u> won't see it hurts! I keep hoping - I don't know - common sense tells me nothing can make this have a happy ending. Perhaps it will just - stop.

<u>Mar. 16</u> -The night of the party. It has been a wildly stormy day with a down pour of rain, but it cleared somewhat by evening.

Dorrance is even nicer than I thought and very romantic looking. The party was at Prof. Boynton's in Toggle Hollow. The Congregational minister, Mr. Farnham was there, and he is something brand new in ministers! Young, tall, handsome with wavy golden brown hair and grey blue eyes. The girls will be consumed with jealousy when I tell them he danced with me several times.

I had a rather sophisticated dress, black, rather traily in points, with a silver girdle and a silver pond lily smashed flat on one side. It added years to my appearance and was much admired.

I think Annette likes Dorrance. Poor kid! And he doesn't even see her. It must be terrible to be gone on someone who doesn't feel that way at all, and it is strange that it has never happened to me. If I like a boy he promptly likes me twice as much as I like him - except Joe - I've never fathomed him.

Dorrance - I hardly know what to say about him. Everyone likes him - there is nothing of the dead bunny about him. Somehow he is quieter, more serious, more worth while than any of the others. I have never known anyone like him. I like him a lot.

<u>Mar. 17</u> -St. Patrick's Day Dance at the Community House. Joe was there. We didn't speak: he wouldn't and I <u>couldn't</u>.

At the end of the first dance Cill told me Ray Hatfield said he had a bad crush on me, but was afraid to let me know. He meant we've known each other so long if he acted any differently I might laugh at him; so he took this way of broaching the subject which is just like him. Ray is the Rev. Byron Ulrich Hatfield's son who married Mother and Ase. The Family won't make a fuss if I go around with him and he isn't a bit nicer than Joe, though better bred. Minister's son or not, he is always in hot water. Seems to me Jesse James was the son of a Baptist minister too.

Well, I was bored and I smiled at him just to see what would happen. He asked for the next dance and could he take me out at Intermission, and could he take me home. Except with Joe I never like to date up early in the evening, so I told him I wasn't going home, but was spending the night with Cill, which was true. I thought that would discourage him as Cill lives in the opposite direction and his father hadn't let him take the automobile. However, it didn't; he said he wanted to come anyway.

Dorrance was there, although he didn't dance. Also Marcus and Milton. Milt went home with me from somewhere and hasn't recovered from it yet, though I have given him no further encouragement. Joe was watching me and I knew he knew I was having anything but a good time - and positively hated him.

At the end there was a stupid mix-up. Marcus, Milt and Ray all thought they were taking me home. Dorrance came up too, but when he saw the others he sort of grinned and kept on going. Everyone and his brother, but Joe. Oh <u>why</u> wasn't he waiting too!

<u>Mar. 27</u> - For all the fun I have I might as well stop going to parties or dances! Joe was at the party last night. I wore a new rose colored dress with little puffed sleeves made entirely of narrow lace and I wondered if he liked it. I thought of other parties and wanted to die. The hardest thing I ever did was to pretend I didn't care what he did or whom he noticed. If he was out of the room for more than a minute I felt <u>ill</u>. But I would not speak first.

Ray was there. He had come straight from basket-ball practice and though he had <u>presumably</u> had a shower when he changed, he smelled hot and sweaty. I hated to let him kiss me. However, like Junior, he likes opposition. The difference there is in men! Joe becomes furious and stand-offish if I show the least bit of indifference.

Anyway, it was a ghastly party and I was glad when it was over.

<u>Mar. 29</u> - School closed today for Easter Holidays - ten days. When the bus drew in this afternoon we poured down to the C.H. We quite often do, providing we've a nickle to buy a chocolate bar at the C.H. to ward off starvation until supper time. I was penniless, but Toby wasn't, so I let him feed me.

We found Glad deep in a forbidden book and she looked up nervous as a cat when Toby crept up in back of her and said, "<u>Oh</u> my dear child! That immoral book! Some of the passages are just <u>too</u> revolting."

"Pig," she retorted. "Don't bother me."

Tetia was dreamily eating a chocolate and looking altogether lovely, while Kat was trying the effect of a barbarous ornament destined for a new dress.

Soon the social room was filled and the cubby-hole jammed. Bill Brown started playing his uke while Joe and Gelo gave their famous, rowdy Apache dance. We laughed until we ached. Ralphy Powers, the colored boy, came in and we got him to play the piano, because while he doesn't know one note from another he gets a savage rhythm that makes you think of tom-toms and heathen rites. Some of the kids had pocket combs and they played on them and one boy even had a harmonica. It was swell. We danced and sang and got crazier and crazier. And then Toby had an idea. He pushed me into a chair, probably because I am the smallest and easiest to carry and he and Bud lifted it aloft.

Someone gave me a string of beads to put around my forehead and a ruler for a sceptre. Then everyone fell in behind, the combs, the harmonica, and the uke and we wound in and out thru all the rooms, upstairs and down, with more and more joining in until there was quite a procession. We were laughing and having a perfectly swell time when in walked Freddy Godfrey, the assistant director who had left a peaceful C.H. to run over to the post office and came back to what he called Bedlam let loose. "Thank God some of the old hens didn't walk in on this!" he said devoutly. "Now calm down! You kids don't mean any harm, but you gotta think of how things look! They say this place is a regular rough house, that you do here what you can't do at home. If they'd seen this! Holy Moses. I'd be out of a job."

Suddenly everything went flat and we felt foolish. We hadn't thought of anything but fun, yet when we looked back at it, it seemed silly - not fun at all.

Apr. 2 - Junior and Emily were down yesterday. He says we will have a good time this summer, for he is coming down <u>often</u> and <u>without</u> Emily. Somehow I felt cross with myself for not liking him more when in so many ways he is absolutely right for me. He is becoming rather attractive without being good looking, and I approve his rangy build. He will be a big man if he ever fills out, but never a fat one, and his towsled hair colored hair can turn grey without altering his appearance to any extent.

When Priscilla and Emily were making fudge, he scooped me up in his arms. I hoped the old feeling would be gone, because he <u>is</u> my kind, and it would be so divinely simple. So, I didn't stiffen, or pull away and when he recovered from his momentary surprise - well, it was no use: I hated it.

"It's no use, let me go!" I creid, breaking away, or trying to.

"You're notional," he answered calmly, paying no attention to my struggles.

The use of that word so favored by Grandmother, made me want to like him. I thought miserably that I could understand if I found him repellent, which I don't! There is an odd, perverse attraction, especially when I haven't seen him for a long time.

"Oh Junior!" I said despairingly, half laughing. "I can't help it."

<u>April 3</u> - Spring is here. All winter I was eager for a Spring and summer with Joe, and now it has come I am bleak as November. Nights when we literally <u>froze</u>, I thought of that white moon- light night on the lake with Junior. If we could have had that! Or a night heavy with the

scent of seringa and roses, the sea shimmering in the distance. Certainly no one can say it was due to moon majic and romantic settings.

Our crowd went to Columbus Hall last night. Of course Joe was there. I wish I could tell what he is thinking! That darn poker face has me completely puzzled.

One of his sisters was there and she gave me one of her pert, to-Hell-with-you glances. I rather expected her to look smug and satisfied, but she seemed as insolent and resentful as ever.

Dorrance came home with me, although Marcus and Milt who seem to be working as a pair, tried to get in ahead of him. He is the most worth while boy I have ever known, and what he sees in me I don't know.

We stopped in the Greek's on the way home where most of my crowd was having the usual sundaes and sodas.

"My, my!" John the Greek said as he slapped a college ice down in front of me. "You gotta a new boy friend?"

The gang roared at that, darn 'em.

Apr. 4 - To-morrow Mary and I are going to visit at Williams Memorial. Dorrance, Bill, Toby and Ren are going to meet Cill, Leona, Mary and I and take us to a show in the afternoon.

Milt asked if he couldn't come too! I wish to heaven I had never accepted that powder compact: it was just the encouragement he needed.

April 5 - Had rather a good time, though it ended flatly, somehow. And to make it annoying, Milt came too. Toby was sore and we had one of our rare scraps.

We saw the show at the Capitol, and the vaudeville was just vulgar enough to please the boys. Honestly, men make me sick!

April 6 - B.Y.P.U. gave a supper and we went over to Toby's house afterwards. Just our crowd, I mean. Fun!

Herman brought his drums, Bill his uke, Dorrance his violin and Ren his violin, but when they all played there was no one but Toby to dance with and we wore him out in no time! So they gave it up and made the player piano do. Some of the girls smoke, and I shall just as soon as I can get some to practice on in private. Strangely enough Dorrance is lots broader minded and more tolerant than Joe. I didn't think he was a wet smack, but one can never tell.

April 7 - I told Mother I was going to smoke and I preferred that she know. She made no objection, but asked me to limit myself. Very fair of her.

April 8 - I hadn't dressed this morning before the phone rang: it was Bill. I drawled such a sleepy hello he said he felt like going back to bed again. He had been out late too, but his father who is a Scout Master and very Spartan, brought him out of bed with a dash of cold water at 6:30.

An Account of My Life

Yesterday <u>was</u> a full day. Our dance at the C.H. was all that could be desired. Of course Alice being chairman took all the credit, while we did all the work.

We spent the afternoon ransacking the C.H. stores for decorations. And then we prepared the punch. The boys usually do that, but because the dance was given in competition with the one to be given by the boys later, we couldn't ask them. I never squeezed so many lemons before and may I never again!

There was a supper at the Episcopal parish house (Bill's church) and he, Cill, Dorrance and I went together. Good food - and did Bill eat! His mother is away on a visit and he and his father are keeping house. He says his father is alright over a campfire, but in a house he is a flop and that he never knew there were so many plain and fancy ways of burning things.

From there we went to the dance, which was a success as the boys generously admitted, while maintaining theirs would be better.

Joe was there, darn him! He comes, he doesn't speak, and he simply spoils my fun.

When I got home I fell into bed rouge and all. Mother says I left a trail of confetti all thru the house.

<u>April 10</u> - Ugh! To-day coming from the C.H. I passed a boy of the Pool Room specie. He is one of Joe's crowd. I don't know his name - he has some sort of a nickname I believe - and he looks like the picture of a typical dissipated youth in a sex and advice to girls book. In a slouchy, sallow way he is good-looking. I hear there are girls who think he is positively fascinating. I don't.

"How about going somewhere, sometime?" he asked, not even troubling to remove his cigarette from the corner of his mouth.

"You know the answer," I answered. "The same goes for any of your cronies who may be curious."

"Okey," he said indifferently. "It's a free country, ain't it."

<u>April 16</u> - Last night we went down to Tetia's. Made fudge over the living-room fire. It came out perfectly vile - too many cooks, I guess.

Alice acts as if she expected her cigarette to go off in her face any minute. Oh I'm a cat, but she has been clawing me plenty, lately, Dorrance of course.

Babe and Billy were in bed, but they came down in their pajamas and there was no sending them back.

Dorrance is worth fifty Joes, and I know it.

<u>April 18</u> - Last night the C.H. kept open house to celebrate its 3rd anniversary with dancing from nine to eleven and everything free of charge. The orchestra was composed of Ren, Freddie Whipple, Herman, Albert Geyer and Dorrance. I love "The Dance of the Wooden Soldiers."

1923

Someone filled in for him while he had one dance with me - "Three O'Clock in the Morning."

Bud tried to plead for Joe, but I wouldn't listen. Queer how he sticks in my mind while I find myself liking Dorrance better everyday. Why can't I be satisfied? I was never wholly satisfied with Joe.

<u>Apr.21</u> Dance at C.H. Had the darndest time getting ready: everything went wrong. A buckle came off my slippers and my girdle of jade green taffeta was all wrong. Grandma came down to see how I looked in my new dress and she scolded at my flighty ways.

"Give me that buckle and I'll see what I can do with it, while your Mother fixes your sash. Good land it is worse than fitting a ship to sea."

I got into shape just as Dorrance rang the bell. She likes Dorrance though she regrets that he is "half foreigner" - German to be exact. I kissed her goodnight as I wouldn't be seeing her again that night, and half the way down the street I tried to puzzle out what that good smell about her <u>is</u>. It's not scent or powder, but a combined odor of apples, clean, startched clothes and I don't know what else.

Joe wasn't at the Dance. Bud says he has a bad cold and if I had any heart at all I'd at least telephone him. Well, I won't.

This was the Boys' Dance. They trimmed the dance hall yesterday afternoon and put us out when we made needed suggestions. The decorations were amusing if nothing else: red and pink! Some of crepe streamers were twisted, some weren't: some were looped and some tight. As a final touch the lights were covered with red paper and the whole place looked as if on fire. It was enough to give one convulsions. They must have done it on purpose, although I have heard Toby say pink and red looked pretty much alike to him.

My dress was just about the prettiest one there, and Hobart Siswick says his father says I am "a cute kid."

Dorrance is so different from the others - so restful. I never realized how tired I am.

Little, old Rhody Hancock came to the dance as usual. She sat watching us, nodding her head and tapping her feet, while she beamed upon us happily. She is so dainty and pink cheeked and queer. Queer people always fascinate me. Rhody is related to one of our best families and it is a great trial to Isabel to have her haunting the place, but there is nothing she can do about it - no one, not even Isabel, could be cruel to old Rhody who isn't one to take even the broadest hints. She not only comes for the music and the dancing, she carries a basket which we fill with what is left of the refreshments.

We regard her with particular interest, because ridiculous as it seems, little pink Rhody is, or was, a Scarlet Woman. At present she is living with John Smith, jokingly called the Horseradish King. He calls her his housekeeper rather grandly, for they have only a few rooms in a dilapidated house. She helps him make horse radish, putting it in glass jars which she collects from her customers as well as from dumps.

Our house is one of her stopping places - in fact she and Grandmother are old friends.

Queer to hear them calling each other Rhody and Mill. Blessed are the simple minded! Rhody is the only completely happy person I have ever known.

When Grandmother tells me old Lelia Bentley was once a pretty girl, I listen almost unbelievingly, but when she says Rhody was "pretty as a pink." I can believe it. She still is. She has always been poverty poor, always worked hard, never taken any care of herself, never has any pretty clothes, and yet she has a better skin than any of us, and if I make anywhere near as good looking an old woman as she is, I shall count myself favoured.

<u>May 5th</u> Tetia and I walked up to Cill's this afternoon. The cedars were lovely and we sat in the little old burying ground smoking and talking for hours. Cill and Tetia are clever - Tetia the cleverest, I suspect, although I don't <u>know</u>. We talked on all manner of serious subjects and while they led inevitably to disagreements, sometimes violent, we enjoyed ourselves.

Dorrance came in the evening. He happened to ask me about the burning of the Fiery Cross in our yard - it was gabbed about all over town at the time, of course. I don't remember the date, but one night a few of Ase's friends burned a small cross on the edge of our lawn sometime around midnight, as a joke, knowing Ase's attitude in regards to the Klu-Klux-Klan.

I don't think either Dr Lou or Kirk actually did it, but Ase seemed to think the idea originated with them. At any rate it tickled his particular brand of humor.

The cross was <u>not</u> a gigantic affair, nor was it set up by the Klan as a warning. We were <u>not</u> frightened for the simple reason none of us knew a thing about it until the next morning when Ase saw the charred remains and, not being a fool, guessed in a minute. After he had been to the Club he was certain.

As far as I know, that is all there was to it, but try to convince anyone!

Some said Ase had received repeated warnings from the Klan. Nonsense! Of course he <u>was</u> on the opposite side of the fence being his usual argumentative self. The Butcher, the Baker, the Candlestick Maker joined what he called the Sheet Brigade: he likewise called them moronic thrill chasers, sadistic show-offs which didn't set too well on some stomachs.

I certainly picked a swell time to go around with a Catholic!

Ase, to do him justice, never objected to Joe because of the Klan, while Joe and I ignored the issue by mutual consent.

1923

Dorrance seems to think Ase took a brave stand. I don't know; all I know is, he has always been on the opposite side and usually right in the long run.

He was against our entering the war and it was a downright unhealthy state of mind; and now he is cursing Pres. Harding up hill and down dale, not sparing Mrs. Harding whom he calls a so-and-so.

May 7 - When a boy is handsome, popular and amusing, it is easy enough to like him, but what of one who is none of those things - and still possesses an odd attraction?

Gustave is everything I don't like put together: homely, broad, clumsy and slow-moving. I dislike his untidy yellow hair, like thatch on a peasant's hut. He is a peasant. I don't like his small, deep set eyes or his big, sullen mouth with its heavy lips, or his ugly coarse skinned hands and their broad, stubby fingers. Of course he is terribly brilliant - one of those people with intellects and all.

Practically everything I do or say, shocks him, yet he'll tell dirty stories to boys, in clearly audible tones. He likes me, without in the least approving of me. I don't know why I attract him, but I do, and he resents it. He may have a brain, but I am much quicker witted than he - in fact I can think in circles around him, which doesn't please him either.

I suppose he has a certain heavy humor. He plans to go to Harvard and when I looked a trifle surprized he remarked drily, "Don't you think I've brains enough?"

He is always laughing at my smallness and the littleness of my wrists, but he refers to girls some where near his own size as "Cows" - which is rather amusing as he looks like an ox himself and lives on a farm in the back woods somewhere.

One day he squeezed my hand trying to hurt me, but I wouldn't give him the satisfaction of hearing me cry out. When I was half sick with pain he loosened his grips. "You have guts," he said casually - and walked away. I sat their holding my crushed fingers tenderly, angry, sore and rather impressed in spite of myself.

The girls have never fancied him, but they are beginning to think they may have overlooked something. Well, they're welcome! I don't like him, although he does interest me against my will. He has no place in my life - living in the back counry how could he take me anywhere?

Besides he has the nerve to tell me he had "no time for girls." I stuck my nose in the air and said, "I suppose you have a great deal of <u>character</u>. It must be what makes you so unpleasant!"

He chuckled. Mean devil.

May 10 - Last Thursday I spent the early evening at the C. H. Dorrance took me to the second show and we walked afterward. I love the way his hair springs back from his forehead in crisp waves.

The next day - or rather evening we went to the C.H. Dance.

The Family likes him, but they'd welcome almost anyone to get my mind away from Joe.

Last night there was an entertainment at the Episcopal Parish House at which Bill, Ren, Leona, Cill, Dorrance, and I enjoyed ourselves. Dorrance played. Everyone says he has a Future and Eckstein said he would go far.

Spent the afternoon in the Library. While there John Gurnsey came for a book. He is a dour, glum, individual with grizzled hair and an unbalanced mind.

Mr. Wheeler hires him as delivery boy and he stumps all over town with a basket in the crook of his arm. He is surprisingly well read and always grabs the Atlantic Monthly before anyone has read it.

Grandmother says he comes from a good family, his father was editor of the old "Mystic Press." His sister Emma smokes a pipe and lives in Bogue Town.

The Community House - years ago it was a Club House with docks and bathing facilities, a shingled building, far from imposing, but quite good looking. The interior is battered, faded and torn, but we love it. The Library, its low bookshelves filled with well worn books, its long window seat covered in faded blue and that spooky "The Tale of the Dead" by Bochlin over the doorway; the Pool Room, shabby from constant use, its beaver-boarded walls dented and broken; the Social Room, a fireplace at one end, windows opening on the River, a piano, a victrola; the little Cubby Hole, barely large enough for a table and a few chairs which is popular with us (the Director can never understand why we pile in there three deep, while the Social Room is not half filled).

Downstairs there is a Bowling Alley and the gym, besides the square Reception Hall, and another piano. You go thru the Bowling Alley out on to the veranda, past the shower room and then on to the Dock. I forgot to say a little room opens off the Library where the Director has his desk and candy and chewing gum are for sale.

How little I know Grandmother, and I thought no one could know her better!

Milt gave me vanity case not long ago. Now, I have several and besides I don't want to encourage him by using it, so I left it at Grandmother's and forgot about it.

Yesterday she brought it out, asking if I didn't want it.

I said "Lord no. I don't care what you do with it."

She hesitated a moment and asked, "Do you mind if I keep it?"

I looked dumbfounded I guess, because she said quickly. "Not that I'd use the thing, but it is a real pretty little thing."

Grandmother wanting silly, pretty things!

"Of course you may have it," I said, throwing my arms around her and kissing her.

"Go long Soft Soap," she told me, straightening herself out.

Suitable or not, I shall give her a string of red beads for Christmas.

She won't wear them I know, but she can look at them.

Mother says she is mellowing and I think she must be.

Ase says she never should have seen "The Shiek" at her age. He can be funny in a horrid sort of way. Then too she's got him where the skin is off so many times, besides she hasn't mellowed toward him, and never will.

Today Bud stopped me and asked with a grin what I was up to now. At first I thought he meant in reference to Joe and I said "What do you mean?" very haughtily, but it developed that he was talking about Gustave! Seems Gustave asked him about the Community House and hinted that he would like to go to some of the doings if Bud would put him up over night.

I said I didn't know what that had to do with me and Bud laughed and retorted: "Not much you don't! Didn't William hang around me until I brought him to the C.H.?"

"You must be a great drawing-card." I told him solemnly.

He told me to cut it out - hadn't he done plenty for me first and last? Did I or did I not want him to bring him (meaning Gustave), and was I doing it simply to get Joe's goat.

"Don't be silly," I said. "They're hardly in the same class."

May 11 - Opening night at the Casino. Dorrance and I went with Betty and Bud, the boys hiring Cini's car for the purpose. We all rode to Old Mystic for Betty who lives there in the house Charles Q. lived in before his family died and he moved into the little house next to his Museum. The big house is a lovely place built in the days when Charles Q. had money and could indulge in port cochere and private dock.

Betty and Bud were carrying on an old disagreement - at least Betty was, with hints, innuendoes and thinly veined sarcasm which Bud blithely passed over and Dorrance and I tactfully ignored.

There was a good crowd at the Casino and we enjoyed ourselves thoroughly. However, I wish Dorrance would dance with someone beside me - and Betty from courtesy. He doesn't mind having me dance with various ones - in fact he acts pleased and proud that I should be noticed. I verily believe he would never dance but for me.

May 12 - Gladys has let me borrow "*Betty Alden*" which is as good as she said it was.

I asked Dorrance if he had many books. He said his family read very little. Maybe I'll get it into my head that all families are not like my own. We are a reading family, definitely.

Toby, Tetia and Dorrance and I went to the movies this evening and to the Greek's Ice Cream Parlor afterwards. Toby is a comical cuss and Tetia in high spirits which was pleasant as she can pretty well wreck any good time if she takes it into her head to do so.

An Account of My Life

Toby and Dorrance are increasingly intimate to my delightful for both are specially dear to me, though for different reasons. Dorrance had dinner with them last night and Toby's mother said he was as nice a boy as she ever hoped to meet. He is.

May 14 - Our Library doesn't have half the books I want to read and as I can't afford to buy many I have to go without. Cill, Glad and Tetia grumble too, but to the others it simply doesn't matter. I shall never forget how shocked I was years ago when I discovered that Marcus had never seen inside the Mystic Library - almost as shocked as if he had never been to church.

If Toby with his generous allowance cared to read we'd be in clover, but he has never been and never will be a reader in the real sense though the book shelves in his sitting room are loaded with boys books in series - in serried rows one might say.

It must be simply heavenly to send a long list to a book store and receive a box packed with bright new books and crisp clean pages.

May 17 - Dorrance's birthday and a lovely day it has been - not that we did anything spectacular.

Orville Harrold gave a concert at the Baptist Church, Clyde Burrows who is a cousin of mine several degrees removed, appearing with him. Emil Polak was the accompaniest.

Orville Harrold who sings at the Metropolitan in New York has made a protege of Clyde. Everyone was there, the pews filled with Burrowses and allied families - all except Grandmother who flatly refused to upset a good night's sleep to hear "Capitola's son sing."

May 19 - Another dance at the Casino: Betty, Bud, Dorrance and I. It was raining and the car hurtled thru wet darkness. I never felt toward any boy as I do toward Dorrance - a certain tenderness I never knew I possessed.

All the girls who saw or heard Clyde - or both, think I am pretty lucky to have him in the family. Well, I guess I am although I never realized it.

Anyway, I didn't even realize he had become important. Of course I like him, but I love Blanch his sister who is really beautiful. Clyde is awfully nice and has a nice smile and is sort of good looking but I never knew he was such a fine figure until I saw him in evening clothes on a platform.

He really seems to like Mystic although it may be all put on, because it stands to reason a person who knows big cities and is successful would be most awfully bored with it and with us.

I will say that he is just as nice to a kid or a person in her teens as he is to older women. Now that he has been away one would have to get acquainted all over again and I guess he won't hang around Mystic long.

I don't know how old he is - way long in his twenties anyway - maybe his thirties. He says he remembers my eyes from the days when Blanch pushed me in my baby carriage. I wish we weren't related and I wish I were older or he were younger or something. Many girls are women at my age, but I am so small and childish looking.

May 22 - To-night I simply had to stay after school to catch up on my chemistry - I got behind because I hate doing experiments.

Gustave stayed too, not for the same reason you may be sure, but because he likes to work out half a dozen ahead. He gets interested and can't wait for the rest of the class just as I can't read a book in assignments, finishing it the day it is handed out in English class. Well, I was glad to see him, because with his help I could make short work of them. How anyone so dull and doltish can be so brilliant I shall never understand.

I finished the last one, and went to the corridor for my hat and jacket. It was all but deserted, though now and then a boy or girl flitted thru at top speed on the way home. I was reaching for my jacket when I heard Gustave's lumbering tread. Then with no warning, no by your leave or anything he kissed me, pinning me back against the coat hooks. The suddenness of it and the feel of his thick coarse, pale, rubbery lips made me so physically ill I could feel everything in my stomach rising. I have never been kissed in such a horrid, smeary, brutal manner! I wasn't frightened. I was simply furious.

When he finally let me go, I said contemptuously: "You pig!" and rubbed my lips with my handkerchief furiously.

"You can't get away with it," he said, his face an ugly red.

I knew he referred to the fact that I had amused myself by flirting with him. Well, so I have - a little, but only because he is such a lump I couldn't resist seeing if he could come alive! I wouldn't have objected to a kiss - in fact I expected one sooner or later, for he has helped me and we have been paying some attention to one another, but he could have been nice about it - couldn't he!

I shan't be nice to him anymore if I never get an experiment done.

I had thought the next time he asked to take me home I might let him just for the fun of it. I stopped in the dressing-room and rinsed out my mouth.

May 25 - Friday The B.Y.P.U. gave a straw ride last night. Mr. and Mrs. Reynolds acted as chaperones and we were lucky to get them as they are good sports of the see nothing, hear nothing, say nothing variety.

We had a marvellous moonlight night and we went to the ocean. When we jumped from the truck I seized Dorrance's hand and ran along the edge of the waves chanting "The Owl and the Pussycat."

It was wonderful - great stretches with a glittering moonpath. We sat on someone's veranda and talked while we watched the New York boat steam past.

Herman and Toby came stag for reasons best known to themselves and spent their time roaming the beach looking for mischief. Herman stopped to see us, mocking our efforts to be rid of him.

The moonlight went to his head apparently, for he gave a shout and began to leap into the air. "See that big wave?" he squealed. "Did you ever see a nicer wave in your life? I'm going to get it. Come to me, little wavelet." and in he went, clothes and all. And Toby went after him. We laughed until we rolled in the sand.

Herman broke into a little store, a shack, and we helped ourselves to what was left. Toby found a tiny bathing suit and swore he was going to put it on. I shrieked with joy at a mental picture of that long legged idiot in a doll sized bathing suit, but when we found he meant it, we restrained him forcibly.

Herman found a pair of enormous sneakers and they unearthed stale cigarettes, a few cigars and quite a few bottles of soda water.

I read them a short lecture on house breaking, so they left five pennies on the counter. As Toby said, nothing fitted and the candy and cigarettes were stale. We joined the others on the beach where we had hot dogs, rolls and pickles.

We laughed and sang all the way home.

Whenever we passed thru a little sleeping town Toby would lean out of the truck and yell. "The British are coming! Awake and to arms!"

Herman slept peacefully with his feet in my lap.

Dorrance is wonderful: he looked like marble in the moonlight. When he kissed me I thought of Prince Charming, Ladies Fair, and misty castles - all the things I use to dream about.

June 3rd - Sunday - Dorrance has read everything he can get hold of about Kreisler and Elman. We have wonderful talks. Everything takes on new meaning when he knows it too.

I'm changing, I guess, slowly and painfully, but into what I have no way of knowing. I feel different without quite realizing how it has come about. Boys don't interest me - just Dorrance - and I haven't any desire to flirt and dance. Nor do I care whether I am popular or not. I wonder if I shall ever be like I was? - or is it gone forever. Parts of it were nice.

I am fonder of Dorrance than I ever was of Joe - and I am at peace with him, but I have moments of missing Joe. I know that he went his way, more or less, all the time we were seeing one another. I hear things and I don't care. I don't want him back but I am still sore and tender. We are on the outside of one another's lives as completely as before and much more definitely.

Another thing is worrying me sick. I have shoved it in the background for so long that it is an actual struggle to put it into words and on to paper, but I must find it soon. As Joe would say, I am playing ostrich.

I'm not a coward physically - at least I don't think I am, but mentally I am yellow. It is all so strange - If I could - but what's the use. I am holding myself in by sheer force, but when the day comes when it must be known, I shall fly into bits.

On the surface it may seem a simple and trivial thing - this not having enough points to graduate from a little high school, but its the queer, paralyzing mental effect it has upon me. I could graduate. I could easily have made up the points my unbelievable first year cost me - that is, it would have been possible, but I couldn't.

I've got use to going over there at a certain hour in the morning and coming out at a certain time in the afternoon. I can bear that, but I can not make myself stay a moment longer. When the dismissal bell rings I simply grab everything and get out and away. I feel a crawly sensation along my spine until I am out of sight of that school. This is ridiculous," I shiver to myself. "You can find a way out. You could have made up these points little by little months ago." but its no use. I feel numb. I can't talk to anyone - not even Dorrance. I can't talk and its been sheer agony to write this much. Why? What is the matter with me?

From the first day of the first year I have had this peculiar dread, hatred, fear - whatever it is. When I left home mornings I was sick with longing to stay at home. I have envied the cat, Mother, workmen, anyone.

I've had some good teachers and at least two interesting ones, but those first few days seemed to mark me. It is so baffling, so beyond anything I have ever known, or read or heard about.

I'm the star pupil in Ancient History and get 98 or even a 100 % in the exams half the class flunks. I'm not stupid. Yet I have flunked courses terribly and miserably, at the same time doing excellently in other studies.

Girls who simply skin thru will have diplomas - but I won't go back - I won't. I'm petrified with dread of the time which Ase must know. And yet, inspite of the shame, inspite of the writhing fear of his flaying tongue, I haven't done one thing to avert this and I can't. Oh I can't explain even to myself. I hoped anything might happen and lately I've wanted to die. I thought if I could make myself write this, I might feel better, but I don't.

Nothing helps - nothing.

June 14 - Dr. Allyn says I am suffering from nervous exhaustion, that if I don't go slow I'll have a complete breakdown.

June 18 - Mary said Joe told her he hadn't "gotten over me." I am too tired to go thru all that again.

June 19 - I cry an awful lot - weak, meaningless, miserable tears, and that isn't like me. I know now what it means to be "unstrung" - all loose ends - everything jangling. The world has gone hay- wire - I mean I have - I've no balance. I don't know what I want except to get away - if I could get away. Is that cowardice?

An Account of My Life

I feel less restless, less tortured when Dorrance is with me. This isn't unhappiness as I have known it, this deep misery making nothing worth the doing and everything I have done worthless. I wonder if it is worth getting up in the morning - and trivial things like deciding what to wear require a tremendous effort.

The Family knows now that I cannot graduate this year and they know too that I could have done so. When they fire questions at me I can only say, "I don't know, oh I don't know!"

The Principal suggested going thru with it with an unsigned diploma, making up the necessary credits during the summer. I won't I won't. It's shabby - I won't. Not to save my pride or theirs.

Grandma has been an ally. Less concerned than Mother or Ase, she has told them to stop riding me so hard or they'll have something worse to deal with.

It has frightened Mother, remembering Will and his inexplicable act, I suppose; but Ase grants me no mercy. I hate him, but I do not blame him.

There are times when I feel that I am suffocating.

June 29 - I had thought I should never want to write in here again, but the habit is too strong to break.

Ase has bought a copy of Ingersoll's Essays and is reading them to me. When I show a ray of intelligence he remarks that it is damn strange every potential mill girl can graduate while I fail.

July 1 - Dorrance and I are together a lot, I very seldom see Joe which is not as strange as it may seem in view of the fact that I had heard about him for years before our paths crossed. Now there is no school and the C.H. isn't what it was, we have no meeting ground.

I sometimes feel as if the solid earth had been yanked from under me, leaving only Dorrance to hold to somewhere in space.

And if Ase doesn't stop treating me like a moron I shall become one. Maybe I am.

July 4 - Last evening Toby, Tetia, and Dorrance came down. We sat on the veranda for awhile and then walked in Ayres Woods. It was moonlight and as light as day. Fireflies pricked the blackness of the tall cedars and in the little clearing, cool, dew wet grass caught at our ankles. There seemed to be a spell on us, even Toby was silent. I listened for something - the sound of voices where there were no voices, a strange chuckling laugh where there was no laughter, only the brook running swift and clear in the moonlight. The fragrance of honeysuckle reached us long before we came to the place where it looped and matted itself from all limbs to the ground.

"Do you feel as if someone has just left, as if they weren't far away?" Tetia asked, her lovely face beautiful in the clear white light.

"The old gods walk tonight," I said softly. "Maybe."

"I'd believe anything tonight," Toby admitted.

And Dorrance said, "In those white dresses you two look like - I don't know."

"Like Priestesses?"

"Helen Clarke, and you a good Baptist!" Toby was shocked.

So was I, a little. Perhaps I was many things before I was a Baptist. A strangely, lovely evening.

July 10 - Robert Alton has, by a noble gesture reduced me to nothingness. Oh I haven't viewed him with utter hatred for quite some time for the simple reason I have seen little of him during the last year and never at any time viewed him as a Person. I have been hearing reports of his metamorpheses - Mother insisting that he had nice manners and a pleasant smile, while Grandmother said he was the spitting image of Capt. Rhodes (there being no higher praise), all of which I heard and didn't hear.

Well, a few weeks ago I was in Cousin Rhodes office and I happened to remark that if he needed anyone he might try me. After he became convinced that I meant it, he said: "Shucks Helen, I certainly would like to have you, but I don't need but one and Alton helps me out. Its hard sledding for the boy, being without a father and wanting a proper schooling and all. You see, don't you."

I said I did and felt ashamed that I had forgotten Alton. Well, that was all until today. I stopped in to read one of his magazines and he brought it up again by asking cheerfully: "When do you want to start in here, Helen?"

"What about Alton? You don't need to both of us. You really mustn't," I said surprized and incoherent.

"You see," he explained. "When he heard you wanted to come in here he said you could have it, he'd find something somewhere else, most likely."

"Honest?" I asked in awe.

He nodded.

"Frankly, what are his chances of getting anything else? Has he anything in view?"

Cousin Rhodes looked uneasy. "A likely boy shouldn't have much trouble." he remarked.

"That settles it," I said decidedly. "Of course I won't take it."

He rubbed his nose thoughtfully. "Boy's pretty insistent," he remarked. "Guess he considers it settled."

"You shouldn't have agreed!" I wailed. "You know it's all wrong! What kind of a skunk am I? It was only a whim. What possessed him! He never did anything for me before in his life."

"Have you ever asked anything of him," Rhodes asked mildly.

"No," I said reluctantly. "Never. But why should I? We've never been able to get along. He would turn into a saint before my face and eyes."

"He couldn't plague you all his life, could he?" he asked with Burrows reasonableness. "His father wasn't much older than he is when he got married. Don't seem possible. You didn't expect the boy to make faces at you all his life did you?"

I laughed. "He could be a grown up version of a pest couldn't he?"

"Now <u>was</u> he so bad?" he protested mildly. "Just a lively boy."

<u>Darned</u> lively, I thought grimly.

"You know how children are. I guess the time you kicked your Uncle Tracy he never thought you'd grow up to be the nice little girl you are."

"You win," I admitted. "Demons shouldn't throw stones - or something. However I've got to see Alton and have a talk with him. I wish I'd known enough to keep my tongue between my teeth. Where is he?"

It was quite awhile before I ran him down and when I did I stared at him. He is tall, broad shouldered and quite attractive. His red hair has faded to sand as Grandmother said it would, his freckles have almost gone and he no longer squeals. I repeat I stared incredulously.

"I believe we've met before," he said politely.

I gurgled with pleasure. "Oh Alton," I beamed, "You take my breath away. How tall are you? You make me think of a Before and After ad."

He laughed.

Well, I thanked him very nicely and told him how much I appreciated it, but that I couldn't take it. It took a lot of talking but I did it.

He surprized me by telling me my dress was pretty.

"Yes, isn't it!" I agreed, eyeing him in wonder. "It's new."

"Most girls would say, 'This old rag? I've had it for ages.'" he remarked, which made me feel very exceptional. Really, if he weren't a relative I should think he had possibilities.

"Sit down on the wall," he coaxed. "You don't have to hurry do you? Cousin Rhodes won't care, he knows I'm on your trail."

So he did and we talked and ate a chocolate bar or two.

"Why is it?" I complained. "That I never see you anywhere? You must <u>bury</u> yourself. You use to go to parties, why don't you now? You don't even belong to the C.H.?"

"Busy," he said.

"Oh," I looked at him blankly. "Don't you go around with any girl? Why don't you bring her down some night? I could get Dorrance and we'd go somewhere."

"I don't go with any girl."

"Well it's about time you did," I said frankly. "You never have have you? I can't remember you ever liking a girl. Why?"

"Maybe girls don't like me," he grinned.

"Well I'd like to know why not!" I exclaimed indignantly, my family pride up at arms. "You're quite good looking. What more can she ask than nice manners and good family?"

"<u>Who</u> ask?' he teased.

"Any girl."

"You answer that, you're a girl," he suggested.

I became so thoughtful he asked angrily. "Do you think you're running an 'Advice to the Lovelorn' column?"

"Don't be touchy," I said calmly."It's for your own good; you need some social life," and then changing the subject for the moment, "How do you like me?"

"I mean, have I improved? You have. Do you like me now?"

"I always liked you."

"Yes, you did!" I jeered. "You were the bane of my existence. Haven't I calmed down a lot?"

"You've got the devil in your eye as big as a wood chuck," he laughed. And I laughed too.

"Will you go with a girl if I get one?" I asked running over a list of possibilities in my mind.

"I will not," he answered promptly, independent as a hog on ice.

"Alright," I shrugged. "I'm not going to argue. You're too nice."

He looked pleased,. but acted indifferent.

Too bad we couldn't have been friends all these years.

Somehow I have always thought of him as a kid when as a matter of fact he's about two years older than I. I'll be eighteen in September - why he's practically a man grown!

July 22 - Junior down today in a bad temper. "I've heard how you can carry-on, don't think I haven't!" he told me, his eyes hard and accusing.

I looked down the cool, dark well with its fringe of ferns, and knew someone had been telling tales with malicious intent. He isn't really intimate with the crowd here - Emily once said he never cared particularly about coming to Mystic until he met me, and I know he has resisted most efforts to take him into the crowd because with his usual direct manner he made it plain that he came to see me. Cill is the only one who has the opportunity to talk to him or to drop remarks to Emily.

"What do you mean by 'carrying on'?" I asked stiffly. "You know I go around more or less and always have. You can't expect me to be a Sally-sit-by-the-fire in between your visits."

"If I don't get down more, you know why! You think Pa is swell, but you don't know how hard he is. I can't use any of the three cars without his permission - and try to get it! I was even coming down on the train until he made a fool of me in that way he has. And Em suggested a galloping steed and all I heard was young Lochinvars and such foolishness."

"Pa ought to have had someone like Don. I don't give two cents for all the violins and operas and classical stuff in the world. Years ago he found out he couldn't make a musician out of me just by his say so, and he knows it would take a raft of tutors working in relays to get me ready for college, so he is licked. Sure I'm dumb - about the things he thinks important, but there are things I can do and do darn well."

"I believe you are born out of your time and place, Junior," I said thoughtfully.

"Stop calling me Junior," he shouted angrily. "Call me by my name."

"But I don't like 'Jacob,'" I protested.

"Don't give a damn! What do you mean born out of my time and place?"

"Well - if this were the 17th century and there were Indians and wild beasts to fight and a forest to fell and a house to build, no one could ask more than your strength of purpose and your big hands and you rangy body. I can see you building stone walls and felling trees. Maybe I watched when I should have been spinning. Probably I died after the sixth child and you became a "relick" - or was it just the women who became 'relicts.'?"

He looked faintly shocked and very bewildered.

"Do you talk like this - to other fellows?"

"Of course not," I answered impatiently. "Do you think it a part of my usual line?"

There is a feeling of fowling pieces, bibles and witch burning about him.

"Pa got me this place in the hardware store," he said unevenly. "I'm doing alright and he'll set me up someday. He is pretty well satistfied I'm going to be a moneymaker and not the kind to hang around waiting for his money. But I don't earn enough to live on and save and while I'm home I have to do as he says. I wanted to come down here to work, but he wouldn't hear of it. I know more about automobiles that he'll ever know, but the only time he'll let me touch one is when he wants to save himself a garage bill. He says I'll be helling around getting into trouble. He says that's what's wrong with the times - young folks jumping into cars and driving miles away. He says when I buy one I can do as I like, knowing good and well I can't buy one and save at the same time. Sometimes every car will be standing idle, just standing there and he won't let me take one. I'll get one if I have to make it out of a scrap heap or buy one piece by piece! He knows I can too, and when he gets good and ready he'll give me the old Dodge. He's so set in his ways you can talk your head off and not get anywhere. He thinks writing letters and coming down with Em or Bob or the whole family is enough. I've never come down alone, never. I told him so and he just gave me a queer look."

"I've never heard you talk like this before," I said gently.

"I'm no talker. Or letter writer either," he answered shortly. And that, I reflected, is the gospel truth.

"It's awkward," I admitted. "But there is nothing to do about it. You are free to go around with other girls."

"I don't want to," he said obstinately.

I looked down the well and thought, if this were a wishing-well what would I wish? And I didn't know.

"There isn't much sense to anything is there?" I told his reflection. "There are so many girls who would suit you. Why should you like me?"

"You suit me," he scowled.

"But it isn't fair to you - or to me?"

"I'll be down oftener," he promised darkly. "I'll get a car if I have to tie it together with string."

And I thought, if you do I shall like you less and less. There is Dorrance ,too, I sighed.

"You like me don't you?" he asked eying me narrowly.

"Of course! But not that way."

"What way?" he asked, deriving sardonic pleasure from my flush of embarassment.

"The way you feel."

He actually smiled, which puzzled me until something in his eyes furnished the clue. I reflected bitterly that he liked me to be shrinking and stand-offish. I had the very unholy thought that he wouldn't be satisfied a virgin was all she pretended to be unless she whimpered all the way to the altar and yelped all the way to bed.

Honestly, I wanted to laugh, to cry, to swear!

"What you call being 'notional' is really not caring enough," I went on. "How can I make it any plainer? It's not anything that you can overcome."

There was a silence during which I looked away wondering if he understood.

He did. "You are just a kid," he said gruffly. "I never made any fuss until this Wop or Paddy or whatever he is."

It was like coming up against a stone wall!

"Junior," I asnwered desperately. "I could string you along if I didn't like you so well. Let's call it quits before any damage is done. It will come to it eventually."

He was very still, his jaw set. I moved uneasily.

"If we do," he said finally, "It will be for all times. You can't whistle me back when you feel like it."

"I shouldn't try!" I tilted my chin.

"You'd try alright," he said coldly. "If I were around where you could work on me. I shan't be."

The stone wall was going over and I felt a little sick and shaken.

"If you'll let things be as they use to be -" I trailed off miserably.

He shook his head. "No," he said. "If you had said all that in a mad fit I shouldn't take much stock in it, but you weren't mad and I guess you told the truth. I guess I always knew it."

He looked down into my eyes. "I think a lot of you," he said simply.

I met his gaze, but I wasn't far from tears.

After a moment he said: "O.K." - and walked away.

The Family isn't going to like this.

"I know him root and branch," Grandmother said, not long ago.

Oh there's no sense to anything!

An Account of My Life

Point Judith, Sunday Aug. 11 - 10:30 PM. It is odd and exciting to be writing in a place away from home. Constance and I are here at Aunt Hannah's for a week at least, if not longer. Ase and Aunt Hannah would be so pleased if Barbara and I could spend endless, happy summer hours in each other's company. Well, we can't and that's that. She bores me and I annoy her. I am as sorry about it as I can be because I love Point Judith and this farm of Aunt Hannah's passionately. And I don't mind Aunt Hannah's brusque, sarcastic tongue at all.

I shan't let Barbara spoil everything. I'm by the sea - there is a private beach and old acquaintances to renew - the Dr. Keiths - the little old woman who knew Ase and a host of others.

Aug. 14 I put one over on Aunt Hannah which is no easy thing to do! Of course I fooled Barbara too, but that is no achievement. Barbara had of course remarked upon the signet ring I wear and asked about Dorrance in her sneery way. You'd think she simply spent her life returning rings, when as a matter of fact I doubt if she ever had one given her. Then Aunt Hannah began to bait me - not that she doesn't like me deep down, but because it amuses her to pick at people.

Barbara asked if I had anymore "souvenirs" and by the way, wasn't that a man's wrist watch? I must pause to explain that my wrist watch stopped going just before we left Mystic. Mr. Kinney, knowing he couldn't repair it in time, hunted around for something to take its place, but all he could find was a man's wrist watch with a leather strap. I took it.

Constance started to answer Barbara's question - when sieized by a sudden devilish impulse I motioned to her to hush, which she did with her mouth still comically open. There was a momentary hush while I looked perturbed and embarassed.

Aunt H. burst out laughing, "If you hadn't silenced her - I suppose it belongs to one of your many admirers? Does you father know?"

"A man gave it to me," I said dreamily, and felt rewarded by the startled expression on her face.

"No," I spoke gently. "If that were the case, it would be a very much nicer one."

Aunt H. stared, and then she chuckled. Barbara looked from one to the other with a look of utter blankness on her face.

Oh I could have a simply perfect time here, if there were no Barbara! The wind in the trees and the surf and the crying gulls: the fireflies in the garden and the pond white with water lillies; the delicious food and the comfortable old furniture, the people whom I so seldom see, but to whom I belong root and branch. But Barbara! She was always mean. She use to stick pins in me when no one was looking and deny it when I accused her, and yell when I hit her.

Sunday - Home again, a week was enough and more than enough of Cousin Barbara.

We went around quite a bit, Aunt Hannah doing her best to give me a good time and she even gave Barbara the devil for not taking me around and introducing people.

I was happiest roaming the beach with Constance and almost every day we went down to the little store kept by an old woman who still thinks of Ase as a little boy.

One of Ase's fishing boats was named for Helen

Helen's home on Noank Road

Ase's fishing boat named for Constance

1923

Barbara's one and only boy friend called one evening. I considered him crude and awfully countrified. He wore an old red sweater and is named Benjamin. If Barbara could see Joe or Dorrance! However, he has a car which helps. When he asked us to go for a ride I thought nothing of it - it didn't seem to be a question of pairing off. At Wakefield they picked up another boy and Barbara informed me sweetly that they were stopping for <u>his</u> girl at the King Tom Farm.

"Where do I come in on this?" I asked ominously. "What am I supposed to represent: the spectre at the feast, or something?"

Barbara laughed and observed that I was "a perfect <u>scream</u>!"

I regarded her silently and my gaze boded ill.

Well, I said nothing more, simply got to work in a manner of speaking. We were still some way from the Farm and boys <u>had</u> fallen in as short a time. I concentrated on Russell, that was the boy's name and while it was decidedly a race with time, I had him falling to the extent of begging Ben not to stop for the girl. He was quite agonized about it and Ben was willing to oblige, but Barbara wasn't. We <u>had</u> to stop she said.

I had no idea of giving in. I had nothing against this girl never having even set eyes on her, but I had to use Russell for the time being. I couldn't do much with Ben because he was in front with Barbara, but I did what I could.

The Fates were kind to me: the girl wasn't home! Russell whooped with glee and Barbara looked foiled, frustrated and cross.

We drove to Charlestown Beach. It was moonlight and I ran along the shore close to the waves until, rather to my surprise, <u>Ben</u> lumbered after me, caught my hand and ran with me. It was fun! In no time I had Barbara where I wanted her. She couldn't keep him away from me so she became excessively fond of her dear little cousin and stuck like a burr. I'm not ordinarily mean enough to take another girls one and only admirer, especially when he doesn't appeal to me, so I let up on the charm stuff. Not that it did any good! Being new or something effected both boys badly. I remembered what I had put up with from visiting girls and enjoyed myself to the utmost. They laughed at everything I said, thought I was cute, raved about my eyes and tried to crowd one another out. It was really too easy. It gave me solid satisfaction to see Barbara forced to assume the role she had cast me in.

When we got back she told her Mother, the big baby. Aunt H. was half inclined to laugh at me and half angry that I had injured her darling daughter.

"If you'd had any sense," I heard her tell Barbara. "You have seen that she was occupied with someone. You're no match for that one."

"What would <u>you</u> have done," I asked, looking her square in the eyes, "if someone tried to pull a fast one on you."

"Humph," she snorted. "Do you always do such a thorough job?"

Affairs being as they were and likely to get worse both Ben and Russell being severely bitten, I decided I'd had enough. Constance said

An Account of My Life

she'd just as soon go home - she'd done all the things she'd planned to do and Barbara was too bossy.

Barbara hardly concealed her relief when I decided to go back to Mystic. The boys argued, but I had had <u>enough</u>, so finally Ben said well, anyway he would take me home in his car. Russell said h<u>e</u> was coming along too. Barbara who had looked up all the train time tables very pointedly said she guessed she'd come too.

I guess she'd like to marry Ben. Well, with me out of the way she should have no trouble.

On Tuesday we drove to Providence. Aunt Hannah has trouble with her eyes and had an appointment with an East Side specialist. It wasn't a pleasant day as to weather, but I enjoyed myself. I had never been to Providence. I have never been <u>anywhere</u>.

We drove around the city and of course Brown and Pembroke where Cousin Mary graduated. Dr. Keith has a sanitarium on Blackstone Boulevard.

All in all I can't say I am sorry I made the visit, but I can't help moaning inwardly when I think of how perfectly marvellous it might have been.

<u>Aug. 21</u> - To say to-day has been upsetting is to say Joe became a part of it.

We were at the C.H. this afternoon, our crowd, and it was like any other time. Most of the others left around five, but I had promised to meet Cill there so I waited.

After Dorrance left, Jerry and I were alone in the library until Joe came in. I sat very still, my head bent over a magazine, too stubborn to speak.

"What are you thinking of?" he asked at length.

"Why - nothing in particular," I said hastily, too hastily as I realized.

He smiled and I had to admit he was carrying it off better than I. I watched him draw circles on the desk blotter and took a deep breath.

Whether in answer to some sign or because we were disturbing him, Jerry picked up his book and departed to the social room.

"Say something," I demanded.

I wanted to beat my hands and <u>wail</u>, but I forced myself to answer calmly.

"We don't seem to get over this very quickly, do we?"

"They say the first hundred years are the hardest," he jibed.

"Well, what are we going to do about it?" I demanded, my patience splintering to bits.

"This is your move, you tell me."

"Oh!" I cried angrily. "You are making this as hard as possible from sheer perversity. Wh<u>y</u> can't I hate you?"

"What am I suppose to say - or do?" he mocked as I glared at him.

1923

"You told one of the girls - I mean you hinted that if a date were arranged - Well, anyway, did you mean it?"

"Sure. I was still feeling a dream," he said bluntly. "And you weren't so thick with the Grimes kid."

"Couldn't we be friends - maybe go to a dance - that sort of thing?"

"No we can't. You know that as well as I do."

The silence was thick enough to cut, it spread and spread.

"I don't know whether its the weather, or you, but I am worn to a frazzle," I sighed, pushing the hair from my forehead.

He drew me against him gently until my head was on his shoulder, and he kissed me gently at first, and then as if he would never get enough, until that wild, sweet majic was with us again.

After a time he told me to look at him and when I did he caught his breath and put his face against my hair.

"What are we going to do?" I asked presently.

"Dunno."

"It's been awful," I signed, moving away from him.

"Yeah!" he jeered. "Didn't take you long before you were going strong."

All manner of thoughts coursed thru my mind, while a sickening feeling that things had changed settled over me.

He looked the same, but he was different - or I was. I wondered what I could tell Dorrance and felt a sharp pang. I couldn't help noticing Joe's finger nails, ugly and not quite clean. I didn't like the smell of the stuff on his hair.

"Kiss me" I said. "I don't want to think."

He did, and it was wonderful, thrilling, yet somehow displeasing.

"I must go," I told him. "If we should be seen like this, the whole Community House would rock."

And I put my finger on his cheek bone for no reason other than I felt impelled to do so.

He shivered and caught my hand. "Haven't you bedevilled me enough?" he said roughly.

I stood up, patting my hair in shape.

"If you think so, I guess I have," I told him.

Standing close beside me, he smiled that slow smile of his. "You're a wonderful gal," he said looking straight into my eyes.

"Why?"

"Because I say so.

"I think you are a pretty wonderful guy." I tried to smile. And then I walked away, my back stiff and straight.

<u>Aug. 23</u> - Dorrance said this evening that he and Joe had been to the movies together. I don't understand anything anymore. If I could get away-

<u>Aug. 25</u> - I have had a letter from Russell.

"Just a rag and a bone and hank of hair," said Ase, brushing his rough cheek against mine.

I giggled.

"It's funny," he agreed, but as I went into a gale of laughter, added aggrievedly, "But not <u>that</u> funny! How do you know but what I've got the makings of a great lover."

He says Rowland is here: he's late this year. Toby doesn't like him. Well, I do - and I don't.

<u>Aug. 22</u> - I have a conviction that Marcus is destined to pop up in my life every so often. This time I really thought he was all over it - he has been going around with different girls, not of our crowd, and I saw so little of him I'd forgotten him.

I saw him today, and as usual he irritated me until I hurt him. I don't <u>like</u> to hurt him! I really like him in the abstract, but that look of dog-like devotion makes me sad, mad and bad.

<u>Aug. 29</u> - Wednesday Rowland drove up this afternoon in his grandfather's big car. He had come to take me for a drive he said, but I couldn't go as Dorrance was coming any minute. I'll admit I was tempted. Rowland never looked handsomer or more appealing in his life, and I couldn't help thinking a drive in a comfortable car preferable to an afternoon on the veranda.

I don't think I should have hesitated had it been any boy but Dorrance, I hate to hurt Dorrance, that's the long and short of it.

And then I saw him coming around the corner - it's a long walk from his house. I looked at Rowland so calm and sure of himself and my mind was made up.

"Sorry Rowland, but I have a previous engagement," I said.

He drove away sulkily, but he'll be back.

I should like to record that I turned to Dorrance with love in my eyes, but as a matter of fact I didn't. Inspite of myself I was rather curt with him and he, having an average amount of penetration guessed what it was all about.

"If you'd rather be with him say so," he snapped.

<u>Aug. 31</u> Rowland came down to-day. So did Dorrance. Rowland couldn't sneer at him as he did at Marcus, so he ignored him, whereupon Dorrance opened up a book and settled down to read.

I knew they were trying to out stay one another and was rather amused. But it was Rowland who gave in - his quick temper and impetuous manners getting the better of him.

I probably shan't see him again this summer. Next summer: Let the Fates decide.

<u>Sept. 2</u> A sad day - not trajic, just sad. Everyone seemed to catch the feeling except Johnny and nothing can sadden him.

1923

Toby is going away to Andover very soon. After S.S. a few of us gathered together outside and decided to meet at Cill's this afternoon.

"Let's get together for the last time," Toby sighed - and added, "the last time this summer, I mean."

"For Pete's sake!" Johnny squealed. "You'd think you were going to your own funeral instead of away to school, you lucky dog. There'll be vacations, I guess!"

Toby brightened a little, but relapsed into gloom. I felt a pang. Oh we'll get together for awhile, I daresay, but we have come to the parting of our ways. He is the first of our inner most circle to go, that's all.

"How dare you look the way I feel," he said, slapping me on the back, which is his way of bringing cheer to the soul.

"Let's get the Sunday dinners over with and meet at Cill's."

Later in the afternoon we got together again. We had the house to ourselves and were glad. The shades were partly drawn to keep out the sun and there were ferns in the fireplace. We piled on to the sofa as we always do, Toby hogging most of the room and leaving the rest of us to perch as best we could.

We laughed and joked for a while, but Toby kept sighing so gustily we began to sigh ourselves. All except Johnnie who thought Toby queer past human understanding.

"Gosh, <u>do</u> you suppose things will ever be the same?" Toby moaned dismally.

"No," I said truthfully. "You know they can't be." He glared at me.

"What's all this weeping fare-well stuff about?" Johnny demanded in disgust. "You're not going to darkest Africa, you know."

"Things change so," Cill said sadly. "Just think Toby, You and Helen and I have been together all our lives: Sunday School, Young People's, the C.H., School - of course I didn't go to Stonington but - why you and Helen <u>have</u> been together all your lives, haven't you!"

"We met when we were a year old," I announced. "That is, formally. I daresay we were wheeled past one another's baby carriages before that. But we met at Cradle Roll Exercises."

"Honest? What did I say?" Toby asked.

"Where have you been all my life," I shot back promptly and watched him roll with laughter.

"I wore my rose-bud bonnet," he simpered, reaching for my hair and rumpling it until I howled with fury and fell upon him with my fists.

"Remember our one and only quarrel?" he asked.

"Yes," I said darkly, "I do. You thought I was telling your Mother things about you. I've never forgiven you."

"I didn't think so," he groaned. "I've told you a million times! Only there was a leak somewhere and she saw so much of you. I never thought of Ren."

"So! Go on!" I said menacingly.

305

An Account of My Life

"Why in heck did I bring this up!" he howled as I grabbed a clump of straight sandy hair in each hand.

After a while he complained that he was practically sick to his stomach.

"It's so seldom you are depressed you don't know what it feels like," I scoffed.

"I'll make you a drink of peppermint tea," Cill offered.

"I don't care if you do," he said sadly. "I kind of like the stuff."

A bit later, after he had drained the cup he seemed to become aware of my sad face.

"Say, do you feel bad about me going Henny-Penny?" he asked suddenly.

"Sad as the devil and you know it," I returned morosely.

"But it won't make any difference," he insisted anxiously. "We'll write and there are vacations."

"It will be different."

"How do you get that way! Going to forget me the minute I'm out of sight?"

"You know it's not that," I protested angrily. "Hasn't it dawned on you that you are about to make new friends and learn any number of things while we won't? We've shared things all our lives, but from now on we go different ways: we're bound to!"

"I won't make any new friends as good as my old," he declared grandly.

"They'll fit your life better."

"Nuts, simply nuts!" he raved, flinging his arms around wildly. "Cill do you believe this drivel?"

She hesitated and he began to roar. "You girls give me one solid pain."

"Don't be an ass," I sniffed.

"Gee," he collapsed suddenly. "Do you really feel bad."

"Of course I'm glad you're getting out and all that, but I hate to see things breaking up."

"So do I," he said sadly. "I hope I break a leg or something."

Johnny could bear no more. "Say will you saps wipe each others noses!" he asked elegantly. "Talk about funerals."

Sept. 5 - Emily hasn't written since Junior and I came to the parting of our ways. Cill says she has owed her a letter for months and doesn't even come over the garden wall when she is here. I feel sore and hurt about the whole thing, for I sincerely like Mr. and Mrs. G. and Emily. Something must have been said. They are so old fashioned they seem to regard it in the light of a broken engagement.

Sunday, Emily was down. Cill talked with her for a few minutes. Junior wasn't there and when Cill asked where he was, Emily said acidulously, "Where he always is now, running around with a hard boiled nurse."

1923

And in reference to me, "I could wring that little devil's neck cheerfully."

Cill seemed a little upset by it all. When I won't talk she says uneasily: "You never liked him anyway!"

She is unhappy about Bob, so I let it go at that. I think if I had fully realized it meant losing them all I shouldn't have done it - told Junior the truth, I mean.

I have been burning a stack of Junior's letters - Emily's too.

<u>Sept. 17</u> - I am eighteen years old to-day and my life seems at sixes and sevens - whatever that means. To put it in a hard-boiled way I was a fool to break with Junior.

Not that I miss him or that he could be little more than incidental, but because I miss Norwich and Mr. G and Emily and all that went into making that period in my life pleasant. It's too late to do anything now. Oh I could, I suppose! No matter how rocky Junior may appear to be I could manage that part of it I am confident. But I am eighteen now and every year would bring me closer to the question.

Although I hated to betray myself I did ask Cill what Mr. G. thought - how he felt about me. Emily and her Mother I know will never quite forgive me though why, I can't see.

"Oh," said Cill. "How <u>would</u> he feel? He always thought you just about right. That makes Em sore. He says it was inevitable from the beginning, plain enough for anyone to see."

"I thought he'd see," I answered quietly. "After all I guess that's all that matters."

"He said," she went on. "that you'd have brought a little color and excitement into Jr's life, but it was in the cards that it couldn't be."

"I can imagine Em's answer to that - and her mother's too." I spoke lightly, but something throbbed in me like an aching tooth.

"Well," Cill seemed reluctant but I don't think she really was. "They are old fashioned you know. I guess they think a really nice girl couldn't have upset Jr. so badly. And at first they thought you were shy and quiet and all that."

"And now they are convinced I was up to deviltry from the first. Well, maybe I was."

"After all," Cill said virtuously. "They are pretty proud, and to have you prefer a ---"

"Never mind that!" I warned. "And by the way, how was Junior kept so fully and probably eroneously informed?"

She had the grace to color. "I never talked about you! I may have mentioned you."

"It doesn't matter," I said. "It was simply brought to a head sooner than it might have been."

An Account of My Life

"You are queer," she told me. "You don't care one earthly bit about Junior, but I think you really feel bad about Mr. G - that little old man! Honestly, it's funny."

Maybe it is. He was a friend and I should have liked him for a father. I haven't known quite the same inner companionship since Daddy, my grandfather died. Of course it's funny! Whoever heard of anyone marrying to obtain a father-in-law! It is funny - I'm laughing - and my eyes are smarting.

Oct. 20 - The theme I wrote for Dorrance has had quite a success. He says his English teacher had read it aloud to half the school and shown it to the other half and he feels an utter fool.

"It was too good," he said accusingly. "I told you not to make it too good. I copied it so fast I hardly realized. If Miss D wasn't dumb she'd know I couldn't write a witty thing like that."

Oct. 21 - I hope this King Tut fad has about run its course. At first we were simply crazy over the jewelry and the general influence on clothes and accessories. I have taken off my wide silver bracelet with its Egyptian pattern and Tetia is ripping off the buckle Kat gave her.

Oct. 27 - Glad and I took a long tramp in the woods in search of bittersweet. It was so beautiful I felt that I must share it with Dorrance to-day. So, we walked down the narrow path bordered by slim birches and frosty ferns. There were bayberry bushes with their grey clusters huddled humbly at the foot of a flaming tree, here and there were late sprays of maiden tresses, waxy white and poignantly sweet.

Nov. 24 - Saturday - Toby is home with a cold. Said he had a vacation coming and he wasn't going to get stuck in the school infirmary if he knew it.

He was abed until he heard my voice whereupon he raced downstairs in his pajamas, not bothering with his dressing gown to his mother's horror.

After he had padded around for awhile and then stretched out on the hearth at my feet.

We talked and were cozily warm, but after awhile there were no new topics. I could tell him amusing incidents, he could tell me funny things, but there were no new experiences shared.

Nov. 25 - Dorrance has been in Providence visiting his aunt. He came down as soon as he got home.

"Helen," he said, "It just isn't living away from you."

Nov. 20 - Wednesday Had a scrap with Dorrance. He won't argue, so it didn't amount to much. He is the most reasonable person in the world,

1923

which isn't much fun when I feel unreasonable or as Joe would put it "contrary on purpose."

Dorrance is awfully good looking - wavy hair with golden lights, deep set blue eyes. The girls would be crazy over him if he'd lift a finger.

Queer that I should fill his mind. I'm not worth it.

I've never felt the same toward anyone - I can't describe it. I should have known him before I knew Joe, perhaps. <u>No.</u>

I try to please him and find myself gladly doing little things for him, and I think of him a great deal and wonder what he sees in me.

Grandmother says I am "better behaved." I feel sort of washed out. It's wicked to wish time away, but I shan't be sorry when this year is a long way in back of me.

<u>Dec. 14</u> Thur. I'm glad I went. Dorrance never played better. I am referring to an entertainment at the Methodist Church.

Ken Hunter was there and was awfully nice to me. He is studying to be an elocutionist.

Wore a new dress, sand colored with tight waist and full skirt bordered with dark fur. The short puffed sleeves were rose satin. My hat is sort of poke-ish and lined with rose velvet.

Ken said I looked as though I ought to be in an oval black frame.

Dorrance never gets jealous - just acts pleased if I am specially noticed. Not that he has any cause, but I <u>have</u> known people to be jealous without cause.

Howard and Joe nearly had a row the other day. I wasn't present, but I heard about it.

Seems Howard asked what I was "like." "She's told me where to get off so many times I'm curious. Is she always that way or doesn't she like my type? <u>You</u> ought to be able to put me wise."

"She's not like that and she can't bear you, you lousy, little coot." Joe told him pleasantly. "Now do you know?"

<u>Christmas Eve</u> Trimmed the tree this evening. I love the scent of fir and the fragile smoothness of bright balls. A year ago - well, a year ago I didn't have Dorrance.

<u>Christmas Day</u> Dorrance gave me candy and Russel sent me a book Grandmother gave a string of carved ivory beads, they are all the rage now. There were many other things including a blue silk umbrella and money from the Aunts.

Cill has a portable victrola - Marion made the house a present of it and several records. There was a blazing log fire and we sat on the hearth with a bowl of russet apples. The bayberry candles were lighted on the mantle and we sniffed their fragrance while we listened to "The Indian Lament."

1924

Jan. 1, 1924

Books I have read this past year
Lummox by Fanny Hurst
Doctor Nye [by] Joseph Lincoln
Bread [by] Frank Norris
The Enchanted April - "Elizabeth"
Excellent movies I have seen
Covered Wagon
Green Goddess
Hunchback of Notre Dame

July 11 - They've torn down the little old Peace Grant house on Main Street to make room for a stucco business building and a lunch wagon. It hurts!
Grandmother says it was ever so - Mystic isn't what it was when she was young, and her Mother said the same before her. Oh I know! But it still hurts.

July 15 - Col. Perce has given Toby the Buick roadster and he and Tetia and Dorrance & I get around quite a bit. Tetia gets lovelier everyday. Somehow it never occurs to me to envy her as I might a merely pretty girl.

July 19 - Marion, Glad, Harold, Dorrance and I spent the afternoon on the tennis courts. Dead tired. Though I admit the fault in me, I cannot like games. Expect Dorrance in a few minutes. Thought I would write in here to use up time, but I am too restless.

July 21 - Dorrance is playing at Lords Point and I am so restless I can not contain myself. Saw Clyde Burrows in Gene's store. He gets more attractive every year and remains just as nice.

July 23 - Rehearsal at Pond's which means Dorrance won't be down. Queer - I don't like to dance or flirt anymore and I am only eighteen.

July 26 - Tennis this afternoon. How I hate that hot, sticky messy feeling. The only pleasant part is the bath and clean clothes after.
The girls would be wild over Dorrance if he gave them the least encouragement, but he can't see anyone but me. Why? I'm dull.

Sept. 18 - Yesterday was my birthday: nineteen years old. I never spent a more drab, uninteresting day in my life - until Dorrance came in the evening.
It has been cold and grey with a thin, disheartening drizzle of rain.

An Account of My Life

Mother had a headache and the crossness that goes with one, while Ase had indigestion and snarled like a bear with a sore paw. Of course my presents: money, a dress, books, but I was indigo blue until Dorrance came.

No candy from Junior, but an adorable butterfly locket from Dorrance.

<u>Sept. 20</u> - The Prince of Wales seems to be sweeping the country before him. I might do a bit of foolish dreaming myself, if I were sixteen and there was no Dorrance, but as it is I leave it to the school girls and the silly married women.

I can't help envying the girls who are in a position to meet him.

So few princes are prince-like, so few princesses are lovely, so few queens are regal, it is not strange that the world loves one who gives substance to the old fairy-tales.

I have no reason to believe I could interest prince or potentate and yet I am sure that I could! Verily, I <u>am</u> a damn fool.

<u>Sept. 25</u> - Have been rereading Gertrude Atherton's "*Black Oxen.*"

<u>Oct. 8</u> - Dorrance's violin means almost everything to him, but there is no money, and it takes so much time to earn it. He says with me he can't fail.

<u>Oct. 20</u> - Ase has asked me to make another copy of the Clarke genealogy for some relative. The line dates back to John Clarke of Westhorpe Manor, Suffolkshire, 1559.

<u>Nov. 4</u> - I want a blue velvet dress this winter - no, deep winery red, I guess. I had a blue velvet years ago for Dancing School. I remember the well-to-do Spicer girls from Noank regarded it with envy. How can a rich man be a skinflint?

<u>Dec. 1</u> - Am reading Edna Ferber's "*So Big*" and find it interesting.

Ase reads "*Main Street*" and "*Babbitt*" over and over with savage delight. I think he feels that they are the books he might have written.

<u>Dec. 25</u> - I hoped this would be a white Christmas and so it is, with a multitude of feathery flakes swirling in the air.

Cill and Glad were down this morning and I spent the afternoon with them. Dorrance came in the evening bearing a slim red and gold copy of Carrie's "Mary Rose."

He also brought and left a stack of Prof. Eckstein's music. I do my plodding best but I am not a good accompanist, nor any where nearly good enough for him.

Is there anything in the world I can do well? I am not even good fun anymore. Ase says I have gone under a cloud. But why?

1925

Jan. 1st 1925 - Dec. 25 - 1925
19 yrs of age

New books read during the past year
The White Monkey - Galsworthy
The Little French Girl - Sedgwick
The Green Hat - Michael Arlen (detest the man)
So Big - Ferber

Jan. 1 - All day the snow has fallen silently and now a howling wind is blowing it into drifts. What a night to be at sea!
I thought Dorrance would never be able to come, for it's a long walk clear across the town, but he did. Read "*Romula*" together and ate fudge.

Jan. 24 - I suppose I should record the Eclipse of the sun which took place today. The newspapers have been full of it for weeks and as this part of Connecticut was directly in its path, New London, Noank, Mystic and Westerly have been over run with scientists.
Thomas Edison was said to be in Westerly and a great crowd of people went over only to find it a false alarm.
The *Los Angeles*, the dirigible, hovered over the Sound like an astral minded whale; and special trains ran for the benefit of students from various schools and colleges who accepted the invitation of Connecticut College to view it from its campus and other vantage points.
The partiality was scheduled for a little past eight and arrived a few minutes later according to Grandma's kitchen clock which wags its waggish way despite eclipses. I am afraid Ase was the only one of us who was intelligently interested. Because we possessed but one pair of dark glasses and it was of course next to impossible to buy a pair, he smoked bits of glass from the old lantern, lecturing me at the same time.
He decided that the Ledge was the best place from which to view the spectacle.
Grandma was provoked because she said I'd catch my "never-get-over" - my throat has been sore for several days - and refused to come out doors herself. She views anything out of the ordinary as being open to suspicion.
After she had piled sweaters, coats, shawls, and mufflers on me and finished off with her little shoulder cape I was allowed to go out, waddling like a duck, admitting herself that I couldn't carry any more canvas.
Fort Rachel was black with people and the sun cast violet shadows on the snow. The piercing cold knifed thru my layers and layers of clothing and left me naked, while the sun blazed so bright it frightened one and the

smoked glass rubbed off on our faces, making the best known countenances weird and unknown.

I couldn't help thinking how immensely frightening it would be if it hadn't been explained and press agented all along the way: bits of the Connecticut Yankee passed thru my mind.

It was interesting and awesome to watch the moon darken the sun bit by bit - and I liked the sky with its few bright stars and the snow with its strangely tinted shadows. We had never felt such bitter, icy cold: dead people can't be much colder.

The shadows gathered quickly until it seemed like midnight, but a midnight clearer, colder and more unearthly, than any I have ever known.

In the N.E. the sky remained faintly flushed, while in the S.E. three brilliant stars shone like lamps. When the sun was entirely behind the moon, the wonderful corona rimmed the moon with splendour. I felt that we should have thrown ourselves flat on the ground.

Feb. 7th - Monday night Dorrance and I plan to hear Pablo Casal at the Buckeley Auditorium in New London. And on the 18th Kriesler is coming! Such riches!

Feb. 10 - Heard Casal last night. We arrived early, but I like to watch the audience assemble. Dorrance said I looked prettier than anyone, which was foolish of course, though very pleasant to hear. Pablo Casal hasn't Mr. Kreisler's personality, but he is a fine musician in every sense.

I don't know enough to discuss the program intelligently - somehow it doesn't seem to matter; it's enough to shut one's eyes and feel the music seeping into one.

We took the trolley car, changing at the Bridge to the bus. A warm night, thick and foggy.

Feb. 14 - Floyd Collins is still trapped in a cave in Kentucky. The newspapers are full of it and everyone is talking. Ase disgusted says it is a dull time for newspapers when they have to resort to such measures. "A damn fool snoops into something, gets pinned by a rock, and can't get out. Reporters with nothing better to do play it for all its worth. Men have died in caves before this and worms have eaten them, without the great American public caring a damn."

Just the same it is terrible.

Feb. 16 - The rescue workers have reached him; he is dead.

March 2 - Monday - Last night we were at the table when the telephone rang. Ase answered it. When he came back he said to me. "There is a vacancy in Howard's office [at the Rossie Velvet Mill]. He says you can have the job if you want it. I told him you'd probably not earn your salt, but he seems to think it won't hurt for you to try it. Want it? Fifteen a week."

"I guess so," I replied. "When?"

"To-morrow," he looked at me keenly. "Scared? You don't have to if you don't want to, you know."

"I'll try it," I said.

"I'll come with you and see you settled."

"You will not!" I exclaimed. "Do you think I'm a kid going to kindergarten?"

Well, then, I must go with Howard.

I said very firmly that if I went with anyone it would be Cill.

"Always been glad I got the girl that job," he observed, apparently giving in. "She's a good worker."

As soon as the dishes were done, I got Cill on the phone. I rather expected her to be pleased, but she wasn't in the least; in fact she showed plainly that she didn't like the idea of having me in the office a bit. Oh, I didn't get it at first! But by the time she hinted I wouldn't like the work and advised me to think it over before deciding, I began to wonder. When I suggested meeting her in the morning she extended half a dozen flimsy reasons why it would not be practical; she was starting at a different hour - we lived too far apart to make connections easily. I interrupted her long enough to remind her that the same distance had always existed and we had thought nothing of covering it several times a day. Then she said she was going to row over with some friends. Of course, if I wanted to come along too -

"Why don't you say you don't want me?" I asked contemptuously. "I had the idea we were friends and usually did things to-gether. Anyone would think I was taking something away from you. It may have been your job, but you've got a better one, haven't you?"

"Oh, don't be <u>silly</u>!" she laughed, protesting, apologizing, but not retracting her excuses. I was bitterly hurt. As I was to have her job - she is taking the place of a girl who is leaving to be married and was to "break me in," the prospects didn't look too bright. What it was all about I couldn't guess, nor can I now.

I started out alone this morning, meeting Howard who was simply grand to me. He took me thru the mills, a vast place of crashing machinery. Everywhere were men, staring men. But the finishing room was almost as bad, dozens of pair of feminine eyes, some curious, some friendly, and some inimical, among them those of Joe's sister.

The office was somewhat better, although one girl managed to inform me that several girls who had made applications for my job months ago, had been passed over. I knew nothing about it and told her so.

"Well, its no skin off my nose," she shrugged. "I'm just telling you."

I gathered that because Howard is a friend of the family, I am to be considered "a pet." Then too, Grandmother is a stock-holder, though only a small one, I should think. It seems that Howard doesn't usually take the time to show a new girl, especially such small fry as I.

I felt pretty helpless and hopeless, especially as Cill was perfectly devilish to me.

Finally one of the clerk's said, "For God's sake, Priscilla, Give the girl a chance. You're supposed to be breaking her in."

The dull flush covering her face showed the shot had struck home. I understood perfectly. Knowing the first day was bound to be hard, she was intent upon making it so hellish there would be no second day.

One time when she went into the mill leaving me to cope with a buzzing switchboard, Howard himself came over and straightened me out.

When Cill returned and found him there she looked rather frightened and began to explain.

"If you find you haven't the time to teach Helen I shall have to get Cora to do it," he said very quietly. "I thought you understood that your new job didn't start until you had broken her in to your work."

After that she attended to me with resentment concealed only when Howard was about, but by that time I was too numb to care.

One of the men said to her, "Tough luck having to let that switch board out of your hands."

I knew by her angry twitch that she had got the point of the remark, although it doesn't seem to make sense. Howard's was the one friendly face in a strange world. It is queer what a single day can do to one. I can't remember how long I have known him casually as an youngish-oldish friend of Ase's. I couldn't have described him beyond saying he was medium height and very blond and always pleasant - and now he emerges as a grand person. I never counted on him - why should I, he is a busy man, but I did count on Cill who has been my friend so many years.

My work is very simple once one gets the hang of it: it would have to be for I have had no training. I can type enough to make out loom tickets, I can answer the phone, and in a short time I should be able to manipulate the small switch-board without making such apalling mistakes. It was the longest day I ever put in and by late afternoon my head ached, my back ached and my ears were sore from putting on and taking off ear phones.

At last it was five o'clock. Cill got her things together, saying nothing about walking home to-gether, ignoring me unless I spoke to her.

One cat of a girl said maliciously, "I thought you and Priscilla were old friends!"

"So did I," I said clearly.

Cill flushed and walked away.

What have I <u>done</u>? We've been good friends - evening after evening we've met to talk of a thousand things. Oh Cill, we've had our scraps, our squabbles, we've hurt one another and made up with complete abasement, but I didn't think you'd ever turn on me in this way.

What has gotten into her to change her so amazingly?

1925

March 20 - Friday - I knew Ase thought highly of Howard's intelligence and personality, but I never gave it a thought before I came into the office. If I have lost a friend in Cill I have gained a much better one in him. We walk or ride together quite frequently. I have never known an older man and find it stimulating.

Cill and I have never regained our old footing.

"You know you were never half-trained," Nate said the other day. "I wonder you didn't complain to Howard."

I didn't answer, knowing Nate to be a confirmed mischief-maker; but I thought of the first day Cill left me on my own without telling me half the things I should have been told. Someone calling from New York with an accent thick enough to cut with a knife, the switch-board buzzing in a dozen places while I tried to understand him. I thought of the S.O.S.'s I had sent her only to be ignored and of the times, when with the clatter of a pencil to the desk, an ejaculation of annoyance meant to be overheard, a rush to the switch-board and an efficient purring and manipulation of plugs, she would straighten out the mess and return to her desk, without a word; and of the times when forced to ask her a question she would assume a patient what-a-fool-she-is expression that was entirely unwarranted.

Cora who wasn't married for a week or so after I came into the office and who had trained Cill in the beginning, dropped into the office now and then. She wasn't supposed to bother with me and, fearing to offend Cill, who if she didn't want to bother with me didn't want anyone else to either, kept her hands off until one day when Cill, carefully up to her ears in work refused to hear my question.

"I'm not doing anything," Cora said. "If you don't mind, Cill, I'll explain."

Cill did mind, but Cora came over to my desk anyway.

Several times after that when Cill was too busy, or on one of her long visits to the Chemical Room, Cora sat beside me and talked of feuds, of differences between heads, of when it was best to call a certain department, of the best way to approach Mr. A. and how to manage grumpy Mr. B. She explained the code book and showed me a quicker way to turn out the loom tickets: she taught me how to tinker the balky old typewriter into shape when it rebelled and told Howard I should have a new one.

"Cill was so good as this sort of thing, I don't shine by comparison," I told her ruefully.

"She was very good and quick," Cora admitted. "I broke her in gradually at the switch-board until she had become use to the loom tickets. Leaving a half-finished ticket to work at the switchboard is liable to cause mistakes. I never left her alone until she had complete self-confidence and could cope with it alone."

"I wish you had taken me on," I told her." It's hard to regain self-confidence once it is lost."

"Priscilla isn't a good teacher," Cora said quietly.

317

Which is true, but I know and they know, Cill deliberately made it as hard for me as possible.

<u>Mar.24</u> - I know now what is ailing Cill and I was dumb not to guess before.

To go back, Cill had been in the office only a short time when she became acquainted with Bill B., the assistant chemist, a man well along in his thirties, unmarried and of a philandering turn of mind. He likes girls, almost any kind of a girl and he has no intentions of marrying. Every new girl is a challenge to him, a well of possible delights. He doesn't carry any affair to the danger point: simply takes a girl around, flatters her, basks in her admiration and eventually tires.

Gladys and I have disliked him from the first, or at least his effect on Cill, growing angry and helpless in the face of her evident infatuation. She didn't call it that - he had taught her the word `platonic' and she used it in the face of our jeers.

When we came across some snapshots in bathing suits we told her we hardly thought them platonic poses, at which she snatched them from us, calling us dirty devils.

Just when she fell madly in love with him I can't say - for madly is the only word. Cill never does anything by halves; she is so intense. There was Bob who wriggled out because her too frequent and insistent letters were bothering him. Junior told me that himself. And there was Herman. Even Toby wasn't sure of her friendship remaining as such. He has known her as long as he has me, but if he took her home from somewhere she'd seem to expect it the next time and pretty soon she made his casual attentions seemed significant.

And now, she is frightening Bill B. She goes to the laboratory on every pretext and often with none. She way-lays him, she writes notes to him, she phones him. She does everything possible calculated to make a man of his type shy away. She knows it and can't seem to help it.

Someone told me that when Howard announced I was coming into the office, Nate said mockingly, "Look out, Priscilla! You know Bill's weakness and this Clarke kid is a cute little thing."

1925

The Thames River, New London, on Boat Race Day

Yale crew practices for annual boat race

Helen at Ocean Beach, New London

An Account of My Life

Of course, she knew she couldn't keep a new girl from coming in, but apparently she intended to keep me out at least. You'd think she would mind me less than an unknown girl, because she must known how I regard him. She has asked me a dozen times if I like him etc., she watches my face when I talk with him on the phone. I've told her ad nauseum that I do not like the man, but she expects me to see him through her infatuated eyes.

He has a slight lisp and on his tongue she is "Prithilla." A lisping fool approaching baldness! When she <u>does</u> have a lucid interval and sees that I scorn the man, she becomes angry with me because I <u>don't</u> find him attractive.

<u>Mar. 30</u> - I hope Cill is satisfied! Up until a few days ago she had nothing on which to feed her suspicions. Bill B. knows quite well I don't care a snap of my fingers for him, but I must admit the novelty of it appeals to him. Nate says its a grand game of Cill chasing Bill and Bill chasing me, but as usual he exaggerates.

Bill will sometimes try to make a phone conversation take a personal turn, but I simply laugh and hang up. Cill thinks my tactics especially designed to fit his case and lead him on. She says I don't talk to him over the phone so he'll come into the office on some pretext!

And if I <u>do</u> talk to him on the phone she looks daggers. If she'd have the sense to let the poor fool get this out of his system! All in all she has been pretty impossible, digging me with catty remarks daily that keep alive a slow burning in me all the time.

One noon Bill was on the bus and as he usually drives his own car, I wondered. Nearly all the way the bus was jammed full, but as one by one the passengers got off, he worked nearer my end until he gained the seat beside. I didn't welcome him warmly, but I was civil.

That was all there was to it, but for several noons it has been the same. He had told me his car was in the garage undergoing repairs. At the end of the week, I said, "You car must have been a complete wreck." He laughed.

He asked if I would ride with him when he got it out and I said `no' flatly: whereupon he remarked that a car was a nuisance and he preferred the bus. Well, I can't forbid him the use of a public conveyance, and I can't always prevent him from sitting with me. I don't take his cues which baffles and intrigues him. Frankly, it is rather fun bothering him. I bet I could lead him a dance. But I'm not going to. He'd give me a good time, but he'd expect pay if only in small coin and he appeals to me about as much as a head of cabbage.

Of course, Cill heard about it almost at once - and the fur flew! I controlled myself fairly well until finally I let loose.

"If I wanted to wreck my life," I spit out, "I'd want a villian who doesn't lisp and isn't a silly girl chasing fool!"

She walked away blind with rage.

1925

Friends! What <u>are</u> friends. We've eaten together, slept together, walked together and dressed together. We've talked half the night and gone to sleep with our arms around each other. We've never quarrelled over boys because we have seldom been attracted to the same ones - or rather she makes a point of never liking any boy I like, <u>after</u> he shows any leaning in my direction: from then on she points out everything wrong about him.

She has given me a rotten deal and all because she has given love to a man who plainly doesn't want it. She <u>is</u> suffering there is no denying that, she has become sallow and haggard and takes aspirin continuously. I'm <u>sorry</u>, but I can't do any more than I am doing.

Yesterday, I found I had no bus token or any money to buy one, so Howard paid my fare. To-night, I slipped one in his hand. "What's this?" he asked. "Take it back you ridiculous child."

"Won't you accept this token of my esteem?" I coaxed.

"I will, gladly," he chuckled as he pocketed it. "How about stopping in for a sundae as a very small token of my esteem?"

Aren't you pandering to what you believe to be my school girl tastes, or do you really want one?" I asked suspiciously.

"Do you think a man loses his taste for sweet things after he reaches the venerable forties, Little Ase?"

"Well, in that case," I dropped my eyes. "Yes, thank you."

When I kept an unprecedented silence over my sundae, he spoke jokingly.

"Penny for your thoughts. Does ice cream always bring on a reflective mood?"

"I was thinking," I sighed. "that I had had millions of sundaes with boys, but never a cocktail with a man."

He laughed, looked at me oddly, and said, "I hope you are not thinking of a certain person who would be only to glad to take you out!"

"I'm not," I assured him. "It bores me just to look at him. It's always that way! Here I am nineteen and never been in a speak easy."

"You aren't - er suggesting -" he looked serious, yet half inclined to laugh.

"You?" I supplied frankly. "I would if I thought it would do me any good. What good is a Family Friend!"

"I am beginning not to like my role," he said drily.

<u>April 3</u> - The office isn't large and I have no way of knowing if it is typical or not.

There is Minnie, Howard's secretary, a large, placid German girl, capable and conscientous. She is even tempered, has no temper as I understand the word, although one sometimes glimpses an ugly streak beneath her glass-like calm. Except for a spoiled younger sister whom she adores and pampers, she seems to care for no one. She reads "The New York Times" most carefully with special time spent on the book reviews, so, I quote, "I'll know what to read." She added that she never bothered to read a book unless it had been reviewed favorably, because it would be a waste of time. There is an unintelligent, rather ghastly efficiency about her.

"What do you do when reviewers disagree?" I asked curiously.

"I read but one paper," she said sensibly.

One time I told Howard a little story about old "Mighty" Mitchell who goes on the *Constance C.*

If Mighty could read or write he'd make a crack reporter, because he has a nose for news and mysterious ways of getting it in advance. When Ethel Godfrey decided to open a little hat shop, he knew about it as soon as she did.

"Say, Asy," he said. "I just heard Ethel is going to set up a military shop."

Howard laughed, but there was no sound from Minnie. We had returned to our work when Minnie spoke slowly and thoughtfully.

"Oh, he meant millinery."

Howard and I exchanged one wild glance and bit back our laughter.

But she can make lightning calculations, while I am counting on my fingers. Her manner toward Howard contains deference in proportion to his salary; my manner toward him shocks her. I shall never forget her face the morning she came in early and found me trimming the frayed edge of his cuff with manicure scissors.

"Hello, Minnie," Howard held out the other wrist to me. "Repair work under way. That damn laundry makes mince-meat of them."

"I can give you the name of a good laundry," she said practically.

"I'm sure you can," he responded politely, then, feeling the prick of the scissors, "You little devil, did you do that on purpose?"

"I'm not sure, but I think so," I said. "It was the merest little snick."

"There's no such word as `snick,'" Minnie put in.

"Oh there must be," I looked at her. "It comes from snickersnee. You know - 'as he squirmed and struggled, and gurgled and guzzled, I drew my snickersnee?' That proves it, I guess."

At her severe manner Howard stopped laughing and became very business-like.

I'm not cut out for business, I guess.

When Howard is buried in work he is a different man and I have seen enough to admire his quick, sure, scrupuosly fair decisions - he is too big for his job and every one knows it, but I cannot stand on ceremony with him. He is just Howard who knows Ase, and has become my friend.

With all the bickering and small jealousies in that office every one unites in agreeing that he is a prince.

There is Julia, Mr. F.'s stenographer. She is not pretty, nor yet homely, but she is the office slattern. If Mr. F didn't look like a heap of soiled linen himself he would never tolerate her, excellent stenographer that she is. She intends to get married, as soon as possible, is warm hearted, quick witted and humorous in a Rabelaissan sort of way. Her slip hangs below her dress hem, her clothes while clean enough are literally thrown on. There is usually some one telling her to straighten her stocking seams and upon ocassion Howard has remarked half amused, half irritated, "For God's sake Julia, haul up the flag!" She laughs good naturedly and gives a half hearted, wholly unconcealed tug at the offending garment. We rather like one another, although there doesn't seem to be anything on which we can get together.

Winnie, besides typing for anyone and everything, has dealings with the Loom Book. She is tall, Irish and handsome except for an over large mouth and upper lip so short it bares the gum when she smiles. She has blue, black hair, smoky grey blue eyes, sooty eyelashes and a rose petal skin. She is in love with Mr. F's private secretary. Mr. F. has a daughter who is plain, unmarried and not too young. He wants Bill N. for her, Winnie wants Bill N., and Bill N. wants what Mr. F's daughter will bring, but pauses to look at Winnie and to listen to her lovely, lazy laughter.

Ralph, is one of the so called Greenmanville gang and has worked up from the mill to the office. He is homely, red headed, freckled, vulgar, shrewd, amusing and likable.

Bill H. (there does seem to be a plethora of Bills!), the pay-roll boss, is a fat little man, sometimes kindly, often malicious and either way repellent so far as women are concerned. His body seems to throw heat like a stove, his blunt, fat fingers are always hot.

Ruth, works with him on the pay roll. She is an adopted child, her foster parents live in Noank where Mr. S. has a small barber shop. Knowing nothing about her real parents, she draws upon her imagination, and while she is grateful to her foster parents she is quite convinced that she was born in a superior class. Sometimes I wonder. She is slim and she carries her head well; her hands are long, her feet so narrow she has her shoes made to order.

She is almost pretty, her pale gold hair silky and soft, her eyes a deep brown, but there is something in her expression which keeps her from prettiness - a queer furtiveness, an odd resemblance to a street gamin, the sharp, darting glances from eyes that can look almost beady. She is sharp too in other ways. Although her vocabulary is strictly limited, she speaks in a precise clear cut way; she never reads, but she watches, listens and takes for her own anything she can use. When she makes a pithy remark one wonders immediately where she heard it.

I might add that she seldom makes the mistake of leaving off quotation marks when the author is within ear shot! She is also one of those provoking people to whom dirt cannot stick: her hair, her skin and her hands are invariably immaculate; her clothes are in good taste and she is completely dainty in detail. So fastidious a soft chocolate bar or a crushed sandwich will fill her with distaste, she literally chases after every, greasy, dirty, coarse-mouthed mill hand who chances to take her fancy. I have seen her out in the mill supposedly on an errand, giggling and flirting behind a towering pile of packing cases.

Harold, Ralph's brother, is a shipping clerk. Good looking, nineteen I should say, brown hair, grey eyes, he is a likeable boy most of the time. Unlike Ralph, Harold is always looking for slights, taking offense when none was intended - that sort of person. He loves scandal and boasts that he knows inside stories about every old family in town including my own. And he is forever asserting loudly that he is "as good as anybody."

I've left Nate for the last because he is in a class by himself. When the afternoon's work begins to drag all the men and boys are in the habit of telling risque stories the length of the room, but the things Nate says are obscene and not funny at all. Some are so bad a dead silence falls. Perhaps Harold or Ralph will start to laugh, but the sound dies away in the dead quiet. It takes a pretty filthy story to floor Julia who knows a goodly number herself, but even she is silent. Nate glories in it. Nothing pleases him more than to see the girls bending over their work in various stages of disgust and embarassment, the men exchanging uneasy glances with one another.

They are told when Howard is out of the office. He likes an off color story as well as the next one but he would not permit obscenity. There isn't anything one can do about Nate, for if one tries to stop him, he coils his nasty tongue around that person. I know because I have tried.

If a girl feels ill and goes to the Rest Room he watches her out of sight and then makes some knowing comment. A woman can't become pregnant without him following the various stages avidly: and if a poor little mill girl finds herself in trouble there is no detail that escapes him. Fortunately he has to devote some of his attention to work, but to see him meekly answering their questions and cringingly taking their abuse is as disgusting as his incessant bullying of the office boy. He could and would make life intolerable for me but he fears Howard.

<u>Apr. 4</u> - "You girls now days know everything," Ase remarked with sarcasm. "so I suppose you know about Howard and Mrs. X."

"Oh that," I said, amused. "Who doesn't?"

Although it was not the maidenly answer he would have liked, he controlled himself, and suggested that I see less of Howard outside the office.

"Why?" I asked. "Is she getting her dander up?"

"Don't flatter yourself she would consider a snip like you a menace," he snapped. "I am thinking of the speech of people."

"H m-m-m." I said. "<u>She</u> never has; if she had she would have shriveled to an ash long ago."

"And what," he thundered, "do you know about such things?"

"I know she has had one affair after another," I answered promptly. "Women talk but accept her. Her husband lets it go on under his nose and you and all the men tell how clever, how witty she is. I know she has the best automobiles and the nicest fur coats in town and that she goes everywhere and has a darn good time. Wages of sin, my eye!"

"Listen to your daughter!" Ase yelled turning in despair to Mother.

"I hear her," she replied calmly. "It's true enough, isn't it?"

I don't know who was the more amazed - Ase or I.

"Are you upholding your daughter -" he choked.

"I hope your daughter," Mother threaded her needle expertly, "has too much sense to lose her head over a man at least twice her age and if she hasn't I trust Howard. He is a nice man even if that hussy has got her nails in him. As for what she may think of a decent friendship I don't care. You've brought home enough of her bright amusing remarks to last me a life time."

There was paralyzed silence while she snipped a thread.

"She was always as homely as a mud turtle and now she shows her age," she went on. "Naturally she knows anxious moments. Personally, I think you should be ashamed of yourself for putting thoughts in your daughter's head that were put into yours by that trollop."

Ase gave her a wild look and departed, banging the door.

I gazed at her reflectively realizing anew how little one can know about a parent.

April 10 - Desks were being tidied, eyes were cast at the clock, it lacked a few minutes to five and the hands seemed glued to the bland white face so slowly did they move.

I took a late batch of special tickets to Howard's desk, stacking them neatly at his elbow. Minnie was in Mr. F.'s office, and he motioned for me to sit in her chair across from him while he checked them.

There being nothing of interest on Minnie's desk, I looked across to his which she keeps almost as impossible tidy as her own. I watched his white hands with their short, well kept nails, and looked at his fair, receding hair.

"Alright," he shuffled them together expertly. "Leo can take them out."

As I reached for them, his eyes met mine and as if in answer to something he said.

"Yes! - you little devil, but I'm not going to."

It was so unexpected I blinked; then tingled; then laughed.

May 16 Minnie left Howard flat - I can't remember just when because time drags yet manages to fly at the same time. Anyway, she had a position in a New London office offered to her, so she gave a short notice and left.

Beaulah Watrous, a Quakeress, has taken her place. I have known her more or less all my life. She seems to be very fond of me, I should say she admired me if I were in any way admirable.

This noon she asked me if I would like a short drive - she has a ramshackled old fliver with a home made license plate tied on with a string. So we drove thru Old Mystic, its sleepy houses smothered in lilac

An Account of My Life

bloom. Gnarled apple trees bowed with years of patient bearing were laden with bloom, and the road flecked with the snow of their blowing petals. I should be used to this sort of beauty, but somehow after hours of smelling the reek of the dye house, it goes to my head and makes me mad with delight. Beulah was pleased with my enjoyment. She says she wishes she could feel things so intensely. "It certainly is a pretty drive," she agreed.

This evening while talking to Ase I happened to speak of certain imponderables.

"Never heard you use that word before," he remarked keenly. "I doubt if you and that boy who hangs out here every night make use of it. Whats its source, Howard?"

"Yes," I said. "We talk on many subjects."

"It's a wise father that knows his own daughter," he grunted.

"Or his wife," I said mischievously.

"Women!" he snorted. "Fools."

May 17 - To-day is Dorrance's birthday. We spent the day in Cliffs Woods, a gloriously warm, blue and gold day, a gift from the gods.

Violets bordered the path, white birch trees stretching slim arms aloft, held a canopy of misty green over our heads, tiny white violets peeped from the brookside, while the brook itself, limpid and brown, rippled in its shadow dappled way, and dog wood flowered on every side.

Up where the old Jonathan Jesse place use to be, we found lilacs just beginning to bloom. In their years of growing wild they have become tinier and have gained a peculiarly spicy fragrance all their own.

Dorrance is the only boy I have ever known who feels beauty like a stinging lash.

May 20 - When Cill first got her job in the office and before Bill B. made her blind to everything else, she use to talk about the office force to me. She hadn't known Howard at all before she went there and she was impressed by his courtesy and his kindliness. I recall one night sitting in the cedars - Cill, Glad and I. She had been giving verbal sketches of this one and that and she finally said of Howard, frowning in a puzzled way. "I simply cannot figure him out. I expected him to be a different sort all together. To women of his age he seems to have sex appeal - and always women who are terrific that way themselves. Now, what do women like that see in him? He could pass for a school teacher, white and blond and sort of dry. He is only ordinary height and weight, thin nosed and thin lipped - and glasses! Now I ask you! Take that type like your Cousin Gene. He doesn't appeal to us, but you can see why older women go for him in a big way. But Howard! What fatal attraction can he have?"

"Maybe it's like white heat - a white flame - oh you know," I said idly.

Glad and I laughed at such rubbish, but Cill considered it seriously. "Well," she agreed. "that's as near as one can come to it."

Now that I know him I can't think of a better comparison than that chance shot I gave over a year ago.

June 18 - Thursday Dorrance graduated this evening from Stonington High. Went over with his Mother, Father and an assortment of Aunts, one who came from Providence for the occassion.

He played - and so much better than any of the other (so called) violinists, he recieved thundering applause. I am not exagerating.

No one but Dorrance could make me go there again. I haven't been there since I left and felt the same surge of sickness.

When we were leaving a little girl ran up to us and thrust a rosebud in his hand.

June 21 - This afternoon when I came down the path from Grandmother's house I discovered Howard on the front veranda with Ase. I don't know exactly why I felt surprized for I have seen him there before and passed by with the barest of greetings. Somehow it is as if he had been reborn full grown before my face and eyes: certainly the man I use to think him and the man I know are two different people. He wore white flannels and a dark blue jacket, which set off his ash blond hair, and he looked clean to the bone. I try to imagine him as a young man, but I can't: I think he was born looking exactly as he does now.

He liked my pale yellow dress and said so, which gave a decided lift to my spirits. I took little part in the political discussion which didn't interest me, but came to life when the topic veered to books. As usual Ase grew cross when my opinions didn't jibe with his, and so he said, "You should thank the immortal gods Howard, that you have been spared the discomfort of a conceited, spoiled, teen age daughter."

I sensed that Howard didn't care a great deal for that remark. After all, he *is* a lot younger than Ase, although I suppose he could have had a daughter my age if he had got at it early enough. At any rate, he laughed as he remarked, "Ase, you don't deserve such a charming daughter."

"Bah!" said Ase, looking at me under knitting brows. "Don't smirk."

I had forgotten that the gang was to meet at Toby's, so I prepared to go when reminded by an indignant phone call, and was pleased to find Howard meant to walk to the house with me. I told him I hoped he would come again soon and that I much preferred him to Peter Marcus.

"Don't you like him?" he teased. "I thought girls were fascinated by artists."

"I like meat rare, not raw," I said tersely. He laughed, but he looked pleased.

When we parted I held out my hand to my complete surprize and was further surprized that anything as pale and dry looking could feel as hot and alive as his hand.

An Account of My Life

I was conscious of a distinct mental let-down at Toby's. <u>Never</u> have boys seemed so young and inconsequential.

<u>July 5</u> - I think Dorrance and I shall remember last night always - the most glorious 4th of July we have ever known. It was moonlit and wonderful and we spent it on the beach with rockets gracefully curving over our heads and the yellow bubbles of fire balloons sailing on their way. Roman candles burst into colored stars spattering the moonglade. There was the sound of breaking waves and distant laughter, and the touch of night cooled sands. It was well after midnight when we turned toward home.

When Dorrance kissed me hard, all the intermittent deviltry died out of me. Is this love? Or is it simply moonlight.

<u>July 23</u> - An afternoon at Watch Hill. Dorrance and I found an isolated spot where we talked and dreamed all afternoon. The waves were an exquisite jade green edged with lace.

The Scopes Trial is our daily newspaper fare with Darrow going the theory of evolution one better by making a monkey of Bryan.

<u>Aug. 18</u> - An excursion boat, the "*Mackinac*", returning from Newport to Pawtucket, blew up killing many: a boiler explosion.

There were young people like us, happy and tired, then in a flash, Death - and all their hopes and dreams dead in their scalded bodies.

<u>Aug. 26</u> - I am deathly tired of the office, but there is nothing I can do about it. Ase preserves the fiction that I work because I am bored at home, while as a matter of fact he can no longer afford to support me. His health is poor, though Kirk tells him brutally that he is a confirmed hypocondriac. He has always been difficult to live with and now he is nothing short of devilish.

It is hot in the mill these August days, inspite of awnings and electric fans. The mill itself is little short of an inferno. When I see workers literally drenched in sweat I hot and sticky myself. Bill H. says I am wasting my sympathy. "Those Polacks don't know any better." I can't help pitying them, but when I smell their sour sweat I cannot love my fellow man.

The heat doesn't improve the dispositions in the office and there is almost incessant bickering whenever Howard is engaged elsewhere. Sometimes in the last dragging hours, when our hands stick to everything and our fingers smear the typewriter keys, and the switch-board buzzes like a nest of enraged hornets, and Nate starts his sly, insidious talk I want to walk out into the clean, cool sea until I drown. If it were not for Howard I could not endure the place.

Even Harold who is little more than office boy, becomes unbearable at times.

1925

"Must be swell to be rich," he jeered one day as the Camp Mystic girls clopped by on horseback. "I'd like to see every last one of them working out in the mill."

"What good would that do you?" I asked contemptuously. "You'd still be you."

Sept. 4 - The U.S. Navy Dirigible, "*Shenandoah*" split apart in a thunderstorm.

Grandmother says everyone knows they aren't safe.

Sept. 17 - Twenty years old and a woman, although Howard insists I am still a child.

Oct. 5 - Autumn, and the river banks are scarlet and gold. There are crispy mornings and sunsets that are a flaming glory behind the dark cedars. Howard says he hasn't really looked at a sunset in years, until this year.

Oct. 10 - Dorrance and I saw a play in New London last night called "The First Fiddle." I like the old Lyceum, the shabbiest, ugliest and oldest theatre in the city - and to me the most interesting. The hangings are of dusty crimson velvet, the dirt ingrained carpet worn threadbare, but it is still every inch a theatre, not a movie house. We had dinner at a Chinese restaurant and laughed a great deal over our bowls of chow mein.

Oct. 17 - Well, Bill B. has interested himself elsewhere, thank God, and though Cill's heart aches we are friends again.

"I should have known you wouldn't appeal to him," she said.

"Cill," I told her firmly. "Anything untried and in skirts appeals to him."

Nov. - Tonight while Howard and I were walking home enjoying the crisp air after the stuffy office, we met Mrs. X, the woman in question.

I noticed with satisfaction that she looked haggard, sallow and old, and then felt ashamed of myself, for she is very likable. I don't think Howard fancied the situation though he carried it off cooly enough.

She has been a poacher all her life, never counting the cost to any one or sparing any woman's feelings.

He is doing me an immense lot of good, I feel; I need a mature, wise, kind, interesting friend and I think I am doing him good too - at least he laughs more than he use to, acts younger and wears gayer neckties.

Naturally I never mention Mrs. X in connection with him, but as we see her constantly it is impossible to refrain from speaking her name.

"Do you dislike her so much?" he asked one time seeing an expression flit on my face.

"No," I admitted. "I rather like her - in a resentful sort of way."

"Except that I am better looking and a generation younger," I went on thoughtfully, "we are something alike, don't you think?"

"God, no!" he said, looking startled.

Nov. 17 - I've felt tired and dispirited for a week, sick to death of my cramping boundaries, of this small town, sick to death of the everlasting sameness, and so, with Howard for an audience, I exploded into rebellious recklessness.

I said I didn't want to go home to supper, I wanted to get into an automobile and drive for hours until tired and hungry I could drop in at a cozy, wayside inn on a long, black road.

"Old and rambling," I went on. "An open fire. Lobster I think and caviar. Soft lights and logs burning."

"You draw an inviting picture," he admitted.

"I am not the type to go off the deep end like Cill," I said reasonably. "And you are no sentimental school boy."

"That I am not," he spoke feelingly.

"Can't two people enjoy one anothers company without becoming involved?"

He looked at me and I found myself blushing which is a thing I seldom do.

"Dangerously involved?" I ammended.

"Little Ase," he said. "We are dangerously involved right now."

Dec. 27 - Now that I am alone I feel fidgety and nervous, my thoughts chaotic.

I told Howard I had a point blank question to ask and I hoped he'd answer it.

He said it was good of me to warn him that my finger was on the trigger, I hadn't always been so considerate.

"Is it," I asked, "Because of Ase, or because you have come all over noble all at once, or because you don't like me well enough?"

"Curiosity and variety?"

"A little of everything," I admitted honestly. "I hope you don't think I have a crush on you, because I haven't. Neither am I in love with you. It is as near as I can make out a combination of real liking, plus a certain amount of attraction.

"Plus excitement, having heard enough to whet you curiosity and pique your variety," he added dryly.

"Perhaps," I conceded. "What does it add up to? I want to know."

He was silent for a few minutes and then he said, "Helen, before you came into the office I saw you downtown one day just as I had a hundred times. You tossed a "hello" and kept on, but I turned to look at you.

Ase had said you were bored and at loose ends. When a vacancy came up I sent for you. You were so unaware of me it amused me. You were entertaining and more challenging than you realized. Naturally, I argued it wouldn't harm you -

"Would it?" I asked.

"You'd take my word!"

"Well," I said. "I'm asking."

"My dear, I can't sell you a bill of goods. I am over twice your age and I have no money. There would be no escape from the vicious gossip."

"Does everything have to be grim, realistic and horrid," I demanded.

"Suppose we dined and danced, had cocktails and kissed. I want adult fun, sophisticated pleasure. I like you, I like to be with you. I want to be gay."

"<u>Could</u> you be `gay' with your reputation gone? I've none to lose. But you? Don't you realize that if we were seen there'd be one construction put upon it. Whether it was warrented or not? And by God, it would be!"

"You!" I said bitterly. "One of the few men who haven't conformed and been buried under a pile of diapers! You, becoming prosy and dull!"

At that his face lost its paleness under a spreading tide of red, and his fingers gripped above my elbow like iron.

"Listen Helen," his voice was tight. "I've told you what to expect from gossip which you might as well know will be merited. I've indulged myself for more years than you have lived, and my present self control won't stand up under too much provocation. Now you know how things stand. Think it over."

Then he gave my hand a quick, hard squeeze and walked away.

Well, where do I go from here?

1926

January 1, 1926 - 20 years old

<u>New Years Eve</u> -
I don't think I've ever known such a misery of discontent.
Even Dorrance cannot change it.
Last week, Mrs. Morgan told me to drop in some evening if the "Rondo" gave me trouble, so I dropped in this evening. Toby let me in, dressed for a New Year's dance. He greeted me with outstretched hands.
"You are better looking than ever. How's Dorrance? Do I look swell, I ask you?"
"You do," I answered honestly, admiring his new dinner jacket. "Magnificent."
He preened for several minutes. "So you really think I look swell?"
"Absolutely," I solemnly affirmed. "Who is she?"
"Aw," he blushed. "Well as a matter of fact its Virginia. Tetia and I are off for keeps. You know sometimes it strikes me funny weve never had a crush on each other. You and me, I mean."
"I did once," I admitted, sinking into a chair.
"No kidding?" he was delighted. "When?"
"In the third grade."
He howled at that. "Gosh, Helen, there's a world full of girls to kiss, but no one like you. Where are you going tonight? Dorrance, I suppose?"
"Yes, but we're not going anywhere."
"Why not? Don't you know its New Year's Eve?" he demanded.
"There is nothing worth going to in town," I reminded him. "And you can't get far without a car. And if you think I'm hinting I'll kill you. Hadn't you better get started? Musn't be late for a date."
"I won't be," he brushed that aside impatiently. "I'll just drive faster. Now what's the idea? You've changed. You use to be a sweet little dancing, laughing fool and about my favorite woman. What's happened?"
"<u>You've</u> changed," I reminded him.
"Never mind <u>me</u>. It's you. What the heck are you working in that office for?"
"What else is there for me to do?" I asked. "The bunch is split in pieces. Everything has changed. The C.H. is on the rocks. I'd die of boredom at home."
"Why can't you get away? Gee, it's a shame for you to rot in this burg."
"Well," I said thoughtfully. "I'm not a determined, work my-way combination of grit and vaulting ambition."
Well, heck!" Toby expostulated. "I'm not either."
"You've got your own money - or will have," I answered drily. "I haven't - and I'm not a good risk. But why all this on the eve of a party?

Darling, the Lord never meant you to worry. Bless you my little man, and get a wiggle on. Look at that clock!"

He let out a yelp of consternation and wound his white, silk muffler around his neck.

"Just the same, Clarkie," he said, shrugging into his coat. "I wish you were coming to-night. Don't do anything I wouldn't! And give my regards to Dorrance."

He banged out the door sending back a wild "Goodnight. See you soon."

Mrs. Morgan listened to the roadster roar down the drive way.

"That boy!" she sighed. "He'll break his neck one of these days. I'm so glad he has gotten over Tetia. She treated him terribly, kept him upset all the time. Now Virginia is a sweet girl -

I listened, making the appropriate responses.

"Toby thinks the world of you," she sighed sentimentally. "If he ever gets some of this craziness out of his system!"

"They say no man can be a brother who isn't one," I said. "But that's how I think of him. They don't come any grander than Toby."

For the first time in my life I don't face the new year with eagerness, in fact if I feel anything definite it is uneasiness. What a purposeless, rudderless person I am!

There is no peace or real happiness at home with Ase behaving like a mad man the greater part of the time, and I hate the office and the problems connected with it. The only haven of refuge is in Dorrance's arms, and it will be so long before we can marry.

I tell myself that this year is unusually important to me in as much as there are decisions I must make, decisions that will effect my whole life, and never have I felt so ignorant and ill equipped.

Jan. 17 - Tonight Dorrance brought me a ring: two pearls and a diamond. "It's not really an engagement ring," he said, "not nearly fine enough, but I'd like it if you'd look upon it as one."

I know only one thing; life would be unendurable without him. I could go on like this letting the real thing slip thru my fingers - changing, seeking, experimenting - like that dream I use to have of pennies, or sometimes pencils, in which I found one only to drop it for another and so on, awaking empty handed. I know so little and there is so much to learn! However, I choose to learn it with Dorrance who has so much to learn and so far to go.

Jan. 18 - There is no explaining Ase, other than that he is mad! After all the fuss I thought he'd be glad of my decision, but he is furious. I <u>cannot</u> stand much more of him! I want to go to Providence with Dorrance where his aunt has found an opening for him, and probably could do the same for me: but at that, Grandmother and Mother register horror. I don't know what they think they are averting, but they have already written the engagement announcement for the paper. I <u>must</u> tell Howard before it appears. Lord, I wish I were good and dead!

<u>Jan. 19</u> This morning I held my ring finger out to Howard silently.

"Pretty little thing," he said absently, having been called upon before to admire dresses and ornaments. Then he looked at me hard and said in a different tone of voice, "Is this an engagement ring?"

"Yes," I said.

"That boy? Helen!"

I nodded.

He picked up some loose papers, shoved his chair back with a scraping sound and walked out of the office.

The bell rang, the last few stragglers scurried to their seats. I put thru a call to New York. One of the girls noticed the ring on my finger: I knew what she thought, but said nothing. I let them buzz and speculate and giggle. Then I told them. Or one might say, I dropped a bomb shell.

At the close of the day Howard and I walked out together chatting pleasantly to their further mystification.

"A line of camels sway thru the thyme scented streets. Their bells murmur of deserts and their loads are wrapped in carpets hand woven in the women's tents...a donkey whose striped saddle-bags are swollen with golden fruit...the tinkle of jewelled anklets..." And from this window snow melting in discolored patches and a line of mud spattered trucks groaning up the hill."

<u>Feb. 3</u> - Dorrance has gone to Providence to take an opening his Aunt has found for him. I can't see why I can't go too and get some sort of a job: but the Family is up in arms at the bare idea.

"Jesus Christ!" Ase swore. "Is there anyting else you can think of to make talk! You get yourself engaged without warning to a boy still wet behind the years: you go on with a very unwise friendship, if it can be called that, and to top it you have that fool Marcus now a married man, hanging around."

"He sometimes sits, with me on the bus - Marcus," I said wearily. "That's all."

They seem lacking in penetration: I should be much safer in Providence. But of the course the idea is they can keep an eye on me here.

The only person who is kind and gentle, who understands my blind attempt to get my feet under me is Howard.

<u>Feb. 10</u> - It is being said openly that Howard has broken with Mrs. X. I don't think he has seen much of her for quite some time if the truth be told. I've known from the way she looked at me. When she told Ase he had a "very clever daughter," I knew.

The engagement doesn't fool her, she thinks. Hasn't she used marriage as a cover for years? Does she really think I could do to Dorrance what she has done to her husband - make him the laughing stock of the village!

Mar. 14 - To-day Howard told me he was contemplating a new opening in another town.
"I shall miss you - beyond words," I said, looking away. "You've been good to me and very dear. It's done a lot for me - knowing you."
"A part of your education," he suggested drily.
"Oh, please!" I put out my hand. "I shall always think you wonderful. I feel so much - only."
"That's all right, my dear," he answered.

Apr. 17 - Days, days, just days. I pick up a pen to write - and I can't write. Dorrance seems to like Providence fairly well. He is playing in a jazz orchestra and taking lessons with Prof. Ladd when not working in the office at Brown and Sharpe. We write almost every day. Oh merciful God, but I am lonely!

May 16 - I am going to Providence tonight on the 8:26. Dorrance's Aunt has asked me down for the week-end. I have had a special hair-do in New London.

May 19 - Back home after a pleasant week-end. It was as if the world shook back in place. He seems to have a steadying effect on me, although my effect on him appears to be the opposite.
The Aunt is nice enough, the business woman type with an attractive apartment, a permanent, a husband and a narrow little world of her own.
Saturday, Dorrance took me to the theatre - the Albee - where we saw "Dancing Mothers." We were very happy - when left alone.
Providence doesn't thrill me particularly, but at least it is a change.
I have never experienced such an agonizing feeling as when my train pulled out and Dorrance was left behind.
We had one good talk at least. He had so studiously avoided Harold's name I purposely dragged it into the open. He admitted he was a "little jealous" of him - "not in the regular way, but because you seem to worship him."
"It's not quite that," I flushed. "I admire him and look up to him, that's about all."
"I've never known him very well," he said. "And he always seemed a good sort, but I don't see anything so wonderful about him. Plenty of people think just the opposite."
"Then they don't know him as I know him. You'll have to take my word for it, he has been a wonderful friend to me."
"Well, why not?" Dorrance shot back. "He's known you a long time and I guess you've been a good friend to him."

I said nothing. "Don't get the idea I've got a down on him," he said anxiously. "If I had a fit everytime some guy looked at you I'd be in a fit most of the time. After all you are going to marry me, so to hell with them. You are, aren't you?"

"Of course," I leaned against him.

"Soon?"

"It's crazy, but then I do crazy things."

And then we kissed.

<u>Saturday May 29</u> - Dorrance and I were married this afternoon. He brought a ring from Providence and asked "Will you?" and I answered, "Why not!"

Finish this later. Everything is stewed up and bubbling merrily.

Next day -

To go back: It was a beautiful day and as nothing seemed to hinder he went over to the Town Hall for a license. It was closed so he came back and we went to Groton Long Point where Latham Avery, whom we supposed to be the town clerk, lives, although we had no idea where. Odd that I should be married to a man as nearly like I imagined young Latham to be ... and by an old man bearing the same name. I suppose he is some sort of a relative, too.

There aren't many cottages open on the Point this early in the season and we thought it would be a comparatively simply matter to find it; it wasn't.

I began to get nervous. After a while we met a small boy who directed us to Mr. Latham's house, where we found him planting seeds. He is white haired and wrinkled, with a fund of humor and, fortunately for us, a love of romance.

He was bending over a wheel-barrow as we approached.

"What can I do for you?" he smiled, and seemed to doff a plumed hat.

"A license," said Dorrance.

"And what kind?"

"Marriage," Dorrance replied as casually as possible.

"Well now, ain't that too bad," he said, rubbing his chin with an earth stained old hand. "You see, I'm not town clerk anymore. You want Bailey. When did you plan to get married, anyway?"

"This afternoon," said Dorrance.

"Come into the house and set a spell," he asked us. And when we were seated. "I'm afraid Bailey has gone out of town - Memorial Day and all, but I'll see what I can do for you. Guess I'll telephone and see."

He did, and found Mr. Bailey very much out of town.

"Hold on," he cried, as we started to get up from our chairs. "I'll try Miss Fitch, his assistant. Maybe she'll open the Town Hall if I ask her to. She's got the right to issue a license."

He couldn't get her on the phone, but evidently entering into the spirit of the thing, drove us to Noank where she lives. And all the way I waged a mental battle - afraid we couldn't get the license and feel perfect fools - and afraid we could get it. I daresay Dorrance was waging a similar battle.

It was a beautiful drive - the ocean blue on the one side and the scent of lilacs and apple blossoms heavy in the air.

In a few minutes we were in Noank and Miss Fitch had expressed her willingness to do all she could. A short drive back and we were at the Town Hall

As Mr. Avery knows Ase I thought it very sporting of him not to ask questions: and when Dorrance offered to pay for the toll calls he had put in on our business, he chuckled and told us to forget it.

"And if you don't locate a minister before they shut up for the night, come back to me and I'll marry you," he added handsomely.

Miss Fitch smilingly told us she "wouldn't have missed it for anything."

On the way home we stopped at Rev. Hatfield's. He married Mother and Ase and was my one concession to the Family Pride: for I knew they would never forgive a Justice of the Peace.

Mrs. Hatfield was at home too, and if she thought it odd, said nothing. Now that I think of it, it seems that the marriage was destined to take place. So many things might have prevented us and nothing did. It is one thing to run away and marry among strangers, but quite another to go among friends and not meet with questions. I can't explain it.

Mrs. Hatfield asked us to stay to supper, saying Ray would be in any minute - but we thanked them and left.

The ceremony was very short and dream like, and through it all I felt hungry for food, which is certainly not romantic!

We walked home in the lovely spring twilight and were happy with one another.

"I suppose the Families will raise merry hell," I said, reflectively.

"Probably at first, but who cares?" Dorrance answered carelessly.

And they did. Mother was the most sensible. Ase was furious, but blessed it as a legitimate chance to rave. Grandmother, poor dear, felt eternally disgraced and accused me of having no family pride. None of my people had ever done such a thing and there would be "talk." Besides I could have had such a pretty wedding. I couldn't tell her that that was what I wanted to avoid - that weddings make me sick.

And then, Dorrance's people. Claire and Joe were staying with his parents for the holidays and she had to stick in her oar.

Mr. and Mrs. Grimes were simply stunned, but Claire was stinging mad. She had never met Mother, but she breezed into the affair, all sails set.

I knew then that I had always wanted to dislike her and was secretly glad of a chance to work up a lather.

"I suppose you know this outrageous marriage can be annulled," she opened fire.

An Account of My Life

"Not by you," I said cooly.

"I don't believe you have a certificate! How can you. You're under age!"

"We lied," I replied blandly.

It went on for hours, until they had talked themselves out.

At length Claire announced that she was going and as no voice was raised to say her nay, she flounced out mad as a wet hen, but not before she hissed at Dorrance.

"You're coming home with us!"

"The Hell I am!" Dorrance said succintly and to the point.

The following announcement appeared in
The New London Day on June 1, 1926

Capt. and Mrs. Ase Clark of 12 Noank Road, announce the marriage of their daughter, Helen May Clarke, to Dorance H. Grimes, son of Mr. and Mrs. Samuel Grimes of Mistuxet Avenue. The ceremony was performed by the Rev. B.U. Hatfield, May 29. They will reside in Providence.

Afterword

Helen and Dorrance were married for 63 years until Helen's death in 1987. They did not have children. Dorrance is currently living in Groton Connecticut.

Constance was married briefly to a Rhode Island cousin and then made a career in New York. She died at 68 in 1974.

Helen's grandmother and her father, Ase, both died in 1928. Her mother, Allie, died at age 65 in 1943.

Helen, Constance, Grandmother, Allie and Daddy (Helen's grandfather) are all buried on the Hill lot in Elm Grove Cemetery on Route 27 in Mystic, Connecticut.

Ase is buried in the Clarke plot in River Bend Cemetery in Westerly Rhode Island.

Aug. 25 – A horrid rainy day and no fun whatsoever. Grandma says all I think of is fun and someday I will realize that life is a vale of tears more or less.
It is still thundering and I am reading "The Fall of the House of Usher" by Edgar Allen Poe. I like dark, romantic stories, but I do not want to suffer so much as he did in order to write them. I also like to hear the rain on the tin roof of the ell while I am reading them.
Aug. 26 – Mrs. Morgan hasn't come to give me my piano lesson, but I don't care. Something has detained her no doubt. Mother bought some cloth to make me two smocks. She is smocking the pumpkin yellow one in brown and the blue one in lemon yellow.
I guess this Diary isn't going to be worth keeping, because nothing exciting ever happens to me..

As a young woman Helen copied her childhood journals into loose-leaf notebooks. Above is a sample of the hand-written text which was transcribed to produce this book.

Index

—A—

Allen/Allyn, Dr., 40, 42, 103, 172, 291
Allyn, Gurd, 17, 112
Appleman, Will, 66, 80
Arbuckle, Fatty, 27, 78
Armistice, 85, 200
Ashby Street, 107, 117
Assembly Hall, 76, 80, 85, 87, 129
Atlantic Beach, 96, 227
Avery, Dell, 43, 44, 98
Avery, Latham, 100, 160, 336
Ayres Woods, 21, 155, 292

—B—

Bank Street, 66
Baptist Young People's Union, 95, 96, 108, 109, 114, 145, 199, 215, 228, 245, 281, 289
Bara, Theda, 92
Barrymore, John, 162
Bates, Rev. Welcome, 16
Batty, Earl, 134
Beebe, Carolyn, 45
Benham, Ida Whipple, 118
Bentley, Leil, 62, 76, 112, 113, 284
Bindloss Brook, 140
blacksmith, 33
Blacksmith Shop, 64, 93
Block Island, 156
Boarding House (Mrs. Benjamin's), 65, 185, 189
Boat Race (Yale-Harvard), 141, 179, 180, 182, 187, 215
Bogue Town, 97, 98, 99, 286
Bradley, Bob, 44, 46
Braxton, Welcome, 61, 97
Breed, Dink, 78, 109
Broadway School, 139, 179
Brown, Danny, 129, 209, 210
Brown, Happy, 20, 74
Brown, Jim, 29, 65, 70, 128, 153

Buckeley, Mrs. Frank, 44
Burnett, Joanna, 74, 81, 104
Burrows Burying Ground, 21, 196, 197
Burrows Coal Company, 17, 98
Burrows Street, 82, 185, 256
Burrows [ship] yard, 170
Burrows, Aborn, 67
Burrows, Ambrose, 44, 80, 156
Burrows, Ben, 98
Burrows, Calista, 66
Burrows, Clyde, 288, 311
Burrows, Daniel, 76
Burrows, Desire, 121
Burrows, Margaret, 107
Burrows, Mary, 196, 197
Burrows, Nathan, 82
Burrows, Rhodes, 72, 80, 82, 150, 256
Burrows, Robert, 45, 80, 153

—C—

Cameron, Charles, 34
Camp Fire Girls, 123
Camp Mystic, 190, 329
Car Barn, 92, 196, 197
Carver, Mildred, 27, 111
Casino, 81, 287, 288
Central Hall, 34
Charlestown, 49, 301
Chase, Clara, 74
Chatauqua, 145, 182
Chesebro, Jimmie, 167
Chesebro, Sam, 110
Christian Endeavor, 102, 103, 136, 252
Cliff woods, 157, 166, 225, 326
Cliff, Mr., 65
Clyde, Mr & Mrs, 57
Coats, Miss, 115, 157, 160, 178
Colby, Alice, 98, 121, 202, 275
Coleman, Roland/Rowland, 116, 187, 227, 244
college ice, 139, 141, 281

Index

Collins, Mabel, 59
Columbus Hall, 233, 281
Community House, 130, 184, 187, 200, 202, 242, 244, 251, 264, 272, 278, 282, 285, 286, 287, 292, 294, 302, 303
Congdon, Dr., 70
Congregational Church, 110, 127, 168, 231, 275
Coogan, Jackie, 190
Copp, Brenton, 107
cradle factory, 44
Crary, Capt. Jesse, 49, 156
Crary, Nell, 23, 49, 94
Cromwell, Lewis, 77, 130
Cutler, Mr. & Mrs., 144

—D—

D.O. Richmond's boat yard, 170
Davie, John, 62
Day Light Saving Time, 133
Deans Mill, 153, 187, 209
Decoration Day, 23, 24
Dennison's Store, 271
Dennison, Lady Anne, 161
Dennison, Malviny, 61
Devil Foot Hill, 145
Dr. Coat's Pills, 107
Draw Bridge, 71
Duhaimes, 93, 190

—E—

Eastern Point, 219
Ebenezer Morgan's Ice Cream Parlor, 32
Eclipse, 313
Edgecomb, Raymond, 79
Eldredge, Charles Q., 230, 287
Elm Grove, 24, 25, 116, 133
Ennaking, Joseph, 189

—F—

Fiedler, Annie, 142
Fish Farm, 153

Fish, Fannie, 49
Fish, Hattie, 228
Fish, Jessie, 74
Fish, Sands, 154
Fish, Warren, 154, 198
Fishers Island, 152, 192
Fishtown, 139
Fitch, Mary, 48
Five Corners, 64, 92
Foote, Bertha, 185
Fort Hill, 100, 110, 196, 210
Fort Rachel, 155, 313

—G—

Gallup, Mr & Mrs, 203, 216, 232
Ganu, Jerry, 29, 34
Gates, Emily, 65, 184
George, Ed, 107
German Club, 265
Germany, 20, 22
Gilbert Block, 33, 34, 71
Gish, Lillian, 210
Glory Band, 161, 162, 166, 199
Gluck, Alma, 192
Godfrey, Freddy, 280
Gravel Street, 49, 62, 171
Greek's (The), 260, 281, 287
Greene, Miss, 103, 104, 105, 107, 109
Greenman, George, 185
Groton, 62, 152, 168, 178, 203, 220
Groton Heights, Battle of, 168
Groton Iron Works, 178
Groton Long Point, 336
Gurnsey, Emma, 98
Gypsies, 18

—H—

Haley's Woods, 18
Haley, Juliet, 65, 198, 227, 228
Halfway House, 150
Hancock, Rhody, 283
Happyland Dance Hall, 223
Hatfield, Raymond, 141

Index

Hatfield, Rev. Byron U., 141, 278, 337
Heath, Judge, 65
Heath, Mr., 65, 108
Hempstead, Mary, 196
High School, 74, 99, 102
High Street, 45, 117, 184
Hinckley, Judge, 151, 152
Hollaway, Zella, 61
Holmes, Capt., 64, 171
Horseradish King (The), 283
Hoxsie House, 17, 28

—I—

ice cream, 32, 36, 194, 321
ice pond, 205
influenza, 75

—J—

Jesse, Jonathan, 157, 158, 326
John Mason monument, 157, 225

—K—

Kaiser (Wilhelm), 20, 80
Keeler, Mary Hannah Packer, 97
Kretzer, 54, 70, 75, 81, 92, 240

—L—

Lantern Hill, 231
Latham Street, 94
Lathrop Engine Co., 256
Lathrop, Annie, 33
Laurel Hill, 203
livery stable, 29
Lover's Leap, 145

—M—

Mahoney, Bob, 77
Main[e]'s Store, 53, 71, 92, 196
Maine, Harold, 114
Mallory [ship] yard, 171
Marcus, Peter, 208, 327
Mason's Island, 227

Mason, Capt. John, 212, 225
Maxson's Beach, 36, 46
Mayo, Lib, 16
McManus, Camelia, 200
Meeting House Hill, 44, 150
Mercer, Irv, 76
Methodist Church, 176, 202, 309
Miner, Elder, 24, 48, 111, 118
Mitchell, Mighty, 44, 191, 322
Mohican Hotel, 180
Montgomery, L. M., 121, 153, 167, 170, 199
Morgan, Capt., 29
Morgan, Evans, 28, 65, 67, 152, 243
Mosher, Mr., 65
Mosher, Teddy, 184, 243
Mr. Iver's store, 189, 194
Mullaney, Mike, 128
Mystic & Noank Library, 48, 91, 95, 121, 141, 151, 166, 171, 187, 190, 215, 256, 286, 288
Mystic Academy, 15, 20, 57, 65, 66, 74, 90, 99, 103, 104, 108, 111, 166, 184, 190, 209
Mystic Bank, 152
Mystic Island, 191
Mystic Theatre, 190, 209
Mystic Valley Water Co., 188

—N—

New London, 25, 26, 27, 34, 54, 66, 81, 99, 117, 122, 142, 152, 178, 180, 181, 201, 212, 215, 313, 314, 325, 329, 335
Noank, 28, 36, 37, 70, 96, 97, 115, 126, 145, 172, 227, 239, 312, 313, 323, 336
Norwich, 194, 196, 197, 199, 203, 210, 211, 216, 225, 252, 260, 307
Noyes Store, 34, 76, 142
Nye, Miss, 74, 87, 103

—O—

Ocean Beach, 54, 99, 186
Old Mystic, 58, 287, 325

Index

Orchard Lane, 30
organ grinder, 18
Osborne, Annie Eugenie, 121
Osborne, Rev., 136, 137, 143, 175, 190, 246, 253

—*P*—

Packer Burying Ground, 100, 196
Packer's Tar Soap, 117
Packer, George, 93
Packer, John Green, 57, 65, 94, 96, 123
Packer, Laura, 117
Packer, Mary Hannah, 197
Packer, Tony, 37, 42
Packer, Uncle Dan, 93, 117
Palmer, Capt. Nathaniel, 111
Partridge, Caro, 151
Payne, Kenneth, 22, 70, 82, 190
Peace Grant house, 311
Peace Meeting, 110, 153
Pecore, Thaddeus, 71
Pendleton Yards, 170
Penfield, May, 21
Perkins, Kate, 99
Pistol Point, 170, 172
Plant, Morton, 219
Point Judith, 48, 298
Porter's Rock, 145, 212
Post, Ernest, 152
Potter, Cort, 71
Powers, Ralphy, 51, 279
Prentice, Ruby, 15, 74
Price, Hollis, 66
Prince of Wales, 130, 312
privy, 16, 46, 135, 151
Providence, 62, 95, 302, 308, 327, 333, 334, 335, 336
Putnam, 69, 127, 156, 197

—*Q*—

Quakertown, 53, 116

—*R*—

Raferty, Mike, 131
Randall, Jedediah, 196, 197
Rathbun, Lib, 271
Rathburn, Fred, 48
Reynolds, Nurse, 28, 40
Richmond, Linda, 125
Rickerman, Annie, 74
Riker, Annie, 48
Rossie Velvet Mill, 314
Rotten Row, 96, 97, 98

—*S*—

scarlet fever, 59, 170, 177
Seamon, Calista, 65
Sebastien, Sol, 44
Shellnick, Hans, 22
Shelter Island, 190
Skipper Street, 77, 126, 146, 150
Slack, Grandmother, 156
Slaughter House Hill, 150, 187
Smith, Albany, 96
Smith, Harold, 200
Soldiers Monument, 25
South County [R.I.], 95
Spenser, Romey, 52
Spicer, Capt., 151, 171, 256
Stanton Farm, 137
Stanton's Hill, 116
Stanton, Frank, 137
Stanton, Giles, 137
Starr Lane, 190
Stillman, Dr. Charles, 39, 82, 133, 165, 208, 209, 212, 267, 269, 275, 284, 328
Stonington, 34, 111, 122, 129, 145, 197, 214, 227, 327
Stowe, Percy, 39
Sunday School, 138
Sunday School (Union Baptist Church), 60, 95, 96, 102, 127, 128, 129, 157, 201, 244, 305

344

—T—

Thomas, Capt. Herb, 17
Three Hills, 120, 126, 256
Tift, Mr. and Mrs., 45
Tingleys, 52
Town Hall, 37, 336
trolley, 24, 25, 28, 34, 37, 43, 79, 91, 96, 112, 118, 121, 126, 173, 177, 178, 201, 203, 205, 216, 227, 314
Tucker, Charles & Hannah, 48, 138, 298

U

Uncas Lodge, 231
Union Baptist Church, 65, 236, 288, 167, 173
Unknown Soldier, 200

—V—

Valentino, Rudolph, 205, 209, 211, 214

—W—

Watch Hill, 328
Water Street, 92, 97
Watrous, Beaulah, 325
Watson, Mr., 30
Webb, Ann Judd, 23
Weeks, Emily, 117
Wells, Mildred, 36
West Mystic, 44, 81, 90
West Mystic Avenue, 150
Westerly, 34, 114, 132, 161, 227, 313
Wheeler's Drug Store, 36
Wheeler, Dick, 201
Whipple, Fred, 98
Wilcox, Elias, 133, 242, 243
Wilcox, Howard, 72
Wilcox, Nancy, 57
Wild Cat Ledge, 46
Williams, Bert, 59
Williams, Charles P., 39
Williams, Connie, 74
Willow Point, 81
World Wide Guild, 107, 115, 121, 156, 185